The Labour Party and Foreign Policy

The foreign p[...]l in most
histories of th[...]from the
party's origin[...]ons. Yet
nothing has be[...]'s history
than the party'[...]ship to its
domestic prog[...]

Much more[...]pestuous
conference de[...]spect for
Governmental[...]approach
to foreign and[...]en said to
stem from a fa[...]osition of
Labour Cabine[...]ce considerations, as wa[...]ng within
Labour Gover[...]s of these
periods in offi[...]uestions.

- But what [...]
- Did it sub[...]?
- Were its l[...]?
- Did they [...]
- Did Labou[...]
- Or does it[...]

The Labour P[...]enetrating
new study of th[...]ns, which
probes the past, present and future of the party's approach to the international stage. This comprehensive and up-to-date book is recommended
for undergraduate and postgraduate courses in British politics and
European history.

John Callaghan is Professor of Politics at the University of
Wolverhampton, UK.

The Labour Party and Foreign Policy

A history

John Callaghan

Routledge
Taylor & Francis Group

LONDON AND NEW YORK

First published 2007
by Routledge
2 Park Square, Milton Park, Abingdon, Oxon OX14 4RN

Simultaneously published in the USA and Canada
by Routledge
270 Madison Avenue, New York, NY 10016

*Routledge is an imprint of the Taylor & Francis Group,
an informa business*

© 2007 John Callaghan

Typeset in Times New Roman by
Florence Production Ltd, Stoodleigh, Devon
Printed and bound in Great Britain by
The Cromwell Press, Trowbridge, Wiltshire

British Library Cataloguing in Publication Data
A catalogue record for this book is available
from the British Library

Library of Congress Cataloging in Publication Data
Callaghan, John.
    The Labour Party and foreign policy : a history / John Callaghan.
        p. cm.
    Includes bibliographical references and index.
    1. Labour Party (Great Britain) – History.   2. Great Britain –
Foreign relations.   I. Title.
    JN1129.L32C27 2007
    327.41–dc22   2006032945

ISBN10: 0–415–24695–4 (hbk)
ISBN10: 0–415–24696–2 (pbk)
ISBN10: 0–203–64712–2 (ebk)

ISBN13: 978–0–415–24695–8 (hbk)
ISBN13: 978–0–415–24696–5 (pbk)
ISBN13: 978–0–203–64712–7 (ebk)

Contents

Acknowledgements

I would like to thank the Lipman–Miliband Trust for financial support in researching this book. Thanks are also due to Jim Tomlinson and Mark Phythian and the librarians and archivists of the Labour Party and the Modern Records Centre (University of Warwick) for help in finding documents. I should also record my appreciation of the staff at the National Archive at Kew; the British Library; the Institute of Historical Research and Senate House Library, University of London; the library of the Institute of Social History, Amsterdam; the Working Class Movement Library, Salford University; the US National Archive at the University of Maryland; and finally, but not least, the staff at the library of the University of Wolverhampton.

1 Party and Liberal nation

When I first entered the House of Commons there was a myth, a prevalent myth. It was to the effect that although the Labour Members of Parliament could reasonably be expected to know something about engineering, or about mining, there were two subjects on which they were completely ignorant: foreign affairs, and how to make war. It was always understood that those were the special prerogatives of the Tories, and their attitude has not changed very much.

(Nye Bevan, speaking at the 1958 Labour Party conference)

The Labour Party

The Labour Representation Committee (LRC) was formed in February 1900 for the purpose, as its name indicates, of promoting independent working-class representation in Parliament. It was not the outcome of a struggle for a socialist party. Socialists like Keir Hardie had certainly worked for its creation in the belief that their own prospects depended on an intimate alliance with the trade unions. But the unions themselves were led by men whose disenchantment with the Liberal Party, as a vehicle for their interests, did not entail a disenchantment with liberalism. For almost three decades after the Second Reform Act of 1867 the 'labour interest' clung to the Gladstonian Liberal Party, making the most of the restricted franchise and its own poor finances. This attachment was loosened as it became clear that the individual and collective interests of trade unionists could not be fulfilled by the Liberal organisations. The broad coalition of British progressive politics was not broad enough to adopt working-class men as its parliamentary candidates even after the doubling of the electorate in 1884. Yet the expectations of the established unions, the growth of new unions among the unskilled, and the rise of class consciousness increasingly rendered this state of affairs intolerable, especially when the legal status of the unions was called into question in the 1890s.[1]

The leaders of the LRC, mostly former Liberals, set out then to defend organised labour alongside the Liberal Party in Parliament. This generation and its outlook dominated the Labour Party (as it became known from the general election of 1906) for the first third of the twentieth century. It took the First World War to create the circumstances in which Labour adopted a socialist objective (in 1918) and a world economic crisis – involving the ignominious collapse of a minority Labour Government – before socialism became the party's dominant discourse in the 1930s. Another national crisis – the Second World War – was required to generate the circumstances in which Labour could win its first parliamentary majority – and all this in a country in which the working class, Labour's 'natural' constituency, represented about 75 per cent of the population. These jolts to the system, though milestones in the development of Labour politics, were nevertheless contained, in that they were unable to shift the deepest convictions of Labour politics, some of which had long roots in British society as it developed in the second half of the nineteenth century. Foremost among them was the belief that legitimate politics was conducted within the existing constitutional framework and institutional structures of the British system. This testified to the dominating authority of both Crown and Parliament as the impartial defenders of the rules of the political game. McKibbin suggests that an important component of this hegemony was upper-class adherence to the rules of the system with the result that the working class was, among other benefits, subject to neither the coercion nor the incorporation which threatened its continental counterparts.[2] Instead there was a large degree of self-sufficiency and independence in the voluntary associations of the working class which adapted to and even prospered in the conditions of late Victorian capitalism.

Though class divisions ran deep, British society was relatively free of grievances which could alienate a large section of the population from the state. The massive stresses generated by the Industrial Revolution in the first half of the nineteenth century had also receded. A certain degree of prosperity and stability characterised the second half of the century, during which the working class experienced a rise in living standards and was able to extract benefits such as free collective bargaining. From 1875 the existing craft unions enjoyed a legal basis that was unique in Europe. But the unions represented only 15 per cent of the employed workforce as late as 1900. Much of the rest of the working class lay beyond their reach, especially women, those in domestic service, shop-workers and the penny capitalists of London. Others were difficult to reach because of the seasonal or casual nature of their employment, or their dispersal in small-scale enterprises which fostered employer paternalism and the deference of the workforce. There is no evidence that these circumstances were any more obstructive of class solidarity and organisation than was true in continental Europe. But there is evidence that by 1900, having no major linguistic, sectarian, or national differences among them, the British were more easily united in their patriotism, their support for the monarchy, the armed forces and the Empire.[3]

After the franchise extension of 1867 it was the Conservative Party which enthusiastically associated itself with the defence and promotion of these institutions and beliefs. By the time the Labour Party came into existence the Tories had already had considerable experience in the art of depicting their opponents (the Gladstonian Liberal Party) as unsound in relation to the national-imperial virtues. Once Labour emerged as the primary opposition party in 1918, the Conservatives lost no time adding 'socialism' to the list of unpatriotic evils which had to be guarded against. Judged by their ability to form governments and command much of the working-class vote – a fact which Labour's parliamentary leaders were bound to be impressed by – the Conservative Party's success in the period 1916–45 owed a great deal to these cross-class issues. Universal suffrage, far from heralding the end of the Tories, opened up a period of unprecedented governmental dominance for them. While Labour's national leaders struggled after 1918 to promote the party as a national rather than a sectional interest, the Conservatives successfully mobilised the fears, prejudices and aspirations of 'the public' against it.[4] In part this differential is explicable with reference to the organic link between the unions and the Labour Party, especially when we remember that the unions, though a declining force from 1920, had done enough between 1910 and 1920 to thoroughly antagonise the middle class and help drive most of it into the Conservative Party. But if Labour was handicapped by its close association with a sectional interest, the Conservative Party held the advantage of standing for values and beliefs which permeated all classes. Thus while the unions never managed to organise more than 45 per cent of the inter-war workforce, the Conservatives – with double the individual membership of the Labour Party by 1925 – could capture as much as 55 per cent of the working-class vote and thus build on and reinforce the undoubted social unity of their middle-class core supporters in class-divided England (and Scotland).

Colonies

Colonial rivalries generated repeated crises between the Great Powers in the last two decades of the nineteenth century in the context of a competitive struggle to annex new colonies, especially in Africa.[5] The first decade of the twentieth century produced even more vivid evidence than hitherto – certainly for the British public – of an arms race that might lead to war in Europe. The precise impact on the public of this virtually continuous narrative of British imperial adventure and Great Power tension is hard to gauge.[6] But there is no doubt that it was subject to a barrage of imperialist propaganda from both of the principal political parties, all of the governments formed between 1880 and 1914, most, if not all, of the churches, various pressure groups (such as the Navy League), most of the press – including the jingoist mass circulation *Daily Mail* – as well as the permanent institutions of the state, such as the armed forces and the monarchy. The least result that might be expected from this organised chorus was a reinforcement of the nationalist and racist prejudices so evident to foreign observers and 'most welcome to many political parties on the Continent' with a national mission of their own.[7] Nor was this purely for the benefit of the lower middle class and the masses beneath them in the social hierarchy. The political and intellectual leadership of the country at the *fin de siècle* routinely explained levels of civilisation in terms of race and worried about the fitness of the British imperial race to carry the burden of Empire. The mania in these circles for 'national efficiency' and eugenics was undoubtedly related to fears that Britain might fall behind in the struggle between nations.[8] The result was that 'a Social Darwinistic tone . . . permeate[d] virtually all the writings of . . . imperialist politicians and intellectuals' in the quarter century before 1914.[9]

The relevance of all of this for the Labour Party begins with the fact that it was born into this context, as was the working class and its organised, trade union minority, which was re-made in the last quarter of the nineteenth century. It had once been possible to criticise British imperialism as a huge system of outdoor relief for the aristocracy – an unwanted, unnecessary, liability. Politicians such as Richard Cobden and John Bright were famous for having done so and still had an intellectual following in the Liberal Party, though the Liberal Imperialists were ascendant by 1892.[10] But the days of Britain's unchallenged commercial supremacy were over by the time the fight for independent labour representation began. Politicians might still profess conviction in the virtues of free trade imperialism and in 1877–8 Gladstone could even advise against further expansion of the empire, arguing that Britain had already swallowed more territory than it could digest and was in danger of forgetting that the source of its material power was domestic industry, not overseas expansion.[11] But Gladstone's intervention was a rare exception, even for him. For he also believed, in company with virtually the whole of the political class, that the British were inherently an imperial race, that their 'dominant passion' was extended Empire and that such overseas interventions as the British government thought fit were a natural feature of the civilised order.[12] Disraeli and the Tories, in Gladstone's view, simply erred by making the wrong moral choices in relation to Empire by pursuing a reckless policy of adventure and prestige designed to 'set up false phantoms of glory' among the British people.

Despite the increasing hegemony of the imperial mentality in British society the Liberal Party continued to act as home for those who took a more critical view of British foreign policy than the Conservative Party was wont to do. To the Manchester Liberalism of Cobden and Bright there was added a critique of imperialism inspired by the self-promotion of the Tories as the popular party of its aggressively patriotic wing. Of course Liberals could respond to the Tory rhetoric – which depicted them as weak-kneed idealists and pacifists, if not actual traitors to the national interest – in a variety of ways. The Liberal tradition also had space for the Palmerstonian approach to international relations which was prepared to undertake intervention abroad on ethical grounds. This was simply one variant of the British tendency to intercalate morality and foreign policy. As Richard Crossman, the Labour MP, described it in 1956, Labour drew from a tradition which held that 'power politics are wicked and must be subjugated to the rule of law; that Britain must stand for applying morality in international affairs and, in particular, for helping small nations to achieve their independence; that rich and fortunate nations have an obligation to raise up the backward colonial peoples; that the elector everywhere wants peace if only the politician will allow it; that what [the] British above all hate is a bully who breaks the law'.[13] It was easier to imagine the British Empire being consistent with these sentiments if one thought of it as the advanced guard of a movement to bring commerce, Christianity, free trade and liberalism to the peoples of the world. This is what the Liberal imperialists did. British imperialism gained in popularity during the 1880s and 1890s in part at least because of its supposed civilising mission and by the beginning of the twentieth century both major political parties stood for its maintenance and even extension. But the attraction of an ethical foreign policy was more keenly felt within the Liberal coalition than among the Tories, especially on the Radical wing of the party which was strongly inclined to deprecate British involvement in continental power politics. It was here that the greatest outrage had been felt in response to the 'Bulgarian Horrors' of 1876 and to the cynical realism which lay behind official indifference to them.[14] The popular agitation which erupted in 1876 has been aptly described as 'the greatest public incursion into the official conduct of foreign affairs in British history'.[15]

It was undoubtedly related to the great Nonconformist revival of the 1860s. The feeling that British foreign policy should be informed by moral considerations exercised a strong attraction for the Nonconformist conscience, as did the conviction that the Great Powers should act in concert, not unilaterally. Turkey's violent suppression of a peasant revolt in the Balkan domains of the Ottoman Empire brutally contradicted these principles and caused a moral outrage in Britain when Disraeli publicly made light of the atrocities in the summer of 1876. British interests, it seemed, were only concerned with the maintenance of the Ottomans as an obstacle to Russian expansionism. The nature of Ottoman rule in the region was an irrelevant consideration according to this way of thinking. But this 'realist' mentality excited an unprecedented extra-Parliamentary agitation whose intensity surprised contemporaries. The episode is instructive on a number of counts. The Conservative Party itself was the least affected section of public opinion. The agitation was strongest in the constituencies containing a strong Nonconformist presence, in local Liberal associations and working-class organisations. Once it began, Gladstone ended his self-imposed retirement to lead the popular opposition. But Gladstone's denunciatory rhetoric obscured the fact that he supported all the essentials of British policy in the region. What is of more interest in the present context is the evidence that the disaffection he sought to lead sprang from a novel conjuncture composed of a newly enlarged electorate, four-fifths of whom were enfranchised as recently as 1867; together with an innovative, graphic and sensationalist popular journalism; and a Nonconformist constituency which retained the vigour of its 1860s revival, particularly among the Liberal intelligentsia and the 'new' men steeped in the tradition of Radicalism. The public also consisted of many men who had been disappointed by their exclusion from the franchise extension of 1867, as well as those irreligious prole-tarians who attended the flourishing working-class clubs of London. The politically frustrated were also most likely to be the ones feeling the economic downturn as the period of mid-Victorian prosperity came to an end in the heavy industries.

By September 1876 Gladstone was able to address crowds of up to ten thousand on the question of British foreign policy. But this first phase of the agitation gave way to a very different mood. By November an Anglo-Russian war seemed likely when Russia confronted Britain's ally Turkey. Radicals now found themselves in the uncomfortable position of supporting reactionary Russia in its stand-off with Turkey. They were also in danger of lending their support to a country with which Britain might soon go to war. When Russia invaded Turkey in April 1877 the patriotic newspapers in Britain did everything to stir sympathy for the 'gallant Turk'. While working-class groups became involved in anti-war agitation, there was also evidence of jingoism – in fact the word was coined at this time from the words of a popular song inspired by a defiant speech of Disraeli's declaring that Britain would fight to defend its imperial interests if it had to. A bellicose nationalism came to prevail by December 1877 as the Turkish armies seemed on the point of collapse. Big anti-Russian demonstrations were held throughout the country with working-class support. Anti-war meetings were attacked by mobs – men from the Woolwich Arsenal being prominent in breaking up a Trafalgar Square meeting on 31 January 1878. Large pro-war demonstrations were held during February and Gladstone's London home was among those which were attacked.[16]

Whereas the Nonconformists had dominated the original anti-Turkish agitation, the working class was more prominent in the anti-war demonstrations of the winter of 1877–8. But it was also present in the pro-war demonstrations. Some of the organisers of the anti-war camp, like the Radical journalist W. T. Stead, initially felt that the bellicose lobby had been routed by this first show of strength. But their judgement was premature and reckoned without the pro-war mobilisation of the Conservatives and the jingo fervour which tried to isolate liberals like Gladstone as traitors. It has been interpreted as a lesson in how masses of people could be mobilised behind Crown, Empire and Conservatism and how pacifist and neutralist sentiment could be driven underground. Soon 'the sense of defeat was nearly total' among the anti-war activists.[17]

Of course Britain was still very far from being a democracy in 1876 – the electorate of just under two and a half million voters represented only one in three adult men. Even after a further extension of the franchise in 1884, four out of 10 men of voting age were still ineligible, as was the entire adult female population. But the Conservative Party had been quicker than the Liberal Party to create constituency organisations and party-sponsored social clubs with which to reach and influence the enfranchised. Disraeli, the architect of the 1867 Reform Act, was ahead of his party in seeing the need to find cross-class issues if the Tories were to remain in business. It was not that he, or anyone else, had a coherent programme in mind for this purpose. But since his Crystal Palace speech of 1872 Disraeli had taken the trouble to paint the Liberals in treasonous colours, play up his own imperial sentiments, and connect the Conservatives in popular perceptions to the nation and patriotism. In so doing he helped to identify the party with strong defence policies and the glories of Empire and promoted the sense of the British as a favoured race with global power.

The rhetoric and intentions of politicians such as Disraeli and Lord Salisbury would not have been enough to achieve these outcomes on their own. They were assisted by the continuous succession of events in which British arms and imperial prestige were glorified – events in which the politicians sometimes played a decisive hand. But many other initiatives contributed to these outcomes, some taken by enthusiastic imperialists outside the metropolitan Government and beyond its immediate control. The upshot was that Disraeli's Government presided over wars in Afghanistan (1878–9); the annexation of a Boer republic, the Transvaal (1877); the Kaffir War of 1877–8; a war with the Zulus (1879), conceived as the next step in the federation of all the parts of south Africa which the British coveted; the occupation of Cyprus (1878); the purchase of shares in the Suez Canal Company (1875); and the imposition of new financial controls on the Khedive of Egypt. These measures followed hard on the heels of the annexation of the Fiji Islands (1874), occupation of the Malay Peninsula (1874–5) and the Suez Canal Zone (1875). Gladstone proposed to restore good conduct in imperial affairs when he succeeded Disraeli in 1880. Faced with instability in Egypt and the Sudan, however, he nevertheless despatched gunboats and soldiers to restore order, setting in train a sequence of events that led to the bombardment of Alexandria and the battle of Tel-el-Kebir (1882), the fall of Khartoum (1885) and the final defeat of the Mahdist movement at Omdurman in the Sudan (1898). An essential component of the 'order' Gladstone wanted to restore was the financial order which enabled the Khedive to go on paying 66 per cent of Egypt's revenues in servicing debt held by foreigners, many of them British. The origin of most of this debt was the ruinously expensive Suez Canal, the main burden of which was borne by Egypt on borrowed money. Gladstone himself was a bondholder, owning stock worth £17,100 before he ordered the invasion of 1882 – stock worth £24,600 soon after it.[18] His biographer observes that it would be 'crude and simplistic' to infer any personal corruption in Gladstone's decision to use force. Perhaps he is right, though it may indicate how deep the corruption ran that the Prime Minister displayed no embarrassment in view of the selfish interests involved. It is certainly worth noting that, as Matthews puts it, 'the absence of any sense of peculiarity or incongruity simply heightens the naturalness of the British occupation and of the inherent, almost unselfconscious relationship of capital and imperial policy' in Gladstone's mind and that of his peers.[19] Nor should we forget that Gladstone represented the sceptical pole of the imperialist spectrum within the British ruling class.

But it is clear that the days were over when Britain's supremacy could rest on extensive informal arrangements overseas, untroubled by competitors. In inter-imperialist rivalry some commentators have found the annexationist dynamic of the 1880s and 1890s, though others perceive 'expansion for expansion's sake' to be the 'central political idea of imperialism', as of other forms of totalitarianism, driving the Great Powers on the collision course which led to August 1914.[20] The expansion of the British empire thus continued apace under governments of both parties; Somaliland (1884), New Guinea and Mandalay (1885),

North Borneo (1888), Northern Rhodesia (1889), Nyasaland (1891), Kenya and Southern Rhodesia (1895), Benin (1897), and Nigeria (1899). Colourful and one-sided wars were fought along the way, supplying a wealth of copy for the newspapers and popular stories of exotic enemies and British military victories. After the Jameson Raid of 1895 the pace quickened in South Africa; two years later many of the imperial assets were put on public display at Queen Victoria's Diamond Jubilee celebrations; in 1898 General Gordon's death at Khartoum was avenged by victory at the battle of Omdurman, where the Maxim gun extinguished the Islamic revolt begun in 1881. There was always something imperial in the national drama. Meanwhile the rationale for expansion was often the defence of existing possessions, according to which the defence of what we have involves the acquisition of territory which lies next to it; and this logic was both cause and effect of the spate of annexations which spread across Africa during the 1890s. No one yet talked in terms of 'salami tactics' or 'domino theory' to explain this process. Blocking the ambitions of imperialist rivals in any case commanded widespread support in a country that regarded its own imperial rule as uniquely selfless and benign. The scepticism which Gladstone expressed in 1877 and which had caused Karl Marx twenty years earlier to ask if the cost of India might exceed its imperial benefits, was now, to all intents and purposes, extinguished in governing circles.[21] Instead both parties found room for a growing number of self-avowed imperialists in their parliamentary leaderships while advocates of withdrawal from empire were virtually unheard of. Leading Tories such as Lord Randolph Churchill justified new territorial acquisitions (such as Upper Burma) in explicitly commercial terms and, though no attempt was made to calculate the costs and benefits, it was widely supposed that empire formed an essential foundation of Britain's comparative economic advantage. This commonsense could only be reinforced by the behaviour of Britain's Great Power rivals, which generally made the same assumption. Gladstone's argument about the domestic sources of Britain's economic might was almost forgotten and there was plenty of economic ideology, or 'political economy', which led to the opposite conclusion; namely, that it was necessary to use political power to acquire and maintain colonial commerce and investment in order to sustain the vigour of British industry.[22] Experience pointed to the same conclusions. By the 1890s 'What is common to almost all of the colonial disputes is that they were the consequences – unintended perhaps yet inevitable – of *economic* expansionism. The same long-term processes which were causing many British merchants and investors to shift their gaze from Europe to the "underdeveloped" world were also responsible for German penetration of those same regions.'[23]

Thus when the Labour Representation Committee was formed the British state was an imperial state at the financial and commercial centre of the capitalist world economy. Britain's premier position had been built on the basis of its industrial and trading supremacy in the first six or seven decades of the nineteenth century, together with its ability to police the world with the Royal Navy, assisted by a global network of strategic military bases. A vast free trade area had been constructed under British rules and protection. Overwhelming force was frequently used against peoples who refused this dispensation.[24] None of these subjects could be allowed to disturb the international monetary system, based on sterling and British fidelity to the Gold Standard. The City of London supplied the banking and insurance facilities which lubricated the system and Britain supplied two-thirds of the merchant marine in which international trade was carried. In the wake of the growth of German and American economic power in the 1880s an argument developed, however, which cast doubt on the future utility of this free trade system and held out the prospect of a more systematic exploitation of the imperial assets. By 1906 Joseph Chamberlain had played a major part in convincing most of the Conservative Party that some form of closed imperial bloc was the way forward. The Conservatives, though defeated in the general election of that year, remained tempted by this vision throughout the inter-war period. The infant Labour Party, however, rarely wavered in its opposition to this form of imperialism. Instead it gave its support to the old Liberal position of free trade. This had been the ruling 'common sense' in Britain since the repeal of the Corn Laws in 1846.

This free trade ideology was often justified in terms of cheap food for the working class and on this basis it seems to have been popular with the voters of 1906. It was certainly the gospel of the Labour Party and most of the trade unions. But its appeal had other dimensions. It enabled its devotees to persuade themselves that the British Empire, while constituted on this basis, benefited all of its subjects, since all would share in the fruits of trade. Then there was the fact that the costs of running the Empire were minimised and devolved to the localities, whereas great imperial bureaucracies and large standing armies seemed implicit in the alternative Chamberlainite empire, as they already were in the protectionist German Empire. The empire Labour looked kindly on already contained largely self-governing colonies evolving to independence – the largely white dominions of Canada, Australia, South Africa and New Zealand. It was attractive to think that the British merely exercised a trusteeship on behalf of all the peoples of the Empire. Eventually all would be guided to self-government. Until then Britain would protect and develop its charges, economically, morally, and politically. This was the acceptable face of Empire and many on the centre-left of British politics sincerely believed in it. For decades past missionaries and evangelicals had seen the British Empire as a great civilising opportunity. Politicians were happy to project it this way, particularly those of them imbued with the same Christian ideology as the reformers, as so many Nonconformist Liberals and Labour men were.[25] But this belief in Britain's benign imperial rule also derived from belief in the superior standards of British government and culture; and this brings us back to the points already made above about the patriotism of the unions, the working class and the Labour Party – they too believed in British government. The British capacity to 'moralise' self-interest and represent it as an enlightened humanitarianism played a role here. It often amused and irritated foreign observers. It is said that US imperialists at the beginning of the twenty-first century 'divide into two groups – those who advocate unconstrained, unilateral American domination of the world (couched sometimes in terms of following in the footsteps of the British Empire) and those who call for an imperialism devoted to "humanitarian" objectives'.[26] British imperialists of 1900 would recognise the distinction, but not the perception of the British Empire as a system based on force – a perception common even among its current American friends.

Rapacious imperialism was firmly associated with foreigners at the beginning of the twentieth century. Between 1903 and 1913 E. D. Morel, the Liberal (later, Labour) activist, led the campaign to expose atrocities in the Congo perpetrated by King Leopold of the Belgians.[27] The systematic exploitation of the local population by forced labour, and the extreme violence with which this was carried out, made the Congo the paradigmatic case of how not to conduct colonial rule. For progressive thinkers in Britain, like Morel, preservation of the native welfare became a paramount concern, and this was thought to be compatible with forms of indirect colonial rule as practised by the British in West Africa, notably in Northern Nigeria during Frederick Lugard's time as High Commissioner from 1900. During the inter-war period this became official doctrine and was codified by Lugard himself in 1922 – by which time he had become Britain's representative on the League of Nations' Permanent Mandates Commission. Lugard's rationale for British policy asserted that the colonial power exercised a 'dual mandate' on behalf of progress and native protection. Thus the metropolitan trusteeship meant that the 'industrial classes' could enrich themselves, and in doing so help the natives on to 'a higher plane' by eliminating barbarism and cruelty, without destroying the fabric of native societies on which the efficacy of indirect rule depended.[28] In practice this meant utilising the large, centralised political and religious structures found in such places as the Indian subcontinent and Northern Nigeria and thereby enlisting local power-holders in the maintenance of British rule. It also meant inventing such structures where they did not already exist, as in Kenya where tribal leaders were nominees of the colonial power.[29] In either case such interests might be expected to join with the British to retard the rate of social and political change, though this was not really the intention of progressives who took up the cause of native paramountcy in the inter-war years. They were aware, however, of the difficulty of reconciling the preservation of native rights and welfare with the needs of commerce and free trade.[30] Once 'native paramountcy' became official doctrine and even Conservative Governments asserted that native rights would be made to prevail in the event of a conflict of interests between metropolitan and indigenous claims, the job of Labour's colonial experts was largely seen as one of defending this principle, as Sidney Webb set out to do as Colonial Secretary in 1929.

Boer War

The South African War (1899–1902) certainly shook the prevailing complacency. There was every reason why it should have done so. The conflict was blatantly provoked by imperialists working for the Conservative Government. The conduct of the war was both shameful and embarrassing. Around 22,000 British soldiers died fighting a community of farmers and self-trained guerrillas. Here was the embarrassment – at British military incompetence in the face of these amateurs. To overcome them the British built concentration camps – the first in history – in which at least 28,000 Boer civilians (mostly women and children) died, together with 14–20,000 tribal peoples. Here was the shame. But this time there was no spontaneous outrage to compare with the events of 1876 and the mass opposition to the 'Bulgarian Atrocities'. The religious sects were at best divided while those Radicals, Liberals and Labour people who protested against the war, and were mis-named 'pro-Boers', fell a long way short of wanting a Boer victory. Few of them even demanded a British withdrawal. Nevertheless, there were among the dissidents critics of imperialism who identified the aristocracy of finance capital, operating secretly, as both the prime mover and principal beneficiary of the policy of greed, reckless adventure and national prestige which, they believed, had led to the South African conflict.[31] The critics highlighted the evils of secret diplomacy which allowed this irresponsible faction to corrupt policy. But even the critics accepted the need for civilisation to exercise a trusteeship over the 'lower races'.[32] Most of them had no argument with the capitalist system itself and accepted that the war had to be won. In fact they believed in the virtues of free trade and the 'Open Door', as it came to be known, whilst objecting to specific consequences of the restless search for investment opportunities which free trade and the Open

Door encouraged. Their arguments were riddled in contradictions. Yet there is no doubting that the 'pro-Boer' alliance, uniting the socialist Independent Labour Party (ILP) with Liberals such as Lloyd George, was genuinely outraged by British bullying and thuggery. Keir Hardie was one of those Labour men who campaigned against the war and the first annual conference of the Labour Representation Committee demanded a cessation of hostilities, attributing the conflict to the 'corrupt agitation of the Transvaal mineowners'.

The silence of the churches – compared to 1876 – was noted with dismay by the dissidents. Yet evidence was brought to light, despite an official policy of deception, that the British had destroyed 30,000 homes, burnt churches, schools and libraries, killed livestock, destroyed agricultural implements, broken irrigation dams and generally denuded the countryside. Instead of outrage a succession of leading churchmen pronounced their satisfaction regarding the leniency and kindness of the British forces towards their enemy. Few of these people publicly expressed contrition when the war was over, even though the facts could hardly be disputed. Those who did condemn the war from the pulpit were told that they represented 'a contemptible minority of a minority'.[33] What was certainly true was that with the exception of the Quakers, only minorities took the dissident position within the Nonconformist sects. It was further evidence of the sweeping tide of pro-imperialist sentiment of the previous twenty years and of the conversion of the sects to the missionary mentality.

The socialists, by contrast, were increasingly critical of foreign and imperial policies.[34] Though the Fabian Society generally stood aloof from pronouncing on issues of foreign policy until the Boer War crisis forced its hand, the socialists of the SDF had a long history of thinking about such matters. In 1881 Hyndman, its founder, actually took a scheme for the democratic reorganisation of the Empire to Disraeli. Hostility towards imperialism, as a policy of military expansion and ruthless exploitation, informed his *England for All* (1881). His party waged campaigns over Ireland and land reform; against the 'bondholders war' in the Sudan; and against the exploitation of India and the ravages of British policy on the subcontinent, which helped to turn droughts into catastrophic famines. The smaller Socialist League, set up by William Morris in 1884 after a split in the SDF, also kept anti-imperialist concerns to the fore, but it was a declining force after 1895 and folded up in 1901. Within the SDF the majority took the view that the Boer War was a capitalist conspiracy but leaders such as Belfort Bax and Theodore Rothstein never developed a fully coherent theory of what was taking place. The same might be said of most ILP socialists who continued to support the idea that British free trade imperialism was, or could become, a progressive influence in the world. Some socialists had gone further and supported the war. Robert Blatchford, best-selling author of *Merrie England*, and one of the best propagandists of socialism in Britain during the 1890s, emerged as a patriot and imperialist. He later became a zealous campaigner for military preparedness against the threat from Germany and published a series of articles for the *Daily Mail* on this theme from 1909.[35] But he was not alone in his belief in the virtuous character of the British Empire. Leading self-avowed socialists were not unknown among the jingos, the racists, and the chauvinists. Hyndman himself was a staunch supporter of the British Empire and a rabid Germanophobe. He was quick to oppose the Boer War as a Jewish, financial conspiracy.[36] But he offered no criticism of those socialists – like Blatchford and George Bernard Shaw – who supported the British Empire. This was because he shared their view that the British Empire – the white Dominions and India were what he had in mind – was founded on justice and liberty. The war was repugnant to him because it betrayed that legacy.[37] As it dragged on Hyndman openly worried that the Empire was facing decay and might actually face defeat in South Africa.

The socialist Fabian Society, whose leaders were actually more sympathetic to the protectionist ideas of Joseph Chamberlain than to the gospel of free trade imperialism, defended the war on both realist and idealist grounds. They pronounced it inevitable in a world of power politics but – as the least offensive imperialism on offer – also insisted that the success of the British Empire in South Africa was desirable to ensure its continuation as a relatively humane force around the globe.[38] A racial element, often implicit in such judgements, was sometimes made explicit even among the socialist minority of the Labour Party. Anti-semitism, for example, was a recurring theme among critics of the South African war and by no means confined to Hyndman.[39] Sidney and Beatrice Webb, who admired the racial efficiency of the Germans and the Japanese, were inclined to explain the misfortunes of the British and Chinese in terms of their racial shortcomings.[40] What is the use of an Empire, Sidney asked at the peak of the campaign for 'national efficiency', 'if it does not breed and maintain in the truest and fullest sense of the word an Imperial race?'[41] No doubt such views were informed by widespread prejudices and fashionable doctrines at the turn of the century. But it is quite wrong to believe that they were universal, as Hyndman's numerous critics in the SDF and the resignations of the Webbs' critics from the Fabian Society demonstrated at the time. The point being made here is rather that if the socialist minority contained racists and supporters of the British Empire, we may safely suppose that the trade unions which formed the bulk of the Labour Party's members, finances and organisational resources contained even more.

Tom Quelch, a veteran of the British Socialist Party who embarked on the transition to Communism in 1920, certainly seemed to think so. When the British delegates to the second congress of the Communist International were told to take anti-imperialism seriously, Quelch replied that the workers of Great Britain would consider it treason if they followed Lenin's instructions.[42] He was convinced that socialists would have to tread very carefully in this area if they were to avoid complete marginality. But then Quelch himself was capable of racist thinking as other socialists had pointed out during the First World War, when he complained of the use of 'jolly coons' as strikebreakers.[43] Racist prejudices like these placed one inside the mainstream – even the socialist and progressivist mainstream. Colonial workers were, as cheap labour, often perceived as a threat.[44] They also constituted those 'non-adult races' which were assumed to be unfit for self-government. Even their protectors might subscribe to these assumptions. E. D. Morel[45] – undoubtedly an indefatigable campaigner against colonial atrocities in the Congo and often a perceptive critic of British foreign policy – is an example. In an attempt to stir the wrath of the Labour Party about the French invasion of Germany in 1922, he dwelt on the horrors allegedly perpetrated by their black soldiers, using every sexual-racial stereotype in the process.[46] Morel was a gifted journalist and a veteran campaigner against the exploitation of Africans. His racism on this occasion provoked criticism on the German Communist left, but passed unnoticed among the TUC conference delegates to whom his pamphlet was distributed free of charge in 1920. Perhaps the real significance of this episode is that George Lansbury's *Daily Herald*, then in its socialist heyday, ran the original story; Lansbury himself drew attention to the 'black savages' which France had 'thrust' into the heart of Germany; and other ILP socialists favourably reviewed the pamphlet and moved resolutions drawing attention to the 'dangerous and degrading practice' of using black troops in Europe.

The leading socialists within the Labour Party before 1914 were of course not the leaders of the Fabian Society nor of the SDF. Keir Hardie, Ramsay MacDonald, and Philip Snowden had all been 'pro-Boers' during the South African war. They had all made the transition from 'advanced Liberalism' to the idea of a Labour Party after experiencing personal frustration in their political careers at the hands of the Liberal Party and this was something they shared with many of the trade union officials and former trade union officials, such as Arthur Henderson, who turned to the cause of independent labour representation.[47] Hardie and Mac-Donald both showed an interest in foreign affairs, so did Henderson, particularly after the First World War. The first two visited the Dominions and India and wrote books based on their impressions. They saw the need for Labour to improve its standing as a party capable of governing an empire. They also made sympathetic remarks about the future self-government of parts of the Empire and generally stressed the humanitarian motives which governed, or ought to govern, imperial affairs. In common with other democrats (such as Morel) they preferred 'indirect rule', imagining, for example, an India that was allowed to manage its own affairs while remaining a voluntary dominion of the Empire. The socialists who found their way into the leadership of the infant Labour Party, like Hardie and MacDonald, generally stressed the need for a new morality of brotherhood. This was the essence of their 'ethical socialism', whose intellectual weakness was the lack of an analytical edge and strategic project. They could already imagine a voluntary commonwealth, in place of an Empire, but had no real idea how it was to be achieved and little or no idea about the centrifugal forces pulling apart the existing imperial fabric. Conceiving the British state as a neutral and benign instrument fit for the purpose of domestic social reform, they had no difficulty believing in its value overseas; the peoples of the Empire could hope for no better custodian of their long-term interests, as long as it was in the right hands.

For practical purposes advanced Liberalism continued to supply these men with ideas about foreign policy and the government of empire, just as the Liberal Party tended to lead them in Parliament in the years before the First World War. Imperialism – as a policy of further annexations or a closed trading bloc – might be viewed as an atavistic impulse and evidence of the disproportionate power of the aristocracy in the armed forces, governments and diplomatic services of Europe. It could also be viewed as having something to do with capitalism. The Boer War, as we have seen, supplied evidence to its British critics of the mischievous role of finance capital and business interests. British politics had long supplied evidence of differing conceptions of empire. But if nasty imperialism was the work of sinister vested interests, enlightened imperialism might follow if only enlightened men formed the government at Westminster. Labour was the legatee of that progressive element which said in effect: the British Empire is a fact of life, one that already contains outstanding successes such as the white Dominions, let us set about governing it as a 'trusteeship' so that future generations of its peoples might govern themselves with the advantages enjoyed by the British and their kith and kin abroad. Ramsay MacDonald had to point out to the 1907 Stuttgart congress of the Second International – to the evident surprise of some of them – that some parts of the British Empire were already self-governing. Like his counterparts in the Netherlands, Germany and France, MacDonald was trying to develop, at least ideationally, a conception of empire that would build on this democratic element.[48] He also had to work alongside Labour men – as did the continental social democrats – who frankly argued that Empire enabled the working class to achieve a higher standard of living than would otherwise be possible. It was to be defended – even expanded – for that reason.[49] Within the Labour Party and the trade unions J. H. Thomas (Colonial Secretary) in the 1920s, and Ernest Bevin (Foreign Secretary) in the 1940s, were prominent exponents of such views. This was simply one of the more obvious contradictions of Britain's 'enlightened' role – as the cotton unions had demonstrated when they lined up with the employers to advocate the conscious deindustrialisation of India.[50]

By 1900 it was conventionally assumed that Empire had made Britain a Great Power, so entangled with its industry, commerce, finance and defence had it become. But if one assumed the integrity and stability of the Empire, it was possible to think of international relations as a question chiefly of Great Power relationships and most Radical thinking took this view. Since the 1880s the old Concert of Europe, by which the Great Powers had sought to regulate their affairs, had fallen into disuse. The two Hague Conferences of 1899 and 1907 were partial attempts to establish arbitration agreements between particular states and establish rules concerning armaments and war. Liberal critics of secret diplomacy and the balance of power hoped that the Hague conferences were evidence of an evolution towards a system of world-wide arbitration and conciliation that would avoid war. But they frequently drew attention to practices which threatened, as Norman Angell[51] put it in 1912, 'an immense European war involving millions of men'.[52] Similar fears informed criticisms of Britain's friendship with Tsarist Russia, after the Anglo-Russian Entente of 1907 and the resolutions at Labour's 1912, 1913 and 1914 annual conferences which protested against militarism, the threat of conscription and the government's 'anti-German policy'. Radicals like Angell and H. N. Brailsford wanted open, public discussion of foreign policy because without an educated public opinion schemes of international courts and arbitration were bound to fail. Labour, they could see, might become central to this project because as Angell observed 'the question of public opinion is mainly a question of the worker'.[53] As things actually stood Great Power relations were given to crises that might lead to a general war in which Britain was allied with France against Germany. Yet if a dispute between France and Germany over another annexation of African territory had brought about this outcome in 1912: 'The country was in the completest ignorance of the whole thing and, if war had broken out, millions in this country would not have known what it was about. Our real obligation in the matter dated presumably from some secret arrangement . . . an arrangement which has never come before Parliament, to which the people of this country have never given their consent, and about which they have never been consulted. The whole thing would have been the result of secret deals and bargains, the work of diplomatic and financial cliques operating in the dark, and playing with the lives of millions . . . On these matters involving questions of life and death the peoples are still less of ciphers than were the serfs in the squabbles of feudal chiefs . . . The whole situation is one of the amazing anomalies of our time, and if democracy has any meaning whatever it must assert itself and its principles in just those questions of life and death.'[54]

The advanced liberals and many of the socialists within the Labour Party concurred with this analysis. Even a Liberal Imperialist like Lord Rosebery worried that the conduct of foreign policy employed methods so secret and precarious that the outbreak of a major war might be accompanied by profound problems of obtaining popular legitimacy. Foreign policy, it seemed to the critics, was increasingly treated as a residual executive authority of the Crown, unassailable by Parliament. The question of the arms race was obviously connected to these problems. Philip Snowden's speech on the naval estimates in 1914 explicitly linked the dark 'understanding with France' to the naval build-up which he described as a menace to the peace of the world; and he warned that Labour would not feel obliged to support any future Expeditionary Force.[55] Thus Labour spokesmen criticised the endemic practice of excluding the British public from the debate over foreign policy, which was conducted within a very narrow elite. Other socialists focused on the arms traders, who were depicted as cosmopolitan, monopoly capitalists with only bogus patriotic credentials. Collectively, rather like the 'military–industrial complex' referred to by President Eisenhower in 1958, they were seen as a danger to democracy, though one that nationalisation of the industry might overcome.[56] Progressives and pacifists objected to 'preparations of war' represented by the arms race and the scare campaigns and anti-German sentiments of the right-wing press and pressure groups.

The continental parties of the socialist Second International contained factions that equated capitalism and war much more strongly than this. In such circles talk of international arbitration was virtually meaningless and the prospect of open diplomacy a non-starter, especially for those of them operating in the Tsarist and Austro-Hungarian Empires. But the Second International was also led by men whose views about international relations were not much different from those of advanced liberalism, especially those of them living in the more liberal states. All of the socialist parties had begun to think about war on a regular basis from 1904. The Russo-Japanese War of 1904–5 was of direct interest to two of the national sections and it coincided with talk of another war between France and Germany, after the Kaiser's visit to Tangier in the spring of

1905. This was stimulus enough. The Labour Party – an anomaly in ideological terms – was only admitted to the International in 1907, against the wishes of members who complained about its Liberalism. But on questions of international relations the Labour Party's doubtful ideological credentials were no disadvantage. Both liberals and socialists in Britain – a country in which the boundaries between these ideologies were especially porous[57] – had been aware of the problem of the growing capacities of states to fight destructive wars and both were conscious of the numerous and growing points of conflict between the Great Powers. Ideas of international arbitration and arms controls grew in this context, so did international pacifism of the sort represented in Britain by the National Peace Council from 1908.[58]

In reality a number of distinct policies were conflated as pacifism,[59] including the rejection of conventional defence and foreign policy nostrums; support for disarmament or appeasement; opposition to 'unnecessary' or unjust wars; socialist, liberal and radical internationalism; war-resistance (by general strike or other forms of civil disobedience); collective security; and moral objection (or conscientious objection) to war *per se*. Most of these positions amounted to the conviction that priority must be given to the prevention, even abolition, of war rather than the absolutist view that war was always ethically wrong and insupportable. War resistance had both socialist and liberal variants in Britain. Socialist anti-militarism stressed the capitalist provenance of wars, while liberals might stress the roots of war in nationalist, irrationalist and undemocratic tendencies. But these were permeable ideologies in Britain and there was much overlap of view. Alliances of socialists and liberals, for example, opposed conscription on libertarian grounds but also because they feared militarism as an antidemocratic and reactionary force.[60]

The socialists also produced a range of suggestions designed to address capitalist militarism, but even these were often not much different from the ideas of advanced liberals. All could agree that imperialism, militarism and chauvinism were bad things in the abstract but there was plenty of scope for disagreement about how they were best tackled. Some argued that nothing short of revolution and socialism would suffice; others preached isolationism or strict pacifism and/or disarmament; or argued for the replacement of standing armies by citizens' militias – a proposal favoured by the SDF in Britain.[61] Socialists were still everywhere excluded from government and even where there was a large socialist presence in Parliament, as in Germany, it was not able to do much to influence foreign policy. This was one obvious reason for the abstract and academic content of so much of what they had to say about defence and foreign policy.

The Second International became famous for its resolutions on war and its inability to prevent it or even stand above the dramatic upsurge of rival nationalisms in August 1914. All the main parties had factions or groups within them which spanned the ideological spectrum from Marxist revolutionary ideology to liberal and even conservative values and beliefs. But the greatest working for pragmatism in the British and German parties was the trade union organisations and in the case of the Labour Party the economic and social interests of the organised working class loomed much larger than other matters. In France the socialists had a much weaker relationship with the unions and it was here that syndicalism was strongest, with its myth of the transformative potential of the general strike. Divisions within the French left on the efficacy of the general strike as a measure against war were transferred to the Stuttgart congress of the International in 1907, reopening an issue raised as early as 1893 at Zurich. Those who saw that a future war between the Great Powers would be on the scale imagined by Engels – a scale likely to weaken the capitalist state – reasoned, as Lenin and Rosa Luxemburg reasoned, that such a war supplied the occasion for the 'overthrow of class rule'. But others feared that seizing this opportunity was just as likely to produce the destruction of the party that took the revolutionary initiative. The compromise which was adopted at Stuttgart committed the parties to very little. The matter was raised again three years later, at Copenhagen, and on this occasion Keir Hardie joined others in urging that a general strike should commence if war were declared. But nothing could better illustrate the emptiness of such gestures; Hardie belonged to the party that was least likely to observe any resolution of the Second International, let alone one calling for a general strike to prevent war.

Even in Germany, where the largest Marxist party existed, the routine of trade union and parliamentary work was accustoming socialists to the practice of reform and compromise. Where the national parties were tiny and ineffectual, with no parliamentary representation or very little, it cost nothing to gesture against war and such parties continued to do so right up to the crisis of 1914. We have seen that the Labour Representation Committee (LRC) came into existence in 1900 at the time when an inglorious and divisive imperialist war was taking place in South Africa. But the LRC came into existence to address a rather narrow range of domestic matters and, though it proved impossible to ignore issues of British foreign policy altogether, there was no great sense of urgency to formulate a specifically Labour view on the Boer War, nor was one expected of it. Most of the people associated with the cause of independent labour representation were content to follow the lead supplied by the different factions and personalities of the Liberal Party. Within this 'progressive alliance' – the spectrum of like-minded socialists and liberals which emerged in the 1880s and 1890s[62] – could be found most of the viewpoints which divided the centre-left in the years up to 1914.

Conclusions

Such evidence as we possess, then, suggests that the LRC had entered a world in which the forces of militarism, nationalism and imperialism were succeeding. The British public had grown accustomed to colonial wars and the right of Britain to intervene when it saw fit in the affairs of the 'backward peoples' had become largely uncontroversial. Patriotism was increasingly mobilised by the state to defend its imperialist interests. The new phenomenon of working-class jingoism, at once royalist and racist and aligned with the Conservative Party, grew stronger from the 1880s.[63] It became increasingly difficult to disconnect patriotism from support for the institutional status quo represented by the Crown-in-Parliament in Britain and the glorification of British arms and empire. Dissentients were a small minority, 'their voices . . . all but drowned in the general imperial clamour of the Chamberlainite era', unable to make an impression on the forces arrayed against them in 1900.[64] From the outset Labour attracted elements aligned both with the liberal tradition of internationalism and pacifism which resisted jingoism and, to a much smaller extent, that socialist tradition which appealed to class solidarity and working-class internationalism. But the largest point of overlap among British political parties was the unshakeable conviction that the British Empire was a force for good in the world and the basis for Britain's Great Power status. The fact that this position was increasingly claimed by other nation states with imperial interests and that inter-imperialist rivalries intensified as the nineteenth century closed only served to heighten the consciousness of Britain's special place in the world. The old Concert of Europe had withered, international arbitration was increasingly ignored and an assertive nationalism became the dominant theme throughout Europe. States made their preparations to survive international conflicts with ever bigger armies, more sophisticated weapons and better military plans. Germany enacted its Second Naval Law in 1900, thus precipitating an arms race with Britain, in the year of Labour's birth. By this time the standing armies and war potential of the continental Great Powers had been steadily increasing for the previous twenty-five years.[65] Britain, having the luxury of island insulation, responded to the quest for military superiority by strengthening its navy and even among the leading socialists there was support for, even insistence on, the naval arms race.

Thus the growth of pro-imperialist sentiment, after 1880, blunted, where it failed to eliminate, the critical edge of Liberalism and

Nonconformism in relation to Britain's colonial role.[66] The militarisation of British society and the ruling assumptions of Britain's imperial manifest destiny eroded pacifism, divided the Nonconformist sects and isolated dissidents as eccentrics and deviants.[67] By 1900 Nonconformity was often associated with the promotion of a benign view of the British Empire, not least because of its growing appetite for overseas missionary work. Political Nonconformity was in any case dying by this time and certainly did not survive the First World War.[68] Some Radicals, Nonconformists and socialists, though small in number, nevertheless continued to believe that deviations from a moral foreign policy (such as the Jameson Raid, 1895–6) were both reckless and sinister, sometimes representing these acts as the folly of particular vainglorious politicians, at other times promoting the selfish sectional interest of an aristocratic caste, international Jewry or an economic faction such as finance capital. In 1906 the Liberal economist J. A. Hobson[69] developed this last argument in his internationally acclaimed *Imperialism*.

Popular prejudices, which Hobson himself was not entirely free from, were little troubled by the analytical niceties of *Imperialism*. The milieu in which oppositional ideas could be nurtured was small and not simply because of the transformation of Nonconformity. Britain was also at the weaker end of the spectrum of social democratic strength, a relevant consideration when estimating the prospects for an alternative to the dominant perspectives on British foreign policy. Many contemporaries, however, took the view that growing economic interdependence between the Great Powers made major wars increasingly unlikely and certainly of little economic value even to the victor.[70] Since the brief but decisive Franco-Prussian war of 1870 Europe had been free of such conflicts. The British, controlling an empire which they perceived as a force for good in the world and protected by their offshore position and the Royal Navy from the need for a large standing army and conscription, were perhaps especially inclined to complacent consensus on foreign policy and defence issues. Since the socialist revival of the 1880s such groups as the Fabian Society, the Social Democratic Federation and the Independent Labour Party contained individuals who took a different view. The argument that capitalism promoted war, not peace as Cobdenite liberals maintained, was always at least an element in the debates of these groups and sometimes the dominant view. The Labour Party would find a place for such people but it was not until the 1930s that their views became the regnant ideology in the organisation.

When war began in August 1914 the Labour Party had around 1,600,000 affiliated members and received affiliation fees representing a further 30,000 members of the ILP and 3,304 for the Fabian Society. The British Socialist Party[71] joined as an affiliated organisation in January

1916 claiming 10,000 members. Allowing for understatement of the individual membership, Cole calculated that the three socialist societies had at most 65,000 members between them.[72] He also observed that the Labour Party had some sort of local organisation in only 158 areas, except where the ILP was its de facto representative.[73] Most of Labour's local organisations were trades councils and only 65 were designed for specifically political, rather than industrial, work. In some respects, then, Labour was barely a party at all. It had certainly not had much time to think about foreign policy, but the membership did expect to have a say in such matters, if only through the party's annual conference, the forum of its inner-party democracy.[74]

2   The First World War

Eight to ten million soldiers will swallow each other up and in doing so eat all Europe more bare than any swarm of locusts. The devastation of the Thirty Years' War compressed into the space of three or four years and extending over the whole continent; famine, sickness, want, brutalizing the army and the mass of the population; irrevocable confusion of our artificial structure of trade, industry and credit, ending in general bankruptcy; collapse of the old states and their traditional statecraft, so that crowns will roll by dozens in the gutter and no one be found to pick them up; it is absolutely impossible to predict where it will all end and who will emerge from the struggle as victor. Only one result is absolutely certain: general exhaustion and the establishment of the conditions for the final victory of the working class.

(Engels, 1887)[1]

War in his imagination was something, a source of news and emotion, that happened in a restricted area, called the Seat of War. But now the whole atmosphere was the Seat of War, and every land a cockpit. So closely had the nations raced along the path of research and invention, so secret and yet so parallel had been their plans and acquisitions.

(H. G. Wells, *The War in the Air*, 1908)

The July crisis

We saw in the first chapter that at Stuttgart in 1907 and again at Copenhagen in 1910 the International affirmed its opposition to any war involving the Great Powers.[2] The parties agreed 'to use every effort to prevent war by all means which seem to them most appropriate' and if the war nevertheless broke out (in a clause added on Lenin's and Luxemburg's urgings), to intervene to bring it promptly to an end and use their energies to exploit any political and economic crisis thus created to hasten the fall of capitalism. There was no suggestion that such a war could be a just war, or a war of national defence, or that opinion on the war would be influenced by who started it, who was right or wrong or that it mattered who won or lost the war. As the July crisis unfolded the socialist press in Europe warned against a general conflagration. On 25 July, the day Austria–Hungary declared war on Serbia, *Vorwarts* correctly anticipated the way the alliance system could lead to this very outcome.[3] Militarism and secret diplomacy were indicted by all and every one of the principal leaders who attended the Bureau of the International when it met to consider the problem in Brussels on the 29th. A successful open-air mass meeting only served to disguise the fact that no practical decisions were taken other than to call for more demonstrations.

The Parliamentary Labour Party (PLP) met on 30 July to express its support (as Jean Jaurès had done at Brussels) for Sir Edward Grey's attempts to mediate between Serbia and Austria and to say that 'on no account will this country be dragged into the European conflict in which, as the Prime Minister has stated, we have no direct interest, and the Party calls upon all Labour organisations in the country to watch events vigilantly so as to oppose if need be in the most effective way any action which may involve us in war'.[4] Under the auspices of the British Section of the International Socialist Bureau, a demonstration was held in Trafalgar Square on 1 August to oppose war and a manifesto was issued to the same effect. Keir Hardie and Arthur Henderson both called for peace. MacDonald met Grey on 3 August, the day when British mobilisation began, with instructions to ask that everything should be done to keep Britain out of a European war. War was nevertheless declared the next day in the traditional way – with no reference to Parliament. On 5 August Labour's Executive blamed this outcome on secret diplomacy. The parliamentary group nevertheless voted for war credits just hours later and after several meetings a majority of the leadership decided that 'under the circumstances it was impossible for this country to have remained neutral'. This was hardly a ringing endorsement, but it was enough. By this time the German SPD had voted overwhelmingly to support war credits in the Reichstag, and some of its deputies, like Hugo Haase, suppressed their own views for the sake of party unity.

A Labour circular issued on 7 August, repeating the Executive's first reaction, continued to express serious reservations. It attributed the conflict to balance of power politics pursued by traditional diplomacy. The Foreign Secretary was named as a particular culprit for having committed Britain to France without the involvement of Parliament, much less with the knowledge of the people. The German socialists, meanwhile, told themselves that they were involved in a defence of their home-land against Russian barbarism and reaction. In France there was little opposition among the socialists for war credits even before the German declaration of war on 3 August; thereafter support for war credits was unanimous. Here was another war of national defence. But what was Britain's purpose? The Labour circular suggested that there were very serious misgivings among party leaders that Britain had been pitched into the war because of diplomatic blunders. Indeed this is what some Liberals also believed and there were five resignations from the Government over the issue. In practical terms, however, the Labour Party and its affiliated trade unions would soon show that they were firm in their resolve to support the war effort, once presented with the fact of war as they were from 4 August. The party's first real preparation for its impact was established the next day when the War Emergency Workers' National Committee was set up to tackle the economic and social problems generated by war. It met throughout the war years and in Cole's judgement helped to prevent a split within the leadership as it kept pro- and anti-war factions working together for the next four years.[5] MacDonald nevertheless resigned as party Chairman and Arthur Henderson, the Chief Whip, took over his job.

Yet Henderson, like MacDonald, also belonged to the Union of Democratic Control (UDC), an organisation created in the second week of August 1914 by a collection of Liberals and ILP people who questioned Britain's participation in the conflict and wanted to set about analysing the conditions for a just and stable peace. Henderson thus managed to lead Labour's support of the war effort while associating himself with dissidents who believed that the war was the avoidable outcome of secret diplomacy and balance of power politics. It seems that Victor Adler was right: the leader of the Austrian social democrats (who also voted for war credits) said that it was incomprehensible not to identify with one's country in war; and it was incomprehensible as a social democrat to do so 'without being racked with pain'.[6] In Britain tormented socialists such as MacDonald were fortunate in having bolder liberal allies than their counterparts abroad and it was these liberal allies who turned their minds to reform of the international system. They did so by a variety of initiatives including those taken in 1915 by G. Lowes Dickinson[7] and Lord Bryce,[8] by the Fabian Society and the League of Nations Society, as well as by individuals within the UDC. But it was the UDC which exercised most influence upon the Labour Party by the end of the war.

Until the end of August 1914 Labour managed to combine official expressions of dissent with the vote for war credits and change of leader. Practical expressions of support for the war soon prevailed, accurately reflecting the balance of opinion within a party which the trade unions dominated. During the last two weeks of August the Executive took steps to promote enlistment to the armed forces and agreed to a political truce for the duration of the conflict. The TUC had already agreed to an industrial truce. The ILP, by contrast, appeared to have no doubt that the war was wrong and issued a statement on 13 August expressing solidarity with the German socialists, while blaming the war on militarism and secret diplomacy. It drew on pacifist as well as socialist objections to the war but also on Radical arguments of the sort expressed by MacDonald, who blamed the war on vested interests. Five of its seven MPs[9] were anti-war, as were most of its membership, but a pro-war minority survived within it, including its chairman Fred Jowett. At the beginning of 1915 the National Administrative Council of the ILP reported that 124 branches or divisional councils of the party supported this anti-war lead, while only 11 took a pro-war stance. There was no anti-war campaign, however, except in the pages of *Labour Leader* under Brockway's editorship. The ILP eventually expressed its unified opposition to the war in a pacifist resolution supported by its 1916 annual conference. The BSP likewise took time to formulate a position that would stick. Initially supporting the recruitment campaign, much of the membership rebelled against its pro-war leaders but it took until 1916 before the likes of Hyndman and Blatchford were forced to resign, forming a rival pro-war National Socialist Party. The Fabian Society took no collective position, but was clearly split on the issue with most of the old guard taking a patriotic view. Meanwhile a minority of feminists actively opposed the war and Sylvia Pankhurst's Women's International League was able to organise about 3,500 of them by the end of 1916.[10] Opponents of the war could also be found in the unions, especially among the younger militants such as A. A. Purcell, Manchester organiser of the National Amalgamated Furnishing Trades Association, and a member of the BSP left wing; and the 21-year-old James Figgins, a critic of J. H. Thomas within the National Union of Railwaymen who went on to be elected its first left-wing leader in 1948; and the young Will Lawther of the miners, who was so opposed to the war that he even refused to subscribe to the Red Cross. Ernest Bevin, one of the dockers' national organisers in 1914, was by contrast critical of both the super patriots as well as those who were strongly against the war.

The critics and sceptics were vastly outnumbered, however, by those who took a patriotic stance and even men who had no confidence in the official explanations for the war, such as Hardie and MacDonald, were soon reconciled to the idea that now that it had started it had to be fought to a finish – the view of most UDC members too. The opinions of the pro-war trade unionists, and the MPs elected under trade union auspices, simply hardened in the course of August and September. By 15 October, when *The British Labour Party and the War* was published, it was possible for the pro-war majority of the party and trade unions to blame the outbreak of the war on Germany and to justify their total commitment to its defeat. The winning formula was defence of Belgian neutrality, and the defence of democracy against German militarism. Though Labour's annual conference, scheduled for January 1915, was abandoned, the ILP – losing members because of the crisis, rather than gaining them – met as usual that Easter and reiterated its opposition to the recruitment campaign. The gap between the pro- and anti-war sides had widened and there was no doubt that pro-war people held a large majority of the Labour Party.

The union leaders who supported the war included icons of the movement such as Ben Tillett who became a national institution by virtue of countless recruitment speeches and visits to the Front; and Will Thorne, veteran of the SDF, co-founder with Tillett of the Gasworkers and General Labourers union in March 1889, who joined the 1st volunteer battalion of the Essex regiment, a unit in which he became lieutenant-colonel. Thorne was sent to Russia in 1917 to do what he could to keep it in the war. Then there were foundation members of the party such as Arthur Hayday of the National Union of General Workers, who belonged to the patriotic wing of the BSP and was to serve on wartime tribunals, set up under the Military Service Act, in which he was the scourge of shirkers posing as conscientious objectors; George Barnes of the Engineers, a foundation member of the ILP who helped to recruit skilled engineers for war work and joined the coalition government as minister for pensions in December 1916, later succeeding Henderson in the war Cabinet as minister without portfolio in August 1917; William Adamson, general secretary of the Fife Miners' Association, who became chair of the PLP in succession to Arthur Henderson in October 1917; J. R. Clynes, foundation member of the ILP, who served on the food commission in 1917; James Sexton, general secretary of the dock labourers' union, whose distaste for the anti-war socialists led him, as it did John Davis, general secretary of the Brassworkers, to briefly favour the creation of a 'trade union' labour party to be rid of them in 1918. The practical pro-war side also included men like Tom Shaw of the International Federation of Textile Workers who acted as director of national service for the west midland region and Harry Gosling, president of the National Transport Workers' Federation, who served on wartime committees concerned with the transport of men, munitions and food supplies.

On 14 February 1915 the inter-Allied conference of socialist and labour parties unanimously agreed – despite the weight of patriotic sentiment which it represented – that it could not ignore 'the profound general causes of the European conflict, itself a monstrous product of the antagonisms which tear asunder capitalist society and of the policy of Colonial dependencies and aggressive Imperialism . . . in which every Government has its share of responsibility'. While victory for German Imperialism, it claimed, 'would be the defeat and the destruction of democracy and liberty in Europe', there could be no justification for the 'economic crushing of Germany' when the war was finished. It was the Governments of Germany and Austria that were at fault, not the people of those countries. The socialists of the Allied countries, the conference concluded, 'demand that Belgium shall be liberated . . . that throughout all Europe, from Alsace–Lorraine to the Balkans, those populations that have been annexed by force shall receive the right to freely dispose of themselves'. The resolution then affirmed that the delegates were 'inflexibly resolved to fight until victory'; but also that they stood opposed to 'any attempt to transform this defensive war into a war of conquest'. The conference thus set down the ideological limits of the war – which was to be for 'popular liberty', 'unity', 'independence' and the 'autonomy of the nations in the peaceful Federation of the United States of Europe and the world'.[11] It was not to be an excuse for merely crushing Germany.

The dissidents

In the first two years of the war 2.7 million men volunteered. The nation was united behind the war effort. But there were reasons to doubt that enthusiasm for the war was quite as extensive as the authorities maintained. The war was justified in terms of lending a hand to the victim (Belgium) of unprovoked aggression. The authorities felt obliged, in other words, to moralise the conflict. In an age of approaching democracy there was, perhaps, no other way to gain legitimacy for the war – governments ever since 1914 have certainly made this assumption. But this meant that democratic publics, repeatedly exposed to such propaganda, would fall into outrage if it turned out that wars were actually conducted for other reasons – such as balance of power considerations or the acquisition of territory. Many liberal internationalists supported the war because, as Martin Ceadal observes, they concluded that 'the wrong committed by Germany on Belgium outweigh[ed] the contributory negligence of British foreign policy in consequence of its imperialism, irrationalism, secret diplomacy, arms trading, and capitalism about which peace activists had been complaining since the turn of the century'.[12] They took the celebrated view of H. G. Wells – that it was the war to end war. There was thus no incompatibility between support for the war on these grounds and support for a future League of Nations, which G. L. Dickinson was calling for from as early as September 1914. Thus the quest to prevent future wars was by no means the preoccupation only of the open critics of the conflict begun on 4 August 1914. Furthermore, as Wells himself demonstrated in *Mr Britling Sees It Through* (1916), as the war wore on its initial rationale wore thin, and doubts and misgivings increased. The authorities were careful not to rely on the persuasiveness of their anti-Prussianist arguments. Prussian methods were adopted in Britain, according to the critics. Indeed, one author argues that 'it is difficult to understand the spirit of persecution and repression which permeated Britain' at this time.[13] Official secrecy was intensified. Censorship was strict. The Defence of the Realm Act was invoked to suppress anti-war activity. Socialists and pacifists were imprisoned. The elements of compulsion increased in number and degree as the war extended its life. The lives of individuals became more regimented as power was increasingly centralised. *Habeas corpus* was suspended, war resisters were subject to various forms of vilification as well as state repression (MacDonald and Bertrand Russell were well-known victims). The secret police expanded the net of surveillance.

Throughout the course of the conflict small groups of dissidents created new campaigning organisations to oppose various aspects of it. They had to because the pre-war peace societies were thrown into confusion when the war began. Even among Quakers as many as a third of males of military age ended up in military service.[14] The Peace Society effectively acquiesced in the war, the National Peace Council was divided, the International Arbitration League justified the war as a struggle against militarism, and the churches enthusiastically rallied to its support. New organisations were created to fill the void including some of those already mentioned such as the League of Nations Society, the Women's International League, the Fellowship of Reconciliation and the No-Conscription Fellowship. Only the last two were strictly pacifist. Ceadal suggests the neutralism of the UDC drew not only upon isolationist sentiment (which was John Burns' reason for resigning from the Cabinet); but also hatred of Tsarism; as well as 'a cultural partiality among intellectuals towards Germany' (John Morley, who resigned from the Cabinet with Burns, is offered as an example).[15] The decision to bring neutralists together was taken by C. P. Trevelyan, a junior minister in the Liberal Government, who resigned on 5 August.[16] He was joined by Norman Angell, MacDonald, E. D. Morel and Arthur Ponsonby[17] as founder members. These men were not really interested in a League of Nations; they believed Britain's involvement in the war was unnecessary and held to old Radical doctrines of British isolationism. But later members, such as Arthur Henderson who was elected to the general council of the UDC in November 1914, favoured an international council of sorts and some, such as Angell, realised that a form of permanent collective security was necessary to avoid future wars and that the old radicalism was obsolete. Leonard Woolf wrote that the demand for some sort of international authority was 'continually upon the lips or pens of a large number of more or less intelligent persons of every variety of beliefs' within months of the outbreak of the war'.[18] Foremost among these was Lowes Dickinson, who joined the UDC in October 1914, J. A. Hobson, H. N. Brailsford,[19] the Bryce Group – which included Ponsonby and Graham Wallas, as well as Lowes Dickinson, Woolf and Lord Bryce himself. The League of Nations Society was set up in March 1915 by these people but kept a low profile until 1917.

Many more people opposed compulsory military service than opposed the war itself. Anti-conscription elements could be found in the Liberal Party, in the unions, the ILP, the left wing of the Labour Party and in religious and pacifist societies. The Irish also opposed it.[20] The No-Conscription Fellowship, set up by Fenner Brockway, Bertrand Russell and Clifford Allen in November 1914, tried to coordinate this opposition and from January 1916 sought the repeal of the Military Service Act. But the vast majority of people accepted that an efficient prosecution of the war was always likely to lead to conscription. The authorities also took the precaution of exempting Ireland and thus defusing the opposition of most of the one million Irish living in Britain, as well as their compatriots at home who were increasingly drawn to Sinn Fein in the second half of the conflict. In the event there were only 16,500 conscientious objectors officially recorded. The vast majority of those who doubted the necessity for British involvement or who opposed the war on other grounds were nevertheless brought into the war effort. Even the radical neutralists of the UDC fell into this category and did not, for example, oppose conscription, though they were moved to campaign for a negotiated peace from March 1916. The opponents of war had to wait until 1917 before things began to improve from their perspective, largely because war-weariness, the Russian Revolution, the exposure of the secret treaties, and the entry of the USA into the war encouraged the Labour Party to adopt an outlook that was very similar to the UDC's, thus reconciling the war critics within its ranks and the majority of war supporters.

The mysterious forces which drove Britain to war and turned a regional dispute in the Balkans into a general conflagration appeared unstoppable to many observers. Perhaps it was for this reason that so many people came to believe in the necessity of mastering them to ensure a just peace. Even the Labour manifesto of 15 October 1914 held out the prospect of future international concord based on new machineries of arbitration. The Union of Democratic Control went much further by proclaiming four guiding principles. First, that there should be no territorial adjustments without the consent of the peoples concerned. Second, that parliamentary sanction was required for any treaty, arrangement or undertaking entered into by Great Britain. Third, that British foreign policy should eschew the balance of power and aim for the establishment of a Concert of the Powers and some sort of International Council, operating in public for the arbitration of international disputes, together with an international court capable of interpretation and enforcement. Finally, the UDC insisted that the peace settlement should aim for the drastic reduction, by consent, of the armaments of the belligerents and arrangements for the nationalisation of the weapons industries and the control of their exports. In May 1916 J. A. Hobson added a fifth principle intended to eliminate economic warfare by the promotion of 'free commercial intercourse among all nations by expanding the principle of the Open Door'.[21]

Norman Angell, writing before the end of 1914, acknowledged that popular support for the war in Britain had been mobilised for the elimination of 'the evil doctrine of Nietzcheanism and brute force'. 'The immense majority', he believed, wanted to free Europe from this menace and 'end the nightmare of militarism' and 'worship of the war god'.[22] The war was thus not so much against another nation as against an 'evil spirit'. The idea that Britain was engaged in a 'spiritual conflict' was endorsed by all shades of pro-war domestic political opinion – Liberal, Conservative, and Labour – with the Prime Minister, Herbert Asquith, and *The Times* among the most conspicuous advocates of this doctrine. Some even went so far, as H. G. Wells and Professor Gilbert Murray,[23] in arguing not only that defeat of Germany would secure the goals of extinguishing militarism, but that victory for the Entente would liberate the Russians from autocracy. Angell, whose own preferences were neutralist in August 1914, agreed with the received wisdom to the extent that he believed it to be in the best interests of mankind that the Allies should win. There was, he said, 'not the faintest risk of the nation wavering on that point'. But Angell also argued that crushing Germany would not achieve the desired results; on the contrary, it would 'leave us in a worse condition than before the war, expose us to a renewal at no distant date, fasten the shackles of militarism more firmly than ever upon the long-suffering peoples of Europe'.[24]

Angell realised that even if the Allies were to kill a quarter of a million German soldiers, which he thought a 'very large estimate', they could not eliminate Germany.[25] Germany would survive to fight another day, even if partitioned. Partition itself would solve nothing, it would simply multiply the number of undemocratic provinces containing rebellious peoples and perhaps revive French militarism. Of all the peoples of Europe, Angell argued, the Germans were most nearly allied to the British 'in race and blood', 'in moral outlook, in their attitude to the things which really matter'. But he realised that people had forgotten all of this and other arguments would be needed to counter the official rhetoric of 'crushing Germany' and of 'wiping' her off the map. People were already talking in 1914 of the return of Alsace–Lorraine to France, of a new Poland at Germany's expense, of the transfer of the German colonies, the destruction of her fleet, the dethronement of the Kaiser and the dismemberment of Austria. Angell spoke for the UDC in objecting to these prescriptions, arguing that without Germany's cooperation and consent no peace would endure, much less one so punitive. States showed powers of recuperation in the past, they would do so in the future. Germany would recover and since history showed that the mutability of alliances was extreme there was no prospect of a stable coalition of states to prevent its vengeful resurgence. The Germans themselves had demonstrated both truths after Jena and Auerstadt; indeed German nationalism had flourished in the nineteenth century only after the Prussian armies were crushed by Napoleon. No destruction of the German cities and industries now, in Angell's judgement, would stop their revival 'within a very few years'.

Nor would the balance of power suffice. To secure peace by a deterrent armed force was doomed to fail precisely because it appealed to every state, and one state's defensive measures were another's chief security threat. No balance was thus possible, rather a perpetual instability and threat of war. The only answer, according to Angell, was to eliminate 'Prussianism' as a state of mind affecting all the Great Powers. This would involve recognition that 'the struggle for political power' was 'a barren and evil thing'. The Allies upon victory would need to promote mutual cooperation, 'a frank recognition that nations do form a society'. The Germans may well have started the war as Allied propaganda said they had, Angell allowed, but the people of Germany thought of themselves as combatants in a defensive war. One-third of them were allied to social democracy which had fought Prussianism at every turn. The Germans did not monopolise the militarist mentality, it was found everywhere.

G. Lowes Dickinson put the point even more forcefully for American readers in December 1914.[26] If the war had been caused by militarism, by secret diplomacy and intrigue, the peace that followed could only be secured by an extension of democracy to international relations. Foreign policy would have to come under democratic scrutiny, the self-determination of nations had to be established as a cardinal principle, armaments had to be subject to national and international controls and the nations had to submit their disputes to arbitration and conciliation by a 'League of Europe'. Woodrow Wilson, the President of the USA, was receptive to these arguments, as indeed were many of his compatriots who saw the European political leaders as greedy imperialists and representatives of self-serving, rather reactionary, even discredited, elites. Most of the Americans who held these views, it should be pointed out, including

Wilson, took an altogether more constructive view of the foreign interventions of the USA, such as those in pre-war Central America. These were always depicted as disinterested attempts to restore order or promote democracy. Likewise American foreign economic policy was always packaged in the anodyne language of free trade. Like the British, the Americans were adept at moralising their own foreign policy; the connections between, say, free trade and gun boat diplomacy were rarely mentioned. As neutrals at the start of the Great War, however, the Americans held the moral high ground in the eyes of most of the war's liberal and socialist critics.

Some of these critics quickly turned to the issue raised by Lowes Dickinson – an international league of states that would prevent wars in the future. Despite all the talk in these circles of the profound causes of war – imperialism, militarism and capitalism – their logic, in common with the arguments of the peace movement of the inter-war years, centred on the perception that wars were avoidable. This rather suggests that there was something about the First World War which persuaded them that it need not have happened. It was the paradigm of the First World War – the war that could have been avoided – which informed the debate on war prevention for the next quarter century. The Fabian Society, for example, set up an International Agreements Committee in January 1915 in order to investigate methods for maintaining peace. Leonard Woolf was commissioned to turn the Committee's research into a book. A conference was held in May 1915 to discuss the findings of the research and Hobson and Lowes Dickinson were among those who participated in its debates. In July the *New Statesman* published two articles deriving from these discussions as 'Suggestions for the Prevention of War'. After another conference involving members of the Bryce group Woolf published *International Government* in 1916, one of the handful of seminal publications which can be said to have guided the creators of the League of Nations.

Woolf found four major categories for the causes of war: disputes arising from legal or quasi-legal differences; those stemming from economic relationships; those arising from administrative or political relationships; and those arising from questions of national honour. Like the leading Fabians, he saw government as a regulatory activity. International government therefore meant international regulation. Just as the Webbs and Shaw were convinced that established social and economic trends pointed towards a more collectivist society in the future, so Woolf outlined the evolution of global social and economic activity and the evolution of institutions designed to regulate and coordinate it. The beginnings of international government already existed in this view as international law evolved in precision and scope and the number and responsibilities of international organisations multiplied.[27] Dozens of organisations had already been established to permit international co-operation for specific purposes, whether in business, medicine, communications or other specialisms. Global commerce, in Woolf's view, drove global integration forward, forcing states to make global rules and regulations, to promote standardisation, establish ethical practices and devise a host of other principles. The British Empire was an advanced expression of this process.

These attempts to facilitate and direct global activities did not involve an unacceptable surrender of national interests, in the Fabian view. International government already existed in embryo and Woolf provided examples of its operation since the beginning of the nineteenth century – such as the post-1815 Great Power Concert; the destruction of the Turkish fleet by the Powers in 1821 (to protect Greece); and the mediation over the Balkan revolt against Ottoman rule in 1876, and the related Congress of Berlin. International adjudication, he argued, was becoming more realistic as illustrated by the arbitration which followed the Dogger Bank incident of October 1904, when the Russian fleet fired on Swedish and British vessels which they mistook for Japanese belligerents. Woolf was optimistic that states could take these developments further so that they might define issues on which they would be prepared to submit to the arbitration and conciliation of a supranational organisation. An International Court would have to be established for the resolution of all such justiciable disputes, that is, disputes deriving from matters of international law. But he also saw that the international order needed to be upset legally from time to time to prevent it from functioning as a defence of the status quo, and for this an International Conference or Council was required, over-representing the Great Powers, so that certain non-justiciable matters could be resolved politically. In these cases the parties to the dispute would be required to submit to a cooling-off period of twelve months, which would give time for conciliation and the investigation of causes. Economic sanctions would be used against states failing to comply and in the last resort, Woolf argued, the world association of states would oblige its members to take military action against a transgressor. Woolf admitted that the objective internationalising changes which he identified ran well ahead of political consciousness in that there was as yet no international psychology corresponding to these developments. Few felt or thought internationally, much less perceived themselves as world citizens. Woolf assumed that the evolution of international organisation was destined to supplant rather than coexist with power politics and the balance of power system, but he offered no evidence for this optimism. He was right, however, to see that national sovereignty was inevitably eroded by certain international developments and his thinking reached similar conclusions to those later embedded in the League of Nations' Covenant with regard to the outlawing of aggression, the use of economic sanctions, the need to make common cause against rogue states, the distinction between justiciable and non-justiciable disputes, the need for arbitration, cooling-off periods, and so on.

The basic idea of the Fabians, widely accepted today, was that international organisation was a feasible and useful way to promote common interests and reduce international friction. This was a revolutionary notion in 1915, certainly by contrast with the conservative pre-war view of war as an inevitable almost natural phenomenon. Woolf was already thinking in terms of a collective security system ultimately based on economic and military sanctions in 1915. Others would soon join him in this, such as Arthur Henderson. But the surrender of any portion of national sovereignty was utterly alien to most members of the political establishment and even some of those concerned to prevent future wars could not bring themselves to advocate it. The group under Lord Bryce's presidency is a case in point. Its modest proposal was that states should keep their sovereignty but in future be bound by treaty obligations to keep the peace. The signatories of this social contract would be obliged to submit all justiciable disputes to The Hague Court of Arbitration and accept its findings. War would be prevented by cooling-off periods, impartial study of disputes and the moral authority deriving from impartial rulings. No automatic sanctions were envisaged for states refusing to accept such rulings. Yet despite the modesty of their proposals it was not until 1917 that the group felt confident enough to publish these ideas in Britain. But others were bolder and made their views known from the beginning of the conflict

For H. N. Brailsford, for example, the fact that the statesmen of Europe had been forced to justify the decisions of August 1914 in terms of national defence only served to underline the modern necessity of appealing to popular idealism in an age of democracy or near-democracy. Even the White Paper (*Denkschrift*), in which the official German position was set out, contained hardly so much as an incidental reference to France – whose threatened extinction served as one of Britain's justifications for entering the conflict – but rather focused its justification for the war exclusively on national defence against Russia. This was to repeat the logic of both Bethman–Hollweg's speech to the Reichstag and Hugo Haase's on behalf of the Social Democrats.[28] It was clear that these were the only terms on which the people could support war. But the destruction of militarism, according to Brailsford, would depend on them awakening from the widespread delusions with which they had been fed. Any victor's peace would merely defer the problem of militarism for another day. Any attempt to load Germany 'with indemnities, lop it of its provinces, encircle it with triumphant allies' would eventually result in an even bigger struggle to recover its standing in the world. 'No punishment could prevent the German people from remaining the best-organised, best-educated, and one of the most prolific of European races' according to Brailsford. A settlement which left them angry, embittered and cherishing revenge would last five, ten or twenty years, but no more. 'The future will stretch before us, a new phase of the ruinous armed peace, destined to end, after further years of anger and waste, in another war of revenge.'[29]

Brailsford argued that the broad fact about the war was that it was the postponed sequel of the Balkan war of 1912, when the Balkan League was formed under Russian guidance, as much against Austria as against Turkey. Even in 1912 the German press was full of scare stories predicting that the Slavs would hold predominant military power by 1916. The *Denkschrift* depicted Serbia as a tool of Russian policy and Brailsford agreed with it, seeing in preparations for a united Slav assault on Austria the main explanation for Germany's readiness to challenge Russia. The war was thus 'a co-operative crime' combining Russian ambitions and German fears. Further contributions to the European war, Brailsford argued, were made by statesmen who miscalculated Russia's prepared-ness to fight and Britain's commitment to neutrality. In any case, he reasoned, 'A preventive war, if it is not a crime as inexcusable as a war of naked aggression, is always a folly.'[30] Germany compounded the folly by violating Belgian neutrality. But moral responsibility for the 'universal war' which ensued was in Brailsford's opinion to be shared between Russia and Germany. Rejecting the 'parochial' view that the war was all about Belgian neutrality or the extinction of France, Brailsford saw it as primarily a Russo-German affair which would end logically 'in a melting of all frontiers of the East, and the settlement by force of arms of the question whether its destinies shall be governed by Germany or Russia'.[31] As such it was both barbarous and utterly remote from any real interest of Britain's. The fact that Britain was allied to Russia – an 'unscrupulous and incalculable Empire' – was incomprehensible; and only a 'mechanical fatality' had forced France, Russia's ally since 1894, to enter the war in its support. Thus for both Britain and France the outcome was irrational. For Brailsford, clear-sighted statesmanship now demanded of the British that they negotiate for peace before the conflict was allowed to drag the country into a prolonged fight over an issue of supreme irrelevance to the British Empire – who would exercise mastery in the Balkans.

It should be clear from these summaries that dissident opinion on the nature of the war did not always agree; but 'Diplomacy has failed'[32] was one of the slogans which united it. The blame fell upon statesmen who encouraged the arms race. But the remedy had also to go to the method of conducting foreign affairs which ran contrary to the spirit of democracy. This was a method based upon a small, exclusive elite working in conditions of secrecy inimical to accountability and public scrutiny. Constitutionally the British executive was allowed an unlimited discretion. The Crown prerogative which modern Prime Ministers exercised had worried some leading politicians precisely for this reason. Lord Rosebery, the Liberal imperialist, for example, observed in 1912 how difficult it was to know precisely what obligations the country had entered into 'in regard to which . . . anyone can predicate that they involve an immediate liability to a gigantic war in certain circumstances which are by no means unlikely to occur.'[33] If such an outcome was thrust upon an ignorant people, how would it react, he wondered? Austen Chamberlain, taking a Conservative view, expressed similar concerns in February 1914; the secrecy encompassing foreign relations prejudiced a successful mobilisation of popular support when an emergency finally arrived. For UDC activists like Arthur Ponsonby these anxieties merely illustrated the larger point. A British Foreign Secretary was exempt from parliamentary scrutiny of the sort which every other Minister was subjected to. Nor was he confronted by an informed Cabinet. 'In his own sphere', Ponsonby concluded, 'he is to all intents and purposes an autocrat', especially if the Opposition agrees with his policy (as the Conservatives approved Grey's policy before August 1914). In these increasingly common circumstances there would not even be a debate on the general lines of policy. Indeed 'the modern practice' was precisely to keep foreign affairs out of the arena of party politics altogether and thus exempt it from critical scrutiny.

The Foreign Office bureaucracy of diplomats and first-class clerks consisted of about 160 financially independent individuals in 1914, winners in a process that began with nomination and selection, before progressing to competitive examination. The larger portion of this socially unrepresentative group then remained abroad, moving in high official society to ensure that their complete ignorance of public opinion in the host country was as profound as their ignorance of opinion in Britain. Ponsonby suggested abolition of the income test and open examination in order to recruit a more representative foreign office official. This was not a very radical proposal. Ponsonby actually accepted the conventions of Cabinet and Ministerial responsibility – though these arguably contributed to the secrecy and centralism which lay at the root of the problem. He simply hoped that the Commons might scrutinise foreign policy more effectively if the Foreign Office Vote was discussed annually over two days. In this way, he thought, Parliamentary sanction would become a prerequisite for any foreign treaty and Parliament, like the

American Senate, would ultimately determine a declaration of war, rather than leaving it in the hands of the Prime Minister and Foreign Secretary. Gladstone had expressed his sympathy for similar suggestions almost thirty years earlier. As long ago as 19 March 1886, a parliamentary motion had been put down calling for an end to the practice of conducting foreign adventures – wars, annexations, contracts obligating Great Britain and the like – of which Parliament was not even informed, let alone consulted. But the gesture fell short of practical support. Ponsonby demanded in 1914 a permanent Cabinet Committee on Foreign Affairs, so at least the nominal executive would have an idea of policy in this area. He could also see the benefit of a Foreign Affairs Committee, empowered to scrutinise the Government's conduct in this area. But his analysis of the problem hinted at the need for bigger changes. For:

> when there is a body of military and naval experts with uncontrolled authority formulating strategic schemes, not necessarily confined to defensive operations, it is practically certain that they will sooner or later exercise an influence on policy behind the scenes, and instead of being the servants of the Executive, they will become its masters, although they have no representative character whatever.[34]

It is remarkable how rapidly criticism of the structure of power in Britain and the secrecy with which it operated dropped out of Labour and Liberal discourse once the war was over – testimony, it would seem, to the strength of devotion to the 'Westminster model'. The idea of a League of Nations, as it briefly became the panacea for world peace in 1918, may also have served to distract attention from the structure of domestic political power. If, as Asquith said in a speech delivered in Dublin in September 1914, the central purpose of the war was 'the substitution for force . . . of a real European partnership, based on the recognition of equal right, and established and enforced by the common rule' the League, in the imagination of its advocates, was to embody a modern, durable Concert of Europe for collective security and peace. J. A. Hobson was one of its most persuasive advocates within the UDC. In February 1915 he argued at length that the alternative to such a League would be preparations for another war.[35] In his view this was not a choice between utopia and the grim reality of inevitable conflict. Hobson, like Leonard Woolf and others, believed that practical measures of international regulation had already been adopted which pointed the way forward. He cited the Hague Conventions as evidence of the steps already taken to promote voluntary arbitration in international relations via a machinery of international law and conventions – judicial, legislative and even administrative. Then there was that even larger network of arrangements governing economic intercourse between nations which had been constructed since 1870. An even bigger conception of inter-nationalism was now required to deal with problems as they arose, building on these earlier steps but expanding in ambition to embrace preventive measures. Thus whereas the Congress of Berlin in 1885 had merely partitioned colonies and decided spheres of influence for Central Africa on an *ad hoc* basis, the new dispensation would provide permanent mechanisms for dealing with such disputes.[36]

A mutual guarantee against aggression among the Powers would be at the heart of it, guaranteeing the independence and territorial integrity of all of them. Theodore Roosevelt had championed this idea of the world order well before the war broke out. Hobson envisaged, as did the former President, an undertaking between the Powers to submit all differences between them to certain arbitration and conciliation procedures conducted by impartial tribunal. The tribunal would have the power to secure submission of all issues and acceptance of all awards. But Hobson and his co-thinkers in the UDC wanted to democratise these arrangements. The central organ of the League of Nations would have to be an elected general council and not consist merely of the *ad hoc* meetings of Foreign Ministers. It would be invested with wider functions than the preservation of peace, such as the furtherance of international cooperation in matters of trade, finance, hygiene, labour law, transport, communications, phil-anthropy and science. Its powers would depend upon the sanctions and guarantees by which the signatory nations supported the processes of arbitration and conciliation. In this regard its success would depend on renunciation of the national 'right' to make war. The founding treaty of the League would have to stipulate that its members would declare war against any member state which commenced hostilities. The moral force of the League would meanwhile reside in its democratic and open character. The Council would represent peoples not states-as-Powers. The League would concern itself with relations between peoples not relations between states-as-Powers.

Here Hobson touched upon the issue already raised by Ponsonby: namely the corruption of professional diplomacy in its methods and goals, its socially unrepresentative character and the apparent ease with which it could be influenced by 'small, powerful, organised groups or castes within each nation', be they aristocracies or modern financiers and arms dealers. In practice international relations had been the shifting secret interplay of these group-forces.[37] Hobson proposed that some method of direct or indirect election would enable the people to elect the governing Council of the League so that 'men of experience and reputation' from all walks of life could conduct its business. This meant that the promotion of democracy among the more backward nations was a pre-requisite of their membership of the League. Yet Hobson could already see in 1915 that competing alliances would not be avoided in the future if countries such as Germany and Russia were excluded from the League's membership; it would simply be a League of Conquerors without them. Thus the inclusion of all eight Great Powers was a basic requirement of its foundation. Beyond that Hobson envisaged its extension 'to all other civilised nations' – at least the 47 states that were signatories to the Hague Conventions of 1907. But these could not be regarded as equals. States such as Britain and France would have to have greater representation than small states such as Serbia, Siam or Paraguay. Hobson acknowledged the danger that these arrangements could be seen as world government by the imperialist Powers but was unable to counter the charge with more than an expression of hope that such degeneration could be avoided.

Party divisions

These UDC arguments were circulating among the organisations affiliated to the Labour Party from the moment the war broke out; indeed they drew on themes that had been familiar to the progressive alliance since the Boer War, as we saw in chapter 1. Though August 1914 saw the Labour Party embark on a long period of cooperation with the state in the transformation of Britain for the purposes of total war, the labour movement was never entirely convinced by the Establishment's account of how the war had begun, what it was about and how it could be avoided in future. The equivocal language of August 1914 continued to surface from time to time well into the next year. Doomed attempts to bring representatives of the social democrats together from all the belligerent countries (German occupation of France made this an impossible condition for the French socialists) led to the conference of the Allied countries in London on 14 February 1915, which we have already mentioned. Here it was resolved that 'a victory for German imperialism would be the defeat and destruction of democracy and liberty in Europe'. Thus the delegates were 'inflexibly resolved to fight until victory is achieved'. But they also made clear that the origins of the war had their roots in the 'antagonisms' of capitalist society and 'the policy of colonial dependencies and aggressive imperialism' in which every Government had its share of responsibility. The equivocation continued when they asserted that the socialists of the Allied nations 'do not pursue the political and economic crushing of Germany'. They were at war with the governments not the people of the Central Powers. They wanted to liberate and compensate Belgium and France and they wanted a European order determined by the people themselves, not by annexations. Secret diplomacy would have to be suppressed and 'some international authority' was needed 'to settle points of difference among the nations by compulsory conciliation and arbitration, and to compel all nations to maintain peace'. They looked forward to the day when a united working class would once again fight militarism and capitalist imperialism and the nations would come together 'in the peaceful federation of the United States of Europe and the world'.[38]

It was of course clear from the beginning that this sort of thing was far too radical for many of the Labour Party's leading trade unionists. The International Socialist Bureau tried to get a representative from the Labour Party to meet representatives of the other parties (once again the French refused to meet with German social democrats) 'to confer upon matters affecting the war' later in 1915. But when Henderson had to drop out of the proposed delegation of two (with Ramsay MacDonald), upon entering the Coalition Government, John Hodge MP declined to replace him and the party Executive decided that no representatives of the British section should go to the meeting scheduled to take place in The Hague. When Labour considered a formal response to the manifesto of 'the pacifist sections' of the German socialists it was decided by majority vote that no action would be taken.[39] Many trade unionists simply took the view that the British case was just and had to be supported without equivocation. The voluntary industrial truce became a formal agreement between the TUC and the government in March 1915; then in July it was made a statutory requirement to accept arbitration of disputes and 'dilution' of the workforce when the government and employers saw fit to rapidly induct unskilled labour in essential industries. Arthur Henderson entered the coalition in May 1915 with the support of the TUC – and the opposition of the ILP. Within weeks of this further step of incorporation, however, 200,000 South Wales miners defied the law by taking strike action; this was not evidence of political dissent but it was hardly evidence of unqualified patriotism either.

Labour's first wartime annual conference did not take place until January 1916, so sparing the party, perhaps, from the acrimony and division which would surely have attended such a meeting in late 1914 or early 1915. When conference met some three months had already passed since the TUC (September 1915) made clear its opposition to military conscription. A special congress of party and trade union representatives, invoking the threat of resignation from the coalition, came to the same decision. Labour overwhelmingly rejected conscription again at Bristol in 1916. It then turned to its first discussion of the war – nearly 18 months since the conflict began. It focused on a resolution identical to one supported by the TUC (with only a handful of dissentients). This considered that the actions taken by the Government were 'fully justified'. It also denounced German atrocities in Belgium and pledged the conference 'to assist the Government as far as possible in the successful prosecution of the War'– a sentiment which persuaded Labour to accept conscription four months later. In moving the resolution James Sexton of the Dock Labourers argued that anything was preferable to a German victory but he also appealed to the delegates' sense that the sacrifices being made would make future working-class claims on the state 'so irresistible that no one could refuse their fair share in the products of the country' – a point which was pursued in July by an Allied Trade Union Conference meeting in Leeds.[40] In seconding the resolution George Milligan, also of the Dock Labourers, warned that no trade unionist would 'dare' to go back to his men and say that he had voted against the war. In any case he was one of those who could not understand how anyone could oppose the war. MacDonald, who spoke next in the debate, was widely believed to hold pacifist opinions. In fact he took the view that though the Government had blundered by taking Britain into the war, it must be fought to a successful conclusion. He urged tolerance of dissent and avoidance of permanent division. He said that they were too late to discuss the origins of the war and too early to pronounce a final judgement. None of them, according to MacDonald, wanted the Germans to win. How could they when they had always opposed every charac-teristic of 'Prussianism' which had been stamping upon 'the peoples of Europe'. But he reminded them that they had supported resolutions in the recent past deploring secret diplomacy as well as arguments which located the origins of war in balance of power doctrines. He thus implied that the war was something they had to endure, faithful to their country, but in no way approving of the decisions that had led to it.

It was all too subtle for some of the speakers who followed MacDonald who wanted to know where he stood and what he was doing for the war effort. They maintained there was nothing confusing about the party's stance; according to one of its MPs 'the whole weight of the influence of the Parliamentary Party had been in the direction of standing by this country in this War and prosecuting it to a successful finish'.[41] The unions which had supported the war effort with barely a murmur of dissent were more representative of the party, it was now asserted, than 'the small coterie of the Independent Labour Party'. But other delegates pointed out that it was possible to be for the war and their country without having to believe that the Government's decisions had been 'fully justified' as the resolution maintained. (Thousands of striking workers on the Clyde made the same point more forcefully in March and their leaders on the Clyde Workers' Committee were rounded up for deportation.) One speaker observed that the sort of unqualified support for the war entailed by the resolution could obviously lead the party to agree to forms of compulsion such as national conscription. (The violent suppression of the nationalist rebellion in Dublin later that Easter was another example of 'compulsion' to come.) R. C. Wallhead of the ILP pointed out that his party opposed the war for the same reasons the Labour Party had opposed it before 4 August 1914. The war was the outcome of a bad foreign diplomacy conducted by Grey behind the backs of his countrymen. No new evidence had arisen since the July crisis to revise that original opinion. Indeed the ILP, at its own conference in April, voted with only three dissentients to take the pacifist view that socialists should 'refuse support to every war entered into by any Government'. The war had converted some socialists indelibly to this position, as the career of a future Labour leader, George Lansbury, would illustrate.[42] But most of the speakers at the TUC and Labour conferences of 1915–16 were more concerned about the effects that any equivocation would have on public opinion; in their view the party had to be seen to be supporting the war. Even a self-avowed opponent of the war, who wanted to see 'the traitors' who had caused it 'wrecked in the middle of the Pacific', nevertheless thought that it would 'have to be fought to the bitter end'. And it was probably in this spirit, rather than one of impassioned patriotism, that the majority of delegates supported the resolution.

An attempt to get the TUC to support an ILP-inspired resolution against the war in September 1916 was overwhelmingly and predictably defeated. In December Henderson joined the new War Cabinet and five more Labour men took lesser positions in Lloyd George's government. It was just at this moment that President Wilson issued a Peace Note and so forced the question of Allied war aims into public debate. The defeated ILP resolution was put to the Labour Party conference in January 1917, just weeks later. It argued that the permanence of the peace settlement depended upon the influence wielded by the working class through the International Socialist Bureau and the speedy reconstitution of the Second International. Bruce Glasier moved the resolution, which forecast annexations if capitalist diplomacy was allowed to have its way. (This was a suggestion made more than once by Woodrow Wilson himself.) Will Thorne countered Glasier with an amendment, which was carried by a two-thirds majority, reminding the delegates that Germany started the war and that the war should be fought to the finish. But even this allowed that the socialist and trade union organisations of the Allies should meet simultaneously with the Peace Congress, to make sure that a just peace was concluded.[43] The discussion picked up this point that 'Labour must have a voice in the settlement of peace terms'. Both MacDonald and Glasier reminded the conference that 'a very important German socialist minority' had representatives in jail and had a long record of opposition to German militarism. But the main point was that if Labour was to have a say in the peace it needed to do it 'as an international force'. The resolution was nevertheless defeated by a two-thirds majority.

The conference also rejected a BSP resolution explaining that the war was 'essentially imperialist in character' and declaring that it would be in the best interests of the working class if it was speedily terminated. But a significant step was taken when the conference unanimously agreed to support a League of Nations once the war was over. This was now firmly associated with Wilson and the USA, as well as the UDC. Wilson's attempts to act as a mediator during the period of American neutrality had been continuously thwarted by both sides to the conflict, dedicated as they were to total victory and the territorial prizes that went with it. He nevertheless began to emerge as the champion of a democratic peace settlement based on the absence of annexations and indemnities, control of the arms race and the armaments industries. The feeling was abroad that the future peace of nations depended on some sort of international body with the power to enforce international agreements and arbitrate disputes. It already united American socialists, liberals and pacifists and would soon have the same impact in Britain.[44] In these circles a programme for a constructive peace was developed in early 1915 and it bore a strong resemblance to the thinking of the UDC in Britain. Wilson identified himself with this programme in all essentials.

League of Nations

The American left was not alone in advocating compulsory arbitration, and the rule of international legal precedents, or the use of coercive sanctions to keep the peace. Some Conservatives on both sides of the Atlantic could also see the value of these arrangements, including Teddy Roosevelt, Senator Taft and the group in Britain around Lord Bryce, the former Ambassador to the United States. These people were generally protective of national sovereignty and not at all interested in disarmament, the democratic control of foreign policy or the self-determination of nations. Nor were they concerned with a negotiated peace without indemnities and annexations. A militant nationalism was compatible with their limited proposals for collective security. The British Cabinet considered the idea of a League within this sort of limited framework in the summer of 1915, just before Wilson, as Philip Snowden observed, publicly aligned himself with the arguments of the UDC.[45] In the presidential campaign of 1916 Wilson transformed the more radical case into a national agenda and US membership of a League of Nations became one of his declared objectives.

By the end of 1916 Germany – hoping to keep the territories in Eastern Europe which it had already conquered, and concerned to manage growing unrest among the Social Democrats at home – announced an official interest in the idea of a League. But the formation of the Lloyd George coalition in Britain, a largely Conservative and markedly imperialist administration, signalled Britain's intention to prosecute the war more effectively. Thus while Wilson argued for a 'peace without victory' the belligerents pressed on regardless. Wilson's supporters in the USA took it that the first cracks had appeared on the Allied side when the Labour Party conference of January 1917 unanimously supported 'an international League to enforce the maintenance of Peace'.[46] By happy coincidence Wilson had delivered his Peace without Victory speech the day before the conference began (22 January) and the delegates stood cheering when it was read to them. So while the Labour conference voted overwhelmingly to support the view that Germany started the war and Britain must fight it to the finish, they also endorsed the President's denunciations of militarism, imperialism and secret diplomacy. In France Wilson's address met with a similar reception within the socialist party.

At the end of the month, however, American intervention on the side of the Allies moved noticeably closer. Germany's renewed U-boat campaign and the discovery of the 'Zimmermann telegram', calling upon Mexico to declare war on the USA, turned American public opinion against the Central Powers. By this time the Allies were financially indebted to both the US Government and to American bankers. Wilson calculated that the US would be able to mould the peace settlement on the basis of financial coercion as well as the moral authority it would derive by entering the conflict on the side of democracy and 'the people'. Before the USA could act, however, revolution in Russia in February 1917 added the voice of the Petrograd Soviet to the call for a peace without indemnities and annexations. Around the same time a Labour Party deputation presented Lloyd George with a list of demands for social reconstruction compiled by Sidney Webb's War Emergency Workers' National Committee. While Labour tried to raise a social agenda at home, Arthur Balfour, the British Foreign Secretary, was obliged to officially inform Wilson of the Allies' secret treaties, when the USA entered the war on the side of the Allies in April. The President lost no time reiterating his demand for a peace without victory, knowing now, rather than merely assuming, that the Allies had all along planned for annexations and indemnities.

In the course of 1917 the Executive of the Labour Party was forced to respond to Wilson and to the revolutions in Russia. Opposition to the war had been growing everywhere, most dramatically in Russia of course, but also in Germany with the strikes of March and April, and in France where troops mutinied after the spring offensive on the western front.

Various attempts had been made throughout the conflict to bring trade unionists and socialists together. The Labour Party only attended those involving the Allied countries, as we have seen. But other meetings took place without it, notably at Zimmerwald in September 1915 and Kienthal in April 1916 where unrepresentative groups of socialists – notably including members of the Russian left – agreed on the need to pressurise governments to end the war and secure a peace without annexations and indemnities. Early in 1917 the Dutch and Scandinavian socialist parties, meeting in a committee chaired by Hjalmar Branting, conceived the idea of a conference of the socialist parties of the belligerent countries, to be held at Stockholm, with a view to formulating peace terms.[47] By March 1917 the question of war aims was difficult to ignore both because of President Wilson and the fact that supporters of the Zimmerwald majority were now prominent in the Petrograd Soviet. The revolutionary events in Russia were celebrated at the Albert Hall in London that April and a United Socialist Committee, comprised chiefly of ILP and BSP members, was formed to plan a convention to examine the implications for Britain.[48] The Albert Hall rally had been like a revivalist meeting in its support for both the Russian Revolution and a peace without annexations and indemnities. The mood infected May Day and demonstrators in some cities carried banners denouncing the war and calling for peace.[49] Enthusiasm for the Russian events was evidence of popular war-weariness in Britain and the hope that the conflict was coming to an end. Labour was still divided over the issue of a conference involving representatives from the Central Powers, however, but decided in May to send a delegation (which included MacDonald) to consult with the Russian socialists about it.[50] A change of government in Russia saw the rise of Kerensky and a demand from his Provisional Government that the Allies urgently needed to meet to discuss war aims. It was at this point that Lloyd George instructed Arthur Henderson to visit Britain's faltering ally, now in danger of dropping out of the struggle against the Central Powers, and to report back on the steps required to prevent it negotiating a separate peace.

While Henderson was still in Russia the Petrograd Soviet added its voice to the call for the Stockholm Conference. The Russian Mensheviks and Socialist Revolutionaries wanted a general peace so that they could build on what had already been achieved in ousting the Tsar. They feared a punitive separate peace with Germany and brought real urgency to the proceedings when they met with the British delegation. Henderson returned stressing the strength both of the left and of the anti-war mood in Russia. He was now convinced of the need to find a negotiated peace before the Eastern front collapsed completely and the Russians were forced into a separate peace. At the Labour Party's Executive Henderson argued that the Stockholm Conference – which would only be consultative – was the best way to bring on the peace movement in Germany too, the German and Austrian socialists already having expressed their enthusiasm for it. Indeed a 'Peace Resolution' put before the Reichstag on 19 July, calling for a peace without annexations by Germany, had been supported by 212 votes to 126. In the event Bethman–Hollweg's successor as Chancellor, Dr Michaelis, who had taken up his post just six days earlier, rejected the idea that Germany would seek a negotiated settlement. The British War Cabinet, meanwhile, had already discussed the need to stifle the peace agitation.[51] But a press release issued by a joint meeting of the Parliamentary Committee of the TUC and the Labour Party Executive called on the British Government to explore the Reichstag's proposal. This was used as another opportunity to demand that Lloyd George should declare his commitment to Wilson's war aims, including the League of Nations and the principle of self-determination. The statement observed that 'our generation has been paying a heavy penalty because this principle has been violated or ignored in the peace settlements that have followed previous European wars'.[52]

Labour's Executive also decided that Henderson and MacDonald should travel to France to discuss the idea of a negotiated peace with the French socialists, before an emergency Labour conference could consider the issue on 10 August. The press denounced the trip as a pacifist stunt and it was already clear to Henderson that he would be forced to resign from the War Cabinet if he persisted with the Stockholm idea.[53] He nevertheless went on to secure a large majority in favour of Labour representation at Stockholm at the emergency conference of the party – the first time the affiliated trade unions had wavered from the official 'fight to the finish' line. The conference could not decide on delegates, however, principally because the unions would not accept the involvement of representatives of the affiliated socialist groups, though Labour had no power to stop them going given the principles laid down by the Dutch–Scandinavian organising Committee. Before this matter was resolved news of Henderson's resignation from the War Cabinet was made known. At a reconvened conference the majority in favour of sending delegates to Stockholm was now exceedingly slender (just three thousand votes out of two and a half million cast) – and still the wrangle over delegates continued.[54] Similar problems were encountered in the French socialist party, reflecting majority distrust of the war's long-standing opponents. In the end the governments of both countries refused to grant passports and the Stockholm Conference never took place. But the episode was the clearest demonstration yet that critical thinking about the war was spreading in the organisations of labour. Henderson was replaced in the War Cabinet by another Labour man, George Barnes, and though there was no attempt to break the whole party away from the coalition, the business had begun of preparing the party for the end of the electoral truce and the start of its life as a national party.

The Stockholm Conference focused the attention of socialists at a time when the Allied war leaders still regarded a fight to the finish as the preferred course of action, even though it was obvious that Russia was on its knees and made weaker by Kerensky's attempts to bolster the war effort. Stockholm represented for a time the best hope of those who favoured a negotiated settlement. But these forces finally proved too weak to carry an unequivocal majority of the left in both France and Britain. The Bolshevik Revolution in October 1917 effectively took Russia out of the war and in its wake Henderson, MacDonald and Webb, in consultation with Camille Huysmans of the International Socialist Bureau, finally completed the process begun by the debate around the Stockholm Conference. There is no doubt that the Bolshevik exposure of the secret deals between Britain, France, Italy and Russia for annexations once the war was won reinforced Labour's determination to shape the peace settlement on a different basis. But even before these revelations a TUC resolution, moved by the unlikely alliance of Robert Smillie and Will Thorne in September 1917, demanded a voice for the working class at any future peace conference and was carried by a massive majority. Labour's Executive took this as evidence that the time was right to prepare a statement about war aims – an issue that had generated bitter division within the labour movement as recently as the summer – and present it for ratification to an inter-allied conference as the first step in uniting the left of all the belligerent countries.[55]

Memorandum of War Aims

The *Memorandum of War Aims*,[56] approved by a special conference of the TUC and Labour Party on 28 December, amounted to the UDC analysis of the war. Thorne and Smillie had referred to the sacrifices of the working class as a justification for organised labour's involvement in the peace process, but there were other reasons behind the initiative. There was growing anxiety that while American labour appeared to be in harmony with the professed aims of the American government, European labour was quite unable to claim the same confidence in the governments of Britain, France and Italy. Since the Bolshevik revelations it was apparent that these governments were, according to Camille Huysmans, the secretary of the International Socialist Bureau, 'in opposition to the traditions of our Movement . . . [and in] . . . denial of the moral conceptions which underlie our Movement'.[57] The unsatisfactory reply elicited from the Allies by Wilson's first Peace Note of December

1916 made this divergence intolerable, according to Huysmans. A feeling had developed that a just and speedy peace was being jeopardised. Huysmans was perhaps not alone in despairing of a war 'without positive result', seeing that 'modern war is comparable only to two iron walls, against which the finest flower of our youth are flung to die'.[58] As he observed, a further reason for a statement of war aims was the belief that 'we must meet those who are called our enemies, because if they agree with us on the main lines of our policy . . . they may become our helpers'.[59] A statement of war aims was thus seen as the necessary first step in preparing a consultative international congress that would bring in the German and Austrian social democrats.

The *Memorandum* reiterated the analysis of the war's origins which the first Inter-Allied conference of 14 February 1915 had supported. Echoing Wilson it claimed that 'the fundamental purpose of the British Labour Movement in supporting the continuance of the struggle is that the world may henceforth be made safe for democracy'. To this end it said that the British Labour Movement was 'very largely' dependent 'upon the democratisation of all countries; on the frank abandonment of every form of "Imperialism"; on the suppression of secret diplomacy and on the placing of foreign policy, just as much as home policy, under the control of popularly elected Legislatures; on the absolute responsibility of the Foreign Minister of each country to its Legislature; on such concerted action as may be possible for the universal abolition of compulsory military service in all countries, the common limitation of the costly armaments . . . and the entire abolition of profit-making armament firms, whose pecuniary interests always lie in war scares and rivalry in preparation for war. But it demands in addition that . . . there should be forthwith established a . . . League of Nations.'[60] This League, it said, had to establish a High Court for the settlement of all justiciable disputes between states and a binding commitment by these states that they agree to observe its judgements.

The *Memorandum* rejected a 'war of conquest'. It saw that Germany would have to pay reparations to Belgium and that Belgium would be restored to independence. Reparation for wrongdoing, in this view, had to be applied to wage-earners and peasants 'in homes and employment' as well as for damage to buildings, companies and material property. It wanted the people of Alsace and Lorraine and Poland to determine their own national identity. It applied the same principle to the Balkans, adding that religious freedom and tolerance would be necessary if this was to work. Labour favoured a Balkan federation and customs union. It wanted Palestine free of Turkish domination and open to a Jewish right of return. It could not countenance the return of the former Ottoman provinces in the Middle East to the 'execrated rule of the Turkish Government'. Nor did it want these to become the 'instruments either of exploitation or militarism'. Yet if the self-determination of these 'territories' should be deemed 'impracticable' 'they should be placed for administration in the hands of a Commission' acting for the League of Nations. Similarly all those tropical African territories north of the Zambezi and south of the Sahara should not become the 'booty' of any nation but should become the charge of the proposed League of Nations 'as a single African state' made permanently neutral and giving priority to native protection, welfare and development. Consideration of the views of the people, it added, should enter these calculations, 'when these can be ascertained'.

The *Memorandum* also insisted on the virtue of free trade and the principle of the Open Door. It equated protective tariffs with economic aggression, war, spoliation of the working classes, and the machinations of capitalists, militarists and imperialists. But it also had to concede that the right of each nation to the defence of its own economic interests and the conservation of its own resources could not be denied. There the matter was left, though the implication was that the interests of the world came before those of a particular people. Global standards of working conditions and rights of labour were also stressed. The document foresaw economic hardship at the end of the war resulting from material shortages, dislocation of industry, demobilised servicemen, and attendant unemployment. It demanded public works, pointing out that 'it is now known that in this way it is quite possible for any Government to prevent, if it chooses' involuntary unemployment. The war experience itself had vouchsafed this knowledge.

Winkler shows that the labour movement had also been more concerned than any other party during the war to stress both the open door principle applied to backward areas and the protection of native peoples. This concern seemed to depend on independent international supervision of the peoples and territories in question. It can be traced in the work of writers like Hobson, Morel, Wells and Brailsford, as well as members of the Fabian Society such as Woolf and various contributors to the *New Statesman*. The idea of colonial trusteeship was developed in these circles as they considered the fate of the German colonies. Their reasoning led to the idea that all of Central Africa should be neutralised after the war and administered by an international commission charged with responsibility for both native welfare and open access to the resources of the area. 'Throughout 1917 and 1918 the question was kept alive almost entirely by the efforts of the labor movement', according to Winkler.[61] But the specific notion that a vast African state should be created to serve this purpose had its critics. The ILP doubted that it was possible to administer the vast area proposed for trusteeship as a single state and wondered why British colonies outside the suggested borders would be allowed to function in the old way. No concession was made to these objections when the proposal appeared in the *Memorandum of War Aims*. Snowden had this in mind when he criticised it in *Labour Leader* as evidence of a national, rather than international, mentality. The Inter-Allied Labour and Socialist Conference met in February 1918 in London to discuss the Memorandum but, as the ILP conference noted in April, it again failed to answer these criticisms.[62] It is of little surprise that Labour's parliamentarians had little to say about the actual fate of the European colonies in the House of Commons once the peace settlement created the League of Nations and placed the former German colonies under the supervision of the victorious (now called mandatory) powers. Mild criticism of these arrangements as failing to answer the needs of trusteeship nevertheless found its way into party literature.[63]

On 22 January 1918 the annual conference of the Labour Party was able to welcome the statement on war aims made by Wilson and Lloyd George, but only in so far as they were 'in harmony with the War Aims of the British Labour Movement and make for an honourable and democratic peace'. It demanded a joint statement of war aims from the two governments and it was at this point that Labour called for an inter-allied conference to consider the *Memorandum*. Labour also asked the social democrats and labour organisations of the Central Powers to declare their war aims and pressurise their governments to do the same. It concluded by demanding facilities for an international congress in some neutral country so that working-class opinion 'of all the countries' could be represented. The French and Belgian labour movements came to the same conclusions and in February the inter-allied conference was convened to agree war aims preparatory to invitations to the working-class organisations of the other belligerent countries to 'take part in united action to establish a durable peace ratifying a defeat of Imperialism all over the world'.[64] An indication that these sentiments were gaining ground in Britain is provided by the fact that the UDC had by now a hundred branches and about 100,000 members, together with a further 650,000 members in affiliated organisations.

But there were rival analyses of the war and of how it would end. The Bolshevik Revolution was immediately followed by a declaration of the new government's intent to negotiate a peace settlement based on the very principles associated with President Wilson. Lenin published the Allies' secret treaties to support his claim that the war was a clash of rival imperialisms in which the working class of both sides was merely the cannon fodder. Who could trust Wilson's proposals if this were true? In December 1917, as the Bolsheviks looked set to agree an armistice with Germany, Wilson's annual message to Congress stressed that the President continued to seek a generous and stable peace settlement based on a partnership of nations, including Germany.[65] Labour's *Memorandum of War Aims* was published as a pamphlet just as the rhetorical fight between Lenin and Wilson got underway. The work of the party's Executive was now confessedly 'dominated' by 'its interests in democratic diplomacy'.[66] Foreign affairs had become a necessary obsession. Even Lloyd George was obliged to look interested in the idea of a just and lasting peace, appearing to embrace Wilson's ideas in a speech to the British Trades Union League in January 1918, a speech in which he referred to the right of self-determination of nations and of the need to limit armaments. Three days later Wilson unveiled his 'Fourteen Points' to Congress, its timing very much determined by the pace set by the Bolsheviks, rather than the British Government. Lloyd George would not be able to pretend to support all of these Wilsonian ideas but he knew it was unwise to be seen actively opposing them.

Apart from demanding an open diplomacy, a League of Nations and freedom of the seas, Wilson wanted the removal of all economic trade barriers, reductions in armaments to levels compatible with domestic defence and the impartial adjustment of all colonial claims according to the principle of self-determination. The British Empire could not last a day after the application of such a programme, nor could contemporaneous Allied schemes to intervene in Russia. But the dissenting left in Britain and France gave Wilson virtually their complete support and the active membership of the League of Nations Society in Britain increased markedly. The Cabinet received the Phillimore Report on 3 March, the day the Bolsheviks concluded the rapacious Treaty of Brest-Litovsk with Germany (a treaty which was opposed in the Reichstag only by the anti-war minority socialists of the USPD). With its more palatable proposals for a conservative alliance of the victors which would pledge its members to procedures of arbitration and conciliation the Phillimore Report, composed by Foreign Office officials and experts, avoided the whole question of disarmament, democratic diplomacy, and the issue of sanctions. Unlike Wilson the authors of the report made no provision for compulsory arbitration, self-determination of nations and the equality of states. This made sense to most members of the Cabinet who wanted national sovereignty to remain unscathed by any future international body.[67] Acceptance of the report also ensured that Parliament gave only scant attention to the future Covenant of the League of Nations, since the League was only ever conceived as a modern Concert of Europe by most members of the Cabinet. The Labour Party's enthusiasm for Wilson, by contrast, was such that the American journalist Paul Kellogg, who visited Britain in the spring of 1918, described it as 'the only force in Western Europe competent and desirous of throwing its strength alongside President Wilson's in securing a democratic outcome to the settlement of the war'.[68] By contrast with the British Government, Labour wanted a public debate on British foreign policy. Wilson was told by other American sources in Britain that while Lloyd George had openly laughed at the proposed League, it was Labour, together with most Liberals and radicals, who fervently supported it.[69] Thus in the clash between the Bolsheviks and the White House, Labour was unreservedly behind the latter.

The *Memorandum of War Aims* was expanded, but not significantly altered, by the third inter-allied labour and socialist conference meeting in London in February 1918. The Bolsheviks refused to attend this conference and the Mensheviks were unable to do so (because the Bolsheviks blocked the issuing of passports). The American Federation of Labor was also unable to attend but delegates representing France, Belgium, Italy, Serbia, Bosnia, Romania and South Africa were present and telegrams accepting the *Memorandum* were received from the Canadian Labour Party, the Australian Labour Party, Portugal and Greece. Those present unanimously reaffirmed the Declaration of 14 February 1915 which ascribed profound causes to the war associated with capitalism and imperialism and, while accepting the need to 'fight until victory', rejected a war of conquest. They also repeated their claim that their support for continuance of the struggle was informed by their commitment to a world 'made safe for Democracy'.[70] It was now made clear that the future League of Nations would have to be composed of all independent states, including the Central Powers; these would bring into existence an International High Court and supervise the self-determination of nations; the League would also form an International Legislature representing 'every civilised State'. Refusal of arbitration would signify deliberate aggression and would be met by economic or military coercion by the League. Once again it was emphasised that the efficient operation of the League was dependent on the prior democratisation of all participating nations and the suppression of secret diplomacy by those same democratic states. The 'catastrophe' of 1914 had developed 'inevitably' from 'the old diplomacy and the yearnings after domination by States, or even by peoples'.[71] Since 1914 'imperialist designs' in the contending states had led one government after another to seek territories or economic advantage.

The Conference took the view that the sacrifices of the working classes had been such that at least one representative of Labour and Socialism should be included in the official representation at any Peace Congress, while a Labour and Socialist Conference should meet concurrently with the official congress. This echoed the TUC resolution of September 1917 which had referred to the 'enormous sacrifices in life and liberties' of the workers of Great Britain, sacrifices that 'entitled' them to 'a commanding voice in the settlement of peace'.[72] After the inter-allied conference steps were taken, via the Swedish and Dutch parties, to reach out to the working classes of the Central Powers which had, of course, also made enormous sacrifices. They were now invited to make declarations of peace terms in conformity with the principles of 'no annexations or punitive indemnities, and the right of all people to self-determination'. The purpose of this exercise was 'to ascertain whether or not there exists between the labouring classes of the two groups of belligerent nations common opinions sufficient to make possible a common action against imperialism, and in favour of a democratic peace'. Vandervelde, chairman of the ISB, and Huysmans stressed in their address to the German and Austrian social democrats that the peace terms of Brest-Litovsk on the eastern front stood in complete disregard for these principles. They acknowledged that socialists in both countries had already protested to that effect.

As they waited for the responses of the German and Austrian social democrats Huysmans summed up the position in the following terms:

> The working classes of Europe were opposed to war but were not powerful enough to prevent war. They did not create the system which rendered war inevitable; they did not control the Governments. In all countries the representatives of Labour before the war advocated a policy of disarmament, arbitration, and understanding between States and Nations, and in the discussion on pre-war budgets they have, by agreement, opposed expenditure on armaments. In such circumstances the working classes have no responsibility for the conditions which produce war.[73]

According to Huysmans the working-class parties in all countries voted for war credits 'because they believed in the duty of national self-defence or because they feared an enemy invasion'. Belief in 'united action' survived, however, in the maintenance of the International Socialist Bureau and in the succession of efforts by and gatherings of the neutral parties, the allied parties and the parties of the Central Powers. After the Russian Revolution of March 1917 the question of a general international congress, first raised by the neutral parties at The Hague in September 1916, became 'practical politics' and all the parties affiliated to the ISB accepted it. Only the refusal of Governments to grant passports prevented it from taking place and it was already clear, according to Huysmans, that this refusal had been a grave mistake.

But it soon became clear that the national viewpoint which had prevailed for purposes of fighting the war could not be conjured away by talk of peace. The Austrian *Arbeiter Zeitung* contained the full text of the social democrats' reply on 29 June 1918. Only thirty lines had been struck out by the censor and it was clear that 'the general principles of international social democracy – the League of Nations, no annexations or indemnities, the right of self-determination, and equal economic opportunity for all people' – were perfectly acceptable. However, it was also observed that a democratic regime was not likely to emerge from the defeat of one or other of the groups of imperialist states. The war could not possibly be the means of creating a democratic order in the world. What was wanted was an early peace, brought about by democratic pressure and negotiation. If the war was allowed to resolve the issue it would only breed a desire for revenge and 'consolidate the authority of imperialism and militarism in the countries of the conquerors'.[74] The Austrians also extended the right of self-determination to 'the Colonies' as well as Alsace–Lorraine, Poland and Turkey. They advocated a federal Austria–Hungary and a Balkan union of free peoples. The *Berliner Tageblatt* intimated that the German Majority Socialists, the most patriotic wing of German social democracy (SPD), were prepared to enter negotiations but also opposed the imposition of any war indemnities, including those which took the form of a one-sided obligation to restore the devastated districts affected by the war. They also agreed with the Austrian social democrats about Austria–Hungary and to the list of agreeable reforms – limitation and control of armament production and the like – they added 'international control of straits and oceanic canals', a measure the sea-faring British had curiously omitted to mention.

Heinrich Cunow, editor of the SPD's theoretical magazine *Die Neue Zeit*, analysed the *Memorandum of War Aims* in that journal on 7 June declaring that the party was not inclined to accept 'well-written, pseudo-socialist peace programmes' designed to 'further the aims of Entente Imperialism'.[75] In London it was greeted by the LSI as 'a cantankerous production imputing insincerity and dishonesty to the Allied Socialists right through'. The SPD's failure to oppose Germany's annexations in the East undermined any claim it might have had to the moral high ground. But Cunow, a distinguished Marxist anthropologist, had more than a point. Although the principle of a League of Nations, with compulsory powers of arbitration was acceptable – many demands associated with the *Memorandum* had been part of the common stock of ideas in the International before the war – Cunow pointed out that the SPD had demanded international judicial institutions, including an International Court of Arbitration as long ago as August 1915 in the Reichstag. He also found no difficulty in repeating the usual commitments to arms limitations, limits on conscription and military service, nationalisation of the arms industries and even the creation of citizens' armies. The SPD also supported the idea of democratic parliamentary control of foreign policy. He quoted Bethmann-Hollweg and Pope Benedict XV to show, without trace of irony, that they too supported certain of these general principles. It was evidence, he said, that even circles far removed from socialism wanted a peace without annexations and indemnities and the establishment of a League of Nations. But this was not true of Clemenceau, who still held the reins in France, and openly favoured a peace based on force – as Germany did in the East with the SPD's passive support. Might not the wily Lloyd George eventually take the same position? Cunow also wondered why the proposed system of international control over colonies should be limited to those tropical colonies north of the Zambesi and south of the Sahara. Was it because the 'English and French imperialists and socialists do not think of conceding the full right of self-determination to the people of the other colonies'?[76] Why was the right of self-determination not specifically applied to Ireland, Egypt and India and the former Boer States, and Cyprus and Malta? Why was the demand for 'no indemnities' limited to 'no penal indemnities'? Cunow observed that Germany would have to pay not only for all damage done in Belgium on account of the occupation, and for the devastation of territories conquered by Germany, but also for all damage suffered by ship-owners, freighters, merchants and the dependants of drowned seamen. This he said was presented not as a basis for discussion but as a fundamental principle of justice. Finally Cunow could not see how the dismemberment of Turkey or the disintegration of Austria–Hungary could be effected except by military victory 'intended to further the creation of English world hegemony'.

The more militantly anti-imperialist Independent Social Democrats (USPD), who numbered Karl Kautsky and Eduard Bernstein among their leaders, observed that 'from the beginning of the war we have consistently demanded a peace without annexations or indemnities, based on the right of peoples freely to dispose of themselves'. Unlike the SPD, the USPD favoured an independent Poland (composed of Russian, Austrian and Prussian Poles), a referendum in Alsace–Lorraine, and German reparations for the damage caused in Belgium. But they also observed that the right of self-determination 'is not respected either by the acquisition or by the exchange of colonies'. They argued that the possession of colonies was 'not necessary from the point of view of economic development'. The future peace, furthermore, would not be secured by an international government authority. It could only be secured by a powerful and independent International and the first step required to achieve this 'is the independence of the Socialist parties in relation to the Imperialist Governments' to be demonstrated by a refusal of war credits for those governments which refuse to declare their readiness to enter peace negotiations. These were of course conditions that the British

Labour Party was incapable of meeting. The USPD analysis also exposed the gap that existed on colonial issues between the liberal and Marxist analyses of these issues. Even the neutral countries, in their Stockholm Manifesto, had observations to make which were uncomfortable for the Labour Party – such as a demand for the political independence and economic equality of Ireland.

The neutral Dutch observed that 'the longer this process of mutual exhaustion is continued, the more we must fear that in the end it will be the necessities of the moment that will dictate peace'.[77] Since the Inter-Allied conference the Central Powers had launched a massive military offensive which made significant territorial gains on the western front before it was finally repulsed by the Allies. Then in June the Allies began a counterattack which was to become the decisive offensive of the war. But as late as the last week of October both sides were planning for the 1919 campaigns.[78] It was in this context of endless war perspectives that the Allied labour and socialist parties considered the replies they had received from their counterparts on the other side. As Vandervelde observed to Henderson in August, acceptable responses had come from Austria, Bulgaria, Hungary and the German USPD but not from the German Majority, the 'official' SPD itself. The SPD's declarations and actions did not conform to the conditions laid down in London in February.[79] Meanwhile the propaganda war taking place between Wilson and Lenin was dividing the pre-war socialists of continental Europe. The Labour Party had clearly chosen to support Wilson but Henderson was conscious that Lenin held a good deal of moral authority and could still be the eventual victor if the war dragged on disastrously.

Soviet Russia had withdrawn from the war following the treaty of Brest-Litovsk and in so doing had inspired the left everywhere with the hope that a proletarian revolution could do what the belligerent governments had failed to do – end the war. Any chance of a negotiated settlement was killed by the same event, however, because it allowed the German army to launch the spring offensive in the West which kept momentum until June, by which time popular support for a deal with Germany had evaporated. By August Lenin's government was fighting for survival against invading armies from France, Britain, the USA, and Japan as the Allies attempted to restore the eastern front. This military intervention was deeply unpopular with socialists everywhere and only added to the bitterness which divided the militants from more moderate leaders. Throughout the western front significant Allied advances were made in the summer but by then a German collapse seemed just as likely to occur because of domestic unrest. The Spartacist League was seeking to emulate Lenin in the German cities and the German army, according to General Ludendorff, was already 'heavily infected' with its ideas by the end of September.[80] Two leaders of the SPD were brought into the German Government at the beginning of October in a bid to stabilise the deteriorating situation. The next day a 'Peace Note' was despatched to Wilson but even before it was rejected the Spartacists had met to demand the establishment of a German soviet government. The supposedly impregnable Hindenburg Line was completely over-run by Allied troops as Wilson demanded a German evacuation of all occupied territories. This condition was accepted on 12 October, prompting fears among Allied leaders that an armistice would come before Germany had tasted war within its own frontiers. The disintegration of Austria–Hungary and the appearance of new nation-states – Czechoslovakia, Poland, and Yugoslavia – initially failed, however, to persuade the German government that it was beaten; but at the end of the month first Ludendorff and then the Kaiser deserted their posts in the face of naval mutiny and the imminent collapse of the front. The final armistice came on 11 November as the threat of socialist revolution along Bolshevik lines emerged as a real prospect in Berlin, Vienna and Budapest. That evening 'Lloyd George told his dinner guests that he was all for hanging the Kaiser' while General Pershing, in France, lamented the lost opportunity to force the German army to capitulate in the field of battle.[81]

The war came to an end just as Wilson found himself undermined at home by Republican victories in the Congressional elections of November 1918. Many of his opponents wanted the peace of retribution favoured by the French and British Governments. The Republicans argued that both the constitution and the Monroe Doctrine would be breached by commitments to a League of Nations involving compulsory arbitration and collective security. Like the politicians of Europe they were appalled by the loss of any portion of national sovereignty which the League might entail, any restriction on their ability to arm themselves, any democratic constraint on secret diplomacy. And so they argued that Wilson's proposals would undermine national sovereignty completely. The rapid collapse of Germany opened the way for Wilson's defeat in the determination of the peace. In Britain a nation-wide agitation in favour of Wilson's ideas was launched by the League of Nations Union during the snap general election which Lloyd George called for 14 December. The election, however, produced an even bigger demonstration of national sentiment when Lloyd George successfully exploited his image as the 'man who had won the war' and the coalition was returned to power.[82] The turnout had been low at 58 per cent but the result produced a thumping parliamentary majority for the coalition and defeat for all the prominent opponents of the war. Lloyd George – now an honorary president of the League of Nations Union – had successfully exploited the spirit of vengefulness that hung over the election and called for punishment of both the Kaiser and Germany. Later that month, the Imperial War Cabinet discussed Wilson's diplomacy. Some of its members, including Lloyd George himself, were already wary of too-close an association with French demands and others – like Jan Smuts and Robert Cecil – supported the idea of a League of Nations. Smuts also advocated arms controls and the nationalisation of the armaments industry, just like the Labour Party and the Trades Union Congress. Labour and liberal opinion was also receptive to Smuts' ideas for a system of 'mandates', supposedly committing the colonial powers to a benevolent trusteeship of their overseas possessions – but only the ones taken from defeated Germany. There was clearly a growing constituency in favour of the rule of law in international relations but no very clear idea of how it was to be constituted, what it would contain or how it would be enforced.

But it did not look that way when Wilson arrived at Brest in December. The American President was greeted as a hero in Paris, London, Manchester and Rome by massive crowds of well-wishers as he conducted a brief European tour. In speeches delivered in London, Manchester and Milan Wilson denounced the balance of power, militarism and imperialism and appealed directly to the labour and socialist movements as a force for progress in the world.[83] Popular hopes were still high that a secure peace would follow.

3 Peace in our time

The cost of the First World War was the destruction of the pre-war international order and policy-makers struggled to restore the lost 'normalcy' throughout the 1920s. Britain was weakened by the war effort and was unable to resume its ascendancy in a multilateral, global trading system based on the gold standard. It emerged from the war owing 4.7 billion dollars to the USA, having lost markets and overseas assets. The national debt had grown twelve times over; the direct tax rate was massive by pre-war standards; the exchange rate could only be protected by high interest rates; and government expenditure had grown permanently larger as a proportion of the national income. Some of these problems were addressed by a sustained deflationary policy which contributed to the severity of the slump of 1921 when Britain's industrial production fell by over 18 per cent and foreign trade collapsed by 45 per cent. Unemployment rose to 22 per cent of the insured workforce. All this meant continuous pressure on the value of sterling. Elaborate plans for social reform – including the 'homes fit for heroes' that Lloyd George had promised – were scrapped when the Geddes Committee recommended extreme cuts in public expenditure in February 1922. Yet the political establishment was determined to restore the gold standard at the pre-war parity with the dollar. This was finally accomplished in 1925 but only at the cost of overvaluing sterling by at least 10 per cent and necessitating further wage cuts and deflation. Chronic structural unemployment was exacerbated by these measures. Economic dislocation and crisis was not confined to Britain, of course, but Britain's economic performance relative to that of the world economy was poor and remained so throughout the 1920s. Its share of world trade fell from 30 per cent in 1913 to 20.4 per cent in 1929 and exports never returned to their absolute levels of 1913 during the whole inter-war period.

Labour became the largest of the opposition parties after the general election of 1918 with 59 MPs, all but two of whom were former trade union officials sponsored by trade unions. It was an outcome that disappointed Henderson's professed aims in pushing through the constitutional overhaul of the party earlier in the year, but one that accurately reflected the balance of power within the organisation.[1] Some of the new trade union MPs were returned on a patriotic, anti-German ticket, despite the party's attempts to rise above such sentiments. There had been a nearly sevenfold expansion of Labour candidates in 1918 compared to the general election of December 1910. But the PLP remained small and unimaginative, leaving plenty of scope for criticism from the socialist minority trapped within the union-dominated mass party. The party's foreign policy experts also had to wait before they could air their views in Parliament. All the prominent ILP members were defeated, as were critics of the war associated with the UDC. The Government's majority in the House of Commons increased after the votes were cast; the combined Conservative and Lloyd Georgeite bloc gave it an unassailable 474 seats in the 1918 Parliament.[2]

Labour certainly could not be accused of lagging behind popular radicalism in the general election campaign. Its manifesto referred to the war and its legacy as 'the present world catastrophe', evidence of 'the culmination and collapse of a distinctive industrial civilisation, which the workers will not seek to reconstruct'.[3] Such rhetoric reflected the conviction of all wings of the party that the time had come to eliminate the causes of war and create the conditions for social justice. In domestic policy 'socialisation' of industry commended itself – all the more so in view of the way the war emergency had witnessed the growth of successful state economic intervention with popular support. In international policy Labour wanted to dispense with 'enforced dominion' over subject races and colonies. It also rejected the 'selfish and insular "non-interventionism"' which denied 'our special obligations to our fellow-citizens overseas', claiming that Britain was morally responsible for the care of the 'non-adult races' of the world.[4] Labour stood for imperial 'maintenance and . . . progressive development on the lines of Local Autonomy and "Home Rule All Round"; the fullest respect of the rights of each people, whatever its colour, to all the Democratic Self-Government of which it is capable, and to the proceeds of its own toil upon the resources of its own territorial home; and the closest possible cooperation among all the various members of what has become essentially not an Empire in the old sense, but a Britannic Alliance'.[5]

Labour's left-wing critics argued that this purely verbal formula – given here the flavour of wartime imperial solidarity – was intended to conjure the real Empire away so that the party might be identified with a consensual, patriotic, uncontroversial, and largely fictional Commonwealth.[6] Labour also said it rejected all projects of imperial federation which amounted to schemes of exploitation for the benefit of a 'White Empire'.[7]

It clearly felt that it ought to stress the goal of democratic self-government, 'especially in India', as the manifesto observed. The empire would be nudged towards an 'Alliance of Free Nations'. Labour also wanted the Dominions involved in 'the most confidential deliberations of the Cabinet, so far as Foreign Policy and Imperial Affairs are concerned', but the manifesto was careful to emphasise their complete local autonomy in decision-making. The world had moved on. It would soon become apparent that the sacrifices of the Dominions in the war had sharpened their critical faculties where British foreign policy was concerned.[8] A national movement was developing in India. Ireland was on the brink of independence. Other subject nations would surely follow its lead. With or without President Wilson the USA would remain a critic of the European Empires, as would Labour's own left wing. The rhetoric of a Commonwealth of freely associating states was a necessary fiction and recurring goal in these circumstances.

The party's need to take foreign affairs seriously led to the creation of specialist committees on international and imperial affairs to advise the National Executive Committee. Composed of UDC members, Fabians, critics of the war and even militants who were soon to found the Communist Party, as well as party leaders, the committees testified to the still-amateurish state of Labour's policy-making process, though they enjoyed a certain amount of prestige at their inception.[9] Labour's rejection of the old diplomacy was restated just weeks before the Peace Congress officially opened in Paris on 18 January 1919.[10] There were many problems to address, some of them arising from the Wilsonian rhetoric itself. How was the principle of self-determination of nations to be applied? How was the will of the people to be determined? What was the role of democracy in the future of international relations? The Europeans were upholders of the balance of power and some of them, like Clemenceau, openly defended the idea. Judged by their rhetoric they were more concerned with making Germany pay and stopping the spread of Bolshevism than the transformation of diplomacy. Hunger, disease and economic collapse spread across central Europe as representatives of 29 countries gathered in Paris. But proceedings were dominated by the Great Powers meeting in secret in a Supreme Council and it soon became clear that Wilson was unable to convert his colleagues to his radical view when he agreed to a 15-year military occupation of the Rhineland and even to American participation in an alliance with Britain and France. The peace of the victors, which the UDC had feared, soon began to unfold. Australia wanted New Guinea; Belgium wanted Rwanda and Burundi; Britain wanted Tanganyika and most of the rest of German East Africa in addition to much of the former Ottoman Empire in the Middle East; France made claims on Lebanon, Syria, Togoland and

Cameroon; Greece and Italy wanted parts of Turkey; Italy also demanded parts of Somalia, together with some Austrian and newly created Yugoslav territory, in fulfilment of the secret deal with Britain and Russia known as the Treaty of London (1915); Japan wanted the Shantung peninsula in China (which it obtained) and a racial equality clause in the League of Nations Charter (which was refused); New Zealand wanted Samoa; and South Africa wanted the mandate for German South West Africa. Wars continued after November 1918 in pursuit of such claims. Poland fought Russia for control of the Ukraine; Greece went to war with Turkey over who would have Smyrna and Thrace; fighting armies were spread all over the former Tsarist Empire.

On 28 June, after five months of deliberations, the main part of the Peace Conference was concluded with the signing of the German treaty. Germany and its allies were made to accept full responsibility for the war. Germany lost its navy, its mercantile shipping and its colonies, as well as most of its machinery of war – submarines, aeroplanes, heavy guns and machine guns. It was forced to annul the Treaty of Brest-Litovsk and to give up its claim to Alsace–Lorraine. It was denied the principle of self-determination because millions of Germans who would have voted overwhelmingly for inclusion in the Reich were not allowed to do so and were forced to remain in the newly created states of Poland and Czechoslovakia or much-diminished Austria, now stripped of its imperial pretensions. Virtually the whole of the provinces of West Prussia and of Posen, together with a portion of Silesia, were incorporated into the new Polish state. Between one-third and one-half of Germany's coal mines and two-thirds of its iron mines were surrendered. Germany would also pay an undisclosed reparations bill which Lloyd George massively inflated by adding the cost of military pensions. The figures touted about in 1919 represented a crippling indemnity in the eyes of the Germans themselves, but the final figure of 132 billion gold marks was not settled until the reparations commission reported in 1921.

Labour's ambition to obtain direct representation at Versailles came to nothing. In common with numerous colonial, national, feminist and other groups the organised working class of Europe was locked out of the largely secret proceedings. Instead the left reformist parties met in February at Berne as the Peace Congress deliberated and there demonstrated the 'common agreement' on war aims and 'unified peace policy' which Labour had sought during the previous year and a half.[11] The Berne conference objected to most aspects of the peace settlement agreed in Paris and quickly conveyed its disagreements to Clemenceau and Lloyd George, with Henderson and MacDonald present in the official delegation. The hoped for League of Nations was a sham, according to MacDonald, and a sham was worse than no League at all.[12] It was clear that it would exclude Germany, Austria and Russia. It had no army of its own, no procedures of compulsory arbitration and no commitment to international disarmament. The mandates system was simply a fig-leaf to cover imperialism as usual. Article 10 of the Covenant effectively legitimised the existing division of the world by committing the League to 'respect and preserve' the political and territorial status quo. J. A. Hobson saw it as a 'New Holy Alliance' of the victors.[13] Other critics felt that it was a basis upon which to build. It did, after all, pledge the member states to respect each other's independence and territorial boundaries; it supported the idea of a permanent international court of justice and an International Labour Organisation, to promote decent standards on matters affecting workers; it was also supposed to control arms sales and outlaw slavery. The very fact of its deficiencies implied a reform programme to put them right in the minds of some people. This was certainly the conclusion of Labour's annual conference, which accepted the treaty subject to a campaign to improve its defects.[14] The terms imposed upon Germany, however, had created the sort of peace that would entail humiliation, duress, and intolerable sacrifice, with the prospect of rising resentment leading to new conflicts of arms in the near future. Certainly, this was the way they were seen by Labour's leading foreign policy experts, as well as those former Liberals who were now drawn to the party.

E. D. Morel called it a great personal tragedy for Wilson and a great international tragedy for the world. He argued that the deliberate purpose of the Treaty had been 'the utter ruin of a great people'.[15] It was linked in his mind to the suppression of the 'Socialist Republic' in Hungary in 1919 and the war of intervention against the Bolsheviks in Russia and to the 'callous cynicism' with which whole peoples were consigned to fates not of their choosing, whether in central Europe or in the Middle East. Like Hobson, Morel saw only a concert of the conservative Powers and imagined that the League could now become 'the greatest engine of arbitrary power the world has ever known'. The Treaty had violated 'every essential principle alleged to have inspired the war aims of the Allies'. It was the culminating act of a whole series of betrayals which began when Asquith and Grey assured the House of Commons that Britain had been under no obligations to France and which then continued with a story of the exclusive wickedness of Germany's rulers to culminate in the secret treaties and the war with Bolshevik Russia. He concluded that a general disarmament was now impossible; where one Alsace–Lorraine had existed before 1914, there were now many. The only course of action was to insist on the revision of the Treaty and save the League from utter shipwreck.

The conference of labour and socialist parties meeting at Berne in February 1919, took the same view as Morel. It resolved that a League of Nations accorded with the 'fundamental ideals of the Socialist International' and that the attainment of this socialist ideal was an urgent task if the threat to civilisation represented by war was not to recur. The conference was insistent that such a League would have to represent – even in its 'central organ' – parliaments and peoples, not Cabinets and executives. All independent peoples would have to be represented, while dependent peoples would be 'placed under its protection' and 'encouraged and assisted to fit themselves for membership'. The League would need to abolish all standing armies, but would maintain its own armed force until 'complete disarmament' had been effected. It would create an International Court to settle all disputes and this would have the power to enforce its decisions, including decisions about frontiers. It would maintain the 'open door' policy in the colonies and establish free trade and it would establish and enforce an international labour charter. It was clear, therefore, as the delegates acknowledged, that such a League could only be fully developed to the extent that the power of the working-class movement advanced and 'the working people realise[d] the ideals of Socialism'.[16] Put bluntly, this League of Nations depended on the twin triumph of democracy and socialism.

The permanent commission created at Berne repeated these demands from its Amsterdam base in April 1919, adding that governments needed to adopt the method of open diplomacy championed by Wilson. But it was already apparent that none of 'these conditions have ... yet been realised by the Paris Conference'. Acknowledging the 'uneasiness' caused by the decisions already taken at Paris, the permanent commission resolved to send its Executive Committee (Branting, Henderson and Huysmans) and its Committee of Action (Renaudel, Longuet, MacDonald and Stuart Bunning) to the French capital 'to remain there until the signing of the peace preliminaries'. Meanwhile a flood of resolutions emanated from the permanent commission to reveal the gulf that separated the socialists from the peace-makers.[17] To the demands for a comprehensive international labour charter adopted at Berne were added calls for action to end the Armenian massacres and establish an independent Armenia; opposition to the machinations of the Entente in Asia Minor where the Greeks, with French and British connivance, had occupied Smyrna; support for the right of Germans and Austrians to self-determination; opposition to the separation of the Saar valley, Palatinate and left bank of the Rhine from Germany; opposition to the annexation of Bessarabia by Romania; opposition to Japanese oppression in Korea; support for Estonian and Finnish independence; opposition to Polish occupation of Eastern Galicia; opposition to Bolshevik occupation of Georgia;

condemnation of the annexations of the victorious Great Powers; support for self-determination in Ireland and a Jewish state in Palestine (with protection for ethnic minorities);[18] opposition to anti-semitic discrimination in Romania and White Terror in Hungary; pogroms in Poland; intervention in Russia; and the punitive Rowlatt Acts in India. The list lengthened in the course of 1919, revealing both the idealism and ambition of the assembled socialists as well as the underlying complexity of the war's aftermath.

The victorious Powers were charged with malicious intent to punish Germany and establish a new balance of power even more insecure than the old one. Keynes was not alone in seeing a Carthaginian peace motivated by passion and greed. The Labour Party also believed that in damaging the economic future of Europe the victors had damaged themselves.[19] Most of Labour's leading figures could agree with the argument of *The Economic Consequences of the Peace* that the Treaty, if not the war, had been concerned with 'frontiers and nationalities . . . the balance of power . . . [and] . . . imperial aggrandisements' and the 'enfeeblement of a strong and dangerous enemy'.[20] Wilson, it was clear even to Liberals like Keynes, had provided 'the web of sophistry and Jesuitical exegesis' with which to legitimate the deals brokered at Versailles. Alas, the Fourteen Points had been shown to be hollow. 'Open covenants of peace, openly arrived at' had been promised but not delivered.[21] The nationality principle and self-determination were applied fitfully; there had been no 'free, open-minded and absolutely impartial adjustment of all colonial claims'; economic barriers remained and were even extended; the major capitalist Powers had not allowed Russia 'independent determination of her own political development'; nothing had been done to disturb the armaments manufacturers; neither the Turks nor the former Ottoman provinces were allowed the 'autonomous development' promised by Wilson; and the 'general association of nations' turned out to be a league of states which excluded the Germans, Austrians, Russians, and, in the event, the Americans as well.

The Labour Party had been one of the cheer-leaders of Wilson at the end of 1918 and most of the following year. It had invested heavily in Wilson's rhetoric and retained an interest in making his efforts work, even though it was recognised that much of what he wanted had been thwarted. Wilson had offered a noble meaning for the war by championing an honourable conclusion to it. He persuaded socialists throughout Europe 'to acquiesce for over a year in a relatively unfavourable political status quo for the sake of a supposedly world-transforming peace'.[22] With the help of Wilson the radicalism which was evident in many countries after the Bolshevik Revolution came and went. Even in relatively stable Britain, the National Executive Committee (NEC) of the Labour Party was forced to conclude that the peace treaty was 'defective, not so much because of this or that detail of wrong done, but fundamentally, in that it accepts, and indeed is based on, the very political principles or premises which were the ultimate cause of this war'.[23] Henderson, writing on behalf of the NEC in May 1919, repeated the criticisms made at Berne and concluded that future wars were inscribed in the punitive terms imposed upon Germany. But in common with other critics he intended to work for the reform of the League and the revision of the Treaty. Germany must be invited to join and the League must be rendered democratic by transforming it into a truly representative international Parliament with both deliberative and legislative powers.[24] Such were the basic demands of the UDC, Labour's annual conference, its NEC, and the parties that would form the Labour and Socialist International (LSI) in 1923.[25] Yet when the Treaty came before Parliament the contingent of Labour MPs approved it, subject to only modest criticisms.

The inter-allied labour conferences had always agreed that Germany should pay reparations and accept the immediate responsibility for starting the war. But they also insisted on profound general causes of the war – militarism, imperialism and capitalism – and distinguished between the immediate guilt of an autocratic government, acting in secret, and the innocence of the German people (such as the Social Democrats), who had opposed militarism before 1914. Once the war was over Labour discussions of these issues acknowledged that the German people had been deceived as to the facts of war and had honestly acted in a spirit of self-defence. The socialist and labour parties took the view that a reparation bill of £5,000 million was fair but by the time the victorious Powers finally fixed the reparations bill in 1921 Labour's sympathy for Germany had grown stronger in the context of worsening economic prospects in Britain itself.[26] Class relations, already embittered, deteriorated further. Inflation and a tax burden that was massive by pre-war standards enraged the middle class, already alarmed by the power organised labour had seemingly acquired since 1914. The onset of mass unemployment and deflationary policies did nothing to soften these class antagonisms.

By 1921 casualties of the conflict begun in 1914 exceeded 60 million, when the death toll from the influenza epidemic of 1919, which the war helped to transmit, was added to the total of fatalities, wounded and displaced persons. Even in Britain virtually every family had been affected by the disaster. The socialist parties meeting at Geneva in August 1920 affirmed that the peace had left the world in a state of uncertainty and chaos. They protested that the treaty and those that followed it reflected 'a spirit of imperialism' of the type that had 'presided over the preparation of the world war'.[27] The 'intolerable character' of these treaties, it was said, had stimulated opposition in the defeated nations and a corresponding fear in the victor nations which the 'imperialist governing classes' were ready to exploit again to maintain and reinforce militarism. The congress objected to ongoing interference in Bolshevik Russia as an instance of such militarism. Progress in such matters ultimately depended on working-class control of foreign policy and working-class leadership of the popular pacifist and anti-imperialist movements of various countries. This struggle, according to the congress, was 'not in contradiction to the collaboration of the proletariats in the League of Nations'. But it was their duty to criticise the League's shortcomings, especially Article 12 which reserved the right of nations to make war. The League had to be reformed so that it represented all free peoples and obtained the powers needed to police the world and disarm the nations. It could then revise the Treaty of Versailles to permit, for example, self-determination of nations and a fairer reparations burden for the nations of Central Europe.

The biggest and fastest growing organised force of League supporters in Britain – the League of Nations Union – was not at all inclined to criticise the League. The LNU came into existence in 1918 (the fusion of two pro-League pressure groups formed during the war), just days before the armistice, with only 3,841 members. The entire membership of the pacifist societies outside the LNU was 'well under 10,000' at this time.[28] But growing enthusiasm for the League was evidenced by the fact that the LNU registered 255,469 annual subscribers by 1925 and was by far the largest peace society of the time. It saw its mission to popularise the League and promote the idea of peaceful, collective resolution of conflict, themes which a section of the public was all the more interested in because British and French disarmament failed to materialise after the defeat of Germany and French bellicosity was seen as a persistent problem by the British. While most of the leading left-wing intellectuals in the early 1920s believed that the Treaty and the League betrayed Wilsonian principles, the LNU took the view that the League had to be supported. It self-consciously appealed to the centre ground of British politics and aspired to avoid controversy. So conformist was it that the LNU was happy to depict the League as a valuable prop to the British Empire and the maintenance of the international status quo. Not until the mid-1930s was the LNU able to advance beyond this conservative position.[29]

The LNU trusted in the power of public opinion – British public opinion in particular – and its ability to coerce errant states without resort to arms. In the later 1920s, when optimism on this count was boosted by a relatively pacific international climate, thousands more joined the LNU and membership rose to a peak in 1931 of around 950,000. The

Foreign Office, by contrast, remained deeply sceptical about the League's efficacy throughout the1920s and one thorough analysis of the documentary record for the decade concludes that British Governments made little effort to make the League work.[30] Foreign policy was made in much the old way with the old objectives in mind, though it was often enough presented for popular consumption in ways designed to appeal to the League's supporters.[31] This remained the pattern well into the 1930s, and it surprised no one in the Labour Party that British policy did not add up to a real commitment to the League. As early as the proposed Anglo-French Pact, which Lloyd George floated in 1922, at a time of heightened Franco-German tension, the LNU showed that this could be a realistic option by linking general disarmament to effective collective security through the League, rather than through bilateral alliances of the orthodox sort. Logically this meant a collective armed force. But the individuals who could see this failed to dominate the general propaganda of the LNU. Labour also failed to convey the message that collective security for peace might mean war and in the 1920s circumstances conspired to maintain a growing popularity of the League without the need to face up to this fact. The LNU in particular was so keen to promote the League of Nations that it neglected to educate its own membership and sympathisers – largely composed of Labour and Liberal voters – about the League's structural weaknesses.

The First World War had certainly cured most of the Labour Party of the view that peace depended on alliances and armies; until the mid-1920s the isolationist views of the UDC were influential in the party. But many members also believed that the mere absence of war was not enough – peace depended on an active commitment to international cooperation. The strength of such convictions no doubt reflected Britain's island insularity and its liberal political culture, as well as the effects of the war. In these circles the war was certainly remembered in the overwhelmingly negative terms which remain familiar to this day. These sentiments peaked at the end of the decade and undoubtedly informed the urgency of Labour's liberal internationalists in their efforts to pro-mote cooperation between states and the maintenance of peace through free trade, international law, and the institutions at Geneva. Some of them continued to see various elites and cliques as impediments to this policy, as the old radicals had done, while socialists, like Brailsford, believed that the abolition of capitalism and imperialism was the only secure long-term solution to the problem of war. In the 1920s none of them were faced with the question of whether war resistance should be unconditional or qualified by the needs of national defence, in the event of threats to Britain from a more reactionary aggressor, a problem which the fascist states would pose starkly in the 1930s. Alongside the neutralism and

liberal internationalism of old there was a persistent critique of the League
as a capitalist club and this critique did not as yet distinguish between
types of capitalist state. Occasionally the party was moved to support
resolutions which proposed resistance to any war, as in 1922.[32]

Labour had a growing minority of socialists within its ranks in the
1920s who saw war as the inevitable consequence of capitalism. But
pacifists – in the original sense of people who believed in the desirability
and possibility of settling international disputes without recourse to war
– were more numerous in both the party and the country. The affiliated
trade unions, a better organised and more powerful interest than any other
within the party, were also apt to be more pragmatic and Labour's foreign
policy revisionism was soon connected to the mundane problem of
unemployment in Britain. In 1921 Labour complained that the volume
of Britain's export trade was only 71 per cent of the 1913 figure. Britain
bought little from Europe and sold it even less. The trade with Germany,
Austria and Russia was especially depleted. Germany took barely one-
seventh of the exports which Britain had sent to her before the war. It
was clear, according to the party, that 'the decline of our trade with
Germany, Russia, and Austria would alone account for most of our
present unemployment'.[33] It followed that restoration of this trade had
to be a priority for a future Labour Government. That would mean
revision of the peace treaty, disarmament, and peace with Russia – a
formula of more general applicability to countries, like Poland, in need
of economic assistance. It might also mean inducing the USA to cancel
Britain's war debts, as the first step in a general cancellation of such
burdens. Labour also suggested Austrian union with Germany and a loose
economic federation of all the states of Central Europe.[34] Ironically this
was, arguably, what Germany would have imposed on Central Europe
had she rapidly won the war unopposed by Britain.[35] Labour's leaders
did not make this connection, of course, but they complained of the way
the war had been allowed to drag on in search of the elusive 'knock-out
blow', thus ensuring that the inevitable devastation would be worse than
what was strictly necessary – an outcome compounded by the 'needlessly
postponed' cancellation of the economic blockade of the Central Powers
which led to mass starvation in defeated Germany.

Russia was an even better illustration 'of the wanton loss and suffering
which the policy of our rulers has caused', according to Labour – as
illustrated by the military invasions, British support for anyone and
anything opposed to Bolshevism, and the naval blockade.[36] What was
actually needed, according to Labour, was an Anglo-Russian trade
agreement. Instead it argued that 'the Allies have done all in their power
for three years past to ruin Russia' and 'their purpose was partly
accomplished'. Germany faced a similar disaster. Reparations might be

extracted – by some combination of forced internal loans, inflation, American credit, pawned assets and other short-term devices – but ultimately, sweated German labour would be forced to pay the price. C. R. Buxton reported from his stay with a miner's family in the Ruhr in 1920 that this exploitation was an accomplished fact and that the evidence of excessive working hours and malnutrition was there to be seen.[37] Labour concluded that if this policy was sustained it must 'destroy the race itself, and with it the most productive and the most advanced civilisation of the Continent'.[38] The indemnity was both crippling Germany and utterly useless from the vantage point of unemployed Britons, or Britons employed in industries forced to compete with their sweated German counterparts. Labour proposed that the 'illegitimate' share of reparations claimed by Britain – repayment of war pensions and allowances – should simply be cancelled.

Lloyd George, who conducted Russian affairs in 1920–1, took the same view as that expressed in Labour propaganda – namely that recognition of the regime and the growth of trading links would encourage the Bolsheviks to at least dilute their radicalism, if not abandon it altogether. The Anglo-Russian trade agreement that he helped to broker in March 1921 led to a fourfold expansion of imports from Russia and a 20 per cent growth of British exports in the course of 1922. His thinking, like Labour's, expressed the old Liberal conviction that trade and prosperity promote peace and inter-dependence between nations. Unlike MacDonald, however, he was surrounded by Conservative colleagues who did not share these beliefs when applied to either Germany or Bolshevik Russia.

The Soviet Republic, 1917–20

In his polemic against the Peace Settlement Keynes had seen 'very good' prospects for revolution emanating from the war which he attributed, like Lenin, to 'the projects and politics of militarism and imperialism, of racial and cultural rivalries, of monopolies, restrictions and exclusion'.[39] Lenin established the Third, or Communist, International in Moscow in 1919 on this prospectus, keeping faith with his conviction that the Second International had been exposed as bankrupt in August 1914. The Bolsheviks lost no time in denouncing the Labour and socialist men who voted war credits in their respective parliaments. Henderson and MacDonald were two of a kind in the Bolshevik view and President Wilson had been their spokesman. Unsurprisingly the Bolshevik government was perceived as a problem by Labour leaders from the outset. The annual conference had listened to Maxim Litvinov warn of the threat to soviet democracy posed by the advancing German armies in January 1918, yet Labour officially deplored the peace of Brest-Litovsk two months later, as the Bolsheviks sacrificed territory for political survival. In June Alexander Kerensky, the deposed head of the Russian Provisional Government, addressed a second Labour conference and talked about the 'police terrorism' of the Bolsheviks. Henderson then defended Allied military intervention in Russia at the inter-allied conference of socialist and labour parties in September and supported Kerensky's argument that if Brest-Litovsk was allowed to stand it would signal the collapse of all that was progressive in the first Russian Revolution.

Representations from the Bolsheviks' opponents inside Russia meanwhile complained of a tyranny established by *coup d'état*. Democracy had been destroyed, the Bolsheviks' only motivation was to retain state power, cost what that may. The issue now was whether socialists in the West 'through their apology for the Bolsheviks . . . are becoming the involuntary accomplices of a falsehood unprecedented in history – a criminal attempt to disguise despotic anarchism with the flag of International Socialism'.[40] At no time did the Labour and trade union leadership encourage or participate in any such apology. When preparations began for the inter-allied peace conference, to shadow the real thing in the French capital, the prospect of Russian participation was rejected by Labour. Henderson was careful to stress to Lloyd George, in a respectful memorandum, that the working-class organisations involved in this initiative were strong supporters of the Fourteen Points and only wanted to contribute to a lasting peace.[41]

At Berne in February 1919 Labour threw its considerable weight behind the argument that the Bolshevik regime was incompatible with socialism because of its undemocratic character. Democracy, moreover, was defined in conventional terms – freedom of speech and press, the right of assembly, universal suffrage and a Government responsible to Parliament. Lenin's claim that soviet democracy was qualitatively superior to all of this was thus emphatically rejected. So was any method of socialisation which lacked majority consent and any method of government which enjoyed the support of only one section of the working class. The majority of delegates at Berne aligned themselves with this critique of the Bolsheviks while making it clear that they abhorred the use of Bolshevism as a convenient bogey by reactionary forces across Europe. They also decided to organise a delegation to Russia so that Bolshevism could be fully discussed by the next conference. This was their only concession to the minority of delegates who supported the Adler–Longuet resolution demanding no criticism of the Bolsheviks until the full facts were known.

Though the socialists might repudiate anti-Bolshevik propaganda as a device of the reactionaries of Europe they could do little about it. In Britain Labour was subject to a sustained campaign of vilification by the Lloyd George Coalition precisely on these terms. Labour, according to the thrust of this argument, was simply Bolshevism in disguise. The secret police under Basil Thompson's direction also acted on this assumption. In fact the Labour Party was a bulwark against Communism and always had been, as was privately acknowledged by the likes of Lloyd George. But its leaders, faced with a local Communist Party from the summer of 1920, had not established the ideological boundaries of the party in ways that would protect it against the Communist embrace. The battle to exclude Communists from the Labour membership would thus continue throughout the 1920s. The party's attitude to the Soviet Republic, however, could not have been clearer. Men like Thomas and Clynes had urged lifting the economic blockade as the best way of defeating Bolshevism while MacDonald and Snowden wanted official recognition of the Bolshevik Government almost from the moment it was formed. The party's Russian policy, in short, was diplomatic recognition and trade. Labour had acquiesced in the military intervention against the Bolshevik regime until November 1918; thereafter it became a problem for the party. The report of the NEC put before Labour's annual conference in June 1919 made no reference to the continuing war of intervention, though the party had received many communications and resolutions deploring it. Basil Thompson informed the Cabinet in the spring of 1919 that opposition to intervention was pervasive among the workers.[42] Calls for direct action to stop the war against the Bolshevik regime accumulated in the course of the year and when, in the spring of 1920, Poland attacked the Soviet Union with blatant British and French support, the clamour for direct action intensified. It peaked in August when there was talk of a British declaration of war against Soviet Russia as the Red Army advanced towards Warsaw. The TUC and the Labour Party issued a joint statement on 9 August warning that 'the whole industrial power of the organised workers will be used to defeat this war'.[43]

Spontaneous direct action in the London docks and demonstrations against war suggested that this was no idle threat and the Labour–TUC communiqué may have influenced Lloyd George's advice to Poland to accept the Russian peace terms.[44] The Labour Party membership certainly harboured a reservoir of sympathy for the Soviet Union that could not be denied. For one thing it contained people who made no secret of their conviction that Lenin's Russia was a socialist society in the making. George Lansbury, a future Labour leader, used the *Daily Herald* to propagate this view. But there is no evidence that the demonstrations against war of 1920 were motivated by anything more than war-weariness; for the most part the working class in Britain was unmoved by the struggles unfolding inside Soviet Russia at this time.[45] The Labour leadership continued to emphasise the irrelevance of Bolshevism for socialism in Britain. This view received emphatic endorsement from the report of an official Labour delegation to Soviet Russia which was published in 1920. The report recommended recognition of the regime and better trading links between Russia and Britain, on the grounds that these would promote moderating political tendencies in Moscow. But it was perfectly frank in noting that the one-party dictatorship had stifled such democracy as there had been in 1917 and had transformed previously independent working-class organisations such as the unions and cooperatives into definite parts of the state machinery.[46]

The contradictions of Empire, 1918–29

Though Asquith declared in October 1914 that Britain 'did not covet any people's territory', Labour knew that at least 800,000 square miles of territory had been added to the Empire by 1919.[47] The NEC manifesto of May 1919 also said that the war was 'partly the product of frustrated colonial ambitions', while the peace permanently denied Germany 'the opportunity to become a mandatory'. It was therefore clear that imperialism had had a hand in the whole process. The embryonic LSI (only fully constituted at Hamburg in 1923),[48] like Labour, welcomed the mandates system as a way of protecting 'people unable to stand on their own feet' by entrusting their care to 'the more advanced states that are in a position to exercise the responsibility'. That these were the same states, according to the Labour analysis, which had demonstrated 'imperialist' appetites is a reminder that imperialism was not a structured relationship for Labour, so much as a factional tendency and policy option. Notwithstanding these limitations of comprehension Labour understood enough to formally agree with the other parties of the LSI that the mandates system should involve definite responsibilities and cover all of the colonies, rather than just those of defeated Germany. The reality, as Labour acknowledged, was that the Allies had awarded the mandates to themselves and the League had no independent powers of inspection to ensure that the exceptionally vague terms of the mandate were being honoured.[49]

Labour had very little to say about the newly acquired Empire in the Middle East and the 'mandated' colonies taken from Germany. It was now possible to travel from Cape Town to Rangoon without ever leaving the British dominion, but there was no celebration of these gains and not much mention of them either. They simply became, as the territorial gains of the 1890s had before them, part of the 'fact' of the British Empire before which the self-styled realists deferred on the grounds of a higher responsibility. At a time when Britain was faced with serious problems in Ireland,[50] Egypt,[51] Afghanistan[52] and India[53] it had just acquired millions of new subjects of which it knew little or nothing. Some of these new subjects had been made promises during the war that could only encourage the same nationalist developments which were evident in India and Egypt. The Balfour Declaration of November 1917, for example, promised a Jewish homeland in Palestine; but other state officials had made promises to the Arabs in return for their support against Turkey. The actual division of the Middle East between Britain and France, meanwhile, suggested that the strategists who argued that a bigger British presence was required to block the advance of the Russians towards Constantinople and the Straits had won the day.[54] The Middle East was also thought to be rich in oil and Britain's interest in this commodity had been strong enough for the state to acquire a controlling interest in the Anglo-Persian Oil Company, after the Royal Navy turned to liquid fuel in 1912. A massive refinery was developed under British control at Abadan. Nationalists in Persia opposed the treaty which Britain imposed on the country in August 1919. In Palestine the first post-war violence between Jews and Arabs was recorded around the same time; in Iraq, as in Afghanistan and the Sudan, Britain was forced to use the Royal Air Force to maintain the imperial order.[55] In the Foreign Secretary's words, 'every place is a storm-centre'.[56] The 'fact' of Empire, which the Labour leadership was disposed to accept, entailed acceptance of many other facts, including the fact that it had to be defended. Through this portal Labour would in time be forced to accept aspects of foreign and defence policy which it officially abhorred and meet frustration in matters which it set out to achieve.

Within a few years of the Versailles conference MacDonald and those around him – determined as they were to make Labour an electorally credible force and a much more polished and professional parliamentary group – were stressing the need for managerial competence in Parliament. They were not likely to remain content with the rhetorical positions of 1919, which had been adopted under pressure of exceptional events, at a time when Labour was only just emerging as a functioning political party. An indication of its organisational looseness has already been alluded to – the presence of Marxists and foundation members of the Communist Party like R. Palme Dutt and Robin Page Arnot, alongside Leonard Woolf, MacDonald and Sidney Webb on Labour's advisory committee on international questions in 1919. But there were other problems which added up to a lack of clarity in policy-making and some of these would only be addressed after the 1931 political crisis. Meanwhile, the advisory committee, drawing upon a varied cast which included pacifists, enthusiasts for the League, militant opponents of the League, as well as Marxists and regular contributors such as Will Arnold-Foster and Philip Noel-Baker, supplied the Executive with information, advice, propaganda and guidance for speakers.[57] It performed a role in policy-making, but only at the preparatory stages and when the party was in opposition.[58] It also performed its functions in secret so far as the ordinary party member was concerned. It had reason to complain in 1920 that its deliberations and advice were generally ignored by the parliamentary party, a fact that could be attributed to the dullness of the Labour parliamentary group at the time, which generally avoided international issues. But this impression could not survive for long after MacDonald returned to the parliamentary leadership. It would then become clear that the party leader had little time for abstract views emanating from the advisory committee, particularly those of a rejectionist and revisionist nature in respect of the peace settlement. 'Our task', it said in 1920, 'is not to deflect the Foreign Office a little from its crazy path. Our task is to make the masses understand the ruin wrought in the world by Imperialist Capitalism.'[59] The parliamentary group had little or no use for such an approach, whatever may have been the case elsewhere in the party, bearing in mind the various divisions which made Labour a rather loose federation of special interests at this time.[60]

It is true that in 1918–19 Labour was as near to unanimity as it ever managed to get in its history on the question of its rejection of the peace settlement. Undoubtedly this had much to do with the bitterness which all sections of the organisation felt arising from their sense of betrayal. The League was a particular disappointment, though the German settlement – which preoccupied Morel and his journal *Foreign Affairs* – was not far behind in the menu of grievances. But there is more to Labour's disenchantment than the rather long list of specific disappointments. The routine realities of power politics were no longer perceived as adequate causes for the outbreaks of war, let alone justifications for them. The year 1914 had changed perceptions. 'The notion that aggression is a crime and that wars can be justified only if they ward off aggression or prevent it acquired its practical and even theoretical significance only after the First World War had demonstrated the horribly destructive potential of warfare under conditions of modern technology.'[61] The world had entered the era of total war when war became a matter of national mobilisation and industrial-scale killing. And it had done so because of a 'diplomatic blunder', or series of blunders. Armies and armaments were no longer there to protect civilians but to kill them on a terrifying scale. Defeat in such wars could mean industrial collapse, mass unemployment, widespread starvation and social revolution. Huge scepticism now greeted the claim of the conventional theory of defence, namely that if one wanted to keep the peace one must prepare for war. The arms race was now – more than ever before 1914 – seen as a cause of war and yet war itself was damned for achieving little or nothing of lasting value. Labour's pre-war suspicion of imperialism, chauvinism, military expenditures, secret diplomacy and power politics was thus greatly magnified among the party rank-and-file. So was its pacifism and demands for disarmament, though such sentiments were by no means confined to the left. 'British political parties generally agreed in placing hopes for disarmament above the mean of implementing collective security, in sharp contrast to the French approach.'[62] Labour damned the peace treaty as a victor's settlement unlikely to last, but there was an equally strong conviction within the party that some processes of arbitration and conciliation were required so that future wars could be avoided altogether.

In understanding why the Labour Party gradually came to the view that it would have to make do with the existing League, rather than wait until a reformed version came into existence, its leader's reformist beliefs are obviously important to bear in mind. It is also of some relevance that the electorate never fell in behind Labour's rejectionist and revisionist policies. Instead there were indicators of public hope that the League of Nations would help to prevent future wars. When Labour's thinkers on foreign policy turned to practical questions they could sometimes see the possibilities of useful reforms conducted within the existing institutional arrangements. In 1918, for example, the advisory committee realised that if national armed forces survived, the League would have to possess superior coercive powers to deal with attacks on its members.[63] This suggested reform of the League extant rather than its abandonment. Some of the speeches at the Southport annual conference in 1919 reflected this attitude, including those of the conference chairman, the staunch patriot and miners' union official John McGurk, as well as those of MacDonald and Clynes.[64] In summarising its attitudes to the peace treaty in 1919, party policy statements talked about the need to admit Germany and Austria to the League; about the League supervising the payment of reparations; and of the League exercising major economic functions to guarantee equality of access to raw materials and foodstuffs and to bring all colonies under its protection.[65] Similar arguments were taken up at Lucerne by the embryonic LSI and again in 1920 by the same organisation in Geneva. The proletariat, according to the International, 'cannot in the interests of peace, consider with hostility or indifference the organisation of the League of Nations as created by the Treaty of Versailles, but it is their duty to proclaim its insufficiency and defects, the worst of which is the recognition, in Article 12, of the right to make war'.[66]

But there was no rapid transition to this pragmatic point of view. For one thing there were too many leading thinkers on international affairs within the party who took Morel's view that the League was an instrument for the suppression of Germany and could not be used to reform the peace treaty. More important, the sense of anger and cynicism was kept alive by the constant drip of decisions and events which reinforced the initial bad impressions of February–March 1919; such as the interventions against Bolshevism, the Polish–Russian war, the conflict between Greece and Turkey and the various secondary treaties which assigned mandates and territory and finally reparations to the victors. Under these circumstances a pessimistic mood prevailed into the early 1920s. The temptation to polemicise against the peace settlement was all the stronger in view of the rapid collapse of hopes for a better Britain. These were dashed by both the economic collapse of 1921 and the coalition's deflationary policies which consigned plans for reconstruction to the waste-paper bin. Germany's economic condition was even worse, of course, and the conviction that it had been harshly dealt with grew in this context. At the same time France came to be seen as an intransigent aggressor, particularly in 1922 when the reparations crisis of that year threatened another war. Meanwhile, pacifist and war-resistance sentiment within the ILP and the Labour Party found expression at their respective annual conferences as the French (and Belgians) planned their invasion of the Ruhr. Labour's small parliamentary contingent, composed in the main of former trade union officials until the general election of 1922, had, however, little to say on international affairs, while those who were interested in such matters were not yet in the House. With trade unionists increasingly preoccupied by the deteriorating economic situation, the polemics of the party's experts on international affairs cost little and might even assist those of them who still required a base in the ILP, an organisation which now contained most of the leading members of the UDC. Party leaders also had to contend with popular and party sympathy for the struggling Bolshevik state and could not yet be sure how this might translate into competition on the left of British politics with the infant Communist Party.

Labour's leaders could never be happy with class war arguments, however, and the idea that the League was a 'thieves' kitchen' of the victorious states, simply an expression of the class interests of the imperialists of those countries, was an argument which sat more comfortably with the revolutionary rhetoric of the Communists. The instinct of Labour's leaders was to negotiate, conciliate and reform.[67] In the course of 1922 and 1923 French belligerence and the invasion of the Ruhr became the specific object of these skills, as they were for Baldwin's Conservative Government. In more general terms the League of Nations slotted in with those liberal convictions, so strong among Labour's leaders, which stressed the possibility of piecemeal progress in political affairs based on reason; as well as those beliefs which claimed a material and ethical community of interests between nations and confidence in the pacific tendencies of public opinion – certainly public opinion within the liberal democracies. Thus when war threatened in 1922 the annual conference called upon the League to step in before one of its members (France) invaded Germany. The League began to seem the only hope for that general disarmament which was supposed to have followed the disarmament of Germany. Some members of the party began to realise that French security anxieties had to be accommodated in the meantime – and through the same institutional mechanisms. Henderson was among the first to realise that if the League was to perform the function of maintaining the peace it would have to be able to resort to effective sanctions.[68]

MacDonald, who returned to the House of Commons in November 1922 as an MP, and was soon elevated to the party leadership and overall responsibility for the parliamentary strategy of its 142 MPs, was equally keen on finding a practical policy. As a prospective Prime Minister he would have to consider British and imperial defence requirements and allay suspicions that Labour would discharge this duty to their detriment. At the same time he had to manage a party which contained outright pacifists and socialists of the sort who thought all these problems would disappear 'under socialism'. Snowden's resignation from the ILP National Administrative Council in April 1922 was an early indication that the leaders were beginning to distance themselves from the policies preferred on the left of the party. Snowden had been prominent in the pages of *Labour Leader* as a spokesman on foreign affairs, an avowed pacifist who damned the peace settlement as vehemently as anyone. But by the end of 1922 he was pleading for patience with, and reform of, the League. So too was Henderson. The Ruhr crisis caused concern that the British Government had not used its membership of the League to persuade France to employ collective mechanisms to resolve the reparations problem rather than resort to unilateral force. These thoughts also suggested a practical way for Labour to distinguish itself from the Conservative Government in foreign affairs. MacDonald complained to the House in February 1923, as the French invasion took its course and the German hyper-inflation worsened, that neither France nor Britain had made any real attempt to make the League work.[69] This posture corresponded to advice from within the party that Labour should stop seeing the League as 'a sort of advisory super-state with a will of its own' and wake up to the fact that it was 'simply an association of governments'. This had been said before, of course. But whereas the conclusion drawn in 1919 was purely negative, it was now deduced that Labour's efforts ought to be directed at criticism of the British Government for not making more of the existing League machinery.[70]

This was all about making a more effective case against Government foreign policy in the House of Commons. The issue that was now arising in the minds of Labour's leaders was that of making the existing League function, rather than waiting until all of its 52 members were as convinced as the ILP seemingly was that nothing could be done until the League was reformed. The LSI, greatly influenced by British Labour, adopted the same stance when it met at Hamburg in May.[71]

What if Labour formed a Government? This was the question MacDonald and his allies asked themselves, especially after the 1922 general election consolidated Labour's position as the principal alternative to Stanley Baldwin's Conservative Government. Snowden put the point rhetorically in 1923; many people, he said, had 'grave doubts about the ability of a Labour Government to run the Empire and to conduct international affairs'.[72] They supposed it had 'no strong affection for the Empire, which it regards as the product of commercial greed and Imperialist ambitions. In foreign affairs it is considered to be anti-national ... It is feared that a Labour Government would sacrifice the interests of the Empire and of the nation to its ideal of internationalism.'[73] Snowden assured his readers that 'these fears and misgivings are quite simply without foundation'. He then supplied the following propaganda gift to his left-wing critics:

> The answer is surely to be found in the fact that the vast majority of the Labour Party, at the outbreak of war, forgot their internationalism when they were told that the country was in danger, and became the most patriotic of British citizens. And the minority which opposed the war did so because they believed, and never have men been more abundantly justified by events, that this country had been dragged into war by the cunning machinations of foreign militarists and diplomatists.[74]

Snowden calmed his readers by insisting that 'a Labour Government would be as jealous of national honour, as keenly alive to the great possibilities of Empire Development, and as determined to promote good international relations, as any British Government of the past'. It would regard the Empire as 'a fact' which, with the aid of the right policies, could become 'the greatest instrument for world progress which has ever been created'. Admittedly, he conceded, the dependencies or Crown Colonies presented 'many difficulties'. But withdrawal was not an option – it would simply 'leave them a prey to the predatory designs of other powers'. Snowden seemed to have no doubt that imperialism was predatory when other countries engaged in it and that the termination of a benign British rule could only leave a vacuum which such predatory

Powers would automatically fill. This was the ruling ideology which everyone at Westminster and Whitehall subscribed to, the world war having made no difference either to the practical ignorance of the political class in matters relating to the Empire or their conviction that it stood for service, justice, brotherhood and even the fundamental good of humankind. Snowden's rhetoric was every bit as extravagant as that to be found anywhere else on the political spectrum. What was missing from it was the attention to detailed policy which might give meaning to the phrases associated with Snowden's vision such as 'colonial development', 'native paramountcy', 'humane and just government', Dominions 'as part of the Homeland', and the 'close association' between a Labour Government at Westminster and Labour Governments in Australia, New Zealand, and Canada. Instead there were doubtful assumptions about the mutual advantage of closer British ties with the Dominions and Victorian ideas (shared with the Tories)[75] about emigration from Britain as an answer to a 'profound and menacing problem', though one which Snowden failed to specify any further, despite forecasting that it would be 'forced upon a British Labour Government' in the future.

Snowden was probably alluding to Labour's impotence in the face of chronic unemployment, if not to that steady-state economy prophesied with dread in classical political economy. He argued that when economic stagnation prevailed the surplus population would be encouraged to emigrate to emptier continents. It was an early warning of his rigid orthodoxy in economic ideology that he had recourse to such expedients at a time when deflationary policies prevailed and balanced budgets were prescribed by both the banking authorities and the political elite. But neither Snowden nor MacDonald – the two leading socialists in the party – thought in terms of an active programme of socialist reforms. Rather, socialism would come when the necessary change of heart had taken place and this was as likely as anything to be the result of an evolutionary process in society of long duration. The Darwinian and biological metaphors favoured by MacDonald when discussing the future of socialism certainly did not suggest a parliamentary timetable.[76] But the general election of December 1923, which Baldwin lost on a programme of tariff protection, presented Labour with an opportunity to show what it did believe to be possible, albeit as a minority government. MacDonald was determined to consolidate Labour's position as the only realistic alternative to the Conservative Party.[77] Socialists expected more than this. Even normally hostile commentators on the left expected significant departures in British foreign policy despite the fact that the first Labour Government would be entirely dependent on the tolerance of the Conservative and Liberal parties.[78]

In part these inflated expectations were informed by Labour's pledge to recognise the Soviet Union, as it was now called. But it was also because Labour had stuck to a revisionist line since 1919 in its critique of the Treaty of Versailles. Britain's domestic problems, according to Labour, were related to the international malaise caused by the war. Labour had championed disarmament, the critique of French militarism and the inclusion of Germany and Soviet Russia in the League. The Ruhr crisis, which smouldered throughout 1923, underlined the relevance of these positions and strengthened Labour's claim to possess an understanding of foreign affairs which the Conservative Government lacked. The party's success at the 1922 general election strengthened perceptions of its radicalism in foreign affairs by permitting an influx of war critics into its parliamentary ranks, at a time when another conflict threatened because of the ongoing reparations dispute. Founding members of the UDC, such as E. D. Morel, Arthur Ponsonby, Josiah Wedgwood,[79] Noel Buxton,[80] Charles Rhodes Buxton and Charles Trevelyan now sat on the Labour benches and acted as the party's leading spokesmen on foreign affairs.[81] They were joined by a number of militant socialists, notably the Clydesider group of James Maxton, John Wheatley, David Kirkwood and their co-thinkers. MacDonald, Snowden, Fred Jowett, Lansbury and Webb were also returned in 1922; Henderson had got back at a by-election in 1919 but went against the trend by losing his seat in 1922. He nevertheless remained a powerful force within the leadership. MacDonald, however, emerged as *the* leader with his election to the Party Chairmanship in November 1922.

The professionalisation of the PLP, in part a function of its growth and adaptation to the Westminster system, was signified in the elections of a PLP Executive in 1923 in which trade union officialdom did relatively badly as against the career politicians. The trade unionists who sat on the party's NEC increasingly deferred on most questions to the parliamentarians and support for the leader was generally becoming the best evidence of loyalty to the party for this group of men. Factionalism on the NEC was weak and ideological divisions pitching unions against each other were absent.[82] For some time now there had been monthly meetings between the NEC and the TUC General Council, a symbolic fusion of the two 'wings' of the movement, if nothing more substantial. In a similar spirit the Chairman of the General Council signed the Labour manifestos of 1922, 1923, and 1924. A National Council of Labour was formed in 1921, composed of representatives of the General Council, the NEC and the PLP. In practice it failed to live up to union expectations, but again it symbolised the common purpose of 'the movement'. This was a movement which was going forward. The growth of Labour's vote – 4,438,508 ballots were cast for it in December 1923, or 30.5 per cent of the total – supported the leadership's view of British politics, a view which imagined Labour taking its rightful place in the broader evolution of British democracy and thereby bringing that great constitutional epic to its final maturity.

First minority government

MacDonald formed his government in January 1924 with no less than nine members of the UDC in the Cabinet and a total of fifteen in the Government, though it was made clear that members of the UDC General Council were expected to resign their positions. The Cabinet was con-structed in the conventional way, with MacDonald consulting where he saw fit to do so and then making his own final judgement.[83] There was never any suggestion that the PLP or the wider party might have had a say in its composition. MacDonald actually retained the wartime secretariat, instituted by Lloyd George, under the conservative leadership of Maurice Hankey, and dispensed with the practice of his immediate predecessors in making political appointments to the private office. Yet he was soon noting that officials dominated ministers by swamping them in a morass of detail.[84] The Cabinet also operated according to orthodox precept, stressing secrecy and collective responsibility in relation to outside bodies such as the TUC. MacDonald combined the offices of Prime Minister and Foreign Secretary and performed the functions of the latter secretively and 'in more or less complete detachment from the Cabinet'.[85] With the exception of the Prime Minister and Ponsonby (a junior Minister at the Foreign Office), UDC members were kept well away from foreign policy and Morel was excluded from the Government altogether. Noel Buxton and C. P. Trevelyan entered it as Minister of Agriculture and President of the Board of Trade respectively. Henderson was made Home Secretary and Snowden became Chancellor. MacDonald was able to count on backbench pride in a Labour Government and the solid support of the trade union leaders – men who needed him to succeed if the interests of their own members were to advance.

Another reason why the Cabinet was unlikely to object to a con-servative approach in foreign relations was the fact that all the key positions concerned with defence and foreign policy were held by conservatives. J. H. Thomas, the Colonial Secretary, was a former General Secretary of the National Union of Railwaymen, with a history of political conformity on matters pertaining to Empire;[86] the Liberal Viscount Haldane became chairman of the Committee of Imperial Defence, thus advertising the Government's commitment to continuity; Christopher Birdwood Thomson, a career soldier elevated to the peerage by MacDonald, performed the same function as Secretary for Air; Sir Sydney

Olivier, the Secretary for India, had already demonstrated his orthodoxy during twenty years of overseas postings managing the Empire in the Caribbean, one of its poorest and most neglected corners; Stephen Walsh, the Secretary for War, had loyally served in Lloyd George's wartime coalition; Lord Chelmsford, First Lord of the Admiralty, was a life-long Conservative, a former Viceroy of India who had instigated the repressive Rowlatt Acts of January 1918 (catalyst of Gandhi's first disobedience campaign), and publicly defended the Amristar massacre of April 1919. If MacDonald intended to transmit a signal by these appointments, it was 'business as usual' and political respectability, as defined by the established parties. His Cabinet contained four former Liberals, two Conservatives, and one former Conservative – and at least two additional Conservatives had been invited to join but failed to do so. His message to Indian nationalists, at the beginning of his 10-month period of office, was more explicit; to the Gandhian Congress, constitutionalists to a man, he advised that 'no party in Britain will be cowed by force'. He was intent on demonstrating Labour's 'fitness to govern' and this was how he would go about it.

MacDonald's objective, according to Cowling, was to fashion Labour as 'a responsible instrument of Radical thinking' while maintaining party unity and keeping his own extreme left under control.[87] This was consistent with the policies he had always pursued, such as the secret electoral pact of 1903 with Herbert Gladstone and the Liberal Party; support for Lloyd George's reforms in 1910 and 1914; and support for the wartime coalition governments, even though MacDonald himself had been a virtual pariah since August 1914. MacDonald knew that he had powerful allies for moderation within the party in the form of most of the trade union leaders, many of them suspicious of the ILP and UDC elements in the organisation. More important, he was intent on proving the scaremongers wrong by showing that Labour was not an extremist party. Taking office was a natural extension of the road taken since 1900 and another step perhaps in edging out the Liberals in the two-party system, a perspective which had opened since at least the end of the war. Once the election result became known Labour's leaders took every opportunity to stress their moderate intentions, depicting government as a public service responsibility which they would dutifully carry out. Within the political establishment it was understood that MacDonald and his leading colleagues were not the militants depicted in the press. Even the reactionary King George V could see that Labour in these hands was a barrier to radicalism, not its most likely source. The question was whether MacDonald could control his own 'wild men'. Within a month of its formation the Government had supplied the answer to this question and Leo Amery was able to remark on the fact that Labour

Ministers 'took practically the same view of things as the late Capitalist government'.[88]

The received view, at the end of 1924 – as at the termination of the second MacDonald Government in 1931 – was that Labour's greatest success had been in foreign policy. This necessarily implies some disappointment on the part of ILP socialists and many of those former Liberals and UDC activists whose conversion to Labour had involved 'no sudden revelation of the cogency of socialism, no rejection of past credo', but who now belonged with the 'extremists' in the distance of their remove from the leadership's thinking.[89] Within weeks of taking office MacDonald was alienated from the ILP's *New Leader*, edited by Brailsford, as well as Lansbury's *Daily Herald* and critical individuals such as Morel. Given his objectives, it is ironic that the end of his first Government was associated with Communist scare stories – the Zinoviev Letter, the Campbell case and the opposition to the proposed trade treaties with Soviet Russia, which animated both Parliament and the press. But MacDonald devoted himself to foreign relations, as planned, and few in the Labour Party doubted its importance at a time when the depressed state of the British economy was thought to depend on repairing the international order so grievously damaged by the world war.

The government accordingly claimed credit for brokering the Dawes Plan, an American-inspired bankers' scheme for rescheduling German reparations which the party managers promoted as evidence of a broader international goodwill fostered by MacDonald's diplomacy.[90] MacDonald took office knowing that France had to be convinced that the threat of German *revanchism* could be contained. This problem was related, in both Tory and Labour eyes, to France's excessive concern for its own security. A few prominent Labour figures, including Henderson and Angell, realised that for the League to provide this security it would have to be ready and able to use sanctions.[91] The French were inclined to link this question to compulsory arbitration through the League and the outlawing of 'aggressive wars'. MacDonald himself seems to have believed that international cooperation depended on a new mentality, a new psychology of brotherhood, rather than the institutions of the League. Like so many of his beliefs this enabled him to work within conventional assumptions in the here-and-now. The role of officials in shaping his perceptions would have increased in any case, this being Labour's first experience of government, but the fact that they shared his scepticism about the League reinforced the process of dependency. So did the realisation, which office brought with it, that any progress in international affairs necessarily involved compromises with other states and their preoccupations. In the given context that meant accommodating France in particular, MacDonald's policy with regard to the French 'was not very different from that of Curzon and closely in line with Foreign Office thinking'.[92] His brief was to persuade France to withdraw from the Ruhr while answering their economic demands with the Dawes Report – an initiative that pre-dated the formation of his Government.

Party propaganda talked of a 'first step to reconstruction and revision of the Treaty of Versailles' on the basis of MacDonald's successful efforts to link acceptance of the Dawes deal to French withdrawal from the Ruhr.[93] This covered up the fact that opposition to the Dawes Plan within the Labour Party was strong enough to warrant a warning from the PLP executive, reminding MacDonald that many in the party had 'consistently opposed the policy of reparations'.[94] Many trade unionists remained convinced that it was detrimental to their interests, since the financial stabilisation which Dawes envisaged could further force down German wages and ruin the British coal industry in particular. The other great achievement which Labour frequently referred to was thought to hold out better prospects for domestic economic recovery – the recognition of Soviet Russia; but these prospects proved illusory. Decisions were also taken which demonstrated the Government's commitment to free trade and disarmament. The plan to build a great naval base at Singapore was abandoned. Projected warship construction was cut back and surplus arms were destroyed rather than sold abroad. Government 'spin' on these decisions linked them to MacDonald's success in strengthening the climate of conciliation and arbitration conducive to an effective League of Nations. But much of the administration's effort followed in the tracks of previous governments, such as in adhering to the 'ten year rule' which justified economies in current defence spending on the grounds that there was no prospect of a major war within a decade. When a motion was put before the PLP demanding cancellation of the order to build five cruisers commissioned by the Conservative Government, MacDonald's displeasure ensured that only twelve MPs gave their support to it. MacDonald also refused parliamentary time for Morel's motion on 'the parliamentary control of foreign relations',[95] leaving the PLP Executive to express 'its deep regret' that this shibboleth of the last ten years, which even the TUC General Council supported, should be so lightly cast aside.[96] Instead Ponsonby announced a considerably diluted form of open diplomacy, specifying that all future treaties would be put before Parliament for a period of three weeks to invite discussion in the usual way.

The LNU had welcomed the first Labour Government but relations soon became difficult. Although MacDonald attended the League's fifth Assembly, friction with the LNU was largely the Labour Leader's fault. MacDonald had not only criticised the Covenant since he became leader of the PLP in 1922, he also kept his distance from the LNU leaders. He took the view that they would put the interests of the League before those of Great Britain. The LNU had campaigned for the adoption of the Draft Treaty of Mutual Assistance but MacDonald was opposed to the scheme.[97] The Draft Treaty, prepared by Lord Cecil and Colonel Requin, and accepted by the League Assembly in 1923, obliged signatories to assist victims of aggressive war within their home region, leaving it to the League Council to decide what constituted an aggressive war. The agreement was to be conditional on measures of disarmament by the consenting Powers and envisaged action on this matter over a period of two years. Once the disarmament measures had taken place, if France, for example, was attacked by Germany, then under the terms of the scheme Britain, Belgium and other members of the League in the region would be obliged to come to France's assistance. The French liked this idea as much as British military men and Foreign Office advisors – with imperial commitments in mind and regional commitments all over the globe – disliked it. The scheme had the merit for some of those who thought in terms of war-avoidance, of linking mutual security with disarmament while giving some substance to the idea that the League was a force for the maintenance of peace. But very few Labour thinkers made systematic connections at this stage between arbitration, disarmament and what would be known in the 1930s as collective security. Morel and most of the left saw in the Draft Treaty only the continuation, under another name, of the nefarious alliance system of August 1914. Others were sceptical about any arrangements which seemed to defend the imperialist status quo. A majority of members of the advisory committee on international questions, however, wanted acceptance of the Draft Treaty subject to amendments, including an agreed definition of what constituted an aggressive war. These people were concerned that Labour should encourage the League's efforts. They also thought that acceptance of this approach could be used to lever France into compromise with Germany. But on this question MacDonald and the bulk of the party agreed, and they agreed on rejection, though their motives for doing so varied enormously. Britain's note of rejection – listing an impressive array of problems with the proposal – effectively killed it off in July 1924.[98]

In place of the Draft Treaty the League suggested a plan based on compulsory arbitration, the Protocol for the Pacific Settlement of Disputes, known as the Geneva Protocol, by which nations agreed to put disputes of a judicial character before the Court of International Justice. This plan gained Labour's support from the Opposition benches in 1925, with Henderson a particularly strong advocate, but this time the Conservative Government rejected it – boasting later in the year that the Locarno Pact had in any case solved the problems which the Protocol addressed. Henderson, who was actively involved in the Third Committee of the League Assembly in 1924, concerned with security and disarmament, saw the connections which eluded many Labour activists – namely those between a general disarmament of League members and the League's ability to support arbitration with real sanctions, including military sanctions if arbitration broke down. The Geneva Protocol seemed to embody such thinking when it emerged in October 1924 with the full backing of the League's British delegation. It specified, as Labour's *Memorandum of War Aims* had in 1918, that refusal to submit a dispute to arbitration would be taken as an act of aggression – thus solving the problem of definition – and that such refusal would cause the League to mobilise sanctions against the offending state. But none of these provisions would come into effect until a disarmament conference had been convened and had agreed measures for the reduction of arms. In the event the Labour Government was spared the necessity of deciding what to do about the Geneva Protocol and it was left to the succeeding Conservative Government to reject it outright. But it is clear from the Tory reaction that the service chiefs – conscious as they were of the opportunities for disputes provided by the British Empire – feared that acceptance would injure British interests. Leo Amery observed in the House, looking back on this decision to reject, that the Government's reasoning 'in fact and in substance' amounted to a rejection of Article XVI of the Covenant, the obligation for taking joint action to coerce an aggressor, as much as it rejected the Protocol itself.[99] But in the face of the opposition of the armed forces it is extremely doubtful that MacDonald would have supported the Protocol if his government had survived into 1925 – he had already accepted their arguments in rejecting the Draft Treaty. Instead the Labour Government ended when the opposition parties refused to accept the trade treaties negotiated with the Soviet regime.

For peace and prosperity: but how?

The experience of this first Labour administration is notable in foreign policy terms for effectively ending the post-war influence of the UDC within the party. In part this was because of the loss of so many UDC leaders when the Labour Government was formed, together with Morel's untimely death later in the year. But the experience of Government also brought home the lesson that there could be no peace in Europe unless the tension between France and Germany was resolved. Active involvement in the League thus supplanted isolationism and revisionism as the best way to achieve this outcome. It was a belief which had popular backing. The LNU's membership reached 600,000 by 1926. It became a force to be reckoned with, especially by Labour which stood to profit from the LNU's alienation from the succeeding Conservative Government. In 1927 a major row broke out in Geneva between Britain and the USA when talks to extend the Washington naval agreements[100] to include cruisers failed because Austen Chamberlain, the Foreign Secretary, would not accept the American demand for parity. Britain's rejection of the Draft Treaty, then the Geneva Protocol and now parity in cruisers with the USA all pointed to the survival of the old diplomacy and Viscount Cecil – the anomalous Tory who devoted most of his time to promoting the League – resigned from the Government. The LNU now took up the cause of disarmament. It enthusiastically campaigned for the initiative taken by the US Secretary of State Frank Kellogg who wanted all the nations of the world to sign a treaty renouncing war.

The brief experience of government meanwhile provided the inspiration for sections of the Labour left to investigate practical proposals for dealing with domestic economic problems in a radical way. International policy entered these calculations as part of this domestic project. In 1925 some Labour left-wingers supported imperial protection in the House of Commons. Others had been arguing for some time that the Empire could be developed in such a way that this immense trading bloc could be used to re-flate the world economy and eliminate the sort of damaging competition which allowed underpaid Indian and Chinese labour to displace workers and even whole industries in Britain.[101] Freda Utley invoked the example of the devastated jute industry of Dundee when addressing annual conference about these issues in 1926.[102] Naturally, these dreams of imperial concord drew upon a long tradition of lauding British trusteeship in the dependencies and celebrating 'kith and kin' connections with the self-governing Dominions. The vision of a cooperative Commonwealth, real or prospective, thus acquired a rhetorical urgency in the context of domestic stagnation. Labour talked of the need for closer political and economic ties between the parts of Empire. The annual conference demanded an audit of colonial resources (just as Ernest Bevin was to do as Foreign Secretary in 1947).[103] It was suggested that 'a scientific redistribution of the land' could be accomplished 'to provide an increasing proportion of the food of the population of the British Commonwealth and the raw materials of its industries'.[104] State-aided migration was advocated together with training schemes for prospective migrants. Such measures might then foster a scientific redistribution of population, or so it was argued. Bulk purchasing and marketing boards were seen as part of the solution for cheaper food and improved trade.

Predictable opposition to such schemes came from Communists and others who objected to the false assumptions of complementary interests which were said to obtain in this mythical 'Commonwealth of nations'. Actual conditions of squalor, exploitation, land theft and repression were emphasised by such critics but the overwhelming majority of Labour conference delegates in the 1920s were more impressed by the argument that the Empire existed, could not be erased and should be put to constructive use. Talk of self-determination was premature rhetoric in this view and the left-wing critics were dismissed as hypocrites who conspicuously failed to apply the principle to the Soviet empire. Labour, it was said by the party loyalists, could not even apply self-determination to the Dominions without provoking the wrath of white minorities, so how on earth could they expect it to solve anything on the Asian sub-continent. In any case it was obvious to some Labour supporters that even the poor of India had more chance of improving their condition under a Labour Government in London than by means of national independence on the 'outside' of the Empire.[105] Lansbury, on behalf of the NEC, nevertheless successfully moved a resolution at the 1925 annual conference calling for 'full self-government and self-determination' for India. The debate supported his call for an end to repressive measures (though the late Labour Government had not overlooked them) and Fenner Brockway seconded the resolution by stressing that it was inde-pendence for India that the party had in mind, rather than just dominion status. But the resolution made no reference to 'independence' and even Lansbury expressed the view that India would elect to remain a member of the Commonwealth if it was given the opportunity to decide for itself.

Conference also heard Trevelyan describe the 'high-handed impe-rialism' which governed all of Britain's dealings in the East – Russia, China, Egypt – as he supported a resolution moved by Herbert Morrison of the London County Council demanding British military evacuation from Egypt and the latter's membership of the League of Nations as a fully sovereign state. Neither of these conditions obtained even after the second Labour Government of 1929–31 or, for that matter, by the end of the first majority Labour Government in 1951, twenty-six years later when British troops remained encamped in the Canal Zone. Promises of Egyptian independence had been made on literally dozens of occasions by British Governments since the 1880s. It is tempting to conclude that Morrison's and Trevelyan's arguments were simply the most recent instalments in Labour's tradition of supplying evidence of its own bad faith. Labour's experts on colonialism – such as Norman Leys, Charles Buxton and Leonard Woolf – were perhaps tempted to similar conclusions. Much of their effort condemned Britain's failure to protect natives in the settler colonies of East Africa such as Kenya, where land expropriation, punitive taxes and forced labour undermined traditional structures while depriving the natives of the benefits of modernisation.

Though it was Labour policy to reject the settlers' demands for self-government as contrary to native interests neither of the minority Labour Governments in the inter-war years intervened effectively to protect them. Thus Sidney Webb's promises to prevent further expropriations of land in 1929 came to nothing. Critics within the party also wondered how any trust could be placed in a League of Nations dominated by capitalist states; or in colonial systems in which people were denied the vote; or in mandates which were completely irresponsible; or in talk of 'development' where there was only underdevelopment. It was not the Conservative Party which set these standards of comparison or an unrepresentative extreme left; it was the Labour Party leadership itself – the leadership which, for example, denounced Mussolini as the head of a gangster state and then ceded Jubaland to this same gangster state while in Government.[106] Nor was Labour's addiction to utopian thinking and pronouncement the temporary disability of a political infant or due to the momentary imbalance of war, as might be argued in relation to the debates and pronouncements of 1919. The standards Labour could not keep were repeatedly set at intervals throughout its history. Another example was the repeated talk of disarmament as a party objective in the late 1920s. The credibility gap which was apt to open between word and deed was the inevitable trap for a party comfortable with moralising about foreign policy and yet determined to be the guardian of the national interest as defined by its opponents. But even for most party activists the 'normal' perception of the party, which short spells in office did little to disturb, was that it stood for an 'even-handed justice without distinction of race, creed, or class' on imperial questions – unlike its rivals – and could make a difference even in difficult places such as the settler colonies of East and Southern Africa.[107]

The divergence between the ILP and the leadership was given programmatic form in 1926 when the former adopted *Socialism in Our Time* – the title itself was a provocation to the Darwinian MacDonald. The ILP was so hostile to the existing international order – unable to accept the League or any of the provisions emanating from Versailles – that unilateral disarmament and war-resistance commended themselves to it as the only practical policies at various times in the late 1920s. Others were unhappy with the conduct of foreign policy and some members of the advisory committee recommended reforms to the Westminster decision-making process to minimise the influence of conventional opinion. Ponsonby returned to the issue he had first raised in 1916 and argued that popular control of foreign policy ranked higher than either the reform of the League or proposals for the limitation of armaments.[108] Such reform would involve all treaties receiving parliamentary sanction before ratification, no binding commitments without the approval of the relevant parliaments, and public scrutiny of foreign policy by a Foreign Affairs Committee of the House. Soon afterwards George Young argued for the reform of diplomacy in the belief that Labour 'must have really representative national institutions' as a step towards representative international institutions.[109] While there was no prospect in this view of 'a clean sweep of the men, the methods, and the machinery of the old diplomacy', there was a real danger that like the German social democrats Labour would 'fail to impose its foreign policy through the existing machinery, and will even have to face the machinery being used against it unless a better relationship between Westminster and Whitehall can be established'. The creation of a Foreign Affairs Committee and open entry to the diplomatic service had not been enough in the case of the SPD, according to Young. Bringing in lower-middle-class or working-class recruits, or replacing diplomats with Labour politicians, would also not suffice – they would merely be assimilated to the prevailing ethos. The first thing that was required to democratise diplomacy in Britain, according to Young, was winning an argument that Labour foreign policy was a return to the lofty and efficacious principles of Canning, Cobden, Bright, Gladstone and Campbell-Bannerman. Once Labour was associated with a tradition that had served Britain well – before the perverse practices which led to August 1914 took over – the commitment of the best elements of the present foreign office personnel would be secured. In addition to this the FO would have to be reorganised. The horizontal three-tier class distinctions would be abolished and replaced by vertical divisions corresponding to regional specialisms mirroring the post-imperial political reality of Europe. 'In this way the absolutist authority of the Foreign Office over Foreign Policy, and through foreign policy, over the politics of the country would be brought necessarily and normally to an end.'

All these reform proposals, which MacDonald rejected, bizarrely, as 'subversive in principle' as well as impractical,[110] were reiterated in 1925, that is after the experience of the first Labour Government. Young added various suggestions to strengthen the political as against the official wings of the Foreign Office, including proposals that the Under-Secretary at the Foreign Office should rank above the Permanent Secretary and that the Foreign Secretary should have a 'political' private secretary. He also wanted to see the admission of women to the foreign services.[111] Philip Noel-Baker and Ponsonby also drew attention to the overweening political power of the Committee of Imperial Defence and to the dispro-portionate influence of the military which it facilitated. They proposed to abolish it altogether and replace it by a Cabinet sub-committee.[112]

These debates remained hidden from the party, let alone the electorate. Dissatisfaction with the leadership from within the party seems to have had little or no resonance with the public. Labour's return to Opposition in October 1924 was not all bad news for MacDonald's strategy of moderation and conventional statesmanship. The party had lost forty seats but gained a million additional votes. Its by-election victories and local election gains in the years that followed also helped to keep faith alive in the Fabian vision of the 'inevitability of gradualness'. Peace seemed to be a feasible objective in the second half of the 1920s. In October 1925 the Locarno Pact was agreed between Germany, France, Belgium, Italy and Great Britain. Austen Chamberlain had apparently achieved the impossible and took great credit, even though the pact arose from a German initiative informed by a desire to scupper the Geneva Protocol and prevent France from concluding a military alliance with Britain. Germany was now seemingly reconciled to the post-war frontiers in the West and the demilitarisation of the Rhineland; Germany and France also undertook not to go to war with one another. Locarno also committed Belgium, France and Germany to submit all disputes between them to arbitration; Germany, Poland and Czechoslovakia were subject to the same provision in the East. This Mutual Guarantee Treaty was something new in that it could only work in the absence of permanent blocs and alliances and this is one of the main reasons why the pact was greeted with joy by a world suspicious of such combinations. At first MacDonald denounced Locarno as a betrayal of the Geneva Protocol but then moved on to claim that it was the first step towards its realisation, before changing his mind again to see only a reversion to old-fashioned and discredited alliances. Labour argued that without disarmament the risk of war remained acute, especially in eastern and central Europe on which Locarno was silent so far as former German territory in Poland and Czechoslovakia was concerned. A growing number of people agreed with MacDonald, to judge only from the rising membership of pacifist organisations; but even more people thought that Locarno had eliminated the biggest causes of Franco-German tension.

Just as the parliamentary leadership and the ILP became progressively estranged, as the latter set out in search of an immediate socialist pro-gramme, so were many trade unionists unhappy at the way they had been treated by MacDonald's first government.[113] Defeat in the General Strike of May 1926, however, cured most of them of the belief that there was a syndicalist alternative to MacDonald's methods. The left in the unions was now permanently weakened for the rest of the inter-war period. The parliamentary alternative thus consisted of a choice between the ILP's idea of championing a militant agenda of planning, nationalisation, increased direct taxation and a redistribution of wealth or MacDonald's attempt to promote Labour as a national and classless party pursuing a cautious and conventional left-of-centre politics. MacDonald could generally count on TUC support, so in intra-party terms the ILP challenge

counted for little. Trade union leaders were mistrustful of left opposi-
tionists within their own ranks and were inclined to see the ILP left-
wingers as trouble-makers of the same stripe. Whether Communists or
supporters of Maxton and Cook, such critics denounced the TUC in turn
for class collaboration in the aftermath of the General Strike. Bevin, for
one, learned his aversion to Communists here, in the battles for control
of his own union. More generally, as Baldwin gleefully noted, the unions
had little time for intellectuals. For the TUC leaders Labour was of little
use to the workers as long as it remained in opposition; it had to be in
power if it was to abolish the various legal disabilities, such as the Trades
Disputes Act 1927, which the Conservative Government imposed after
the General Strike. Labour only attracted 30 per cent of the voters but
the number was rising steadily and there was no evidence that it would
rise faster by emphasising socialist and class politics – such at least was
the reasoning of the party power-brokers. In these circumstances if
adopting a 'national' pose and a policy of continuity in imperial affairs
was the price of respectability, there were trade union leaders ready
to pay it.

At the same time Labour addressed the constituency which believed
in a diplomacy of conciliation and peace. This constituency, it claimed,
had plenty to complain about under the Conservatives with 'gunboats to
China, disputes with the USA, collapse of the Geneva conference . . .
the Arcos raid and severance of relations with Soviet Russia'.[114] *Labour
and the Nation* (1928), the product of the leadership's thinking since
1925, declared – in broad brush strokes designed to restate the party's
principles and general aims – that 'the whole structure of peace and of
a foreign policy of cooperation must be built firmly on the foundation
of the League of Nations'. 'Six pillars of peace' were listed as the renunciation of war – necessary 'for the completion of the League Covenant':
disarmament by mutual agreement 'until the abominable modern weapons
of destruction, which threaten the very existence of Western civilisation,
are completely proscribed and abolished'; arbitration via acceptance of
the jurisdiction of the Permanent Court of International Justice; economic
cooperation between nations; publicity – which now took the place of
open diplomacy in Labour's vision of how the House of Commons would
have the final say on all international engagements; and, finally, political
cooperation which Labour understood to mean 'repudiation of all
partial military alliances and groups which now again threaten the peace
of Europe'. Labour also repudiated 'the imperialist policy of domination
and economic exploitation' which was 'creating a revolt of Asia against
Europe' and which it predicted would eventually inspire the same problem
in Africa. It kept faith with free trade. It continued to play up the
significance of trade agreements with Russia, though the Conservative

Government had torn up the last one in 1924. It held out the prospect of future Dominion status to India and reiterated its faith in those schemes for closer economic coordination between Britain and the Dominions which annual conference had considered in 1925. As for the Crown Colonies, the party reiterated its dedication to the principle of native paramountcy and protection while affirming its faith in the forces of progress in these tropical and sub-tropical dependencies.[115]

In reality the sense of security in European affairs had never been stronger than it was after Locarno, even if that was based on false assumptions. It was strengthened by the success of Frank Kellogg's peace initiative which arose when the American secretary of state wittily turned a French proposal for renunciation of war between the two countries into a general demand that all states abandon war as an instrument of national policy. The Russians exploited the same opportunity by proposing that all states scrap their armed forces, though this took the joke too far. In the event fifteen countries, including Britain, signed the Kellogg Pact in August 1928. Meanwhile Henderson put himself at the head of the real enthusiasts for the Geneva Protocol within the party because, unlike MacDonald, he believed that the acceptance of compulsory arbitration, supported by a readiness to employ collective sanctions, including armed force, and measures of national disarmament was the way to secure the peace. One of his protégés, Hugh Dalton, took the view that the League might even be regarded as a transitional stage towards a world state.[116] It was certainly an established fact and the most sophisticated instrument yet conceived with which to manage international relations. Its final form would depend, according to Dalton, on how creatively it was employed. But he imagined the League promoting economic as well as political stability by championing free trade, disarmament and compulsory arbitration backed up by the armed might at its disposal. Like Henderson, Noel-Baker and Will Arnold-Foster, Dalton was one of the first to face squarely the issue of what the League would do in the face of aggression. The issue was thrashed out in meetings of the advisory committee in 1928 revealing the differences between those who placed their faith, like MacDonald and Ponsonby, in disarmament and those who stressed the need for collective force to maintain security through the League.[117]

By the end of the decade one of the things that had gradually slipped from view in Labour's thinking about foreign policy was the critique of the foreign policy establishment which the First World War had done so much to stimulate. In 1916 Ponsonby had drawn attention to the socially unrepresentative nature of this echelon, as we noted in chapter 2. The tendency of Prime Ministers to conduct their own foreign policy simply reinforced the centralisation and secrecy of decision-making. MacDonald's Cabinet 'was seldom troubled' by foreign affairs, according to Sidney Webb and 'no memo, examining a particular problem, and discussing alternative policies was ever circulated'.[118] In 1924 and 1925 the issue of reform had been raised again with specific proposals. But the critical edge in Labour's thinking on this issue was not assisted by the fact that so many of its leading personalities and power-holders were strong admirers of the Westminster system. Such was this admiration, there was no recognition of the fact that the advent of universal suffrage in 1918 was simply grafted on to the pre-war undemocratic institutional order in a way which ensured that the political class was almost as well-protected from democratic scrutiny and accountability as ever before, especially in the foreign services. In a system virtually free from checks and balances on the executive, an elective dictatorship had been created in which Parliament remained powerless on matters of foreign policy, as on so much else. Circumstances after 1918, as it transpired, also allowed a lengthy period of Conservative hegemony on the basis of the electoral arithmetic of a three-party system in which the right could count on at least 200 safe seats and 38 per cent of the vote, while its opponents were divided three ways.

Labour made matters worse by subscribing to the official fictions of empire. MacDonald in particular basked in the conceit according to which Parliament presided over the gradual, almost providential, evolution of those colonial lesser breeds which fate had placed in its charge. The Empire was an unfinished chapter in this Whig theory of history. Acceptance of this ideology made it easier to defer to the wisdom of the people who were its living agents. Personal ties connected virtually everyone in the political establishment with India and, through the public schools, with virtually everyone recruited to administer the Empire.[119] Indeed between 1919 and 1948 one man, Sir Ralph Furse, was charged with finding the appropriate human material for this task, providing, as Cannadine says, 'secure, comfortable, well-paid and essentially ornamental employment opportunities' on a scale which would have surprised John Bright.[120] Labour made no gestures to challenge this system during its periods of office between the wars. Nor did the party draw attention to the continuing aristocratic background and mentality of the men who dominated the inter-war Foreign Office, Colonial Office, Dominions Office and India Office, as well as the armed forces and the diplomatic corps.[121] On the contrary, MacDonald placed his trust in such people. Yet there was every reason to believe that as the bearers of the old Radical tradition Labour might take exception to the exclusive club atmosphere of the Foreign Office or the fact that the scions of landed families monopolised the corps of career diplomats and ambassadors. Recruited young, the personnel of these branches of the state enjoyed an unusual longevity of career. These were also the zones of the political system, furthermore, in which the rules of democracy exercised only a feeble influence. Bound together by common values, a strong sense of their fitness for exercising power and schooled to think in grandiloquent terms about Britain's special place in the world, this elite enjoyed all the conditions of secrecy and permanence of office conducive to the survival of their own complacent assumptions.[122] The delusions about the fascist states fostered by Lord Perth in Rome or Neville Henderson in Berlin may be taken as illustrative evidence. As Leonard Woolf said in 1939 the Civil Service was 'admirable as a peace-time machine for maintaining the status quo without corruption', but in sacrificing everything to correct routine and being 'complacently unaware of [its] remoteness from the outside world' it also represented a 'tenacious and high-minded obstructionism' devoid of creativity.[123]

Labour might have questioned this order instead of subscribing to it. The party began life as the main opposition in the House in 1919 criticising the peace settlement root and branch. Committed to the view, however, that the Empire must be treated as a fact, Labour had adopted the stance since its origins that it should be spoken of as a trusteeship of dependent peoples where it was not yet a union of free peoples. Acceptance of both the fact of Empire and the official view of its purposes soon blunted the edge of Labour's criticism of the peace settlement. Labour never seriously considered British withdrawal from the territories acquired by virtue of the war. Though Britain had been a satisfied Power in 1914, it nevertheless took over an additional 800,000 square miles of territory. In practice Labour was as committed to maintaining these acquisitions as the Conservative Party. Likewise, though Labour initially pointed to the falsity of the 'mandates' which Britain had awarded itself, the criticism was not allowed to affect policy. By the end of the first Labour Government the party's revisionist credentials in respect of the peace settlement were much more like those of Conservative Governments than they had been in 1919–23.

It is true that the Conservative Party continued to voice deeply reactionary views while Labour continued to give expression to more critical views in both the Radical and socialist traditions. This meant, for example, that while Conservatives were more likely to defend General Dyer's orders to shoot around 1,500 unarmed protestors at Amritsar in 1919, Labour Members were more likely to criticise them. The same was true of the Black-and-Tan repression of Irish nationalists; the exclusion of Egyptian nationalists from the peace conference; the military intervention against the Bolshevik Government; the use of mustard gas in Iraq,[124] Afghanistan, Somaliland and Sudan;[125] the imprisonment of nationalists in India; the suppression of nationalists in Egypt in 1924; the expropriation of native lands in Kenya; and so on. But it is also true that such criticisms were sometimes very feeble indeed, the more feeble as they moved from the back benches to the front bench and on into Government.[126] This was to remain the pattern well into the 1950s and up to the point when decolonisation was nearing its conclusion. Somehow the criticisms were never ever able to shift the myth that the brutalities of Empire were exceptions to the rule, the work of bad eggs operating locally and unilaterally, which reflected not at all on the policies pursued at Westminster. This is also Labour's achievement. If it was the logical result of the party's striving to represent the nation, it has to be said that the nation and the national interest remained under a conservative definition.

This might well have reflected popular patriotic views of Empire, as we suggested in chapter 1. Labour's identification with peace policies also had a popular basis. In imperial matters it meant preservation of the status quo and called upon proponents of civil disobedience in India and elsewhere to trust in the benign evolution of constitutional change devised at Westminster. In relations with the other Powers the peace policy called for voluntary collaboration in the League of Nations for the settlement of disputes as well as their acceptance of the permanence of British colonial possessions. It also meant revisions to the peace settlement as it affected Germany in particular. A pacifist strain in public opinion grew in the course of the 1920s, as the trauma of the First World War sank in. But it did not seem to mean withdrawal from any of Britain's overseas commitments, even though Britain's defence requirements were scaled down in the interests of economy from as early as 1919 and the 'ten-year rule', first formalised in 1924 when Churchill became Chancellor, became operative.[127]

Whereas the Tories reacted to Britain's weakened economic position by proposing imperial protection in 1923, Labour never wavered from the policy of free trade and sound money, though individual left-wingers were drawn to the idea of a more systematic exploitation of Empire in 1925. In relation to free trade Labour simply wanted more of it and this formed the largest part of its case for normal relations with Soviet Russia or for increased emigration to the Dominions. But the system of free trade imperialism which had served Britain well since it became state policy in the 1840s could only be restored after 1918 by measures which exacerbated the problems which afflicted Labour's own supporters, such as unemployment. Unemployment began to concern all the parties as the 1920s came to an end and all of them talked of loan-financed public works. Apart from Churchill, most of Baldwin's Conservative Cabinet in 1928 seem to have 'shared Amery's belief that imperial protectionism was the radical solution to unemployment', but there was no conviction that the electorate would support such a policy.[128] With the help of Keynes

Lloyd George fashioned a reflationary programme to seduce the voters in the 1929 general election. The Conservatives answered with a programme which included old nostrums such as emigration and more novel ideas of Empire development. Labour, content to denounce Lloyd George's 'flashy futilities', while stressing the virtues of peace and trade with a little nationalisation of industry, emerged as the largest party with 287 seats. There were signs of economic recovery as MacDonald formed his second minority Labour Government in June and he had every intention of concentrating upon foreign policy and in particular picking up the threads of Labour's emerging special relationship with America.[129]

4 Crisis of liberal internationalism

Within months of the formation of the second Labour Government the international economic situation worsened dramatically. By the summer of 1930 it was clear that the government was powerless in the face of a world recession. Yet the outlook had been far from bleak just a year earlier. Though all parties had talked about the unemployment problem in the general election, MacDonald had been keen to focus on foreign policy and only reluctantly made way for Arthur Henderson to take the position of Foreign Secretary. The Prime Minister nevertheless played an active role in foreign policy and was especially interested in repairing relations with the USA (following their marked deterioration after the collapse of the Geneva naval disarmament conference in 1928) – especially in relation to new proposals for naval arms controls. For his part, Henderson entered office at a time of optimism in international relations and was determined to make the most of the opportunities for disarmament and peace-making which the circumstances of 1929 favoured. Such was Labour's satisfaction with what was actually achieved in 1929–31, party propaganda was still glorying in the foreign policy achievements of MacDonald's second administration in the mid-1930s, long after its domestic record had become a matter for embarrassment.[1]

The party claimed it had effected an 'astonishing transformation in Anglo-American relations and in the degree of prestige enjoyed by the British representatives at Geneva'.[2] The former had deteriorated in the 1920s in the context of naval rivalry and US encroachment on British markets in South America, China, and Japan, as well as conflicts with the US over the control of Middle Eastern oil and world rubber production.[3] But the proximate cause of tension was Britain's failure to comply with American demands for parity in cruisers, which the Conservative Government had resisted. MacDonald bowed to the inevitable – Britain could hardly afford an arms race with the USA – at the London Naval Disarmament Conference in 1930, but he took credit for broadening the discussions to include Japan, Italy and France. Labour promoted his success as a massive economy measure, as well as a blow for world peace and the avoidance of another arms race. It was less keen to publicise British arguments at the London Conference which stressed the needs of British naval capacity given the scale of operations that were required to police the Empire. Meanwhile, Henderson had given prominence to the League by attending all of its sessions and committing Britain to the 'Optional Clause' for compulsory arbitration, another measure which the previous Government resisted. Henderson personally favoured the Geneva Protocol but proceeded cautiously by pressing for the adoption of the Optional Clause in the League's Covenant, which provided for the voluntary acceptance of League jurisdiction in the resolution of legal disputes between nations. Even this modest first step was hedged about with opt-outs to answer discontent with the idea that the Permanent Court of International Justice would be able to interfere in disputes between Britain and her Dominions and other intra-imperial matters. Henderson came away from Geneva as the designated president of the world disarmament conference scheduled to begin in 1932.

Henderson had signalled his pro-League intent by bringing Cecil into the Foreign Office as Chairman of a Committee on League Affairs. Philip Noel-Baker became Henderson's PPS and Hugh Dalton was made Under-Secretary. Against these pro-League influences one has to set MacDonald himself; Maurice Hankey, the long-standing Secretary of the Cabinet; Snowden and the Treasury; the Services, and the departments representing their interests. The public mood and the relatively pacific state of international relations in 1929–30 favoured Henderson. For this was a time when the First World War was popularly remembered – in film, poetry, fiction and autobiography – as a never-to-be-repeated disaster. The prospects for peace, however, looked favourable. German, French and American statesmanship after Locarno seemed as constructive as it had been at any time since the end of the war and progress towards the stabilisation and rescheduling of reparations had been achieved by the Young Plan. At the same time there was a strong expectation that in the event of failure the peace initiatives would give way to another world war even worse than the last one. The bomber would always get through, said Baldwin in November 1932, and anti-war discussions were already reflecting such pessimism, tending to dwell on the bestiality of cata-strophically destructive air-raids, the then height of military barbarism in the imagination of the public.

British 'pressure' thus helped to fix the date for the long-delayed Disarmament Conference in February 1932 and was present in attempts to harmonise the Covenant of the League with the Kellogg–Briand Pact (1928) for the complete renunciation of war as an instrument of state policy.[4] The practical value of international arbitration was allegedly 'proved', according to one Labour pamphlet of 1931, when Henderson secured the reference of the Austro-German Customs Union to the Permanent Court of International Justice. Five months after this event, the Japanese invasion of Manchuria drove a large hole through such claims. But following the apparent success of the Kellogg–Briand Pact, public opinion was at least as hopeful as the politicians claimed to be about the prospects for world disarmament. Labour also boasted that important measures of international economic cooperation, including steps to free trade, had been successfully negotiated at Geneva – a claim which ignored the stampede to protectionism led by the USA, which adopted the Smoot–Hawley tariff in 1930. And staying with the economic theme, Labour restored full diplomatic and trade relations with the Soviet Union – it having been a constant of party propaganda since 1920 that British unemployment was in large measure the result of lost markets, for which the cure was restoration and expansion of 'normal trade'. In practical terms the diplomatic agreement with the USSR did not amount to very much in the areas where it was supposed to count. There was no great expansion of Anglo-Soviet trade and Communist anti-imperialist propaganda – a particular concern of the British – did not abate. In colonial policy, however, there was no notable change of emphasis under Labour. In Egypt and India, to take two examples, nationalist agitation was met by repression and a determination to maintain the British military-strategic and political dispensation, whether that entailed maintenance of the vast military base at Suez, control of the Sudan and the Canal, or exclusion of the Indian National Congress from effective political participation.

The scale of the crisis which faced British politics during the second Labour Government could never be guessed from the party's account of its international achievements. The whole basis of the post-war economic order had collapsed between the financial crash of October 1929 and the following summer, as had the working assumption of all Governments since 1918 – that the pre-war 'normal' might be restored. This was as much a shock to the Prime Minister and his Chancellor of the Exchequer, the utterly orthodox Philip Snowden, as it was to the Governor of the Bank of England and the other exponents of the 'Treasury view'. A succession of deflationary budgets since 1919 had sought to restore 'sound money', stable exchange rates and the Gold Standard. The financial and commercial instability of continental Europe was supposed to depend on these and kindred achievements such as the spread of free trade. In fact the liberal order unravelled at an accelerating rate in the course of 1930 as unemployment reached two million in Britain by August and more than four million in Germany, where the Nazi vote increased from

800,000 in the previous Reichstag elections of 1928, to 6,409,000 in the September 1932 elections. The payment of German reparations – rescheduled for a final time in 1929 – was now effectively finished. Governments everywhere resorted to tariffs and even in Britain the clamour for some form of imperial protectionism swept the Federation of British Industries, just as it did the Conservative Party and the press. Even the TUC began to talk of the desirability of encouraging more imperial trade by interventionist methods. But while some business and trade union leaders blamed an overvalued sterling for British uncompetitiveness, most experts outside the TUC blamed high wages and taxes. In the end, of course, it was pressure for wage and benefit cuts which divided MacDonald's Cabinet in the summer of 1931 leading to the emergence of a National Government with MacDonald at its head. One of its earliest measures was to bring Britain off the Gold Standard and prepare the ground for imperial protection with the signing of the Ottawa Agreements in 1932.

It took a little longer before Britain's imperial strategy – which consisted of hanging on to as much as possible – went the way of the gold standard. Labour had been determined to demonstrate continuity in such matters as an essential part of its attempt to prove its fitness for office. The Empire Labour defended was the one based on indirect rule, native paramountcy, trusteeship, humanitarianism and economic and social development. The manifold contradictions of this vision – how could indirect rule through traditional rulers facilitate economic and social development and how could development be made compatible with protection of the native way of life – were not as important as the benign image of the Empire which the vision served to promote. It was the Conservative Government of 1923 which formally committed Britain to the principle of native paramountcy but Labour was more than content to go along with it. It was consistent with the faith of Edwardian critics of colonialism who trusted that the model of indirect rule, as in West Africa, was compatible with preservation of the native way of life. This model of trusteeship at least served to spotlight the problem posed by settler economies such as those of East Africa where land-grabbing, forced labour and demands for white self-government were obviously in breach of Labour's humanitarian concerns. For all that, however, the party never proposed to redistribute the appropriated land. Sidney Webb, as Colonial Secretary in MacDonald's second Government, thought that by turning a blind eye to the settler monopoly of the best land in Kenya he might be able to begin the process of African political participation. But the settlers rebelled and his White Papers had the guts torn out of them in committee.[5] Meanwhile other voices in the Labour Party, notably Ernest Bevin's and the TUC's, favoured imperial economic development as an answer to Britain's economic problems. The TUC published a report in 1930 calling for such development, showing little concern for either the economic obstacles involved – though these had been cogently explained in objection to Baldwin's protectionism – or for the social costs to Africans. Bevin was the only member of the party to serve on the Development Committee which was set up under the 1929 Colonial Development Act.[6]

Labour alternately objected to the capitalist exploitation of the African colonies and proposed their development; the party sometimes encouraged rapid progress to self-government and at other times spoke more guardedly about it.[7] The emphases also varied according to who was doing the talking – those steeped in the humanitarian tradition, for example, who spoke in Parliament but not from Government, or those steeped in Fabianism or merely pragmatism. The Commonwealth ideal, however, gave all but the extreme left a vested interest in playing down the brute realities of imperialism. For faith in the noble vision to be sustained evidence of repression had to be treated as exceptional and deviant. The more attention was drawn to these unfortunate episodes, the more ridiculous the claim that British rule was based on the consent, or the virtual consent, of the colonial peoples. It was unfortunate for MacDonald that his second government coincided with immense political turbulence in India which threatened to break the consensus on imperial issues which he wanted to share with the Conservative Party leadership. Labour entered office just months before the deadline expired for Gandhi's second great campaign of civil disobedience for Indian independence. Martial law, mass arrests, censorship, violent disturbances, 'conspiracy' trials and the imprisonment of political India – such was the situation on the subcontinent for much of the second Labour Government. The Conservative Party and the press, meanwhile, gave voice to demands for an even greater show of force to teach the nationalists who was boss. Disorder in Palestine, martial law in Jerusalem, the naval suppression of riots in Egypt – following British dismissal of the nationalist premier Nasha Pasha – the collapse of trade talks at the Imperial Conference – all this was insignificant compared to the tumult in and over India.

Evidence from every quarter presented a picture of imperial retreat in the view of imperialist diehards. Since the Washington Conference agreements of 1922 British naval power had been forced into making concessions to the USA and Japan. Good relations with the Dominions increasingly depended on acknowledgement of their sovereign autonomy, eventually given constitutional expression by the Statute of Westminster in 1931. Even the settler colony of Southern Rhodesia had demanded and secured a measure of self-government as early as 1921, though this rested on the white minority and was hardly compatible with protection of the interests of the natives. The same was true of Kenya in which the white minority was already acquiring a reputation for racism, seediness and corruption. The doctrine of 'native paramountcy' had become a matter of such concern for these white settlers, owners of all the best land in the country, that they were demanding dominion status for themselves when Labour entered office. For all the controversy about native rights the Labour Government did nothing to prevent the passage of the Tory-inspired Southern Rhodesia Land Apportionment Act in 1930 which reinforced the privileges of the 48,000-strong white colonialist elite in that country. Meanwhile a mixed policy of concession and force in 'independent' Egypt had failed to satisfy or suppress the nationalists. The same was true in Palestine with the added complication that Britain was unable to meet the expectations of either Arabs or Jews. All of these matters were salient in 1930. Tensions increased as the time approached for an Imperial Conference scheduled to start in October and dominated by the issue of constitutional change in Britain's relationship with the Dominions. A round table conference, arranged for November, brought closer the problem of how to manage constitutional change on the subcontinent. Both conferences were the culmination of long-winded processes begun, respectively, by the Balfour Report in 1926 and the Simon Commission, appointed in 1927. The Labour Government was content to passively support these Conservative initiatives.

Impatient reformers saw only delaying tactics in these arrangements while imperial diehards saw only retreat. Parliament, however, contained more diehards than impatient champions of decolonisation. The political class as a whole shared a powerful perception that British prosperity depended on the markets and products of Empire. The world recession served to strengthen this perception. Political stability in Britain itself was thought to depend on its imperial power[8] as was its military might. These perceptions may well have been wrong or misleading but there is no doubt that they existed. A great deal of official propaganda in the 1920s was devoted to making these connections, including the extravagant British Empire Exhibition at Wembley in 1924.[9] Numerous pressure groups extolled the virtues of Empire and demanded closer links between its dominant parts. Much of the Conservative Party had been persuaded of the need for a more systematic exploitation of these resources since the first decade of the century. This type of militant imperialism grew as the recession deepened. The fact that total British expenditure on the Crown Colonies – the dependencies on which the burden of trusteeship bore most heavily – amounted to just three million pounds in 1930 was not allowed to spoil the fantasy of economic development, or expose its cant.[10] Collaboration between Britain and the Dominions, on which

Labour propaganda had once invested heavily, was almost as problematical. Their economies had rival rather than simply complementary
interests to those of Britain. They had even been reluctant to join the
Empire Marketing Scheme established by Leo Amery in 1927. Yet
MacDonald had made much of imperial unity in 1924 and his successor
as Foreign Secretary, Austen Chamberlain, was fond of asserting its
existence, even though the Imperial Conference of 1926 had struggled
to contain the divergent forces that were actually loosening it, as the
Balfour Report reluctantly acknowledged.

MacDonald complained in 1930 that in foreign policy matters a British
Prime Minister could only speak with certainty on behalf of Britain, yet
at the same time had to think imperially on matters of defence. The
Imperial Conference of 1930–1 dashed hopes that this paradox might be
resolved but MacDonald was privately convinced that the problem lay
with the Irish and South Africans – 'two states and peoples not belonging
to [the] same stock or history', he privately concluded. Nevertheless, he
believed that though the 'British union' had really ended in 1926, it was
necessary to maintain the illusion of unity for the benefit of the rest of
the world, as well as the 'group psychology' so necessary for the maintenance of the Commonwealth itself.[11] Such prejudices were commonplace.
So was MacDonald's anxiety that Britain would be gravely weakened
unless the Dominions supported a common foreign policy. The Labour
Prime Minister shared the Establishment view that British power
depended on the maintenance of Empire and that it faced disintegration
in 1930. The War Office and the Admiralty nevertheless continued to
plan as if the resources of Empire were at Britain's disposal, even after
the Dominions attained a constitutional status to match their practical
sovereignty.[12] The reality was that in many ways the Empire was
becoming more of a liability than an asset, but it seems that the Labour
Government was as incapable of seeing this as its Conservative rivals.
The ten-year rule was proof of the need for defence economies and so
were the Washington Naval Agreement of 1922 and its London successor
of 1930. These agreements averted a naval race with the United States
which Britain could not afford but they did so at the cost of surrendering
the two-power standard and the 1902 alliance with Japan. Absolute naval
dominance had always been trumpeted as the sound military basis for
the British Empire; but it no longer existed. Here was an opportunity
for Labour to take up the case for a realistic reappraisal of Britain's
imperial responsibilities, but it was an opportunity which the second
MacDonald Government was unable to take advantage of.

Under pressure of mounting unemployment Ministers were instead
concerned to promote imperial trade, emigration and efficient marketing
of colonial produce. To this extent the Government shared the growing

fervour for imperial integration. Most members of the Cabinet, however, would not contemplate a retreat from free trade, leaving MacDonald unable to respond to Canadian suggestions of reciprocal trade preferences which were offered at the Imperial Conference. The Prime Minister was grateful that in Lord Irwin (Edward Wood, later Lord Halifax) the Labour Government was blessed with a wise Viceroy at a time when India was moving towards political confrontation. Irwin took the view that the nationalist unrest stemmed from an 'inferiority complex' and a psychology of suspicion and vanity on the part of the nationalist leaders. He therefore proposed to soothe the nationalists by suggesting a 'round table conference' to consider the proposals of the all-British Simon Commission, while employing the Indian princes in their traditional role of reactionary ballast.[13] The Simon Commission, the brain-child of the Tory diehard Lord Birkenhead, had provoked disturbances and boycotts wherever it travelled on the subcontinent in the course of 1928 and 1929. Labour had been represented on the Commission in the person of Clement Attlee but the Indian political leaders had not even been invited to join it. When they drew up constitutional proposals of their own they were simply ignored.[14] Once it became clear that the formation of a Labour Government had made no difference to this process Gandhi announced that a civil disobedience campaign would begin at the start of 1930 unless the British conceded the demand for independence.

By the time the round table talks got underway MacDonald, Irwin and Stanley Baldwin were at one in believing that the cure for Gandhi lay in the elaborate scheme of federated devolution which the Viceroy gradually unfolded to the assembled delegates. This would secure British control of India's economy, defence and external relations at the centre while permitting elections – suitably adapted to express communal loyalties and princely privileges – in the localities. Irwin explained privately to Leo Amery that this 'semblance of responsible government' would pacify India. It was simply a 'façade which will leave the essential mechanism of power still in our hands' while catering for that 'Indian psychology . . . composed in equal parts of vanity, inferiority complex and fear of real responsibility'.[15] Samuel Hoare, leader of the Conservative delegation at the round table conference, expressed similar sentiments to the shadow Cabinet, referring to the plan to concede 'a semblance of responsible government and yet retain in our hands the realities and verities of British control'.[16] This was the bi-partisan policy which MacDonald's second government presided over, doing its best to help Baldwin manage his own extremists along the way.[17] In 1934 Baldwin was still telling Conservative activists that 'you have a good chance of keeping the whole of that subcontinent of India in the Empire for ever'.[18] All of this was obscured by the furore generated by diehard opinion, led by Churchill in the Commons and Lords Rothermere and Beaverbrook in the press,[19] which saw only scuttle and betrayal from Cairo to Calcutta. Yet the Labour Government made extensive use of repression throughout 1930–1 and when constitutional reform was finally presented in a White Paper in 1933 it followed the devious design recommended by Irwin and Simon. Nevertheless the Conservative Central Council and party conference continued to make known their displeasure in 1933 and 1934 when the diehards secured 30–50 per cent of the votes for complete rejection of the proposals.

The world economic crisis placed enormous strains on the Cabinet's faith in the old Radical shibboleth of free trade and the ruling orthodoxy of sound money and balanced budgets. This worried the unions. But the Government's inclination to treat the TUC as a sectional interest caused even more trade union resentment when leading ministers such as Snowden, MacDonald and Thomas made known their conviction that unemployment numbers and benefits were insupportably high and the old slogan of 'work or maintenance' had become redundant. Baldwin and the Conservative Party called for public expenditure cuts, radical reform of unemployment insurance, tariff protection of manufactures, restrictions on food imports and negotiations for imperial preference. By the end of 1930 authoritative figures in banking, industry, politics and journalism were talking of a national emergency of comparable gravity to that of August 1914. The idea of a national government was in the air. Conventional opinion – whether that of business, finance, the civil service, leading experts, journalists, or Opposition MPs – believed that such a government would take the appropriate measures to reduce wages and benefits.

The world crisis

Historians regard 1931 as a turning point. Taylor points out that in doing so they follow contemporary opinion which took the view that the 1920s and 1930s were distinct decades in both mood and substance.[20] The world economic crisis, which closed the 1920s, also opened a period of international volatility which culminated in the Second World War. Commentators have identified the political and economic crisis as the final breakdown of attempts to restore the pre-war 'normalcy'; the final breakdown of the progressive alliance in Britain; the advent of the socialist intellectual in the Labour Party and the beginning of an obsession with ideologies; the beginning of the cult of planning; and the moment of a reassertion of the power of the TUC within the labour movement. It was also the beginning of a change in the international situation – one which the advent of Hitler in January 1933 would dramatically confirm. Already in 1930 the Labour Party was talking about the breakdown of capitalism on an international scale. 'We are not on trial', said MacDonald at the annual conference, 'it is the system under which we live. It has broken down, not only in this little island; it has broken down everywhere as it was bound to break down.'[21] Susan Lawrence, the President of the conference, made the same point to the assembled delegates, as ministers emphasised their impotence in the face of forces beyond their control or responsibility: 'it is not within the power of any single country to deal with the roots of these evils by any purely national policy.'[22] After the formation of the National Government, of course, new elements entered the analysis as the party came to terms with Labour's poor performance in office, culminating in the parting of the ways with MacDonald, Snowden and Thomas.

The President's address at the 1931 TUC stressed the role of 'Political and financial influences of a sinister character, working behind the scenes'.[23] The manifesto of the joint session of the TUC, NEC and PLP argued that 'Forces in finance and politics' were determined to 'attack the standard of living of the workers in order to meet a situation caused by a policy pursued by private banking interests . . . primarily because financial interests have decided that this country is setting a bad example to other countries in taxing the rich to provide for the necessities of the poor.'[24] It concluded that growing unemployment could be expected at home and abroad. The TUC did not allow conspiracy theories of MacDonald's 'betrayal' to obscure what it called 'the fundamental facts of the economic disorder in the world'. By 1931 there were already at least 15 million unemployed in the USA, Germany and Britain added together. The 'capitalist system stands exposed', the TUC declared. For here was a picture of poverty in the midst of plenty and matters were set to deteriorate; 'the present crisis in trade and industry is being used to enforce a demand for the lowering of wage standards, the worsening of conditions of employment, and the restriction of expenditure on . . . social services'. Indeed a 'ruinous course of competitive wage cutting' was threatened which would bring the wealthiest down to the level of the worst paid. The 1931 annual conference of the Labour Party likewise perceived 'a process of world-wide degradation'; this was the latest phase of the crisis generated by the Great War 'with its legacy of political-economic chaos, international debts, reparations, post-war deflation, and the return to the Gold Standard'.[25] All shades of TUC and Labour opinion seemed united in their conviction that the problem was global, endemic to capitalism and solvable only by the transition to a planned socialist order. Within a year of these debates world unemployment was estimated at 25 million, rising to 30 million by 1933. Capitalism was heading for a 'smash' as 'the whole world of industry and finance' succumbed to chaos.[26]

In the immediate aftermath of the formation of the National Government, Labour and the TUC issued a manifesto rejecting all the proposed economies and asserting that:

> we could overcome the immediate difficulty by mobilizing the country's foreign investments by a temporary suspension of the Sinking Fund, by taxing fixed interest-bearing securities and other unearned income . . . and by measures to reduce the burden of War debts.[27]

In reality Labour and trade union statements show that there was much hopeful speculation in the search for alternatives and familiar refrains were often repeated whether they carried conviction or not. The Bristol TUC conference in September 1931 heard calls for disarmament and limits on arms expenditures. On 25 September, four days after Britain left the gold standard, Henderson made a speech at Burnley in which he proposed emergency powers to deal with financial crises; control over the banking system; institute public ownership or control of the 'main industries'; and international agreements to restore trade and credit and promote peace. The Labour conference debate in October referred to the need for 'a new system of finance' and international cooperation, disarmament and an end to war debts and reparations. In the face of protectionism the traditional commitment to free trade and opposition to tariffs was nevertheless reasserted. The participants in these debates knew that the British economy had been subjected to deflationary policies since 1920 and that international monetary disorder and economic dislocation in Europe were legacies of the war. Debt and reparations problems had been destabilising influences on the international economy throughout the past decade. States were increasingly placing national considerations before external equilibrium, following the lead of the biggest, and therefore worst, offender – the USA, which had consistently failed to perform Britain's pre-war international role in world capitalist finance. To call, in these circumstances, for free trade, coordinated tariff reductions, coordinated reflation, wholesale price stability and similar measures, to be arranged by 'international conferences', was to spit against the wind.[28]

The Labour election manifesto issued on 9 October asserted that the capitalist system had broken down and demanded extensive nationalisation of industry, credit and finance to permit 'co-ordinated planning'. In the lurch to the left which followed the breakdown of the Labour Government even the moderate voices contributing to the party's post-mortem – Henderson, Clynes, Pethick Lawrence and Morrison – were united in claiming, as Henderson put it, that socialism was the 'only alternative to the present chaos'. This was a remarkable rhetorical development for an organisation which had hardly mentioned socialism under MacDonald's leadership and was notably restrained on the subject as recently as the 1929 general election. The sense of international crisis and the very absence of convincing practical alternatives to the proposed deflationary policies at home may well explain why Morrison, for example, 'begged' the party 'to make Socialism itself the big, the fundamental, the most acute issue' in the general election.[29] In the absence of convincing reform proposals there was a tendency to protect Labour's identity by resort to the language of socialism. But it is not enough to say that this was in some sense a natural reaction to the crisis and the experience of the second Labour Government.[30] Crises had failed to cause such a shift in the past. Yet only partial explanations of the 1931 reaction can be found in the existing literature. Beer refers to the emergence of a 'socialist generation' during the course of the 1920s, and there is of course evidence to support the claimed development.[31] Taylor talks similarly of 'the creation of a new element in the Labour Party: the left-wing intellectual', a development that 'was basically a revolt of social conscience by intellectual members of the educated class, ashamed of "poverty in the midst of plenty"'.[32] Bassett produces a similar explanation saying that for a few years Labour fell under the influence of 'anti-parliamentary tendencies'.[33] None of this explains why socialism was taken up by the pragmatists and party managers such as Henderson, Clynes, Morrison and the like. The slogan they took into the election was 'we must plan or perish'. Some of their opponents – Churchill for example – had already calculated that a general election was needed precisely in order to crush Labour and thus effect 'the restoration of confidence at home and abroad'.[34] In the chairman's address to the 1931 annual conference the prospect of a crushing defeat for Labour was actually highlighted with the warning that a dictatorship might follow such an outcome.[35] It was not as if any of the concrete proposals contained in the Labour manifesto – such as planning and public ownership – were of any use in addressing the immediate problems facing the country. And they left Labour open to the charge – as Snowden put it – that it was all 'Bolshevism gone mad'. This was a strange development for an organisation that had gone out of its way to refute such claims – the routine propaganda of its opponents – ever since the war. The result was that the National Government partners won the biggest victory of any British general election of the twentieth century, obtaining as much as 55 per cent of the working-class vote and 554 of the 615 seats in the House of Commons. Labour lost 215 of its 267 seats, leaving it with 46 – another 6 were unendorsed seats mostly held by the ILP. Henderson, who now cut a forlorn figure as President of the doomed Disarmament

Conference, and 13 other ex-Cabinet members and 21 former junior ministers and whips were among the defeated.[36] Lansbury, the pacifist, became chairman of the parliamentary party at this moment of its supreme impotence – a moment that was to last for the rest of the decade. There was little Labour could do except to call, as Herbert Morrison did in November, for a policy review 'to evolve concrete remedies . . . to educate the people in constructive socialism'.[37]

Labour's weakness in 1931 can hardly be overstated. Cowling argues that 'the primary question was how best to convince its members that the movement had a future'.[38] Henderson and his colleagues had agreed to almost all the short-term economy measures that were about to be implemented, balking only at the last minute. Their old Radical faith in free trade looked obsolete. A policy re-think was necessary, under the control of the party managers. It was now discovered that prior to 1931 there had been no really effective policy-making process in the party.[39] The crisis naturally led to recriminations, with the ILP in particular finding that MacDonald's leadership had been sustained by 'a community of outlook' which, of course, the ILP flatly rejected.[40] Those wanting to secede from the Labour Party were now strengthened in their convictions. Tawney, who had no intention of leaving the party, perceived its problem to lie in 'a general habit of mind', more concerned with surviving in politics than remembering why it mattered. He saw the need for ideological renewal, but also the need for some of the motivation and discipline which enabled the Russian Communist Party to actually implement the ideas it believed in.[41] So did other intellectuals such as Laski, Brailsford and Cole. After 1931 Cole set up the New Fabian Research Bureau and the Society for Socialist Inquiry and Propaganda (SSIP) and initially promoted the Socialist League as another vehicle for ideological and policy change. There was also the XYZ Group, concerned with the workings of the City of London. The spirit of scientific inquiry and the need for ideological renewal also affected colonial policy, though it was not until 1940 that this was given a home in the Fabian Colonial Bureau. Labour meanwhile received information from the ILO, the LSI and the IFTU – though it had never taken them seriously as sources of policy – as well as specialist pressure groups such as the Socialist Medical Association.

But the important changes, the ones that really mattered for policy-making, were the reorganisation of the NEC sub-committees under Hugh Dalton's control and the revival of the National Joint Council (renamed National Council of Labour in 1934) which enabled the leaders of the TUC to have a big say in the coordination of party and trade union policy. The process of centralisation affected both wings of the movement. In the unions Bevin and Citrine had come to dominate after 1926, as head of the giant Transport and General Workers' Union and General Secretary of the TUC respectively. The militants and their quasi-syndicalist strategy had been defeated by the failure of the General Strike. Falling trade union membership and persistent mass unemployment further weakened the strike weapon in the late 1920s and early 1930s. In these circumstances the Bevin–Citrine leadership stressed moderation and influence through the legitimate channels of parliament and state. Citrine was also the only major figure of the British labour movement to represent Labour at international gatherings of the IFTU (of which he was President) and at joint meetings of the IFTU–LSI. The party's usual representative at the LSI was William Gillies, the organisation's obsessive International Secretary, who was not a heavyweight politician. Bevin had taken the initiative in reviving the NJC before the end of 1931 at a time when there was not even a Shadow Cabinet to act as the collective voice of the PLP. His move ensured that policy discussions were centralised in this union-dominated body, which met prior to meetings of the NEC.[42] The NEC's policy-making sub-committees were dominated by Hugh Dalton, increasingly a realist on matters of foreign policy. We saw in the previous chapter that Dalton had a strong interest in foreign policy and realised before most of his colleagues that the League was useless without the power to enforce its decisions. He was also known to dislike Germany and was one of the first in the leadership to favour rearmament. Dalton, Bevin and Citrine were allies throughout the 1930s.

There was little to cheer them in 1931. The collapse of the liberal political economy discredited most of the ideas that had sustained Labour's view of the world system. As we saw, it left a gap that could be filled with radical rhetoric, as the party's annual conferences demonstrated in the immediate aftermath of MacDonald's 'betrayal'. The void could just as easily be filled by a reversion to conventional ideas in foreign policy but it would take time to convince a party in which socialists held the intellectual initiative. Yet in the face of fascism, protectionism, and the overthrow of international law, the logic of power politics was bound to reassert itself even within the Labour Party – in the fullness of time. But it would take until the mid-1930s before the party as a whole began to face up to the threat posed by aggressive fascist states. The party was meanwhile confused by its faith in contradictory ideas – such as the idea that peace could be secured through the League. This was, hypothetically, a juridical solution to the structural problem of international relations but it existed alongside the idea that the problem was social because it inhered in the character of capitalism and could only be solved by the transition to socialism. Labour's ideas about the world economy, moreover, were purely idealistic and irrelevant to the immediate problems it faced. The British political economy had been successfully geared to the interests of the middle class since 1920. The industrial strength of organised labour had shrunk remorselessly in the same period. Labour's vote had steadily increased up to 1931 but there was no evidence it could break out of its electoral ghetto. Labour knew of no coherent reformist alternatives to the ruling economic orthodoxies, the most pernicious of which was the view that unemployment was to a large extent a function of the dole – a view even Keynes shared. It is true that the 'Living Wage' proposals of the ILP existed – drawn up in the wake of the 1924 minority Government – and that they identified 'underconsumption' as the root of the unemployment problem. But Labour had rejected these ideas in the 1920s and the world slump made them look altogether irrelevant. Nor was there any reason to believe that other left-of-centre parties elsewhere in Europe had any better ideas. The Mueller Government, for example, the last parliamentary government in Germany under a social democrat, elected in May 1928, fell in 1930 in very similar circumstances to those affecting Labour in the summer of 1931. Hjalmar Schacht, the president of the Reichsbank, warned foreign banks against subscribing to a loan which the finance minister, Rudolf Hilferding, was trying to raise in November 1929 to cover the budget deficit. German industry demanded tax cuts and cuts in social spending.[43] There were demands to reduce unemployment benefits and Mueller resigned in March 1930 when the SPD Reichstag *fraktion* refused to support them. The succeeding Bruning government promptly enforced the cuts and deepened Germany's deflationary policy. Another round of unemployment benefit cuts was announced in June 1931, together with emergency orders for reductions in the salaries of state employees.

These experiences fitted the international trend as world trade fell by 65 per cent in the course of the crisis.[44] Terrible political consequences were perceptible in the course of 1930–1, including the spectacular growth of the Nazi electoral following, from 2.6 to 18.3 per cent of the vote since 1928. The Japanese invasion of Manchuria in September 1931, another direct result of the world depression, exposed the weakness of the League of Nations, which still remained the best hope for peace in the opinion of much of the Labour Party.[45] The LNU, which had been slow to respond to the international economic crisis greeted the Japanese aggression with passivity and limp calls for an inquiry. Public interest in the war in China grew with the bombing of Chapei on 20 January 1932 but the LNU was still unable to give a lead and its credibility was badly damaged. This might have been the time for frank recognition of the limits of British influence and power, from an organisation which had set inordinate store by the power of British public opinion in world affairs. Now was the moment to stress that collective security depended on public support for effective sanctions in Britain and France. But it was not forthcoming. Neither the League nor its supporters demonstrated such clear commitments. Membership of the LNU began to fall from 1932. Labour itself was still in two minds, caught between disarmament and isolationist sentiment on the one hand, with all the accompanying rhetoric against war-mongering arms manufacturers and political cliques, and commitment to the League on the other.

Yet the economic crisis threatened to undermine the League's foundations still further. The Labour-supporting *Daily Herald* reported Stanley Hirst, chairman of the party's NEC, returning from a meeting of the LSI in Vienna and declaring that 'the economic crisis . . . threatens to destroy democracy in Central Europe'.[46] In Germany in particular 'the economic crisis was first and foremost a political event: it signalled the collapse of a political experiment' – the end of the Weimar Republic.[47] It was in these circumstances that the Soviet Union – whose experience had always been considered irrelevant by British Labour in the 1920s – now became a matter for study, discussion and even emulation. This was because the Soviet Union had launched the first Five Year Plan in 1928 and seemed immune from the world capitalist crisis. For sections of the Labour Party and trade union movement, Soviet socialism had the priceless merit of actually existing. When delegates to the Labour conferences of 1931 and 1932 referred to 'the socialist state', 'a real plan', 'an ordered plan' or 'our Socialist system', these abstractions acquired credibility – when they might have been dismissed as empty rhetoric in the immediate aftermath of the party's 'betrayal' by its best-known self-avowed socialists, Snowden and MacDonald – because of actually existing Soviet socialism. At a time when the inevitability of Fabian gradualism had been declared redundant by its founders and the 'ethical' socialism of Labour intellectuals such as R. H. Tawney had never looked more irrelevant, and the social democratic parties had nothing but failure to show for their efforts, Soviet socialism kept the cause alive. This is what the Labour MP Arthur Pugh was referring to when he said at the Bristol TUC in 1931: 'A great industrial revolution is taking place before our eyes which transcends anything that occurred a century ago in its magnitude and its potentialities for good or ill of the workpeople.'[48] Ernest Bevin, the next person to speak in the debate, made the reference more explicit when he said, to the applause of the delegates, that:

> cutting right across the world economy today was a new development
> in Russia . . . That new economy involved planning and the attack
> on Russian planning did not arise because of Russian labour condi-
> tions but because its planning was against the old world economy
> of scramble and individualism and profit . . . The portent of that

planning could not be overestimated . . . lining up priests and parsons to denounce Russia did not work.[49]

Despite the evidence – and their own rhetoric – to the contrary, it could be argued that some of the socialists simply did not believe that global forces held the upper hand. There was still a consciousness of Britain as a powerful financial centre and industrial Power able to manage its own affairs. Thus a left-winger like Frank Wise – a leading economics spokesman for the Socialist League[50] – thought in terms of the survival of the City as the centre of world banking even under a socialist dispensation. His reasoning was that a socialist government would be able to 'influence the course of events, both financial and political, in other countries'.[51] In one form or another the British left would continue to count on the country's ability to do that long after the Empire had ceased to matter. The socialists remained persuaded, whether they consciously took the Empire into account or not, of the efficacy of the state, even when the bankers' ramp theory was at its most influential and 1931 was held to be 'the clearest demonstration of the power of capitalism to overthrow a popularly elected government by extra-parliamentary means'.[52] Once again, one only had to look at the Soviet Union – admittedly a massive one-sixth of the earth's surface – to see that socialism in one country was possible. Was Britain that different, however, in the minds of people who had been used to hearing about its great Commonwealth of Nations all of their lives?

If 'the theoreticians . . . were directly inspired by the example of Soviet Russia' because of the Five Year Plan,[53] the idea that Russia was on the side of the workers had a much broader scope than that. Large numbers of ordinary party members and trade unionists could not be indifferent to the fact, as Bevin explained to a conference of the International Transport Workers' federation in Prague in 1932, that in Russia 'we are here dealing with an actual living instance of super-human effort to rebuild a state on socialistic lines'.[54] Twelve months later Hitler became Chancellor in Germany and by the end of 1933 the Soviet Union put out the first tentative feelers for joining the League of Nations and finding 'collective security'. 'It is no accident', proclaimed the NEC in its report on the year 1934–5, 'that Soviet Russia has entered the League, is one of the strongest supporters of collective security and is moving towards Democracy.'[55] Peace, social justice and democracy were linked in Labour minds. This is why there were many reasons why it remained extremely difficult for leading figures in the Labour Party to speak positively about the Soviet Union. Since the foundation of the Bolshevik state the party had denied its relevance for both socialism and the British left. It had condemned Bolshevik violence, criticised the undemocratic nature of the

regime and rejected revolutionary politics. The Soviet franchise in Britain
was held, furthermore, by a small, unpopular, disruptive and aggressive
party to Labour's left which the party leaders did not want to encourage.
Labour was wholly committed to a peaceful, electoral, parliamentary
politics and was bound to defend this orientation in 1931. Any hint
that Labour found aspects of the Soviet Union agreeable would be
seized upon by its rivals. Any opportunities to disrupt the Labour Party
would be seized upon by the Communists. The Labour Party statement
Democracy vs Dictatorship (1933) was only one of many measures
designed to protect Labour from both these evils. In the same year Bevin
was already less confident of his earlier judgement that the stories of
forced labour in the Soviet Union were merely the fabrications of priests
and parsons. He now suggested that this was something on 'which the
international labour movement should be well-informed', implying,
perhaps, that there was doubt on this matter. Yet when Cripps talked of
a central plan and enabling Acts, or Cole talked of 'a unified policy
stemming from central control' as the 'indispensable condition of a
successful expansionist policy',[56] their thinking was inevitably informed
by the Russian example – which was the only evidence that a real socialist
alternative existed. Taylor rightly argued that 'This thinking, when it
started, was almost entirely on economic questions' with unemployment
as the spur. In this context the centralisers and technocrats increasingly
prevailed over their critics. Morrison's idea of a public corporation, for
example, was endorsed by one of Labour's left-wing conferences – that
of 1932. Hugh Dalton, one of those who 'preferred pragmatism to
doctrine' according to his biographer, was one of the converts to Soviet-
style planning in the course of 1931. 'The notion that planning should
involve physical control of resources by a central instrument of
government became one of Dalton's strongest themes in the years that
followed.'[57] The issue, as Barbara Wootton put it in 1934, was *Plan or
No Plan?* and planning depended on experts and physical control. The
Soviet experiment also offered hope for the future – and even socialists
such as Brailsford, who 'constantly denounced the Soviet tyranny', were
dependent on this.[58] Introducing Laski on the occasion of his Conway
Memorial Lecture in 1932 on 'Nationalism and the Future of Civilization',
Brailsford referred to the Russian Revolution's 'imperious call to order
and planning' and the Soviet system's grasp of 'the significance of the
machine', its 'passion for social equality' and its 'sense that the whole
is greater than the parts'.[59]

Few of the socialists inspired by Soviet planning turned to the
Communist Party. Although the crisis was everything that could be hoped
for from the standpoint of Communist doctrine, the party remained a
negligible factor. We have no difficulty accepting that while events

between August 1931 and January 1933 served to strengthen every argument that leftists had ever put for doubting the benefits of capitalism, at the same time denting their confidence in its political institutions, they nevertheless persisted with the old political methods. The 1931 and 1935 general election results showed where the balance of political forces lay in Britain by returning large majorities for the National Government. All but a tiny minority agreed that Bolshevik political methods were both nasty and alien. Thus the vast majority of the politically active militants for socialism remained in the Labour Party. Hugh Gaitskell, for example, though arguing in support of the Soviet regime at the end of 1931, 'saw the Communist Party as just a bunch of impatient comrades' and did not believe in joining any left-wing groups that were not part of the official movement. 'We cannot afford to have sectionalism', Gaitskell argued, even though 'he talked freely to his friends of the revolution, the class war and the class enemy'.[60] What was true for Gaitskell – as well as his future rival Nye Bevan – was true for many more socialists in the Labour Party. Taylor has judged that the economic crisis 'provided the opening through which Communist influence broke into the middle classes'.[61] More important in the longer run, it seems to us, the Soviet experience made possible the dominance of a socialist discourse in the Labour Party in 1931. Thereafter it remained the language of party and trade union debate for decades to come. Orwell described the Soviet Union as 'the real dynamo of the socialist movement' in 1944,[62] but it first emerged in that role in 1931 and Soviet economic planning was still relevant to the left of the Labour Party thirty years later.[63] In the moment of crisis its economic advances were relevant to the whole party. They made faith in socialism possible and seemingly relevant despite Labour's actual political impotence and programmatic irrelevance.

If defeat in 1931 reduced the Labour Party to little more than a rhetorical presence in national politics, no one was more effective in supplying the rhetoric and articulating and representing the activist left's thinking in the 1930s than Harold Laski.[64] Laski combined an academic career at the London School of Economics with an active political involvement in the Labour Party – in which he served on the NEC for 12 years from 1937 – and a prominent role in the Left Book Club from May 1936. After 1931 his views became more radical and when Hitler became German Chancellor Laski's sensitivity to the fragility of democracy and world peace was displayed in everything he published. More than anyone else he scrutinised the compatibility of capitalism and democracy in a succession of influential books and arrived at conclusions which Lenin anticipated twenty years earlier. For Laski, parliamentary democracy increasingly looked like the creation of capitalism in its expanding, competitive, and optimistic early phase, working best when the dominant political parties shared fundamental values, as the Liberals and Tories had done in England before 1914. But the First World War had opened up an epoch of monopoly capitalism characterised by a chronic crisis of profitability and popular legitimacy, the latter best expressed in the socialist challenge. The old parliamentary tolerance, compromise and reasoned debate, based on an underlying consensus of core values, was jeopardised by these developments. The class antagonisms endemic to capitalism had grown fiercer in circumstances of prolonged economic adversity. Fascism was the product of this international trend. It answered the capitalist problem by extinguishing democracy. It was simply 'the expedient adopted by capitalism in distress to defeat the democratic political foundation with which it could be successfully linked in its period of creative expansion'.[65] This was an international problem. International relations, in Laski's post-1931 view, looked very like Lenin's 1916 characterisation of the imperialist epoch as an epoch of wars, civil wars, and revolutions. Democracy was everywhere in retreat as capitalism turned to authoritarian solutions to working-class insubordination.[66]

The central contradiction running through all of Laski's thinking in the 1930s was that between his Leninist reasoning and his non-Leninist conclusions. Laski saw nothing 'more futile than to live as the social democratic parties live, as very notably the English Labour Party lives, in the pathetic belief that it will be able to enact Utopia by the use of the parliamentary machine'.[67] The violent suppression of socialist, working-class, Vienna in 1934 confirmed him in this view. Yet he believed that parliamentary democracy was the only valid system in Britain and hoped that it would prove an exception to his general analysis. His depiction of international relations likewise suggested that fascism was a global response to capitalist crisis and that the international system was headed for another major war. Capitalism, Laski argued, inevitably led to war. His faith in the League of Nations had already withered after the Japanese invasion of Manchuria and was dealt a bigger blow with the creation of a Nazi Germany. But his logic also became more reductionist in the wake of these empirical trends. International peace now seemed to depend on the transition to socialism rather than the League of Nations because capitalism and democracy were incompatible partners and one would have to be eliminated to save the other. Yet just as Laski clung to hope in the viability of British parliamentary institutions, despite an imperious logical pessimism which pointed to their fading relevance, so he admitted that the League was the only hope, even though, as Philip Noel-Baker complained, he spent all his time 'sneering at it, belittling its achievements, using his immense influence and prestige to throw doubt, and indeed despair, into the minds of those who should be furnishing that driving power of public opinion without which the League cannot triumph'.[68] Newman argues that Laski's contradictions reflected the collision between his logic and his democratic preferences.[69] But this only suggests that, in common with many other British socialists at this time, he did not see enough evidence to either support a revolutionary position or to refute the economic reductionism which fed his pessimism.

Nobody could doubt Leonard Woolf's democratic preferences but he too emphasised the contradiction between political democracy and capitalism. In 1933 his reflections on the 'modern state' stressed the virtues of liberal democracy based on the rights of the individual. This, according to Woolf, had been the foundation of the movement for social reform and personal happiness. Neither fascism nor communism were interested in personal happiness in Woolf's view and so whereas the political landscape in 1900 had been 'thoroughly democratic', a time when 'Everyone believed in democracy',[70] in 1933 this was no longer true. Dictatorship had spread and the change had taken place in people's minds as well as in their institutions. By 1939, however, at the conclusion of the treaty between Nazi Germany and Soviet Russia, Woolf argued that 'the Marxian analysis of nineteenth-century European capitalist society is, in its main lines, impregnable'.[71] Up to 1914 Western civilisation had been a 'class civilisation, and therefore unequal'. But it was a progressive civilisation in which violence was rare except in connection with imperialism. Since 1918 the increased scale and savagery of persecutions of opinion, religion and race and the change in attitude towards them in three-quarters of the countries of Europe had been striking. Woolf argued that the roots of the 'class war' lay in the resistance of the middle class to change the economic system in the direction of socialism. Political democracy and economic power were henceforth in contradiction and middle-class liberals and democrats betrayed their own principles in not recognising the fact. Their capitalist system and their sacred rights of property were no longer compatible with liberty and equality.[72] 'Once the civilized themselves and civilization itself begin to hestitate and falter all the barbarians and all our barbarisms raise their heads again' and this, according to Woolf, is what happened at the end of the nineteenth century. The 'social psychology' of Europe had changed and violence, cruelty and intolerance became acceptable.

In Soviet Russia, however, the economic problem had been solved and the Bolsheviks, Woolf argued, 'thereby laid the foundations . . . of what might have been the greatest civilization in human history'. This achievement was all the more important because it had been secured, in Woolf's view, by a Government which had 'exerted a dominating influence' upon the forces of the international left.[73] But the Bolshevik revolution had no place for liberty, equality, tolerance, truth or humanity.

The regime had stabilised as a dictatorship due to 'historical and purely fortuitous circumstances'. Yet in Woolf's view – and this was a persuasive argument for many on the Labour left – the 'ultimate objective' of the Soviet Government placed it 'on the side of civilization and it cannot escape the consequences of its own ultimate beliefs'.[74] It put them, therefore, against the barbarians at the gate – in other words it made the Soviet state an enemy of fascism. The fact that the British Government seemed uninterested in this fact told its own story for Woolf. Neville Chamberlain's foreign policy between 1937 and 1939 'can only be correctly interpreted upon classical Marxist lines . . . The dictators were to him the bulwark of Capitalism against Communism and Russia.'[75] Woolf saw no reason to amend his reasoning when Hitler and Stalin concluded the treaty which kept Russia out of the early stages of the Second World War.

The argument that capitalism and democracy were in fundamental contradiction survived the 1930s, as did the conviction that Soviet economic advances were undermining the Stalinist dictatorship and preparing the foundations of socialist democracy.[76] Left-wing suspicion of the USA and a propensity to give the Soviet Union the benefit of the doubt fed off this logic well into the 1950s and 1960s. Yet even in the 1930s the Labour Party as a whole was never converted to these views. The economic crisis of the 1930s actually affected Britain less severely than elsewhere and the country was one of the first to emerge from it. By 1935 employment and production had risen beyond the 1929 figures and productivity was 20 per cent higher. The real incomes of the working class were rising because of falling prices. Benefits for the unemployed, moreover, were maintained at higher levels than elsewhere in Europe even after the introduction of the household means test. These more favourable conditions may have enabled the country to resist the allure of the political extremes, though the strength of the middle ground in politics could just as well be interpreted as evidence of the strength of the British cultural commitment to parliamentary government. Some Labour politicians, perhaps most of them, took this view and believed that the strength of British democratic values had really saved the day. When Hugh Gaitskell witnessed the crushing of the organised working class in Vienna – the event which confirmed Laski in his pessimism – he 'learnt as never before to value the freedom of British political institutions', according to his biographer.[77] The notion that the British were peculiarly fortunate to have such democratic institutions probably peaked at the end of the Second World War, but was obviously present throughout the 1930s, as other countries succumbed to fascism and various forms of authoritarian government. If the British were especially suited to democracy, other peoples – notably the Germans – might appear to be especially unsuited to it. This was the view of Robert Lord Vansittart, whom MacDonald assisted on his way to becoming Permanent Under-Secretary at the Foreign Office.[78] By the end of the 1930s it was also the view of William Gillies, secretary of Labour's International Sub-committee, George Dallas, its chairman, Hugh Dalton, by now an aspiring foreign secretary, Arthur Greenwood, deputy leader of the party, and Ernest Bevin who became Foreign Secretary in 1945. The mistrust of German militarism and imperialism which had grown during the First World War was revived by Hitler and so too was the defence and celebration of British democracy. More prosaically, one could simply deduce, as Bevin and Citrine had, that the first victims of a fascist or communist victory were free trade unions; the trade unions thus had a massive stake in maintaining parliamentary democracy.

Another rising star of the Labour Party, Evan Durbin, took Laski's observation about the tensions between democracy and capitalism and came to the conclusion that the maintenance of democracy required restraint. In the end it depended, in this view, on the 'emotional balance in the individuals composing a nation'.[79] These insights of Durbin's admittedly came at the end of the 1930s rather than its beginnings, though the times were no less catastrophic for that. 'Uncompromising party programmes' were, however, on this reasoning, products of extremist personalities, rather than extremist times, and such personalities endangered the delicate balance which made democracy possible. For Durbin it was clear that 'the battles upon which the future of democracy depend must be fought within and not between the parties contending for power'. This was what MacDonald (and Baldwin) had arguably realised in the 1920s,[80] ensuring, as Durbin put it, that 'the extremist minority on the Left of the Labour Party' had been subject to 'continuous defeat'.[81] Indeed the function of the Labour Party, from the perspective of a stable political system, might be said to be its power to attract all the utopians, idealists, 'cranks and extremists' (Webb) the better to contain them. Certainly on international issues Labour attracted most of the socialist internationalists, pacifists and idealists while ensuring that they rarely troubled the making of foreign policy. Durbin's observations on the nature of the internal party struggle, as a necessary part of this process, though already relevant to recent history, were made to look prophetic by the epic Cold War battles which racked Labour and the trade unions after 1950.

But Durbin's and Gaitskell's and even Laski's views also serve to underline the point that while the 1930s were certainly catastrophic in many ways, the thinking of Labour politicians was rarely catastrophist in the sense of them pinning their hopes on the collapse of capitalism or of losing faith in liberal democracy. Labour's programmatic statements on international relations reflected this faith and differed very little from those of the 1920s. War was still described as 'senseless and wicked'; national, racial and class barriers were still detestable; international anarchy, as in the manifesto of 1918, was still the fault of capitalism. In 1934 it had to be acknowledged, as it had been in 1919, that 'the only final guarantee of peace [lay] in the development of a Cooperative World Commonwealth of Nations' and the League could only succeed if it evolved in that direction.[82] *For Socialism and Peace*, the party's 'programme of action', thus recommended a foreign policy directed to that end, while sadly acknowledging 'a return to pre-War standards and methods' such as the arms race, the search for military alliances and the balance of power. It thus proposed 'all-round disarmament', abolition of national air forces, nationalisation of the arms trade, the open door in China, the return to free trade, and improved commercial relations with Russia. The only semblance of new thinking was the demand for a 'Peace Act' which 'would bind the Government to submit any dispute with another State to some form of pacific procedure, and not to resort to force as an instrument of national policy; and to report at once to the League and to comply with the League's injunctions on the basis of reciprocity, in case of having to use force in self-defence. The Act would also empower the Government to apply any economic and financial measures necessary to take its share in collective action.' While Labour promised to 'unflinchingly support our Government in all the risks and consequences of fulfilling its duty to take part in collective action against a peace-breaker' it also said that it would 'refuse to serve or support our Government if it were ever condemned as an aggressor by the League'.

The adoption of *Labour's Immediate Programme* (1937) is normally taken as evidence of how the party had moved on since the left swing of 1931–3. The domestic policies of the party had by then eliminated the doctrinal excesses recorded at the start of the decade and closely approximated to those enacted in 1945–51. But on foreign policy the experiences of the period had apparently made no difference; the party still wanted 'to strengthen and reinvigorate the League of Nations as an instrument of international cooperation and Collective Security' while promoting disarmament by international agreement and nationalising the arms industries. There was apparently nothing new to say. But this was not entirely true. In 1932 Labour, the public and the National Government certainly had no appetite for war. When the Disarmament Conference ran into problems in 1933 Labour successfully fought by-elections stressing disarmament, and the party's annual conference called for war-resistance by general strike. The Peace Ballot – shorthand for the National Declaration on the League of Nations and Armaments – was launched in 1934 to demonstrate and reinforce the LNU's base of support in British public opinion. Labour was associated with the ballot nationally, which it described as 'a significant experiment in democratic control of foreign policy and a remarkable demonstration of public support of many of the fundamental principles which inspire the foreign policy of the British Labour Party'.[83] Indeed the NEC declared that the results of the Peace Ballot gave 'an overwhelming popular mandate to Labour's Foreign Policy'. It noted that 'a considerable majority' had expressed support for military measures in support of collective security through the League, though it stressed public approval of 'all-round' disarmament. But the National Government began rearming Britain that year and was also able to draw some comfort from the results of the ballot.

Though frequently invoked as evidence of popular pacifism – along with the East Fulham by-election of 1933[84] and the Oxford Union's rejection of the idea of fighting for King and Country[85] – the ballot was nothing of the sort.[86] By the summer of 1935, when the results were made known, over eleven million votes had been recorded. The language of collective security was just now becoming popular, though the Labour Party and the LNU continued to oppose rearmament. The ballot showed that support for the League of Nations was overwhelming, as was popular approval of disarmament, abolition of national military aircraft, and support for the prohibition of private arms sales and their manufacture. But respondents also voted for collective security, with over 10 million favouring economic and non-military sanctions and 6.8 million supporting military measures in support of this principle. Self-avowed 'christian pacifists' numbered only 17,536, as revealed by the ballot's response to the issue of military enforcement of collective security, though a total of 2,366,184 voted against such measures on other grounds.[87] The fact that this massive survey of opinion was popularly known as the Peace Ballot may indicate that many people believed they were being asked to choose between peace and war. The results of the ballot may also be interpreted as evidence that people still thought of collective security as an alternative to war. Baldwin certainly stressed the Conservatives' commitment to the League in the general election of November 1935 – presumably to increase his chances of winning a majority. The LNU, following British public opinion, had responded to the Italian aggression against Abyssinia a month earlier with strong support for sanctions – in contrast to the Cabinet's reluctance to act (revealed after the election by disclosure of the Hoare–Laval plan to buy-off Italy by conniving in the dismemberment of Abyssinia). Baldwin was dissimulating, and in so far as his deceptions worked they did nothing to encourage clarity of thought in public opinion. The failure of public opinion to react in a similar way to Hitler's remilitarisation of the Rhineland in 1936 may suggest greater fear of another war was aroused by this event than in the crisis of October

1935. It may also reflect some remaining doubts about the justice meted out by the world war. But it may also have been influenced by the obvious failure of collective security in relation to Abyssinia. A resolute stance on the latter, forcing Italy to back down, may have produced a different response to the evidence of Hitler's aggression. It is difficult to be sure on any of these matters.

The events in question certainly forced a constant reappraisal of policy, a process that had begun in 1933. The advent of Hitler generated public discussion of the danger of war with an intensity not seen again until the Munich crisis in 1938.[88] The emergence of a Nazi state during the first eight months of 1933 laid bare the absolute incoherence of Labour's foreign policy, though one should remember that the National Government was no better prepared; less than twelve months earlier Stanley Baldwin had been advocating international abolition of air forces in Cabinet and proposing to take this idea to the Disarmament Conference. After Hitler became Chancellor, of the five Great Powers that were permanent members of the League, three – Germany, Japan, and Italy – were aggressive dictatorships bent on overseas expansion. Two more Great Powers – the USA and Soviet Russia – stood outside the League. Of the remainder – Britain and France – the first was governed by a party which did not believe that the League had any real role to play, though it pretended otherwise. Members of the Labour Party were reaching the same conclusion about the League's bankruptcy. The trouble was, the only real alternative was a military alliance and the party believed that this would bring war closer and at a faster pace.[89] Germany's withdrawal from both the League and the Disarmament Conference at Geneva in October 1933 came just days after the unopposed adoption of a resolution promising mass resistance to war at Labour's Hastings conference. The socialist left was now divided between those who believed that Britain ought to deter Hitler by a strong commitment to collective security, those who believed the League was a failure and those who believed wars between capitalist states were of no interest to the working class except as opportunities for the advance of socialism. The latter position was strengthened by suspicion that the National Government could not be trusted to take a resolutely anti-fascist position; indeed many socialists argued that it had fascist tendencies of its own.[90] But the number of absolute pacifists was small and some of those who continued to use the title – such as Clifford Allen and Norman Angell – recommended an armed collective security after Hitler's accession to power. This commitment to collective deterrence was by far the most popular view on the left by 1934 and it became Labour policy that year. There is no coincidence in the fact that it also became the policy of the Soviet Union, which entered the League in September. The departure of the fascist powers from the League and the entry to it of the Soviet Union rescued Labour's policy from the complete incoherence into which it had been plunged only a year earlier.

But it was not until 1935 that all its supporters were forced to answer the question of whether collective security ultimately rested on the threat of armed action. The Abyssinian crisis forced this discussion. Lansbury and Ponsonby – Labour's leaders respectively in the Commons and Lords – both resigned rather than renounce their pacifist beliefs and accept that the party's commitment to collective security had to involve credible sanctions up to and including war with Mussolini.[91] Lansbury had tied himself in knots when the Commons debated the issue in August, insisting that if he were Prime Minister he would stand by the League but refuse to intervene militarily.[92] Labour's annual conference at Brighton in 1935 took place as the Italian invasion began. The delegates read in the NEC report on the previous year that the party leadership acknowledged that the League had been set up on the assumption that democracy would spread in the world; that membership of the League would be universal; that disarmament would be imposed on its members; that the cult of war was dead; and that capitalism would function successfully. It admitted that none of these assumptions were true in 1935.

A change in attitude was beginning, slowly, to emerge. At the TUC congress of 1934 the General Council had taken the first step. George Gibson, in outlining the TUC's thinking on the League, acknowledged that the League must not be allowed to become a machine 'merely to maintain the status quo'. Some initiatives could be taken through it to address economic and social inequities that currently generated international friction. Peace, however, certainly could not be achieved by unilateral disarmament. The TUC believed that the League could and should become 'an effective police force'.[93] At Margate, in September 1935, just before the Labour annual conference, Citrine reminded TUC delegates of the Labour movement's conviction that 'the maintenance of democratic institutions is an essential factor in the preservation of peace'. The fascist dictatorships had fostered a spirit of militarism and fomented national antagonisms which imperilled world peace. He therefore moved that congress affirm its belief in a 'collective peace system operating within the League of Nations and its determination to take all appropriate action to make that system a reality'.[94] He then called upon the British Government, in cooperation with the League, 'to use all necessary measures provided by the Covenant to prevent Italy's unjust and rapacious attack' upon Abyssinia. The TUC and the Labour Party had also arrived at the conclusion, as they had in 1919, that the colonial issue, brought to world attention again by the Italian mobilisation, could only be dealt with fairly if all colonies were placed within the mandates system and some system of international control could guarantee access to raw material sources for all the countries of the world. This was as close as Labour got to colonial appeasement with annual conference agreeing on some sort of international control of raw material sources guaranteeing open access. As for the immediate situation, Citrine made clear to the delegates that sanctions against Italy meant penalties and they included the possibility of military punishment. This message was clear enough to excite opposition in the debate which followed, including an impassioned statement of pacifism from one of the men who volunteered to join the army in August 1914 and who had vowed never to serve 'King and Country' again – whatever the rationale for war. Citrine nevertheless commanded the support of the congress.

The NEC's review of 1934–5 condemned the National Government for failing to check Japanese aggression in China. It declared that the 'reversion' to power politics – as also symbolised by the Nazi government – had increased the danger of a general war. This could only be averted if acts of aggression were confronted by a collective strength powerful enough to overcome them.[95] Spurred on by the unions led by Bevin, it thus transpired that Labour's annual conference of 1935 followed the TUC's lead and accepted the need for military sanctions in the event of the League standing up to Mussolini. Bevin's attack on Lansbury's pacifism – God and the Christian martyrs having been invoked in the debate – signalled the end of the old man's career as leader of the party, but it took the events of the following year to finish the job of routing pacifism.[96] The party itself was still looking both ways. The League was seen to be ineffective and it was clear that the National Government did not take it seriously. Like Labour the National Government emitted confusing signals, alternately playing-up the League, quietly rearming, by turns seeking to conciliate and check the revisionist fascist dictatorships, while often enough warning that another world war was a disaster that armaments and alliances brought forward, but which had to be avoided. The encroachments on China of Japanese imperialism, the Nazi regime's 'open reversion to power politics', the collapse of the Washington Naval Treaty with the repudiation of 'ratios' by Japan and Britain, the absence of any agreements for the limitation of land and air armaments, the beginnings of a new arms race – all these were taken as signs of an approaching world war in 1935. But Labour still opposed rearmament and was opposed to 'any pact of the kind involving military commitments'. It still believed that the League could be strengthened to prevent war, it still opposed measures that might bring war closer – such as rearmament and military alliances outside the League. Labour still talked about the need for a World Commonwealth on the basis of justice and equality as if it answered the pressing needs of the hour. Yet the leadership admitted that none of the prevailing assumptions of 1919, when the Covenant was framed, were valid in 1935. The economic crisis had fostered protectionism and political reaction; 'It has become clear', the NEC concluded rather desperately, 'that the survival of Democracy and of the idea of peace throughout the world is ultimately bound up with the triumph of Socialism.'[97]

Any residual idea that economic sanctions would suffice to contain and defeat aggression was refuted in the course of 1936. Abyssinia was brutally overcome by Italy; Hitler remilitarised the Rhineland in defiance of the Treaty of Versailles and denounced the Locarno Treaties; and civil war broke out in Spain when the democratically elected government was challenged by a fascist-leaning army led by General Franco. The Labour Party was completely cured of its pacifist illusions by these events, and the tiny minority of absolute pacifists within its ranks exercised no practical influence on its policy or rhetoric. But to the dismay of its own supporters, Labour meekly followed the British Government in adopting a sham 'neutrality' towards the Spanish civil war, despite the fact that the struggle between democracy and fascism was here being joined and almost one million people eventually died in the conflict. Some of Labour's leaders allowed their anti-Communism and mistrust of radicalism to affect their judgement.[98] The party and trade union leaders who gave Labour's support for non-intervention before the mass organisations had been given the chance to consider the issue were men who harboured a strong dislike of the factionalised, revolutionary character of the Spanish republican movement and worried about the absence of moderates of the type they could recognise. Citrine and Bevin also thought in terms of Britain's national interest and the country's unpreparedness for a general war, which they claimed intervention could spark off.[99] Like Dalton they were not strong admirers of Spanish democracy and were easily persuaded that the stability of Leon Blum's Popular Front Government in France depended on non-intervention.[100] This is what Sir Anthony Eden told them and this is what they repeated when they met with the PLP, the NEC and the rest of the General Council on 28 August. There was no question of treating the issue in terms of socialist solidarity. What Citrine, Bevin and Dalton were exercised by was the continued opposition to rearmament within their own party – an opposition which was not helping the country stand up to aggressors.

The TUC conference endorsed the non-intervention policy in September 1936, though not without objections from the floor. Everything was set for a repeat performance at Labour's annual conference in October until the intervention of fraternal delegates from Spain changed the mood of the delegates and forced the party to investigate breaches of non-intervention by the fascist states. The Executive admitted that the fascist rebellion in Spain was being assisted by the Portuguese Government and the three Labour movement executives had already allowed that if neutrality was being violated by Italy and Germany then Britain and France ought to review their positions. In debate at the annual conference Philip Noel-Baker was among those (including Cripps and Lord Strabolgi) who insisted that proof was already available. He also doubted the rationale for neutrality touted by the Labour leadership, namely that supplying arms to the Spanish Government would spark a general war. Meanwhile, in conditions of 'near total international isolation', the Republic was actually forced by the non-intervention policy to buy arms expensively and piecemeal where it could. By 21 October, however, the NCL felt obliged to conclude that the Spanish Government had the right to purchase arms abroad. This policy was then debated at a Labour Movement Conference later in the month which was notable for its rejection of Morrison's motion calling on the British Government to 'permit and facilitate' the supply of arms to Spain. When the NCL met with the IFTU and LSI in Paris in October the representatives agreed that it was intolerable that the government forces could not obtain arms abroad at a time when it was evident that fascist intervention in Spain was effective and making a difference. Again Morrison, supported by Susan Lawrence, put forward a resolution demanding that Britain 'should now permit and facilitate the supply of arms to the Spanish Government'. But once again Citrine prepared a revised motion, adopted unanimously, which merely called upon the British and French Governments to restore full commercial rights for the purchase of munitions.[101]

The majority view within the leadership, expressed as late as March 1937, was that non-intervention was the right policy if only the powers which ignored it could be made to see reason. It was not until the autumn of 1937 that the Labour leadership was instructed by annual conference to launch a campaign against the policy of non-intervention and for the Republic's right to buy arms abroad. The League of Nations had been of no use to Republican Spain, of course, and the Republic had tried to obtain war materials from the western democracies from as early as July 1936. Though Citrine, Bevin and Dalton appear to have believed Eden's version of events, rather than that of the French socialists they consulted in August, the truth was that Leon Blum's Government withdrew its initial promise of support in response to British opposition, as well as that of the Radicals at home. The Republic was seen by the British Government as less reliable than the rebels in guaranteeing the rights of property in Spain, including those of British investors. Within the Cabinet there were strong supporters of the rebels, such as First Lord of the Admiralty, Samuel Hoare, but no strong supporters of the Republic. Conscious of his vulnerable national defences Blum was persuaded by the British to adopt non-intervention on 24 August. A recent study rightly points out that 'as the Axis powers were already intervening with impunity, what the policy amounted to was an arms embargo imposed exclusively against the Republic'.[102] When Negrin became Prime Minister of the Republic in May 1937 the removal of non-intervention was still perceived as its greatest problem in terms of winning the war. Unfortunately for the Republic, Neville Chamberlain replaced Baldwin as Prime Minister in the same month and British foreign policy, determined to find a *modus vivendi* with Italy in the Mediterranean, the better to defend imperial interests, wrongly believed that it had no interest in dropping non-intervention.

The international threat of fascist aggression – vividly illustrated by Mussolini's and Hitler's support for Franco – undoubtedly converted the vast majority of socialists to the view that a war against Hitler would be a just war.[103] As Michael Foot points out, 'Suddenly the claims of international law, class solidarity and the desire to win the Soviet Union as an ally fitted into the same strategy.'[104] Spain seemed an obvious portent to many socialists of a larger conflict to come, clarifying the point that without a successful armed struggle against fascism, socialism had no chance anywhere in Europe. International fascism posed this issue internationally, though the ILP, now seceded from the Labour Party, continued to see a general European war as a war of rival imperialisms rather than the potential people's war stressed by most socialist anti-fascists. A lingering problem, however, even for those converted to the majority view, was whether the National Government would fight such a war. Its lack of enthusiasm for a pact of collective security with France and the Soviet Union – the latter self-evidently anti-fascist in the eyes of many on the left – raised doubts on this matter, as did the professed class sympathy of many of its supporters for Franco's Spain. In these circumstances the old unease about British foreign policy translated into outright opposition to rearmament.

At a meeting of the NCL in March 1936 Attlee outlined various 'Points of Policy' which included the argument that 'the alleged need for more armaments is a confession of failure'.[105] Hitler had just denounced the Locarno Treaties and sent troops into the Rhineland. Attlee believed that peace depended on 'League solidarity and a real attempt to deal with the causes of war'. 'Labour's policy,' he said, 'is twofold – first, support the League system and second, resistance to all capitalist and imperialist wars.' The National Government, under pretence of collective security, was simply providing for national defence – in other words an arms race had begun and a system of alliances and counter-alliances was taking shape under purely nominal League auspices. Attlee's paper showed that he thought the British Government would ultimately go to war as a function of this competitive scramble based on a failure to make capitalism work. He also quoted Baldwin to suggest that warlike preparations were 'futile' in the age of the bomber. The menace of the dictatorships had to be met but the Government was 'following the old path'. What was needed was 'collective action' to prevent war, 'the adjustment of grievances' and a renewal of proposals for disarmament and the internationalisation of air forces in particular.

In May the NCL published *Labour and the Defence of Peace* to call for an assertion of the League against fascist Italy which, by poison gas, indiscriminate murder of the civilian population and aerial bombardment had subdued Abyssinia. Labour still believed that an active peace policy was possible through the League – 'the only existing organisation which can possibly fulfil the task of preserving peace'. Unilateral disarmament would not have helped China and Abyssinia; non-resistance had not saved the Jews of Germany.[106] Alliances would only lead to competitive rearmament; they did not prevent the war of 1914–18, why should they do so now? Isolationism was no longer possible, because of Britain's proximity to Europe in an age of air warfare. Collective security was the best hope for peace. But Labour rejected the 'peace plan' offered by Hitler. It was not clear that Hitler even recognised the rule of law and it was not acceptable if his proposed Western Pact was merely a device to ensure a 'free hand' in Russia. Nevertheless the NCL believed that 'a sincere effort must be made to discover a basis of negotiation with Hitler' without allowing him to dictate the agenda. Labour proposed three things: a world economic conference that would, among other things, consider the issue of access to raw materials and economic exploitation of colonies; security by mutual disarmament; combined, finally, with the creation of a collective armed force under the auspices of the League.

In July the Advisory Committee on International Questions anticipated far-reaching reform proposals for the League and the Covenant from the National Government later that year. The especial danger was that such changes might add up to regional or other pacts pretended to be within the framework of the League, which could then lead to an August 1914 situation.[107] The other possibility was reform of the Covenant and several options of this type were considered. Since 'the ultimate test of the reality of collective security . . . is disarmament and the willingness of members to disarm' revision of Article 8 might seek to reduce this obligation to vanishing point. It was also thought possible that the National Government might want to rid Britain of the obligation to assist victims of aggression by revising Article 10, thus building on the impression created by Manchuria and Abyssinia that this was impossible of attainment anyway. Similarly, revision of Article 16 might make sanctions 'purely permissive instead of obligatory'. The significance of these speculations, which occupied 3–4,000 words, is that they provide evidence of Labour's suspicions that the National Government desired to weaken the obligations of collective defence. But the paper also reveals that its authors knew perfectly well that existing arrangements needed revision if there was to be any real intention to turn the League into an effective collective security system.[108] Article 16 as it stood was 'too dilatory' and in the event of, say, a German attack on Czechoslovakia, 'it would all be over long before economic sanctions could even be thought of'. This pointed to the need for 'special pacts or arrangements guaranteeing immediate military aid in special regions or cases' but the authors believed these were distinguishable from the orthodox alliances favoured by the National Government. They would not be a substitute, they said, for the general obligations of the collective security system. The committee failed to see that this was only a verbal formula since, on Labour's own reasoning, no such 'system' existed. Such a system required an obligation to treat an act of war against one member of the League as an act of war against all and a belief – among aggressors as well as potential victims – that the League would act on this principle. But since Manchuria and Abyssinia that belief 'had been destroyed'. The League was only 'a collective security system on paper . . . which everyone knows will not be applied in practice'. Standing by the League, or even talking of recreating a real League, now sounded 'merely academic and utopian'.[109] And since the National Government's foreign policy, by Labour's own logic, would not be transformed in the desired direction, the League was likely to become more and more discredited and the real alternatives would be made clear in the public mind – either alliances of the peaceful states against the fascists or an attempt at British isolationism.

At the beginning of 1937 the Labour left reacted to its disappointments over Spain at the 1936 annual conference by joining a short-lived 'United Front' campaign with the ILP and the CP. More durable was the launch of *Tribune* which tirelessly opposed rearmament on the grounds that the proto-fascist National Government would never use it against fascism, but might well engage in another imperialist war contrary to working-class interests. This was a Government which had connived in the partition of Abyssinia; held aloof while Spanish democracy was threatened with extinction; displayed no interest in an alliance with the Soviet Union; but manoeuvred for a deal with fascist Italy, while abandoning the pretence of taking the League seriously. Voting against rearmament in this context – bearing in mind that Labour could do nothing to actually prevent rearmament – was purely symbolic; it had been an expression of the party's opposition to such policies, as Nye Bevan argued at the annual conference.

Attlee's Left Book Club publication, *The Labour Party in Perspective*, made the same point earlier in the year, explaining that Labour's opposition to the service estimates was based on the fact that the Government did not show sufficient support for collective security. He recognised that the position of the League had deteriorated since 1934 but stressed that the fascist danger in Britain came from the National Government, observing that 'the speeches of Mr Ramsay MacDonald are full of Fascist ideas and even Fascist phraseology'.[110] Attlee complained that 'the collective peace system is not a reality at the present time' and argued that a Labour Government would rebuild it, 'not as a collateral security for national defence', but as 'a closely knit organisation able to stand against an aggressor'. He asserted that war with the fascist states was not inevitable and might actually be avoided if 'economic solidarity were added to political union' and the League was able to offer prosperity and higher living standards as well as collective security. These were clearly long-term hopes. Attlee accepted that defence requirements involved imperial commitments (to the Dominions and India) which could not be abandoned without a breach of faith. But he stressed that Labour rejected alliances and the balance of power. It favoured collective security – a policy which the National Government had never attempted. What was needed was 'unified direction' of the League's defence forces and the creation of 'an international police force'. In the meantime he acknowledged that it was necessary to ask what general defence principles should be applied to Britain. But he had little to say on this subject beyond the creation of a Ministry of Defence and the mobilisation of the economy using Labour's favourite instruments of planning, collectivism and social justice. Rearmament by the National Government could not be supported until foreign policy was changed because as things stood there was every indication that it would play the old alliances game and thus bring about the very war which Labour was still anxious to avoid.[111]

Labour abstained on rearmament in 1937 rather than vote against it as it usually did. Readers of the *Labour Party in Perspective* could be forgiven for being confused. At annual conference, in September, the NEC, in its report on 'International Policy and Defence', placed rearmament alongside the familiar call for a 'revived and strengthened' League (and closer friendship with the USA). Clynes, speaking for the Executive, pointed out that Labour Governments had provided arms for defence in the past and the voters expected support for defensive arrangements now. The TUC conference had already seen the sense in this position. Others saw it as betrayal. In the debate which followed at the annual conference Sidney Silverman forecast military and industrial conscription as the next steps to war and wanted to know why Labour was no longer linking arms to policy questions. Arms for collective security were permissible but not for national defence. Lansbury seemed to think that a conference offering economic justice to the fascist powers would suffice, so did Arthur Salter. Ponsonby concluded that Labour's opponents could now scoff at its socialist aspirations. It was true that Labour's experts on the Advisory Committee on International Questions had been recommending greater emphasis on 'the necessity for appeasement through international justice' since the beginning of the year and though this had 'always been an integral part of Labour policy' it was especially stressed over the next 18 months.[112] The NEC thus observed that it did not disagree with the need for economic appeasement but added that the aggressors currently had nothing to fear from the League except resolutions. Richard Crossman supported the NEC, arguing that peace would prove elusive 'unless England, France, and Russia are armed, resolute, and believe in themselves'. Bevin saw that the weaker democracies looked to Britain for leadership and security. He personally doubted the utility of colonial appeasement – though he had elaborated the arguments in its favour in his union's journal at the beginning of 1938 and would do so again – but stressed that fascism would not be stopped by words. But Nye Bevan reminded everyone of the old argument that there was no guarantee that fascism would be fought with the weapons acquired by the National Government. The NEC, however, carried the day, declaring that the international system was analogous to a society without a police force; the best democracy extant was British democracy and it was necessary to defend it.

Labour's reappraisal of the efficacy of the League had been provoked by the events of 1936. When Hitler remilitarised the Rhineland the NCL specifically called for 'a close coordination of the policy of Great Britain, France and the Soviet Union' – a military pact by any other name.[113] Clearly the need for a military alliance was becoming difficult to deny, whatever Attlee might be saying for the benefit of members of the Left Book Club. The need for further clarification of Labour's defence policy was also urged by Dalton and Bevin at a meeting of party and union leaders in September 1936.[114] It was this initiative which produced 'International Policy and Defence' which was then put before the TUC and Labour conferences of 1937. But it was not until 1939 that the party openly and unequivocally supported alliances, while all the time demanding that the Soviet Union, together with France, should be brought into a system of collective security. Similarly, while air defence was promoted by experts and Government alike as a cheap deterrent, Labour continued to argue for the abolition of national airforces and for the internationalisation of civil aviation. Only in the course of 1937 was this long-held position dropped.[115]

The first National Government plan for full-scale rearmament, at the end of 1935, identified the shortage of skilled workers in building and engineering and the shortage of the products of skilled workers such as machine tools as the most serious bottlenecks.[116] The government rejected direct interference to restrict civilian production and feared the political and social consequences that might arise from enforcing the dilution of labour. It also feared the consequences for trade if resources were diverted to war production. Practical assistance for the Government from Labour arose at the same time in response to a Home Office circular calling for local authorities to make arrangements for Air Raid Precautions (ARP). Herbert Morrison at the London County Council over-rode objectors who talked about ARP as a delusion encouraging civilians to think that protection against air raids was possible.[117] Cooperation from the unions over 'dilution' was likely to be more difficult to obtain. Recession deepened in the course of 1938 as direct taxes were increased and this made the problem of labour shortages a little easier to manage. But the *Anschluss* in March made matters more urgent. Chamberlain recognised that the urgent cooperation of trade unionists was required and it was at this point that Walter Citrine was mentioned as a useful place to start.[118] Citrine met with the Prime Minister's personal assistant Horace Wilson in March and advised him what Chamberlain should say to the General Council. He also advised that the Labour Party should be excluded from the discussions because its argument that armaments should only be used for collective security would hinder the enlightenment of the General Council rather than assist it. Citrine also wanted to see Chamberlain privately before the proposed meeting between the Prime Minister and the General Council. The meetings duly took place in the recommended order. It was clearly advisable that the AEU executive, whose members would be directly affected by dilution, should not be alienated from the outset because of suspicions that promises had been made on its behalf. In fact the AEU had bitter memories of broken agreements from the First World War and as it informed the Minister for Labour, Sir Thomas Inskip, on 4 April, it also objected to the government's foreign policy – specifically in relation to Spain, collective security, and the League of Nations. Members of the union, Inskip was told, suspected the National Government of covert fascist leanings and hostility towards the Soviet Union, as did the Labour Opposition.[119] In June the AEU Executive rejected the proposed changes in union practices, and relations between the union and the General Council deteriorated. Only in 1939 did the AEU accept dilution.

In 1938 events nevertheless moved very quickly towards war. A joint meeting of the General Council and the NEC in January 1938 proposed a comprehensive embargo on Japan embracing loans and credits and exports and imports – covering most of the metals used in industry and vital sources of energy such as oil. Such coercion would be sustained until Japanese troops were withdrawn from China. It was recognised that the cooperation of the League and the USA would be required to make this policy effective. It was acknowledged that this did not exclude 'a full and sympathetic consideration of Japanese claims in the Pacific and in the sphere of commercial relations'.[120] Once the *Anschluss* of Germany and Austria was completed Hitler quickly turned his attention to Czechoslovakia. In September a Labour NEC leaflet argued that 'Every consideration of democracy ... forbids the dismemberment of the Czechoslovak state by the subjection of the Sudeten German regions to Nazi Government control. British Labour emphatically repudiates the right of the British or any other Government to use diplomatic or other pressure to compel an acceptance of such humiliation.'[121] Before Chamberlain left for Munich Attlee and Greenwood made clear to Halifax that 'the limits of concession to Herr Hitler had been reached' and that 'the gravest view was taken of the fact that no Czech representative would apparently participate in the discussions'. They also argued that 'it would be a great blunder if any action were taken which would alienate the Soviet Government'.[122] This advice was ignored. The Labour leaders also spoke to the Soviet ambassador Ivan Maisky and Jan Masaryk, the Czech Minister in London. Pressure was also brought to bear on the French Government. Once it became clear that the Czechs had submitted to an Anglo-French plan Attlee and Greenwood vigorously protested. A joint meeting of the three executives – PLP, NEC and General Council – on 21 September declared that it had 'read with profound humiliation the statement of the Czech Government issued in Prague today that it has been "forced under irresistible pressure" by both the British and French Governments to accept with pain the proposals elaborated in London . . . This dishonour will not bring us peace. Hitler's ambitions do not stop short at Czechoslovakia. There is no longer a frontier in Europe which is safe.'[123]

At the end of September Chamberlain returned to Britain from Munich having surrendered Czech Sudetenland to Hitler in exchange for peace with Germany. In October 1938 the NEC issued another leaflet entitled 'Labour's Claim to Power: A Supreme National Effort for Peace'. This argued that 'we are back in 1914':'The League of Nations has been reduced to impotence; the system of mutual and collective security among the peaceful nations has been shattered; Russia has been cold-shouldered by the Western Powers; Europe, from the North Sea to the Mediterranean, is now dominated by Germany.'[124] The conclusions drawn from this were that the National Government must go, ARP and the airforce needed to be strengthened and unemployment (standing at 2 million) must be reduced. But compulsion was deemed equally unnecessary for both industrial and military purposes. War could still be avoided 'by removal of genuine grievances' and the rebuilding of the League. In November there was the collective punishment of German Jews on *Kristallnacht*; and before the end of the year it was already apparent that Hitler was set on the dismemberment of Poland.[125] There was growing evidence of public opposition to the National Government as the success of a Popular Front candidate at Bridgwater, with local Labour backing, illustrated in November. Dalton complained to the House of practical problems impeding aircraft production and of a deficit of strategic bombers capable of long-distance raids. The party and the unions also stepped up their involvement in practical defence measures such as Air Raid Precautions. In December the Government announced a voluntary scheme of national service.

During the next three months Franco came to power in Spain and Hitler's armies marched into Prague. At the end of March 1939 Chamberlain guaranteed Poland against German aggression. Meanwhile Labour's Advisory Committee on International Questions reflected on the 'soundness' of the party's policy. It had opposed a punitive peace in 1919 and foretold the rise of a militant Germany if this opposition was ignored. It had stood for revision of the Peace Treaty in the early 1920s, for the inclusion of Germany in the League, for genuine disarmament and for 'a world policy of political and economic appeasement'. Most of this – including the system of collective security – was ignored. 'The National Government pursued precisely the opposite policy; it destroyed and abandoned the League.'[126] It embraced protectionism, 'a variety of economic imperialism', at Ottawa in 1932 and the beggar-thy-neighbour policies which lead to war. But just as in July 1936, so now in March 1939, the advisory committee complained that Labour's alternative had come to be seen as 'academic, unreal and utopian'. The rearmament and aggression of the dictatorships continually increased the imminent danger of war. The party, in these circumstances, was forced to demand that the Government 'stand up to the dictators'. It supported rearmament. But 'its real and fundamental policy' was obscured in the process. It must now contemplate the hour when there will be nothing more to give belonging to others in the appeasement of the fascist Powers. Labour must take the initiative from them by advocating the return to a system of law in exchange for consideration of their 'territorial and economic demands'. While trading in colonies was still ruled out Labour would 'advocate the British Empire making its contribution to justice, economic equality and appeasement as part of the reconstitution of the whole international situation on the basis of law, order, and disarmament'.

The party continued to reject conscription as late as April 1939, when the government introduced a bill in response to the collapse of Prague to German armed forces. In the summer the annual conference debated the international situation along the well-worn paths, largely devoid of inspiration. The NEC resolution talked about staving off the imminent danger of war by the formation of 'a strong group of peaceful powers bound together by pacts of mutual aid against aggression'. It complained about the delay in reaching an accord with France and Soviet Russia and it denounced the betrayal of Spain, Czechoslovakia and the League itself. Action ought to have been taken in 1932 when the Manchurian struggle had just begun. But appeasement, according to Noel-Baker, had been 'a dangerous pathological complaint' instead of a policy. Belatedly a stand was made with guarantees for Poland and Greece. But alliances, though undoubtedly necessary, did not constitute an active policy for peace. This still depended on a rebuilt League and, as Noel-Baker put it, 'the Labour Party will not abandon, now or ever, the vision of a new world order'.[127] Other speakers in the debate still put their trust in 'peace conferences' or the social reconstruction of Europe, or worried that they would soon be fighting so that Britain could retain control of 'Egypt and Iraq and oil', as William Mellor expressed the point.[128] Ernest Bevin brought most of these concerns together in a widely reported speech which, echoing arguments he had returned to on several occasions in the previous eighteen months,[129] said that collective security could never be effective unless all the parties concerned had something to secure.

He wanted to know what the causes of the present world disorder were and suggested that 'the biggest contributor is this country and not Germany, for one of the most potent causes of world disorder has been our dominant financial policy'. He was referring to the policy of deflation, pursued with rigour since 1920. Chamberlain was merely a spokesman for the bankers, the main supporters of appeasement in Bevin's view. The Prime Minister was guilty of trying to fit world events into the requirements of the City of London. Bevin agreed with the resolution in believing in the desirability of a closer relationship with the USA and thought that the quickest way to secure it was through the Empire – the Dominions and Africa in particular – rather than Europe.[130] An 'understanding' with the USA might come about by extending 'the great Commonwealth idea' to make the USA 'a partner, at least economically, even though it may involve a limitation of our sovereignty'. Instead of scrapping the Ottawa Agreement we might expand it, he mused.[131] Collective security and an 'economic Peace Bloc' would go together and be extended to all those willing to cooperate, 'to come within our preference system' and pool 'the whole of the Colonial Empires of the world and their resources':

It would bring the 'Haves' together and they would, in fact, be controlling 90 per cent of the essential raw materials of the world. They would also control 75 per cent of the world population and, in fact, would be the great financial and money powers of the world.[132]

Having pooled their arms, resources and economic power the Peace Bloc would be able to 'pilot the world along towards a World Order'. The colonies would be held in collective trusteeship and the world's resources would be opened up for the benefit of humanity. Without wishing to read too much into Bevin's vision of a new world order, it is possible to see elements of the old Wilsonian argument for the Open Door here, together with more recent 'Keynesian' ideas, with which Bevin was familiar through his work on the Macmillan Committee on Finance and Industry in the years 1929–31. Bevin gave these ideas an imperial dimension, reflecting the common inability of senior Labour politicians to imagine the world without colonies and their conviction – which Bevin made explicit on occasions – that such colonies were vital for maintaining the living standards of British workers. In 1939 there was absolutely no reason to believe that any leading American politicians could share this overtly imperialist view of things. Bevin's vision of a US–UK condominium over the government of the Free World would have to wait until more powerful politicians reworked the idea in the changed circumstances of the late1940s. In the meantime the pressing issue of collective security against Nazi expansionism was already a lost cause. On 23 August the Nazi–Soviet Pact was made public and Hitler was given a free hand to invade Poland.

5   The Second World War

It is a remarkable fact that when Arthur Greenwoood rose to speak in the House of Commons, in response to Neville Chamberlain's last attempt to avoid war with Nazi Germany, on 2 September 1939, a Tory voice called 'Speak for England, Arthur!' The House had expected to hear that Britain had issued Germany with an ultimatum, following its invasion of Poland the day before. Instead it reacted with confusion and some dismay to Chamberlain's announcement of a possible conference with Germany if the latter agreed to withdraw its forces. Greenwood, acting in Attlee's absence, told the Prime Minister that every minute's delay imperilled 'our national interests' and 'our national honour'. After the Commons' debate broke up Greenwood approached Chamberlain to warn him of a parliamentary rebellion unless war were declared the next day. The British ultimatum was duly delivered the following morning. And so it was that the main parliamentary force for the avoidance of war of the last twenty years helped to stiffen the resolve of the Government to fight on. Normally reviled by the Tories as an irresponsible sectional interest Labour spoke for the nation in doing so, with the enthusiastic backing of imperialists like Leo Amery.

Britain had done everything to avoid war but when it came it was seen as a war for democracy, almost an international civil war in which the forces of progress of the last two hundred years were lined up against their nemesis.[1] Many socialists – George Orwell and Tom Wintringham, the founder of the Home Guard, among them – believed that the war had to become a people's war if fascism was to be defeated. While Orwell called for red militias, the Labour intellectual Richard Crossman looked forward to conscription breaking 'the parochial life of the working class', generating a social ferment and undermining the 'social oligarchy' which ran the country. They both expected the conflict to expose the deficiencies of 'the class-army' and give rise to the creation of a 'people's army'.[2] The knowledge that Britain's own ruling class was divided reinforced this view. Woolf advised Labour in September 1939 to advertise itself as an alternative Government until the 'men of Munich' were purged from their posts. The principal war aim, he believed, was the overthrow of Nazism and the emancipation of occupied Europe; but if Labour wished to go further it could pledge itself to root out the architects of Versailles, the enemies of the League, and the supporters of Hitler's 'bloodless victory', while making clear that it would buy no allies 'at the cost of national rights and social justice'.[3]

His advice that Labour should concentrate on the home front to mobilise productive resources for victory and achieve social justice anticipated the course of events, though the 'Guilty Men' remained in positions of power and influence even after the fall of France and the formation of Churchill's coalition Government in the summer of 1940. A denunciation of their malign influence, published in July 1940 by a group of Labour supporters, was a best-seller and went through forty re-printings in the next three years.[4] Popular hatred singled-out Chamberlain, Samuel Hoare and Sir John Simon for particular opprobrium because of their record of appeasement. But advocates of a deal with Hitler, such as Lord Halifax and R. A. Butler, continued to oppose Churchill from within the Government into 1941. In these circles there was still the conviction that Britain's primary national interest – the Empire – was best protected by leaving Hitler to get on with his European conquests. Hitler himself had frequently asserted that he had no quarrel with the British Empire and many on the left in British politics believed that Chamberlain had encouraged him to think that he had a 'free hand' in the East as long as his goal was a war against the Soviet Union.[5] Suspicion of the pro-fascist, anti-Soviet sentiments of the British ruling class had been fuelled by a wealth of circumstantial evidence, including the National Government's stance on Spain and Czechoslovakia, and the failure to bring Russia into an alliance with Britain and France. There was also the *Daily Mail*'s anti-semitism and pro-Hitler sympathies; the admiration expressed for Mussolini within the British political establishment; the royal family's dalliance with the Nazis – and so on. A typical socialist instance of this line of reasoning is provided by Crossman's observation that 'the consultations of representatives of the FBI with Nazi industrial leaders at Dusseldorf during the week of Hitler's occupation of Prague showed that British capitalism was prepared, on the economic side, to support the Nazis in their trade war, even where this meant violation of American interests'.[6] It was acknowledged by the left that Churchill had never believed that a deal with Hitler could be secured, but then Churchill only became Prime Minister on 10 May 1940 – when Labour refused to serve under Chamberlain, and Halifax, Chamberlain's choice as successor, turned down the job.

No one was more determined to preserve the British Empire than Churchill whose record in this department placed him on the diehard wing of Tory reaction in the 1930s. He was determined that the senior Labour figures in his Government would be kept well away from defence and foreign policy. Attlee and Greenwood were given non-departmental posts, Morrison became Minister of Supply, Dalton was sent to Economic Warfare and Bevin was made Minister of Labour. The Labour ministers accordingly took over the domestic front, much as Woolf advised them to do. Thus when the Government made foreign policy choices that were unpopular on the left it was often assumed that the Labour members of the Government privately disapproved and would have behaved differently if they had been able to take the relevant decisions instead of Churchill. Evidence for this view was scanty, though the high-profile mission to India led by Sir Stafford Cripps lent it some credence. In Parliament Nye Bevan, the strongest advocate in the House of the war as a social revolution that would politicise the people if it was fought against the Conservative Party as well as Hitler's Germany, was also the most effective critic of the way the war was actually conducted. As such he was a critic of the political truce and the subordination of Labour within the war Cabinet which gave Churchill control over the ideological struggle and jeopardised the future liberation of Europe and the colonies. *Tribune* gave voice to these perspectives, arguing for a second front, criticising Churchill's conduct of the war, opposing those domestic and overseas measures which strengthened the right, such as the deal with Admiral Darlan in Algeria in 1942 and the Allies' support for the monarchy in Italy after Mussolini's overthrow in July 1943.[7] 'Bevan saw the overthrow of fascism as the historic opportunity for a Europe-wide popular uprising against monarchism, clericalism and reaction of every sort, an opportunity which the British Tories and their American capitalist allies were determined to abort.'[8] This perspective rejected the post-war subjugation of Germany and put its faith in the tide of popular democracy sweeping across liberated Europe. Even Bevan and his supporters were alarmed by the evidence of Soviet *realpolitik* at the beginning of 1945 but they generally saw sense in a neutralised buffer zone in the East of the continent to appease Soviet fears and acknowledge the military realities. The danger of a Cold War was already apparent to Bevan and many other observers among left intellectuals in 1944, as was the futility of British Great Power pretensions in an age in which the USA and the USSR would be dominant. It would be better for Britain, in the view of some of them, to take the lead in creating 'an organic confederation' of West European states.[9] But British actions in Greece, which Ernest Bevin tried to justify at Labour's annual conference of 1944, embarrassed and outraged wide sections of the party and pointed to a different division of the continent.

Chamberlain's declaration of war on 3 September 1939 – like that of 4 August 1914 – automatically committed India to the conflict. Churchill thus inherited the problem of the non-cooperation of the Indian National Congress, which was demanding independence for India. Two offers of cooperation with the British, in September 1939 and the summer of 1940, had come to nothing because the Congress had demanded equality of status for India in return. Churchill, who explicitly excluded the British Empire from the rhetoric of the Atlantic Charter of August 1941, when he and Franklin Roosevelt talked of the 'right of all peoples to choose the form of government under which they will live', was unlikely to succeed where Chamberlain had failed. So when Japanese military advances imperilled India itself after the fall of Singapore in February 1942, he turned to Cripps, the recalled Ambassador to Moscow and pre-war leader of the Popular Front, expelled from the Labour Party for his pains as recently as January 1939. But whatever the public talk of Cripps as the friend of India, and the Tory perceptions of a lurch to the left in British policy, 'the agenda of his mission was ambiguous from the outset'.[10] Gandhi advised Cripps to take the next plane home and within ten days of his arrival Congress concluded that his proposal was not good enough. It amounted to no more than an 'Indianised' Executive Council, advisory to the Viceroy, with the prospect of further post-war constitutional change, too vague to satisfy Indian demands for independence.

A clearer colonial strategy emerged elsewhere in the Empire, drawing upon pre-war thinking and satisfying some of the demands for colonial development put forward by the Labour Party. It had to – the war generated the need for both material assistance from the colonies and devices that would legitimise colonialism. By mid-February 1942, and the fall of Singapore, Japan had taken Hong Kong, Malaysia, Burma and Indonesia, often with a show of local indifference to the defeat of the European imperialists, as in Malaya, sometimes to demonstrations of popular enthusiasm, as in parts of Indonesia. Its slogan of 'Asia for the Asians' undoubtedly struck a popular chord and even though Japanese atrocities in the occupied countries soon exposed its own imperialist face, the anti-imperialist theme of the war continued in the form of an anti-Japanese insurgency throughout Asia. On the Allied side the war was fought in the name of democracy and equality against racist and militarist dictatorships. It mobilised millions of Asians and Africans and raised expectations of self-determination. As during the First World War, Britain extended its occupation of the Middle East, leading to the forced removal of the governments of Egypt and Iraq. Iran was occupied by British and

Soviet troops to secure supply lines between the allies. British armies were also in Syria, Libya and Lebanon as well as old imperial strongholds such as Transjordan and Palestine.

The claim that Britain held its colonies in trusteeship for the native peoples, all the while developing their capacities for self-government, had always been the subject of much scorn and incredulity within the political elite of the USA, as well as sections of the British left. Britain's dependency on the USA from September 1939 and Roosevelt's particular influence, especially after the USA entered the war in December 1941, ensured that this scepticism became relevant to the conduct of British policy. Roosevelt engaged in an 'unceasing public and private campaign aimed at eliminating the European empires and setting the colonial world on the road toward independence'.[11] He toured the colonial world, holding talks with nationalist leaders; he lashed out at the British and French at presidential press conferences for obstructing independence; and damned particular instances of colonialism, such as British Gambia and French Indochina, for supplying 'the most horrible thing I have ever seen in my life . . . plain exploitation of those people'.[12] His alternative was a fully accountable system of international trusteeship and timetables for independence administered by a post-war international organisation. Roosevelt's enthusiasm for this scheme peaked in the winter of 1943–4 but 'the British . . . rejected the proposals outright. They objected in principle to international supervision and accountability for colonial administration.'[13] They responded by trying to prove the sincerity of their own scheme of trusteeship – the Colonial Development and Welfare Act of 1944 was one of the results of this effort. The idea of placing all colonies under an international trusteeship was never realised, in part because the US military objected to it as a threat to their own island bases in the Pacific. Roosevelt was already defeated on this issue by the time Labour's NEC became conscious of the 'bitter conflict going on between the naval imperialists and the internationalists in the American Government about the question of colonial trusteeship'.[14]

The Churchill coalition began to stress the urgency of colonial development. Of course this was not merely to appease foreign critics of Empire. The needs of war made development a practical necessity. The Empire contributed five million troops. Africa became particularly important for strategic and logistical reasons. One recent study observed that 'Almost everywhere the intense pressure for the colonies to produce more goods to meet war needs led to more and more imperial direction over colonial economies.'[15] The British demand for raw materials and foodstuffs in Africa was in many cases secured by coercion, including industrial conscription, as well as higher taxes and prices.[16] It enabled the white settlers of East Africa to promote themselves – in contrast to

African farmers – as representatives of economic efficiency, and be taken seriously. Inevitably they dominated the monopsonist marketing boards and mobilising committees in countries such as Kenya, securing bigger returns for themselves than African producers. Metropolitan companies – such as those which dominated the plantations (plantations which normally escaped the attention of the Labour Party) – generally acquired colonial cash crops cheaply and colonial administrations appropriated the difference between the price paid to the producer and the world market price. The surplus thus obtained was used to develop reserves that helped to finance the British war effort.[17] The living standards of colonial workers were squeezed by a variety of additional devices including production drives, shortages of imports, the controls exerted by both the metropolitan companies and the system of marketing boards created at British instigation, as well as higher taxes and higher import duties.

Some Labour critics of Empire had long believed that the benefits to the natives of British rule were negligible in terms of health, education and prosperity. In the 1920s Leonard Woolf, for example, observed that taxation of indigenous peoples generally exceeded expenditure on them, labour was often akin to slavery, the best land was taken by whites, and so on. He saw that Europe imposed its will upon Asians and Africans in these and other respects. Yet until the mid-1920s, along with many others, he thought the mandates system offered the best hope for progressive change, even though the system had been denounced as a sham from the beginning by his own party. He finally came to the conclusion that trusteeship was indeed phoney because Westerners had no real belief or desire for it.[18] The League of Nations was never empowered so that it acquired the capacity to revoke a mandate, award one, or inspect its responsible discharge. In 1926 Woolf pointed out that very little had been spent on native education and in many cases Europeans had 'deliberately kept the natives uneducated and ignorant . . . In Nigeria the revenue for 1923–4 was £6,260,561, the expenditure on education was £135,866 [that is 2.7 per cent].' In Kenya it was about 2.44 per cent.[19] There were plenty of other examples he could have drawn upon. Of the £1 million earned by Kenyans in registered employment in the years 1920–3, taxes took £750,000.[20] Wages were, of course, remarkably low to begin with; four pence to one shilling per day in the iron mines of Sierra Leone; one shilling per day for a Nigerian coal miner; similar rates of pay in the mines of Northern Rhodesia, the Gold Coast, and South Africa.[21] Alongside the neglect of education and health and the exploitation of the local people, the system of indirect rule normally relied upon local reactionary elites – princes, sheikhs, emirs, chieftains and the like – which did their best to defend feudal and pre-feudal social relations. British colonial administrations generally excluded local peoples from all but the humblest positions. Next to nothing was done, as Woolf observed in the 1940s, to prepare the natives for self-rule. In Kenya, for example, as late as the mid-1940s, 2 Europeans out of the 18 members of the Legislative Council were supposed to represent African interests. In short, though the long-term goal was supposed to be independence, little was being done to prepare the African colonies to cope with such a future.

The world economic crisis of the 1930s made an already feeble return on decades of British rule even worse. Commodity prices collapsed catastrophically – by 70 per cent on the principal cash crops of East Africa, for example, in the years 1929–32. The terms of trade also turned against African producers as the cost of imported manufactures rose. Unemployment also hit Africans in colonial administration. Servicing debt absorbed a growing proportion of state revenues. Tax collections on Africans were intensified. In Kenya in 1931, for example, Europeans paid a total of £42,596, while Africans paid £530,877.[22] Yet expenditure on economic development and social welfare programmes – never more than a few shillings per head of the population in Africa – was cut back.[23] This was an unsatisfactory record which provided critics of Empire – from Moscow to Washington – with plenty of polemical ammunition. There was also the embarrassing fact that the racism practised routinely in many of the British colonies bore a family resemblance to the doctrines of the Nazi regime in Germany, while expansionary imperialist powers like Japan and Italy stressed their own high moral purpose and cultural mission, much as the British had done. Discontent in British colonies, though nothing new, exploded on America's doorstep in the 1930s when a series of labour revolts began in British Honduras and Trinidad in 1934 and spread to British Guiana, St Vincent, St Lucia and St Kitts. By 1938 Jamaica was experiencing sustained unrest, fomented by 'so-called labour leaders',[24] and a royal commission under Lord Moyne was appointed to investigate the causes. Its report of 1939 showed that wages in the countryside were little higher than they had been at the end of slavery. It revealed the verminous, insanitary, overcrowded conditions of the towns; the 'chronic sickness' that was 'common' among the people; the shocking lack of health and educational facilities.[25] The war made this situation even worse, causing food shortages throughout the Caribbean, disrupting trade and generating unemployment. Riots and looting continued, as the NEC was informed at the end of 1942.[26] The Moyne Report was withheld from publication until 1945. But leading figures in the Labour Party knew all about it.

One of its authors was the General Secretary of the TUC, Walter Citrine, an influential voice in the policy-making bodies of the party. We saw in the last chapter that Citrine enjoyed an unofficial advisory role to the National Government on occasions when it had to manage awkward elements in the TUC and the labour movement. Konni Zilliacus, an expert on international affairs working for the League in Geneva, suspected there was more to it than this. He told Philip Noel-Baker in September 1936, 'I've known for some time that Citrine and Gillies were in the pockets of the FO [Foreign Office] and that Hugh [Dalton] was moving in the same direction.'[27] He was thinking about Labour's policy on Spain but his judgement could also apply to aspects of colonial policy. The TUC General Council acknowledged in 1938 that it had set up a Colonial Advisory Committee in December 1937 in response to British Government concerns about the West Indian disturbances. Citrine was joined on this panel by Labour experts on colonial issues such as Arthur Creech Jones. Its main brief was concerned with how best to establish proper unions in the Caribbean.[28] This was an exercise which involved marginalising, if not eliminating, 'unofficial' or spontaneous industrial militancy and its tendency to provide a platform for dangerous nationalists and revolutionaries. Citrine approached the Colonial Office in 1938 formally offering such assistance on a regularised basis.[29] The TUC took the initiative in conferring 'associate' status on colonial unions which met its narrow criteria of *bona fide* trade unionism. Its model rules discouraged grassroots activity and promoted a 'constitutional' and 'responsible' approach. Nye Bevan was unusual among Labour MPs in objecting to these developments, telling the House of Commons in February 1938 that something like a 'National Labour Front' was being proposed for the West Indies, redolent of its National Socialist original.[30] In fact it was in keeping with the TUC's long-standing discouragement of any trade union activities within the British Empire which provided a channel of influence for the Communist Party, notably in relation to India.[31] The TUC made the same assumptions as the Colonial Office about what was 'constitutional' and 'responsible' and from the summer of 1940 the latter enlisted its support in a sustained collaboration which eventually abetted the suppression of radical unions in Sierra Leone, Malaya and Kenya. In 1942 the Colonial Office set up a Colonial Labour Advisory Committee, with TUC participation, to oversee this work which became increasingly important as the war generated conditions in which irresponsible trade unionism spread across Africa. There is little doubt that the TUC wanted to advance the rights of colonial workers; it had long been recognised in British Labour circles, for example, that there was a self-interest in doing so as cheap colonial labour could undermine the rights of British workers. But it is equally clear that the TUC wanted to do nothing that would undermine British colonialism, especially avoiding anything that might foster militant nationalism. It thus acted as an agent of the British state in good conscience and continued to do so after the war and well into the 1950s, when Communism joined nationalism as the twin bugbears of colonial trade unionism.[32]

Meanwhile the refusal of the Indian National Congress to support the war effort, signalled initially by the resignation of the provincial ministries in October 1939, paved the way for the Quit India campaign which Gandhi launched in August 1942 in response to the failure of the Cripps Mission. By the end of 1942 serious disorder had been answered by tens of thousands of arrests in conditions of near martial law. As chair of the Cabinet Committee on India, Attlee had played a part in prompting the Cripps Mission, by devising a scheme for constitutional reform designed to find a way out of the mess. Its failure, and the subsequent escalation of disorder, probably inspired his proposal of September 1942 – echoing Labour discussions of the late 1930s – for future international control and administration of the colonies, much as the Americans wanted.[33] Yet Attlee was at best inconsistent about such matters. If Amery can be believed, the Secretary of State for India received no support from Attlee in Cabinet when he clashed with Churchill in July 1940 for suggesting an offer of Dominion status to India.[34] The subsequent failure of the Cripps Mission seems to have led Attlee to draw pessimistic conclusions about the capacity of Indians for self-rule and he fully supported the policy of repression from August 1942. The war emergency may explain that stance but is less convincing as an explanation for Attlee's concern – shared with Sir Anthony Eden, Viscount Cranborne and Oliver Stanley – that the War Cabinet should do something to correct the 'misguided' American view, in the words of the protestors, that 'there is something archaic in the conception of the British Colonial Empire'. In the same month, December 1942, Arthur Creech Jones also rallied to the defence of British colonial policy in response to American criticism at the 8th Conference of the Institute of Pacific Relations at Mont Tremblant in Canada. Attlee's future Colonial Secretary found himself in alliance with Lord Hailey in defending colonial development as a policy which fulfilled the objectives of Roosevelt's internationally policed trusteeships, without necessitating constitutional reform or timetabled steps to colonial independence. The Armistice and Post-war Committee, which Attlee chaired, closed ranks against the Americans precisely over this issue.[35]

Lord Hailey was the leading colonial expert within the British political establishment, the Lord Lugard of his day. In a very influential report of 1942 he argued that nationalism – which had spread across Asia and the Middle East in the first half of the twentieth century – could be anticipated in Africa, unless the metropolitan power managed to harness the energies of the educated minority.[36] The best chance of doing that, he reasoned, was for Britain to promote colonial economic and social development and involve Africans in public administration at a local level.[37]No doubt the favourable reception which was given to these thoughts within Whitehall owed much to the exigencies of war and the legacies of the Great Depression. The economic development of Africa would answer all these needs. War also brought reformers into Whitehall such as Arthur Creech Jones and Rita Hinden of the Fabian Colonial Bureau. It transformed the political fortunes of the Labour Party by creating the conditions for its landslide victory in the general election of 1945, which produced the first majority Labour Government and enabled Creech Jones and Hinden to influence post-war colonial policy. When Creech Jones addressed a meeting of the Fabian Colonial Bureau in December 1946 he did so to show how Labour had made a difference in this field. It was an impressive speech and yet 'virtually every innovation there mentioned could be shown to have originated in the Colonial Office under the wartime coalition'.[38] The Labour reformers had contributed to a new colonial consensus, if they had not been coopted by it.

The real impact of these policies was not necessarily what their authors wanted. The politically active Africans were very much aware of American and Soviet criticisms of imperialism. Nationalism was given impetus by such pronouncements as the Atlantic Charter.[39] Economic turmoil, however, did at least as much to arouse opposition to British rule, by undermining the local conservatives on which it normally relied. Trade unions and political associations multiplied, as did strikes and 'disturbances'. The literate elite was able to merge its nationalist aspirations with the discontents of the rural and urban poor for the first time. This is the main reason why the flurry of constitutional reform in Africa in the 1940s, under a Labour Government, failed to keep pace with the growth in local expectations. The war led to a more obtrusive British presence. The same was true, again for military as well as economic purposes, in the Middle East where there was a widening cultural gap between the population and the British-sponsored rulers in countries such as Iraq.[40] India's mobilisation for war also stirred discontent, as we have seen, and reinforced the old need for local collaborators. The Muslim League's claim to speak on behalf of the subcontinent's largest religious minority was taken seriously in this context and its demand for Pakistan was formulated and promoted under these circumstances. Among many other changes making for popular discontent in India, the war led to state control of grain marketing, food rationing and price controls in a context of general inflation caused by shortages and hoarding. The Bengal famine of 1943–4, in which three million people died, was blamed on the British, though military censorship did its best to deny that the problem even existed.[41] Labour was the legatee of these and other discontents in 1945.

It was of little surprise that the USA was determined to prise open the British Empire system which it perceived as a closed trading bloc detrimental to the American economy. MacDonald's pre-war efforts to cultivate the Anglo-American relationship had broken down during the world economic crisis when both countries resorted to intensified protectionism. While British recovery led to greater reliance on the Empire and the sterling bloc, the Americans sought recovery by an expansion of trade, from the mid-1930s, which the British system of imperial preference obstructed. Economic rivalry thus intensified in the 1930s. In the first two years of the war isolationist sentiment was strong in the USA, as was the perception that a discredited imperialism continued to inform British policy. The 'cash and carry' legislation which amended the Neutrality Acts only allowed the British to buy weapons from America with gold, securities and the sale of companies. But until the defeat of the French in May 1940 there was no urgency in Washington to support the British war effort unless something could be had in return. In this spirit Roosevelt allowed Britain to take old destroyers in return for rights to naval bases in the Caribbean and Newfoundland. The system of lend-lease was announced in December, though it only became law in March 1941. From the beginning the US was concerned to ensure that lend-leased goods could not assist British exports, particularly in South America, and US companies seized the opportunity this provided to encroach on British markets in places such as Argentina.

Britain's military plight in the summer of 1940 – and the realisation that US interests were imperilled by the Nazi victories on the European continent–swung the mood in America against isolationism and allowed Roosevelt to go beyond active neutrality. American entry into the war had to wait until the Japanese attack on Pearl Harbor in December 1941, however, by which time the British Empire in the Far East was on its last legs. Throughout their involvement in the war, as we have seen, the US leadership kept up pressure against the European Empires which it saw as corrupt and inefficient (as in South East Asia) and damaging to the war effort (as in India). Some members of the British Government, such as Eden and Amery, forecast that the US would emerge as the new world power based on an empire of money and trade. Its foreign economic policy was clearly informed by a commitment to end the system of imperial preference, break the sterling area, and refashion the global economy along free trade lines, with the dollar as the master currency. It was based on the belief that American prosperity depended on an open world economy. The sterling area and imperial preference were necessarily defined as obstacles to the creation of such an open system. The British nevertheless planned for the restoration or reconquest of the 'lost' Asian colonies, while committing themselves – Labour and Tory alike – to an indefinite perspective of their future self-government. This determination was a constant for the duration of the war and extended to the colonial empires of France, Belgium and Holland, in recognition of the need for imperial solidarity in the face of US and Soviet pressures for decolonisation and a common front against the nationalism sweeping the colonial world.[42]

As Britain's exports fell after 1939 members of the sterling area began to accumulate sterling balances in London which represented their export surpluses to Britain and the cost of local military expenditures, all of which were paid for with British IOUs. They were also required to deposit their dollar earnings in London in a 'pool' from which they could make withdrawals to pay for a very restricted range of essential military imports from the USA. British dependencies such as the Gold Coast had no choice under these arrangements but to accept that their sterling balances and dollar earnings were effectively frozen for the duration of the war. Neutral countries were brought into this scheme in so far as their export earnings with Britain could only be spent within the sterling area. US policy-makers saw these discriminatory arrangements as prejudicial to the American economy. Article VII of the lend-lease agreement, which the British signed in February 1941, was intended to force Britain to abandon these arrangements as soon as the war was over. It committed both countries to reduce tariffs and eliminate trade discrimination. British policy-makers, however, envisaged the need for continuation of such practices in the context of an anticipated post-war trade imbalance of disastrous proportions. US export dominance would be as dramatic as Britain's trade deficit. Britain would need its empire as never before if it was ever to recover its economic independence. British policy also sought to preserve London as an international financial centre and this was thought dependent on the maintenance of the sterling area. Both requirements assumed that Britain would remain a world power based on empire. The USA meanwhile managed lend-lease so as to prevent Britain from building up its reserves, even though Britain's debts to the sterling area increased.

The war provided the USA with an opportunity to refashion the international order, while it inevitably exposed economic weaknesses in Britain's position. The Cabinet was warned of Britain's near-exhausted gold reserves as early as 8 September 1939. It was American aid that enabled Britain to continue the struggle against Germany. Britain acquired virtually everything it needed – from dried milk to tanks and machine tools – from America. The abrupt suspension of this economic aid within six days of the Japanese surrender was a sharp reminder of Britain's economic dependency and the real terms of the special relationship. Though American demands were spelt out in Article VII of the lend-lease agreement as 'the elimination of all forms of discrim-inatory treatment in international commerce', considerable friction between the two countries continued to turn on the question of the British Empire's future economic foundation. As the world's biggest trading area, the sterling bloc would have to be reformed if the USA was to realise its own post-war ambitions for an open world economy. This issue kept reappearing in Anglo-American discussions – such as at Bretton Woods in July 1944, where an attempt was made to fashion a multilateral system of payments based on the gold–dollar standard and the operation of such institutions as the International Monetary Fund and World Bank. Of course, the Labour Party was a long-standing supporter of free trade and had criticised the Ottawa Agreements of 1932 from the beginning. But the Labour members of the Cabinet were also well aware of Anglo-American friction on this issue everywhere from Latin America to the Middle East.[43] In practical terms it involved US encroachments on British markets in South America and conflict over oil concessions in Arabia and Iran (where the British and French had controlled things since the San Remo agreement of 1920). Knowledge of this rivalry, sensitivity to Britain's weakened position, and the belief that an independent Great Power role could only be secured on the basis of Empire and renewed economic strength – all these factors inclined Bevin after 1945 to seek ways of reorganising the colonies to make them more economically efficient. Behind the rhetoric of free trade the British continued to hang on to imperial protection well into the 1950s and the Labour Party itself continued to believe in a planned Commonwealth trade as the basis for British prosperity up to the 1964 general election.

These issues of foreign economic policy, entangled though they were with political issues involving Anglo-American relations and the British imperial system, elicited no distinctive party positions. Rather, they were treated as technical issues and matters of national interest. Hugh Dalton, as President of the Board of Trade and a member of the Committee on External Economic Policy, was obviously informed about such matters, and so were the Labour members of the War Cabinet. When divisions in the Cabinet arose Bevin lined up with Conservative opponents of the Article VII agenda to defend imperial preference and British agriculture – a position which enjoyed 'widespread Labour support'.[44] When the scheme for an International Monetary Fund was debated in the House of Commons there was a similar coalition of opponents. Though the reasons given varied between defence of imperial preference and the needs of socialist planning, the resistance was largely tokenistic because all shades of opinion understood the reality of Britain's financial dependency on the US. Yet Labour was just as convinced as the Conservative Party that post-war economic recovery was incompatible with the US agenda of sterling convertibility, the destruction of the sterling area and the abolition of imperial preference. By the time the first majority Labour Government was formed in July 1945 Britain had accumulated a debt of over £3,000 million to other members of the sterling area, largely by virtue of awarding itself credit against wartime expenditures in places like India, but also because it retained the value of export surpluses made by its colonies. In this way India was transformed into Britain's single largest sterling creditor with assets of £1,300 million, though Parliament and the British people were kept in the dark about it until the debt had been amassed.[45] Some £1,200 million was owed to other Commonwealth countries, while Egypt (£400 million) and Iraq (£70 million) accounted for most of the rest. When these sums are set beside the unquantified value of colonial labour brought into the war effort, the five million colonial troops, the rigged prices for colonial produce, the tax increases and other deprivations suffered by local peoples it is clear that the colonial contribution to the British war effort, some of it involuntary, was considerable. Labour's policy, on coming to office in 1945, was to permit the £454 million debt owed to various Crown Colonies, such as the Gold Coast, to rise. By 1951 this debt stood at £928 million as Britain continued with the policy of issuing IOUs to dependencies, such as Malaya, in return for the dollars which they earned from key exports such as rubber, tin and (in Gold Coast's case) cocoa. In this way the cost of British reconstruction was partly borne by others, though this was only rarely observed at the time.[46]

In Iran the Anglo-American rivalry and US encroachment succeeded in discrediting the compliant government of Mohammed Saed, which faced growing opposition from both nationalists and Communists. When the Soviet Union entered its own claim for oil concessions in the five northern provinces of Iran in September 1944, where local Communist forces had grown during the war, Iranian political instability became an issue of the incipient Cold War. Some voices within US policy-making began to see that 'the continuance of the British Empire in reasonable strength is in the strategic interests of the United States'.[47] But this was by no means a settled policy in December 1944; it would take another two years or so before American foreign policy made isolation of the Soviet Union and international Communism the overriding consideration of its design. Even in Britain the Chiefs of Staff conclusion that the Soviet Union represented the main threat to post-war Britain did not command unqualified support and it was advised that their planning should only be spoken about in the most guarded manner – a measure that would not have prevented the Soviet leaders from finding out about them, however, given the prominence of their spies in the British and American political systems. But the British, with an empire to defend, were constantly worried about developments that might disrupt it, and so were rather ahead of the Americans in worrying about the spread of Communism. Aid to the left-wing partisans of Greece, for example, was terminated in 1943 because of fears of the growth of the Communists within the National Liberation Front (EAM) and its army (ELAS). A friendly post-war Greece was considered vital to imperial communications in the eastern Mediterranean and a post-war Communist government in Athens would jeopardise them.

A Cold War policy was thus emerging well before the war ended. The Allied decision to install Marshal Badoglio and King Vittorio Emmanuel III as heads of Government in the Italian south in September 1943, after the fall of Mussolini, was clearly intended to exclude the powerful Italian left as far as possible from any exercise of power. But Stalin did not object to such arrangements. Indeed a year later, at Moscow in December 1944, he entered into an agreement with Churchill – which the absent Roosevelt endorsed by telegram – that he would confine himself to his own sphere of influence in Eastern Europe where the presence of the Red Army was in any case decisive, and allow Britain a similar freedom in Western Europe.[48] This Moscow deal, which Churchill was ready to renege on just four months later,[49] also gave the Soviets unrestricted access to the Mediterranean from the Black Sea, thus necessitating deletion of the Montreaux Convention giving Turkey the right to keep the straits closed. An apparent deal had also been struck over Poland – certainly one that no Polish leader in London would have agreed to – permitting the forced removal of Poles to fit the revised frontiers which Stalin demanded. The first the Labour Party would have discovered about these agreements was the British decision to invade Greece at the end of 1944 when it became apparent that the British army was backing monarchists and fascist collaborators to keep the left from power and doing so with Stalin's silent approval.

The Greek civil war was still in its early stages, however, when Churchill began to back away from the idea of treating the Soviet Union as an equal. The British Government took it for granted that it could act anywhere it liked around the world to secure British imperial interests – an example was the decision to restore French control in Indochina, another – better publicised at the time – was the British intervention in Indonesia on behalf of the Dutch.[50] But the Soviet Union in Eastern Europe and the Mediterranean, let alone the Middle East and Africa, was anathema. When the Big Three met at Yalta in February 1945 they were still preparing to rule the world in partnership. But behind the scenes the British were preparing for confrontation. Five months after Yalta, Sir Orme Sargent, soon to become Permanent Under Secretary at the Foreign Office, had prepared a lengthy briefing paper, 'Stocktaking After

VE Day', in July 1945, just as Labour prepared to take office. The discarding of left-wing wartime allies was far advanced in this thinking. Ernest Bevin, the new Foreign Secretary, would have learned from Sargent's paper that if Britain wanted to remain a great power it had to act like one and that meant: 'we must take the offensive in challenging Communist penetration in as many of the Eastern countries of Europe as possible'.[51] The direction of policy in the later stages of the war thus ensured that foreign affairs would remain at least as contentious within the Labour Party when the war ended as they had been before it began. The collision course with the Soviet Union and the emergence of an Anglo-American alliance would both be deeply unpopular with large sections of the party. Successive waves of disillusionment with the Soviet regime, generated by the Moscow Trials, the Hitler–Stalin pact, and the Soviet winter war against Finland, never completely cured the Labour left of its conviction that the October Revolution had made fundamental and permanent strides of progress which the Stalin regime defended in its own clumsy, brutal, contradictory way.[52] With the entry of the Soviet Union into the war on 22 June 1941 the regime became Britain's only major ally and pro-Soviet sentiment was officially endorsed. The Soviet regime was popularly supported in Britain for the first time in its history and though the authorities tried, they failed to persuade people that Red Army successes had nothing to do with the Soviet social system. At the peak of this pro-Sovietism in January 1942 a public opinion poll found 86 per cent of respondents wanted to see Anglo-Soviet cooperation when the war was over.[53] This mood, sweeping all before it, brought demands for a new trade union international which led the TUC into talks with the Soviet 'unions' and other left-wing organisations such as the American CIO. Together they established a World Federation of Trade Unions (WFTU) in October 1945. It was one of many symptoms of the global shift to the left generated by the war, but also of the USSR's intention to prolong the wartime alliance.

The spokesmen of the socialist left – Laski, Cole, Bevan, Brockway, Emrys Hughes, Kingsley Martin, Konni Zilliacus and many others – continued to see the Soviet Union as an ally as the war drew to a close. The Americans were viewed with rising suspicion in the same quarters.[54] The editorials of the *New Statesman* and *Tribune* concurred with these biases, as did *The Times* under E. H. Carr's direction. In 1941 Cole had already warned that British capitalism would seek to save itself after the war by forming 'the closest possible links' with the USA. This had to be resisted and the best way of doing that was through cooperation with the USSR, 'necessarily the principal rallying point for the forces of Socialism throughout the world'.[55] This argument was given a sophisticated gloss by acknowledgement that Soviet socialism had shown a 'terrible disregard of suffering', had persecuted dissent as treason, had inspired Hitler and the Gestapo, had turned Marxism into a fossilised dogma and so on. Its advocates were dispassionate scientists, or so they thought, not apologists like the Communists, and were ready to admit the manifold failings of Bolshevism – but only to insist on the deeper, stronger, objective forces of progress which the planned, state-owned economy had unleashed and which, in due course, would democratise and humanise the system. When allowance was made for the barbaric elements of the Soviet experiment the solemn truth remained, according to Harold Laski, the celebrated Professor of Government and expert on the American constitution who sat on Labour's NEC, writing in 1944, 'that in the Soviet Union since the October Revolution more men and women have had the opportunity of self-fulfilment than anywhere else in the world'.[56] As for Soviet foreign policy intentions the *New Statesman* and *Tribune* were agreed in the same year that Stalin's plan was to secure friendly buffer zones on his western borders and that to achieve this aim he needed Popular Front governments in those countries 'capable of entering into economic and political arrangements with their neighbours'. All of this was 'quite natural and inevitable' according to Nye Bevan; 'that is the price we have to pay for the bitter recent past'.[57]

In April 1944 Labour's NEC formally approved Dalton's *The International Post-War Settlement* which he had been working on since the late summer of 1943. During 1942 the NEC had denounced German atrocities against Poles, Czechs and Jews. Awareness of 'frightful massacres, tortures and brutalities' only increased thereafter as did the knowledge that they had occurred 'on even a vaster scale against the Russians' (evidence was also to hand that the Russians themselves were implicated in barbarous acts).[58] These facts raised the question of German responsibility for war crimes, as well as empathy for those demanding revenge and harbouring feelings of hatred. 'Many millions of Germans' and not just Party members were 'directly responsible', Dalton wrote, including those in the regular armed forces. Laski and William Gillies, head of Labour's International Department, exchanged views on the nature of this responsibility with the former rejecting a theory of responsibility of the German people as a whole. Dictatorship nullified any talk of the responsibility and obligations of the German people, according to Laski. Attlee had argued much the same in November 1939. But Gillies pointed out that the NEC had declared on 22 July 1942 that 'the organised and bestial atrocities committed by Germany' cast dishonour upon the nation which had acquiesced in them. Other statements had acknowledged the 'conquest of the mind' entailed by the Nazi regime and the prevalence of the mentality necessary for efficient prosecution of 'total war'. To make 'capitalism' responsible, as Laski did, was to empty responsibility of all concrete meaning according to Gillies.[59] In the final draft, however, it was agreed that little was to be gained by debating how many Germans were responsible for war crimes, though 'certainly many millions'. A series of long judicial trials of war criminals should be avoided, Dalton thought, but the idea of returning Gestapo and SS units to the scenes of their crimes in Russia, as suggested at the Moscow Conference, was to be welcome, as was (he privately thought) the summary execution of war criminals in liberated Europe.

All were agreed that the best post-war option was 'a straight-out Anglo-American–Russian alliance' as the hard core of a world organisation. Roosevelt thought much the same, but included China among the world's policemen. There would be no pacifism this time. Britain would be one of the three Great Powers, in Labour's view, 'great both in military and industrial resources of all kinds', on the basis of the Commonwealth, perhaps arming the latter with 'permanent consultative machinery on external policy'. There was no mention of international trusteeship but the usual commitment to colonial development and native welfare was given emphasis and India was to be free to decide its own form of government inside or outside the Commonwealth. There must be 'total disarmament of the defeated states', payment of reparations in kind involving German labour corps, as well as appropriations of fixed capital and raw materials. The Germans would also have to contribute to the financing of such armed forces as were deemed necessary to police the peace. Their economy would have to be subject to 'some form of international control ... at least for a period of years'. A repetition of the inter-war minorities problem would be avoided by transfer of populations to the appropriate home state and discouragement of all agitations for frontier revision.

On the question of Palestine Dalton recorded that most of the International Sub-Committee were 'quite prepared for the transfer of population' to permit the establishment of a Jewish state. Jewish immigration should be allowed so that the Jews became the majority, while the Arabs would be encouraged to move out of Palestine, with appropriate compensation.[60] Dalton thought that the Arabs had plenty of land elsewhere and argued that there was a strong case for a Jewish Palestine extending its boundaries into Egypt or Transjordan, with something to be said for 'throwing open Libya or Eritrea to Jewish settlement as satellites or colonies to Palestine. In any case we must seek to remove Russian dislike of the Palestine experiment and encourage American interest in it and support for it.'[61] Labour's apparent unanimity on the establishment of a Jewish state in Palestine was rooted in views that had set hard in the 1930s. The old Wilsonian idea of self-determination had originally legitimated the call for a Jewish homeland in Palestine in 1919. Though this idea was written into the Palestine mandate, which Britain operated after the dismemberment of the Ottoman Empire, little thought was given to it until the 1930s. Until then the idea of native paramountcy held sway and this directed attention to the Arabs, whose hostility to Zionist settlements was expressed in riots in 1920 and 1921. Sidney Webb's 1930 White Paper on Palestine acknowledged such opposition by proposing restrictions on Jewish land purchases and immigration. After the abandonment of the White Paper, in the face of domestic and international opposition, an orthodoxy was established within the Labour Party which asserted the unity of Arab and Jewish working-class interests under a (Jewish) socialist leadership.[62] Labour thus opposed the first suggestion to partition Palestine when this was put by the Peel Report in 1937. Despite the sustained Arab rebellion of 1937–9 few Labour figures recognised the existence of national sentiment among the Palestinian Arabs, while Jewish national sentiment was more often depicted in terms of the advance of working-class politics through the Jewish trade unions and socialist party, despite the exclusively Jewish composition of Histradut. This pro-Zionist stance was strengthened when Jewish flight from Nazi Germany became an issue after January 1933 – and somewhere other than Britain had to be found to take the refugees. When Labour entered the war coalition it was forced to support Churchill's restrictions on Jewish emigration to Palestine but its leaders made clear that Nazi persecution of the Jews had only strengthened their support for the Zionist project. Dalton's blithe remarks about the Arabs in Palestine were thus representative, rather than personal, biases informed by this old Labour discourse. But if he was casual in his advocacy of the removal of Palestinian Arabs, it should also be remembered that the context was one in which the forced removal of millions of people in Europe seemed inevitable and even a lesser evil, when compared with the old minorities problem of the inter-war years. If Palestine was to become some sort of settler colony, this was also a moment when the settler colonies in East and Southern Africa were enjoying official approval.

There was nothing in Dalton's vision of the post-war world to suggest that Labour would undertake a major rethink of Britain's overseas role. Inside the coalition government Attlee appears to have been alone in questioning Britain's ability 'to police the seas of the world for the benefit of others', as he put it as chairman of the Suez Canal Committee on 20 March 1945. He was answered by Eden on that occasion who described the preservation of Britain's position in the Middle East as 'a matter of life and death to the British Empire'. By the summer Attlee questioned this occupation as a redundant survival of an age when power depended on mastery of the seas rather than, as now, the air. It was an argument he would continue to make until he was finally silenced in 1947. But while he had supporters like Dalton and Cripps who questioned the costs involved in the world role, Attlee did not rally support for his arguments either in the party or in the Cabinet which he formed in July 1945. He was very much an isolated voice among those involved in foreign policy from whose circles most of his Labour colleagues were excluded, even after he himself became Prime Minister.[63]

At Yalta in February 1945 the Big Three discussed the formation of a world organisation (the UN) in which, with China (and even France), they would exercise the dominant role. Germany would be divided into four occupation zones and purged of Nazism. Free elections would be called at the 'earliest possible' time in the occupied territories. Stalin was adamant that for Poland the Committee of National Liberation, made up of Communists and based in Lublin, would form the provisional government – not the London Poles supported by Churchill. The Western Allies appeared to acquiesce in this arrangement, if only in deference to the fact that the Red Army occupied Eastern Europe. But this disguised the fact that the British were already worried by the expansion of Soviet power in Eastern Europe and under Churchill's leadership looked to an Anglo-American partnership as the only way to counter this problem and maintain Britain's world role by steering the US 'for purposes which we regard as good'.[64] Roosevelt was wary of Churchill's motives and was not prepared for a confrontation with Stalin over the future of Poland. But Roosevelt died in April. His successor, Harry Truman, appeared to support the old policy when he recognised the Polish Communist government formed on 5 July 1945, shortly before the Potsdam conference met to decide the fate of post-war Germany. The Yalta deal by which 40,000 square miles of German territory, with a pre-war population of nine million, was incorporated into Poland was also confirmed at Potsdam. All told almost 12 million Germans or people of German descent were expelled from Eastern Europe. The Allies agreed that Germany would not be dismembered but also that the occupiers would be able to take reparations from their own zones and construct new institutions to replace the Nazi political system. In the event the Russians proceeded to loot their zone, further alienating a population that had suffered mass rapes at the hands of the Red Army.

There *was* an expansionary imperialism, as the war drew to a close, but virtually the whole of the British left seemed to think that the culprit was the USA, not the Soviet Union. Michael Foot saw Wall Street as the symbol of an 'arrogant, self-confident, merciless, capitalism'; *Reynolds News* believed President Truman had made 'clear beyond any shadow of a doubt that the men who rule America are determined to go to any length to stop the development of Socialism and to open up the world as a vast colonial area for American capitalism'. By 1945 the USA had virtually doubled the size of its economy in the course of the war, while, as the first meeting of the United Nations Organisation in San Francisco was informed, the Soviet Union was a picture of devastation with 70 per cent of its industrial installations demolished and 1,700 cities and towns virtually razed to the ground, an estimated 20 million dead, 25 million homeless, the survivors afflicted by widespread famine and homelessness.[65] By the late summer of 1945 US and British troops occupied much of Western Europe and the Middle East, Japan, South and South East Asia and much of the Pacific. Africa and Latin America also fell within their spheres of influence and economic domination. The British left found it hard to believe that it was the Soviet Union that was bent on world domination. After only twelve months of peace Laski was able to point to the character of Anglo-American interference in Greece, Italy, Iran, and Turkey, together with American policies in China and Japan, for evidence in support of the idea that the main problem was American imperialism.[66]

6   Great Power strategies

Labour came to power with a majority of 148 seats in July 1945 at a time of great economic and political uncertainty. The war had cost Britain about one-quarter of its national wealth and left it with huge overseas debts and a massive imbalance of trade. There was no sign of a peace treaty. Britain had been massively weakened by war and relations with both of its major allies were under considerable strain. In ideological terms neither the USA nor the Soviet Union had much reason to look kindly on a social democratic Britain and its overseas interests. More important than ideology were conflicts of interest between Britain and both military superpowers. If there was one element of continuity in the situation from the British standpoint it was the conviction that Britain was and must remain a world power based upon its Empire–Commonwealth. None of the Labour ministers publicly dissented from this conviction, though Attlee continued to express reservations about it in private. The Foreign Office, in common with the Chiefs of Staff and the Foreign Secretary, proved immune both to doubts about Britain's ability to pay for the world role and any analysis suggesting that it should be fundamentally rethought in the context of new realities such as the emergence of the two military superpowers and the spread of nationalism in Asia and Africa. The old imperialist consciousness held sway. This geopolitical commitment underlined the British need for a balance of power in Europe, a balance which the defeat of Germany and the expansion of the Soviet Union had upset. Britain's central problem was its inability to provide that balance either alone or in conjunction with other West European states. Its other major problem was the problem of managing the Empire–Commonwealth and the great sterling area trading bloc which overlapped with it. In the Middle East, Asia and Western Europe the greatest threat to these interests was identified as the Soviet Union, rather than a further expansion of leftist and nationalist movements with perhaps only a tenuous connection to it.[1] The only solution for all these problems was to enlist the assistance of the USA, the greatest power in the world and the only one to have emerged from the war stronger in all respects than when it went into it. Bevin's first speech to the House on foreign policy on 20 August 1945, by reflecting these assumptions, provoked a message of thanks from Lord Halifax, noting the essential continuity of policy which the statement implied.[2]

Yet all the economic indicators at the end of the war and all sober prognoses of the immediate future were grim reading for Britain. The sudden cancellation of lend-lease, just days after the defeat of Japan, was a sharp reminder that US support could not be taken for granted. While Labour ministers thought in terms of a gift or, at worst, an interest free loan, Truman's administration expected that any aid to Britain would be conditional on elimination of the sterling area dollar pool, elimination or substantial reduction of imperial preference and cancellation of the sterling balances.[3] Attlee called an emergency meeting on 23 August to decide what to do about the 'financial Dunkirk' which Keynes foresaw. It was already clear to Bevin and Dalton before the British negotiators departed for Washington that a loan (of $5 billion) would be conditional on ratification of the Bretton Woods agreement and acceptance of American commercial policy.[4] London was also disadvantaged by the fact that a socialist government could not expect to arouse the empathy of Congress. Furthermore US politicians were not yet alarmed enough by the Soviet Union and international Communism to downgrade their objections to British imperialism. Bevin was one of the few who confidently expected that this would change in time and that, in the meantime, Britain should make do with a smaller American loan than the one envisaged. Britain should sign up for Bretton Woods, in this view, but otherwise wait for the Americans to come round to the British analysis of international priorities (as they did a year later).[5] The terms for large-scale aid would not then be so onerous. In the event the London end of the British negotiating team only very reluctantly agreed to the American terms for the loan, which included sterling convertibility. The Loan Agreement (and the Bretton Woods Agreement) was forced through the House of Commons in December 1945 with only 29 Labour MPs voting against it, alongside 70 Conservatives. Despite intensified rationing, much of the loan was spent on US imports, a dependency exacerbated by American inflation. When convertibility was implemented in July 1947 a full-blown crisis of sterling commenced which strengthened the case for rapidly reducing Britain's overseas commitments.

When Labour entered office British armed forces were stretched across Europe and the Middle East and helping to restore European colonialism in Indochina and Indonesia.[6] By 1945 Britain owed its dependencies £3,500 million. Under the Labour Government the poorest of these dependencies, the Crown Colonies, saw their sterling credits grow from

£454 million to £928 million as Britain continued to extract dollar earnings for its own immediate benefit. In short, British reconstruction efforts employed a more systematic exploitation of colonies than at any previous time in imperial history.[7] There was development *in* the colonies, but not necessarily *of* the colonies. There was the new indefinite responsibility of occupied Germany and the commitment, which Churchill made in December 1944, to prevent the Communists from coming to power in Greece, which now involved the Labour Government and the TUC in policies which essentially supported a 'one-sided civil war' against the left.[8] British troops could also be found in Austria and Trieste. In Egypt the presence of about 150,000 British troops and various military bases – including the biggest arms dump in the world – were under pressure from a nationalist agitation which wanted to abrogate the 1936 Treaty. In Palestine and India the problem on both sides of the equation was on a larger scale still. The navy had commitments in the Pacific, the Caribbean, the Mediterranean and the Indian Ocean. At the end of 1946 over 1.4 million people still served in the armed forces. Peacetime conscription was introduced in 1947 (and extended in 1948) and the cost of the armed forces amounted to 15 per cent of national income, falling to 8 per cent in 1948. About half of this cost was composed of imperial commitments such as the 20,000-strong garrison in Cyrenaica (modern Libya) – the former Italian colony which Bevin was negotiating to retain as a British base – and the war against Communist insurgency in Malaysia, where the British army would perfect techniques later deployed by the USA in Vietnam. The Cold War threatened to increase these costs further still when the Korean War broke out in June 1950 and Hugh Gaitskell was forced to contemplate a defence bill amounting to 14 per cent of national income.

It would be a mistake to imagine these commitments simply stemmed from forces beyond any British Government's control. Though it is obvious enough that the Labour Government responded to events as and when they occurred, it did so with assumptions, plans and theories. By the time it took office arrangements had already been made in association with the US administration to establish institutions for the management of free trade. Similarly a United Nations Organisation (UNO) had been conceived; its Charter was signed at San Francisco in June 1945, shortly before the Labour Government was formed. By these means the Anglo-American states sought to preserve peace, advance justice and constitute permanent structures for international cooperation. The wartime advance of the Soviet Union into Central Europe, the emergence of mass Communist Parties in Italy, France, Czechoslovakia and Yugoslavia, the post-war instability of Germany and Greece, the progress of the civil war in China, the Soviet presence in northern Iran, and the upsurge of nationalism in much of Asia; all these problems jeopardised both the effectiveness of the UNO and the scope of the Bretton Woods arrangements. US policy-makers in the State Department believed that American prosperity depended on a global application of what used to be called the Open Door policy. Communist autarky stood in the way of this objective, as did the sort of imperial preference schemes that operated within the British Empire. Meanwhile, Foreign Office officials, seemingly unconcerned by massive economic problems at home, worried that if Britain 'ceased to regard [itself] as a World Power' it would 'gradually cease to be one'. Sir Orme Sargent thus advised in July 1945 that 'in the immediate future' Britain had to 'take a stand' in Europe to maintain its interests in Finland, Poland, Czechoslovakia, Austria, Yugoslavia and Bulgaria – all states in which the Soviet Union had a major interest – and maintain 'close and friendly relations with Italy, Greece and Turkey'. Sargent advised that 'in the immediate future we must take the offensive in as many of the Eastern countries of Europe as possible'. He also assumed that the power of the USA had to be enlisted by Britain if Soviet influence was to be curtailed.[9]

Friction between Britain and the Soviet Union over the future of Poland and the holding of free elections in the countries under Red Army occupation had already surfaced at Yalta in February 1945. On the other hand, Stalin had also been given to understand that Eastern Europe was a Soviet sphere of influence. Different interpretations inevitably accompanied these and other deals such as those concerning the future of Germany, the treatment of war criminals, the payment of reparations and so on. Orme Sargent's advice was calculated to increase such friction, though undoubtedly chimed in with the most stubborn theory of them all in British foreign policy; namely that Britain was a Great Power and would remain so on the strength of its imperial world role. Before the result of the British general election was known Attlee, accompanying Churchill to Potsdam in July 1945, witnessed the beginnings of the Cold War as Truman took up the Polish question with Stalin. The wartime alliance was already breaking down now that Germany was defeated and the first successful test of the nuclear bomb – which Stalin was told about while the conference was in session – gave the USA a monopoly of the new super weapon. The next month Attlee set up a secret Cabinet sub-committee on atomic energy which he called the 'Atom Bomb Committee', though most of the Cabinet were unaware of its existence. It is evidence of Attlee's conviction that Britain was and would remain a Great Power. His decision marked the beginning of the process by which Britain acquired its own bomb independently of the USA. The first step was taken before the end of the year, though the decision to go ahead and build atomic weapons was left until January 1947, by which time the USA had signalled its intention to maintain its monopoly position by refusing to share its secrets with Britain. Parliament first heard a vague allusion to these fateful steps only in May 1948.

The British disposition in foreign and defence policy – bold and confident as it was – was not supported by the underlying economic reality that Labour inherited in July 1945, as the Chancellor was all too aware.[10] Exports would have to increase by 75 per cent to correct the balance of payments deficit even if the volume of imports could be kept down to pre-war levels. Rationing was intensified. Britain suffered from shortages of every kind including dollar earnings, manpower and building materials needed for the urgent housing programme. While exports earned just £350 million, total outgoings including military expenditure abroad was running at the rate of £2,000 million per year. A team of officials headed by Keynes negotiated a US loan in December 1945, but this would only become available in July 1947. When it came, much of it was frittered away trying to maintain sterling convertibility. In the light of these facts the Government's determination to maintain Britain as a world power is as impressive as its determination to press ahead with its domestic reform programme, all the more so as the public expectations and pressures which attached to the latter were absent in foreign relations.

Well before the hardening of US attitudes towards the Soviet Union, when Britain's economic problems were still mounting, the new Foreign Secretary, Ernest Bevin, was already following the advice of Orme Sargent and Gladwyn Jebb (assistant Under Secretary and United Nations advisor at the Foreign Office) that to yield, as the latter put it, 'to any Russian demand would clearly mean that we were not prepared to play the part of a Great Power'.[11] This may account for officialdom's (and the Tory Opposition's) high opinion of Bevin who was counted in these circles as one of the best Foreign Secretaries Britain had ever had.[12] Within two months of taking office Bevin, with Jebb at his elbow, was negotiating at the London Council of Foreign Ministers meeting in September 1945 to acquire British control of the former Italian colony of Cyrenaica in North Africa, though Attlee thought it 'an expense we can ill afford'. The USA favoured an international trusteeship rather than a British military base. Only when Molotov, who agreed to the British proposal, insisted on a Russian military base in neighbouring Tripolitania, did Bevin change tack and side with the Americans. In October, at the Soviet Embassy, Molotov accused Bevin of wanting a British monopoly in the Mediterranean to which the Foreign Secretary replied that Britain could not tolerate a 'new military power . . . across the lifeline of the British Empire'.[13] Molotov had a point, however, because the British claimed 'special strategic rights' in Libya. But Foreign Office officials realised that this argument might not convince the USA. One way round this obstacle was to propose the rapid independence of Cyrenaica so that 'we can conclude with her an alliance such as we have had with Egypt'.[14] British confidence on this score was based on the supposed reliability of Sheikh Idris, the Emir of the Senussi, a local collaborator of the sort that Britain had been accustomed to find in 'independent' Egypt, not to mention the many territories under 'indirect rule'. But other suggestions were considered, such as extending the Senussi writ over Tripolitania. Bevin agreed with the ancient South African sage, General Smuts, one of the originators of the mandates idea, that the Soviets having already reduced the Balkans to virtual satellites, and now casting greedy eyes on the Persian Gulf, across a weakened and dependent Iran, it was only a matter of time before they occupied 'a commanding position in the Mediterranean' and undermined Britain's Great Power status. All this would follow if they were allowed a say in any international trusteeship over the former Italian colonies.[15] This had to be blocked at all costs – British control of Gibraltar, Cyprus, Malta, and East Africa was evidently not enough, even though Britain also had troops stationed in Palestine, Egypt and Greece. The Foreign Office was also preparing a case for British control of Italian Somaliland and the Ogaden which would be administered as a single unit together with British Somaliland, but for tactical reasons the idea was not tabled at the Paris meeting of the Council of Foreign Ministers in April 1946.

This was not the posture of a Power that was down and out. These were proposals for increasing British control over the Mediterranean and keeping the UN out. Once again Attlee entered his own reservations, this time arguing that the strategic position of Britain should be conceived as 'an easterly extension of a strategic area the centre of which is the American continent rather than [that of] a Power looking eastwards through the Mediterranean to India and the East'.[16] Such views were never placed before the Cabinet and potential supporters of Attlee – Bevan, Cripps and Dalton – were excluded from the circulation of the relevant discussion papers. An interdepartmental committee, reporting shortly before the Council of Foreign Ministers Paris meeting in 1946, was more representative of Foreign Office opinion and took the same line as Smuts. It particularly disliked the American idea of a five-Power advisory committee to supervise the UN trusteeship of Libya because it would give the Russians a say in the area. The idea that a referendum should be held to test local opinion was dismissed as frankly ludicrous, bearing in mind, as one official observed, that referenda did not always work well even in civilised countries such as Switzerland. Press reports in Cairo, however, were already blaming Britain for obstructing trusteeship and, according to the Commander-in-Chief in the Middle East, General Paget, were having a disturbing effect on the already tense situation in Libya itself.[17] Bevin, advised by the Chiefs of Staff that a Russian presence in North Africa could only 'lower our prestige and lead to unrest among the Arab tribes', went to the Council of Foreign Ministers determined to block the Russians by proposing immediate independence for both Cyrenaica and Tripolitania. But when the Americans came round to the idea that Italy should resume control, he changed tack again by arguing that 'Cyrenaica was vital from the point of view of the British Empire'. This implicitly confirmed Molotov's suspicion that Britain had all along wanted to turn Libya into a new Egypt – that is, an independent state under British military occupation. He was also aware of the British plan for the Horn of Africa, but this was a secondary concern. As late as February 1948 Bevin was still advising the Cabinet in favour of British control in Libya even if this meant giving back Somaliland and Eritrea to the Italians.[18]

Britain's appetite for additional bases in the Mediterranean was seemingly unaffected by the problems it was facing everywhere in the Middle East and may have been sharpened by the imminent loss of India. Oil was a factor as the scramble for rights between Britain and the USA in Iran and Saudi Arabia illustrated. Bases were also a factor; the Chiefs of Staff advising that Russia's own oil fields were more easily hit from bases in the Middle East. Then there was the vacuum problem – Russia, already 'malevolently bent on expansion southwards' into the oil preserves, had to be checked.[19] But Egypt had been repeatedly promised (since 1882) that the British would soon withdraw and there was still no sign of them doing so, despite mounting nationalist agitation. Palestine was rapidly becoming ungovernable and elsewhere in the region the traditional leaders who had always collaborated with Britain were faced with national movements and worse. In Iraq the Communist Party had grown alongside the resurgence of Kurdish separatism. In Iran another Communist Party had become significant especially after the creation of autonomous governments in the Kurdish and Azeri regions (which owed something to the continued presence of the Red Army since the Anglo-Soviet invasion of 1941). Attlee would seem to have had a point, then, when he questioned the military value of the Middle East in January 1947, describing it as a region thin on people, economically weak, and socially and politically unstable.[20] Such considerations counted for little, however, against considerations of prestige, potential vacuums (which the USSR would inevitably fill), oil, sterling balances and the capacity to bomb Soviet cities from Middle Eastern airfields.

Meanwhile the 'Soviet threat' was increasingly taking shape as a unique danger owing to the ideological nature of the Soviet state, bent on world domination. It was observed in Washington even in 1945 that British stock rose as Soviet stock fell and by 1946 the Truman administration had quickly come round to the view that Moscow represented a special menace. Anglo-American differences over the future of Iran accordingly receded when the Soviet Union persisted with its claims for oil concessions.[21] Although Truman had acknowledged Russia's claim on rights of access to the Mediterranean at Potsdam in July 1945, he was accusing it of planning an invasion of Turkey and seizure of the Black Sea straits in January 1946. The British and Americans also concluded that month that the restoration of order in occupied Germany was incompatible with a radical de-Nazification either of the economy or the political administration – or of Soviet reparations from the Ruhr industrial heartland. Evidence of a change in policy towards the USSR was provided by George Kennan's 'long telegram' from the American embassy in Moscow, warning of Soviet expansionism, in February 1946. Frank Roberts, the British ambassador in Moscow, also warned that there might be no limits to Soviet expansionism, particularly in 'the whole zone vital to British security between India and the Dardanelles'.[22] In May the Americans ended Soviet reparations from the Ruhr. In July the British and American zones of occupation were fused; any hopes that the Labour Government might assist the German left on matters of socialisation, works' councils and left unity were henceforth quashed. Stalin's continuing delay in withdrawing Soviet troops from Iran in March 1946, under the terms of the wartime agreement which Britain and the US had already complied with, added to the growing friction between the former allies. That month Churchill made his Fulton Speech warning of an imperilled 'Christian civilisation' in all the countries beyond North America and the British Empire. More than 100 Labour MPs condemned the speech in a House of Commons motion. But more important, the Labour Government had arrived at the same conclusion as Churchill, who probably spoke with its silent support. American political leaders were counselled to the same effect. The US Joint Chiefs of Staff advised the Truman administration that 'the defeat or disintegration of the British Empire would eliminate from Eurasia the last bulwark of resistance between the US and Soviet expansion . . . Militarily, our present position as a world power is of necessity closely interwoven with that of Great Britain.'[23] Signs of dissent from Labour's foreign policy continued to surface within the party with calls for friendship with the Soviet Union at the annual conference and an unprecedented amendment to the King's Speech along these lines, moved by Richard Crossman, and supported by over 50 MPs. The Chancellor of the Exchequer, Hugh Dalton, confined his own misgivings about Bevin's foreign policy to his diary.[24] The misgivings were so widespread that Morgan Phillips, the party's secretary, wrote to all divisional Labour parties in December 1946 to deny the charge that friendship with the

Soviet Union had been sacrificed in the interests of an alliance with the USA.[25]

The Soviet Union withdrew from Iran in April and continued to demobilise its troops so that only three million of the twelve million in uniform remained by 1948. By this time, however, Stalin had responded to the Marshall Plan of June 1947 by tightening his grip on Eastern Europe and the perception and fear of an ideologically driven expansionist empire was heightened in the West. This may have been a factor in forcing Attlee to revise his views on the wisdom of maintaining, let alone increasing, the British presence in the Middle East. Since the spring of 1945 he had expressed scepticism on this issue – opposing the plan for Cyrenaica, favouring international control of the Suez Canal, and expressing doubt on the need for a massive British military presence in Egypt. In March 1946 he confided to a sympathetic Dalton, while Bevin was negotiating to obtain Cyrenaica, that he was 'pressing the Chiefs of Staff and the Defence Committee [to take] a large view of his own, which aims at considerable disengagement from areas where there is a risk of us clashing with the Russians. This would mean giving up any attempt to keep open the passage through the Mediterranean in wartime, and to pull out from all the Middle East, including Egypt, and, of course, from Greece. We should then constitute a line of defence across Africa from Lagos to Kenya and concentrate a large part of our forces in the latter ... we should concentrate a great part of the Commonwealth defence, including many industries, in Australia. We should thus put a wide glacis of desert and Arabs between ourselves and the Russians'. Dalton added that 'This is a very bold and interesting idea and I am inclined to favour it'.[26] On subsequent occasions Attlee also observed that from the Russian viewpoint Egypt was a British satellite and that in an age of aerial warfare this was both superfluous to requirements and a gratuitous provocation to the Russians. The practical problems of colonialism in an age of nationalism could not be ignored either. Dalton thought that 'It is quite clear that we can't go on holding people down against their will, however incompetent they are to govern themselves, for the whole pace, as determined in the East, has quickened in the war years, and it would be a waste both of British men and money to try to hold down any of this crowd against their will. They must be allowed to find their own way ... to what they regard as "freedom" '.[27] Such subversive thoughts had never been allowed to influence policy but after January 1947 they ceased to be expressed. Faced with pressure from Bevin, the Foreign Office and the Chiefs of Staff, Attlee backed down but the context in which he did so was one of increasing polarisation between Washington and Moscow.[28]

The implications were nevertheless clear to contemporaries. Whereas Attlee imagined Britain on the eastern boundary of a strategic zone centred in North America, critics of Bevin's foreign policy from within the Labour Party pointed out in May 1947 that it committed Britain to forward defences all over the globe, under American leadership.[29] A vocal opposition had taken the view since 1941 that Britain should seek to befriend the Soviet Union, rather than the USA. Others, like the *Keep Left* authors, had favoured a socialist 'third force' via some form of European integration.[30] But these had been minority views, lacking specification and significant support at Cabinet level. The larger numbers of critics sympathetic to the Soviet Union melted away as the Cold War intensified, especially after Marshall Aid was announced and Labour's domestic programme began to receive the support of American dollars. Bevin himself was keen to restore Britain's economic independence from the USA – necessarily so for it was obvious that this was a precondition of Britain remaining a Great Power. What is more interesting is how he imagined this could be achieved, and here the ideas he expressed at Labour's annual conference in 1939 resurfaced. The scheme he championed envisaged the economic restoration of Western Europe on the basis of a coordinated development of imperial possessions, especially on the African continent. As he told the French Prime Minister Renadier in September 1947, 'with their populations of 47 million and 40 million respectively and with their vast colonial possessions they [Britain and France] could, if they acted together, be as powerful as either the Soviet Union or the United States'. Bevin stressed that 'they possessed between them supplies of raw materials greater than those of any other country' and he was impressed 'by the number of raw materials [found in the colonies] in which the United States was lacking'.[31]

At the end of the year the time was deemed right for a major propaganda offensive against the Soviet Union. The construction of the Soviet Union as an ideologically driven enemy of the West, manipulating fifth columns in China, Indochina, Malaya, Greece and elsewhere, was already the common stock of officials in the course of 1946.[32] So was the idea that 'social democratic' Britain was a particular object of Soviet loathing because of its rivalry for the allegiance of the working class and colonial peoples. The possibility that anti-colonialism might have independent roots and that British imperial rule might be unpopular because of its own shortcomings was not allowed into the equation. It was, however, timely to spread these biases through and beyond the party and the TUC to the front lines of conflict wherever they might be. In January 1948 Bevin brought the plan before the Cabinet and the Information Research Department (IRD) was born. The British colonies and the colonial world in general were thought to be in need of its close attention. Weiler cites an example of the IRD's propaganda which appeared in the Arab press ostensibly as the work of an independent

Arab observer. It said that Israel had been created as a part of a Soviet 'plot' to dominate the region, using 'the Eastern European Jew, divorced from his ancient faith and wedded to a cynically "practical" ideology'.[33] Appropriate stories were placed for the same anti-Soviet purpose in the Indian and Far Eastern media. The Ministry of Labour meanwhile proposed the British Council as a vehicle for disseminating British values in such matters as trade unionism in the colonies, continuing the good work done by the TUC since 1938 (most recently in Greece). Creech Jones at the Colonial Office also had the 'colonial development' policy to hand to show, *inter alia*, that British imperialism did not exist, that native peoples benefited from British rule, that there was no widespread desire to expel the 'progressive' British from their dependencies, and so on. The Western allies coordinated anti-Communist propaganda aimed at literate Africans. Dissidents within the party who continued to question foreign policy – such as those Labour MPs who sent a telegram in support of Pietro Nenni's pro-Communist socialist party in Italy in 1948 – were threatened with disciplinary action. Some were expelled from the party that year. The TUC called on the unions to remove elected Communists from their positions. Communist-dominated Trades Councils were later closed down and various organisations were established to root out the Communists within the unions.

While these projects were underway other imperial Powers were invited to join the discussion about imperial economic coordination, including Belgium, the Netherlands and South Africa, with Bevin calling for the involvement of Italy and Portugal too. It was made clear from the start that West European economic integration was 'wanted for political reasons, such as combating communism', as well as to secure future economic independence from the USA.[34] Immediately after the Soviet Union formally refused Marshall Aid and its conditions, and the Cold War division of Europe hardened, Bevin and his officials talked of the 'opportunity' which the European Recovery Programme offered to promote 'a union . . . which would have natural cohesion and political reality'. Like the Americans Bevin initially saw a customs union as a necessary step in the restoration of the West European economy and the defeat of Communism.[35] Indeed the US considered that Marshall Aid was to be conditional on such progress and Bevin realised that British cooperation was necessary if Congress was to approve the massive expenditures required. But the British were always clear in their own minds that they wanted nothing to do with a customs union that would compromise the UK's imperial role. The development of colonial resources was seen as 'vital for our long-term viability', in the words of a briefing for the Cabinet Economic Policy Committee.[36] Bevin was perfectly open in his conviction that Britain 'was not just another

European country'; as he told the Americans, at the International Trade Organisation negotiations in Geneva in June 1947, 'through the resources of its empire . . . it could make a contribution to European recovery second only to that of the United States'.[37] As late as October 1948 he was convinced that African development would enable Britain to have the USA 'eating out of our hands' in four to five years time.[38]

By the autumn of 1947 the Treasury, the Foreign Office and the Colonial Office were at one in rejecting European union – raised to the political agenda by the USA and Marshall Aid – not only as a threat to imperial preference and the preservation of the sterling area, but also as inevitably involving a supranational authority. On all these counts the imperial role would be weakened if Britain were forced to join in. Bevin remained convinced that 'some measure of economic unity' in Western Europe was essential to restore its independence from the USA. But he again stressed to the Economic Policy Committee (November 1947) that control 'over important Colonial territories' was vital to the project since they contained 'resources [which] would be available to sustain this new structure'. Stafford Cripps, the Chancellor of the Exchequer, agreed that 'the first step should be the creation of a Customs Union with the Colonial Empire'. His predecessor Hugh Dalton – a man who immediately imagined 'pullulating, poverty-stricken, diseased, nigger communities' when he was offered the Colonial Office in 1950[39] – concurred with the general view among ministers 'that the principal value of any arrangement we might enter into with Western Europe lay in the Colonial resources which this might make available to us'. Harold Wilson, President of the Board of Trade, spoke against a customs union but added 'that it would be inadvisable to appear lukewarm or hostile' to the proposal in view of American support for the idea. In discussion it was observed that 'The United States and Russia would be critical of any arrangements which appeared to involve the exploitation of Colonial areas in the interests of Western Europe, or any restrictions on the development of multilateral trading. It would therefore be inadvisable in any public statement to lay emphasis on the inclusion of Colonial territories within any arrangements that might be contemplated'.[40]

The public statements of Labour politicians were in fact very careful to stress colonial 'development'. Every minister in the Government made speeches extolling the virtues of Britain's overseas economic development policies at a time when the net gain of this activity was very definitely in Britain's favour rather than that of its colonies, though this was naturally obscured by official rhetoric.[41] We have already seen that future problems in African colonies such as the Gold Coast (Ghana) and Kenya were related to the socially disruptive policies Britain pursued in the period between the opening of the war and the end of the Labour

Government, including the doubling of the white settler population in Kenya, the intensification of land theft in that country, widespread shortages and inflation. No doubt Bevin was as sincere as Creech Jones at the Colonial Office in wanting genuine development in Britain's colonies, if only so that Britain could manage the nationalists and secure improved future markets for British goods on the back of rising living standards in Africa and the Middle East. But the capital for major overseas investments could not be found in Britain. Not only was it bedevilled by shortages of every kind in the state sector of the economy, Bevin and the Labour Government had no power to direct the flow of private investments. The vast capital outflow from Labour Britain during the Attlee years was the equivalent of 8 per cent of the national income, but the Dominions took the bulk of it, especially Australia and South Africa.[42] In the Crown Colonies there was net disinvestment. Just £8 million flowed annually under the Colonial Development and Welfare Act, a far greater flow of value came back to Britain. The ill-fated groundnuts scheme in Tanganyika cost £40 million and £86 million was found between 1945 and 1949 to invest in Malaya's rubber plantations and tin mines, these representing the second and fifth largest dollar earners in the sterling area at a time when Labour was desperate to overcome the dollar shortage. But these large-scale projects were exceptions to the rule. The chief devices for colonial development were the sterling balances, the monopsonist trading boards, the physical controls on colonial commerce, higher taxes, production drives, and emigration. Bevin was thinking long-term, of course, when he set out with his plan to raise British living standards and achieve political independence for Britain by colonial development. He was not even sure of the raw material resources which the Empire possessed and had to ask for an inventory to be made highlighting those that were scarce in the United States.[43]

In Africa Government policy, alert to the rising expectations of returning African troops and the need to engage the local population in the planned economic and social development of dependent territories, was geared to a corresponding political development.[44] Africa was 'now the core of [Britain's] colonial position; the only continental space from which we can still hope to draw reserves of economic and military strength'.[45] Yet the period during which it was possible to 'rely on the white man's prestige to govern Africa' was seen to be nearing its end. There was, however, no confidence in the 'class of professional politicians out of touch with the people' that was already said to exist. The answer was to develop an African local government, partly as a way of under-mining would-be national leaders such as Dr Azikiwe, president of the National Council of Nigeria and the Cameroons. Such leaders were said to be not only out of touch with 'the illiterate mass' but capable of fomenting racial conflict. Creech Jones, the most dynamic of Attlee's three Colonial Secretaries, followed the advice of his officials in promoting this policy of linking local government with the twin goal of development and spiking the literate minority of African leaders, unhealthily 'absorbed in the activities of the centre'.[46] The Governor of Kenya, Sir Philip Mitchell, one of the first to respond to his outline of this policy in May 1947, emphasised the danger of 'synthetic nationalisms', inspired by 'current Hindu politics', in the context of the 'spiritual, moral, social, cultural, and economic' backwardness of Africans. In Kenya, he reported, even the tribal chiefs had been created by the British and indigenous administration had not traditionally existed beyond the village circle.[47] Uganda was another territory in which the development of some measure of self-government was seen as problematical for the next generation. Independence for such territories might be centuries away. Even in the Gold Coast (Ghana) 'where Africans are most advanced politically, internal self-government is unlikely to be achieved in much less than a generation'.[48]

Yet it was a recurring theme of official analysis of the African problem that the war had picked up the pace of change and it was no longer possible to think – as in the old days of indirect rule – of the gradual adaptation of traditional societies, carefully preserved against radical outside influences. Apart from the circulation of subversive ideas, such as international demands for accountable trusteeships and even decolonisation, there was also population growth, land shortages, expanding cash crop production and soil deterioration to contend with. It had been found expedient to dispense with the nostrums of indirect rule during the war in order to assist the war effort via increased production. The involvement of talented, non-traditional representatives of African societies had been deemed essential in these circumstances. Creech Jones reminded African Governors in 1948 of world criticism of Britain's purpose in Africa and of the nationalism which threatened to disrupt the dependencies from within.[49] There were even those who said that the Government's development policy was merely a cloak for exploitation – an idea that was rejected by the African Governors' conference that summer, even as it acknowledged 'critical shortages of capital and consumer goods' and worried about the long-term future of cash crops designed to earn or save dollars for Britain. But then, as the Government had repeatedly pointed out, 'British "Imperialism" [was] dead, in so far as it ever existed, except as a slogan used by our critics'.[50]

There had never been any doubt, however, that colonial development could assist in the reconstruction of Britain and in particular put right 'the tremendous unbalance' between the sterling and dollar areas. All three of the Colonial Secretaries appointed by Attlee joined the chorus of Labour Ministers who made these connections. Cripps had stressed that this was 'no short-term difficulty'.[51] 'The further development of African resources was thus crucial and the tempo of development had to be increase[d] out of all recognition', even though Britain would continue to be unable to supply large quantities of the necessary capital goods (rail, port and road facilities, bulldozers, tractors and so on). Britain was 'interested in every method and device that will yield a few thousand tons more of any valuable crop or material', the African Governors were told. The whole of the sterling group and its ability to survive depended upon a rapid African development. No one was in any doubt about 'the probable development of nationalism, racialism and communism in Africa in the next ten years', or of the development of the UN as a vehicle for anti-imperialism.[52] It was seen to be essential, on both counts, that 'government in the Colonies must cease to appear to Colonial peoples as something imposed from outside'.[53] At the same time the needs of development involved stirring up these peoples while demanding greater reliance on white settler communities and the large-scale, efficient farming techniques they were supposed to represent. These were the very communities in East and Southern Africa associated with an externally imposed government that held the local populations back in so many ways. It was asking a lot of local government to solve all these contradictions, much more to fulfil the 'world-wide experiment in nation-building' that was supposed to be Britain's central purpose in the African dependencies.

Middle East

In the face of an acknowledged nationalist agitation throughout the Middle East, Bevin also imagined that it would be possible to broaden Britain's influence in the region 'by developing an economic aid and social policy which would make for prosperity and contentment in the area as a whole'.[54] It would raise the purchasing power of 'the masses' and undercut the nationalism that was potentially lethal to British interests. In approving this policy in October 1945 the Labour Government was again following ideas which had been taken up in Whitehall during the war. In Egypt, however, the government of Sidki Pasha had been calling for the abrogation of the Anglo-Egyptian Treaty of 1936, and the removal of British military bases, even before Labour entered office. The Government continued to resist this demand throughout its term despite recognition of the strength of local feeling and the fact that Britain was asking Egypt to accept a new treaty involving obligations, as Attlee pointed out, that were considered intolerable by members of the Commonwealth – such as accepting Egyptian involvement in war by virtue of decisions taken in London.[55] Egypt, as Field-Marshal Smuts informed the Cabinet, was considered 'a vital link in the British chain of communications through the Mediterranean and the Suez Canal'. For that reason it was essential to retain a British military presence in the country and the right to enter Egypt whenever Britain apprehended an international emergency. This was essential according to advice from the Chiefs of Staff, though as Attlee observed there was no more justification for it than claiming the same rights in continental Europe. Oil rights needed to be protected, he conceded, but stirring up nationalism was not the best way to do it.

The Labour Government thus adopted a policy of stalling and of linking the argument about British military bases with the question of the future of the Sudan on which there were disagreements with Egypt. It was calculated that were the UN to be drawn into the dispute, Britain would receive a more sympathetic hearing on the Sudanese question as long as it was emphasised that Britain stood for the eventual self-government of Sudan at the earliest practicable opportunity (whereas the Egyptians claimed sovereignty over it). It was also recognised that insisting on the validity of the 1936 treaty would serve immediate security interests but probably compound Britain's long-term problems in Egypt when the treaty came up for revision in 1956. By April 1951 the Cabinet was considering how the subject of Middle East defence might involve the USA 'on the basis that the defence of the Middle East was at present very weak and that the western democracies could not afford to allow the oil resources of the Middle East to fall into Soviet hands'.[56] The unilateral nationalisation of the Anglo-Iranian Oil Company by the government of Mohammed Mussadiq in that month gave this thought a particular urgency, though Mussadiq was no Communist. In May it was thought opportune to introduce the Sudan issue into the negotiations with Egypt, though the 'main objective was to prolong discussions in order to gain time'. The US administration also suggested that the Egyptians might be mollified by the supply of arms. It was opposed, however, to the forcible removal of the Iranian Government. Though plans to intervene in Iran were drawn up, the Cabinet realised that the UN would denounce any action as aggression and the new Commonwealth countries would take a similar view. Morrison, by now the Foreign Secretary, following Bevin's illness, favoured the use of force. But it was the US position that the Cabinet felt was decisive; the US would oppose force except if it were needed to save British lives or save the refinery from a Communist Government and Britain 'could not afford to break with the United States on an issue of this kind'.[57] It was hoped that Mussadiq would be replaced by a more favourable government in the near future.

On the question of Palestine Labour had to contend with an incipient civil war between Arabs and Jews and a growing terrorist campaign against British occupying forces, as well as American pressure to massively increase Jewish immigration which in the Cabinet's view would make the situation worse. Some Zionists greeted the advent of a Labour Government as the best opportunity for the realisation of their ambitions.[58] They had every reason to be confident – on the basis of established Labour doctrine since the abandonment of the 1930 White Paper on Palestine. But this was to underestimate the new Foreign Secretary's fidelity to Foreign Office, rather than Labour Party, assumptions. British national interests would not be served by alienating the Arab states. The White Paper on Palestine of 1939 had envisaged an independent Palestine state by 1949 but one in which the Jews would constitute a minority. Jewish immigration to Palestine was running at just above 13,000 monthly when Labour entered office. Bevin, who was worried about Soviet encroachments in the Middle East and North Africa, construed Russian support for a Jewish homeland in Palestine as part of this strategy. The immigration of 'sufficient indoctrinated Jews', he reasoned, would turn Palestine into a Communist state. The Foreign Office advised the Americans accordingly, thereby suggesting that this was more than the prejudice of one man.[59] The danger of Communism in the Middle East was not confined to Palestine in the perceptions of the British Government, of course; Cyprus, Iran and Iraq were all identified as candidates for such a take-over in these years.[60] But the fixation with Soviet power was only the reverse side of the Government's concern to secure British interests in the region and they were identified with the stability and continuity of Britain's Arab friends.

President Truman demanded certificates for the immediate admission of 100,000 Jews from the displaced persons camps in Europe and it was in response to this that the Government set up an Anglo-American committee in January 1946 to investigate the Palestine problem. Its recommendation in May 1946 for the granting of the 100,000 certificates was not to Bevin's liking. Nor was the suggestion of the largest minority of the commission (comprising four of the six Americans) that the mandate be continued. The Labour MP Richard Crossman, who published a book on the commission's work, favoured partition.[61] But only two of the Americans supported him and none of the British. A bi-national state, as the Royal Commission had concluded ten years earlier, was impracticable and in the Cabinet's view remained so. The Government was also convinced that neither side in Palestine considered it acceptable. The problem was that none of the other options looked any more viable. A unitary state was unacceptable to the Zionists, though this was what the Arabs wanted. Partition, creating two independent states, was the only solution the Cabinet could imagine; this had some support among Zionists, but not among the Arab states. Labour's annual conference endorsed the Zionist demand for an independent Jewish state in Palestine in 1946, but the Government felt that it had to keep faith with the Arab states. Failure to do so would result in 'a long period of unrest throughout the Arab world' with formidable military implications, damage to essential oil supplies and communications, and the danger of growing Soviet influence.[62] Oil alone, according to the Chiefs of Staff, 'makes the retention of Arab friendship essential'.[63] An even bigger, indefinite, British military presence in Palestine on the current basis could not be financed by savings from Italy and Greece, since it was already assumed in July 1946 that these commitments would be liquidated to meet other manpower targets. The coming withdrawal from India and, perhaps, Egypt, nevertheless made the Middle East even more essential to Britain's 'defensive strategy' and the Cabinet was told by the Chief of the Air Staff in January 1947 that Palestine remained an important base for 'the mobile reserve of troops'. It was also told that the UN was unlikely to support partition.[64]

While the Arabs continued to reiterate implacable opposition to the creation of a Jewish state in any part of Palestine, the Cabinet was also told that it was doubtful that any scheme of partition acceptable to the Jews would be regarded as defensible by the Labour Government because it would claim a far larger area than the Government thought justifiable. Meanwhile terrorist actions against British troops and civilians increased in the summer of 1946, leading to mass arrests and curfews. Truman reiterated his demand for a relaxation of the immigration controls and called for the creation of 'a viable Jewish state'. The Zionist Organisation of America, responding to Truman, made clear that the whole of mandatory Palestine would alone suffice.[65] Bevin called a conference in London early in 1947 as a last forlorn attempt to find a negotiated settlement. But the Arab delegation rejected the principle of a Jewish state, as well as land sales to Jews and Jewish immigration. It was thus decided in February 1947 that the matter would be referred to the judgement of the General Assembly of the UN and a statement was made to the House of Commons to this effect. Behind the scenes Bevin recommended unconditional withdrawal from Palestine whatever course of action the UN decided upon. On 20 September the Cabinet decided to renounce the Mandate and to reject any settlement involving coercion against one side or the other. Notice was then given that troops would be evacuated by 1 August 1948 at the latest. When the UN decision to recommend a form of partition was taken that November civil war was imminent and there was no plan in place for the enforcement of partition.

Britain's role in the world

Ministers and officials also speculated on the likely results of Britain remaining aloof from Western European economic integration, noting that even in the short run there could be 'devastating competition from the Continent' in certain basic industries such as steel and chemicals. Some officials feared that if Britain stood alone 'we shall just manage to survive as pigmies between two giants' always dependent on one of them – the USA – for protection. Robin Hankey, Head of the Northern Department at the Foreign Office, observed that 'we have not had, in practice, sufficient industry to arm the British Empire for the last twenty-five years and in two wars ... we have only survived because the Americans have made the arms for us and in effect given us the money to pay for them'. Gladwyn Jebb, in the same discussion, talked of the 'dismal choice' of Soviet satellite or poor dependant of the USA which awaited an isolated Britain, but he also saw that 'a Customs Union does not make sense unless it leads on to economic and political union'; this meant losing the Empire and accepting the eventual German domination of Western Europe in perhaps twenty years time. It was seen that 'every long-term economic and strategic argument would seem to be in favour' of European economic integration because it 'would surely offer greater security and stability than any system of military alliances could achieve'. Hankey argued that 'Western Europe as a whole . . . is potentially a Great Power even by modern standards' but he went on to advocate the position which Bevin championed in Cabinet: 'we can, I believe, only meet this situation by actively building up the economic potential of the Empire, and by pressing forward the economic and political reconstruction of Western Europe and also co-ordinating its defence as a whole'.[66]

Bevin obtained Cabinet approval for his plan and persisted throughout 1948 in linking it with resistance to Soviet expansion, mobilisation of African resources and European union to create 'a bloc which, in both population and productive capacity, could stand on an equality with the western hemisphere and Soviet blocs'.[67] It was not until the autumn of 1949 that he reluctantly acknowledged in Cabinet that his 'third force' strategy was dead.[68] In the meantime he learned some hard lessons that had plagued imperial-minded politicians since 1918. There was insufficient political unity in the Commonwealth; the UK could not supply imperial defence requirements on its own; Britain did not possess the capital to develop Africa and the Middle East; and Western Europe could not defend itself without American assistance. The formation of NATO in April 1949 was formal recognition of US hegemony, but its reality had been established during the Second World War and an American 'empire by invitation' was there for the taking in its immediate aftermath.

For the British this did not mean that the world role was finished. Bevin only echoed his officials and virtually the whole political Establishment in Britain in calculating that it was usually possible to reconcile American and British views and in supposing that as the USA took on the burden of global responsibilities it would learn to regard the UK and its Commonwealth as its most reliable and essential friends.[69] Western Europe might well form a Customs Union, but Britain had too much to lose by submerging itself in a mere regional project.

Even after the formation of NATO the alternatives to the Atlantic alliance, as well as its consequences, continued to be discussed. The Cabinet was informed in May 1950 that the notion of Western Europe as a potential 'Middle Power' between American capitalism and Soviet Communism still had its advocates, despite all the steps taken to consolidate the non-Communist world – the Marshall Plan (June 1947), the Brussels Treaty (March 1948), NATO (May 1949) and the Council of Europe (May 1949).[70] Some of these advocates were Americans who supported isolationism. The only serious contenders for this Third Force were Western Europe and its overseas territories. But finding a common policy in the White Commonwealth – let alone the larger European imperium – was fraught with difficulties; there was no strategic coherence in it at all and its defence clearly relied upon the USA, now that sterling and the Royal Navy were less significant than the dollar and the atom bomb. The economic and military weakness of Western Europe was taken as a given and even 'the political will to union must always be doubtful'. The 'inescapable conclusion' was that 'the closest association with the United States' was essential, not only for the purpose of blocking Soviet aggression but also in the interests of Commonwealth solidarity and European unity. The USA would inevitably take the lead, 'but experience has shown that it is usually possible to reconcile British and American views'.[71] If the Americans believed, as the British ambassador to Washington said they did, 'that major policies in the foreign field can be formulated and carried out only with the aid of Britain', then the US must make adjustments to ensure Britain's long-term economic strength.[72] As the Americans took on a bigger world role 'she was becoming increasingly conscious, first that the strength and prosperity of the United Kingdom, both in her own right and as the leading member both of the Commonwealth and of Western Europe, was an essential factor in the security of the United States; and second, that the United States cannot get the main lines of their foreign policy right . . . without our help'.[73] It was therefore contrary to the interests of both countries to injure or take advantage of the other. This, at any rate, was the line to be adopted at the forthcoming London Conferences of May 1950, intended to review the progress of the western alliance. Sterling, the sterling area and the

British colonies were 'the general sources of strength' that, paradoxically enough, required US protection. The sterling area – representing 50 per cent of world trade – had to be 'nursed back to strength', not undermined by experiments in convertibility such as that of August 1947. But the Americans, for their part, continued to warn that the USA would sometimes have to deal with 'Europe' and the UK would not be treated as a special case. If the Commonwealth somehow clashed with a strong Western Europe, the UK would have to demonstrate the reasons for giving the Commonwealth priority.[74]

Foreign Office officials recognised that 'privileged treatment' could not always be expected. Powerful voices in the USA wanted Britain to lead in European integration. There was also the danger of American isolationism. And if Germany were to be rearmed US assistance to Europe would possibly take on a more continental focus (and 'undoubtedly involve help to Spain').[75] French support for the American idea of Western European unity, and in particular a Franco-German leadership role in that venture, could also lead to rival special relationships with the USA. Ministers were advised that 'the Council of Europe must be steered away from seeking a federal system as the immediate solution to Western Europe's difficulties'.[76] Britain would persist with the principle of 'one foot in and one foot out' of Europe. At the Treasury doubts about the UK's ability to maintain both the world role and living standards in Britain continued to be expressed in 1950, as was concern that the UK was deluding both itself and the USA on this question.[77] Cripps complained that the basic economic philosophies of the two countries were entirely different, with the USA continuously pressing for the adoption of free market policies which socialist planners could not agree with (such as convertibility of sterling). Economic independence from the USA was impossible if the UK had to continue borrowing from it. Nor did Cripps like the prospect, under consideration, of Deputies to Foreign Ministers becoming the effective decision-making body inside NATO, committing Finance Ministers and Governments to projects whether they were viable or not.[78] Cripps apparently went on to say that the UK should aim 'at freeing ourselves from the political and economic hegemony of the United States'.[79] Sir Norman Brook reminded Attlee that the Third Force idea had been dead since July 1949.

Withdrawal from India, Ceylon and Burma in 1947; the need for the Americans to take over in Greece and Turkey in the same year; the scuttle from Palestine in 1948 – these strategic retreats were not intended to inaugurate a general de-colonisation process. Disengagement from the subcontinent was a function of the fact that Britain had faced an effective national movement there since the end of the First World War. Labour politicians had individually and collectively expressed sympathy with the ideal of Dominion status for India since the beginning of the twentieth century. Conservative politicians had repeatedly legislated for constitutional change to appease the nationalists, without enduring success. The Second World War further radicalised the subcontinent and brought US influence to bear on the debate about India's future. The War Cabinet had considered the idea that Britain might 'engage in a grand scheme of majestic politics involving direct appeals to Indian peasants and workers over the heads of an "unrepresentative" bourgeois Congress'.[80] Even Cripps, friend of India that he was, thought that:

> If the British Government could enlist the sympathy of the workers and peasants by immediate action on their behalf, the struggle in India would no longer be between Indian and British on a nationalist basis, but between the classes in India on an economic basis. There would thus be a good opportunity to rally the mass of Indian opinion to our side.[81]

The naivety is staggering but, to be generous, was probably born of wartime duress and wishful thinking. What was more enduring was Labour's continuing conviction that the Indian nationalists would settle for something very much like the offer made by Cripps in 1942 – a federal India composed of provinces that would be bound by treaty to Britain, enabling the latter to dominate India's regional security interests. The problem was that Nehru would settle for nothing less than independence while the Muslim League was equally adamant in its demand for a separate Muslim state. By 1946 violent unrest was spreading, especially in the north, but the search for a compromise continued. By the beginning of 1947, however, and the appointment of Mountbatten as Viceroy, the latter was able to insist on a public deadline for the end of British rule and June 1948 was set as the date for withdrawal. Bevin complained of a policy of 'scuttle' but Attlee silenced him in Cabinet by simply asking for 'a practical alternative'.[82] If Bevin was indulging in wishful thinking so had the British strategists who had initially tried to keep India within the sterling area and dependent on British military leadership, allowing London to dispose of Indian armed forces and facilities for British operations in South East Asia.[83] These ambitions had been destroyed – hence Bevin's complaints – and the hasty, improvised withdrawal that took place was not dissimilar to the retreat from Palestine a year later, and in acknowledgement of the same problem of ungovernability.

It was apparent to Attlee that civil war might develop in India as the various parties to negotiations failed to reach agreement in the course of 1946. It was certain, however, that Britain 'could not put back the clock', as Attlee put it, and introduce a period of firm British rule; neither the army nor the administration was any longer capable of this. The Viceroy, Lord Mountbatten, made it clear that the enforcement of British rule would be impossible beyond 31 March 1948. But some members of the Cabinet feared that an announcement of Britain's intention to quit India by a specified date would be perceived as the beginning of the liquidation of the British Empire and would have serious repercussions in Burma, Malaya, the Middle East and elsewhere. Bevin observed that in discussions with Egypt Britain was claiming that it was not practicable to withdraw British troops by 1949; how would this be reconciled with a rapid withdrawal from India by the spring of 1947 as the Viceroy recommended? All were agreed, however, that withdrawal had to be presented as the logical conclusion of an evolutionary process which successive British Governments had contributed to for many years.[84] By May 1947 the Viceroy's judgement about the probability of widespread communal disturbances unless there was a very early announcement of the intention to withdraw was accepted in Cabinet as the best way to 'thrust upon Indians the responsibility of deciding whether or not India shall be divided and in what way'.[85]

Once the loss of India was seen to be inevitable, the Labour Government became more dedicated to the development of the Middle East and East Africa as its replacements, though the original rationale for occupation of these places had been to defend India.[86] The Middle East now became the 'gateway to Africa' and the Indian Ocean which Britain had to defend against supposedly inevitable Soviet incursions. It was also argued that British prestige in the whole of southern Europe, the Balkans and Turkey depended on it and that it was (according to Bevin) of enormous economic value to Britain. As late as the spring of 1948 about 270,000 British troops were deployed in a dozen different countries in the region – this at a time of acute 'manpower' shortage in Britain itself.[87] Advice from the Chiefs of Staff and the Foreign Office, both as seemingly oblivious to Arab national sentiment as they were uninterested in Britain's economic plight, was adamant that the Middle East was a vital 'strategic reserve' into which the Russians would inevitably descend in the event of a British withdrawal.

On colonial matters – as in its attitude to nuclear weapons, European economic integration, the disposition to challenge Soviet hegemony in Eastern Europe and the search for economic independence from the USA – the foreign policy of the Attlee Governments was predicated on the maintenance of Britain's Great Power status on the basis of its Empire–Commonwealth. Growing tensions between the USA and the Soviet Union in the course of 1946, culminating in President Truman's announcement of an American policy of 'containment' of Communism in March 1947, followed by the announcement of Marshall Aid in June of that year, ensured that the basis was laid for a 'special relationship' with the USA – the only Power to have emerged from the Second World War stronger than when it went in. Weak though Britain was in 1945–51 it was substantially stronger than the defeated Axis Powers and France. Its global commitments meant that it could be expected to 'punch above its weight' in the confrontation with Communism. It was for these reasons that the US administration stopped lecturing the British on the evils of colonialism – as Roosevelt had done throughout the war – and began to regard the remnants of Empire as an asset. The suppression of Communist insurgency by the British in Malaysia from 1948 and the successful attempt to pre-empt a Communist victory in Greece from 1944 – not to mention the efforts to restore French and Dutch colonialism in the Far East against nationalist and Communist elements – showed what could be done.

In 1948 Communist parties throughout the world went on the offensive – rhetorical and industrial in Western Europe, military in much of Asia, including Malaya where Britain was in control. Malaya consisted of the Crown Colony Singapore and the Federation of Malaya. The latter consisted of the two British settlements of Penang and Malacca and nine Malay States, ruled over by Sultans under the protection of the British Government. A Malayan Union, providing for strong central government, was proposed by the Labour Government in 1946 but had to be abandoned. The Federation Agreement which replaced it came into existence in January 1948. The problem of governance was made complex by the rival nationalisms which the war against Japan promoted among the (two million) Chinese and (two-and-half million) Malays. The Chinese also suffered from discrimination in the higher ranks of the administration and only one-third of them qualified for citizenship. In June 1948 a state of emergency was declared as the Malayan Communist Party (MCP) initiated an insurgency which was perceived as part of a Kremlin-orchestrated campaign across the whole of Asia, though one with Maoist sympathies. The MCP was almost wholly Chinese, confined to rural areas bordering the jungle and only 8,000 strong. The British identified around 500,000 squatters in these locations who were easily intimidated by the Communists. It resolved therefore to relocate the squatters to 'administered areas', deport thousands of 'undesirable Chinese' and conduct an offensive campaign against the MCP. The protection of the rubber and tin resources of Malaya was of course crucial for the USA, their main consumer, as it was both for the revenues of the Malayan Federation and the UK's dollar spending power.

Britain's management of the Malayan Emergency provided an early illustration of the global division of labour with the USA which the survival of the British Empire–Commonwealth afforded. The fastest growing section of the Foreign Office in 1948 was the IRD.[88] Covert operations against the Communists multiplied on both sides of the Atlantic, consolidating and expanding the intimate relations between British and American secret services established during the war. Faced with the 'Soviet threat' and evidence of Communist expansion the Labour Government left office in 1951 believing that it had taken all necessary measures. There were to be no complaints about the secret services from the Labour Opposition in the 1950s. The last years in power had only seen the threat of another world war grow stronger. In China the Communist armies swept their American-backed 'nationalist' opponents into the sea in the course of 1949. In June 1950 Communist North Korea attacked South Korea, with what was assumed to be the approval of Moscow. The Attlee Government was quick to pledge troops when the UN approved military intervention (in the absence of the Soviet veto in the Security Council). The fact that intervention had UN legitimation, despite US preponderance in the forces actually despatched, was enough to persuade proponents of a socialist foreign policy to support the action – at least at the outset. Labour insisted that prompt action in Korea had 'immensely strengthened [the UN's] authority and prestige' in 'shining contrast' to the pre-war collapse of collective security. Constituency Labour Parties, however, were clearly unsettled. Resolutions on foreign policy – the vast majority on aspects of Anglo-American policies – poured into headquarters at the rate of 70–90 per month between June 1950 and the spring of 1951, double the usual rate and increasingly critical in tone.[89] While the party leadership deduced that 'the peace-loving nations must spend a larger proportion of their resources on building up their strength in arms', constituency activists drew different conclusions.[90] The British military budget already stood at a damaging 7.5 per cent of national income when the Korean War began. Under pressure from the USA, the Cabinet now approved an increase in expenditure from £700 million to £1,800 million for the year, with a further £3,600 million over the next five years. When Hugh Gaitskell became Chancellor of the Exchequer in October 1950 Britain was pressured to raise the projected expenditure to £6,000 million, though the final figure was £4,700 million – or 14 per cent of national income.

By September 1950 the USA was also pressing for German rearmament as part of NATO's unified force under an American commander. Britain's first response was to favour an expanded police force in West Germany but Dean Acheson, US Secretary of State, made acceptance in principle of this demand a condition of US leadership of the unified force and its commitment to West European defence.[91] Britain had already extended national service and increased its troops in West Germany and proposed to double its defence budget over three years, on the assumption of financial assistance from the USA worth £500 million. Bevin was nevertheless converted to German rearmament by the middle of September when he concluded that it was the only way to fulfil his strategy of involving the USA in the defence of Western Europe. NATO was only an organisation on paper and Bevin believed the Americans when they said that the whole project would collapse unless the Europeans agreed to West German rearmament. Though some of his colleagues expressed scepticism about this threat of American withdrawal, the Cabinet was persuaded to follow Bevin's lead, even though it was known that the West German social democrats opposed rearmament, as did a substantial section of public opinion in that country.[92] By 23 September Gladwyn Jebb was able to inform Attlee that he had assured Acheson that 'Britain would resolutely follow the course we had embarked on whatever Government were in office'.[93]

The US intention was to defend Western Europe as far east as possible. Labour ministers recognised that any sea change in British defence strategy which participation in this project implied was dwarfed by the cultural change which the British commitment to this project entailed. The problem was also economic. By the outbreak of the Korean War Britain had declared that it no longer required Marshall Aid. As Britain's Ambassador to Washington, Sir Otto Franks, said, 'we had won our economic independence and seemed likely to be able to keep it'.[94] It was now thought possible for the first time since the war to behave like a Great Power and sustain Britain's world-wide commitments. But the new defence obligations were certain to cause great difficulties for the British economy, increasing its overseas indebtedness, inflating the sterling balances, weakening sterling and threatening to return the British economy to the vicious circle from which it had just escaped. Dependence on the USA would grow again and was likely to last longer because, as Franks observed, 'it is . . . most improbable that the heavy burden of armies and armaments will suddenly be lifted after three years or that defence expenditure will suddenly shrink to something like a pre-Korean level. On the contrary, the prospect is that the burden will remain very heavy for a longer time and therefore that the need for substantial American aid will also be prolonged.' Franks could see that as the US increased its own burdens 'The Americans will be less patient of opinions not exactly coincident with their own'.[95] Once more, he concluded, 'we shall lose the position we were just attaining, the partner in world affairs of the United States. We shall be back again in the European Queue as in 1947.'

The Labour Government was determined that the special relationship with the USA would be maintained and strengthened. The ability to respond quickly and positively to American initiatives, and with cross-party unanimity, was one of the assets Britain brought to the relationship, as well as the diplomatic and military experience derived from long-held global commitments. After Attlee's meetings with Truman in Washington at the end of 1950 success was measured by the administration's conviction, as expressed by the President, General Marshall and Dean Acheson, 'that the United Kingdom was the only real ally on whom they could rely and that they attached great importance to [the UK's] efforts'. The Prime Minister 'welcomed these observations'.[96] In Cabinet Attlee reported that he 'had persuaded the Americans to accept Anglo-American partnership as the mainspring of Atlantic defence'. But he warned:

> Much of the advantage we had gained would be lost if we were now to be treated as merely one of the European countries which were being urged by America to make a larger contribution to the common defence effort. We should align ourselves with the Americans in urging others to do more. One could not ignore the risk, however remote it might seem, that the United States might lose interest in the defence of Europe, if her allies in the North Atlantic Treaty Organisation failed to play their proper part.

> The Prime Minister accordingly proposed that the Foreign Secretary should express general agreement with all that the United States Secretary of State was to say about the urgency of building up the military strength of the West: that he should also emphasise the substantial contributions which the United Kingdom Government had already made: but that he should be authorised to go on to say that the United Kingdom Government, in view of the disturbed and dangerous international situation, had decided to increase and accelerate their defence preparations still further, with the sole object of assisting the Atlantic community and the other nations of the free world to resist aggression and to secure their own safety and freedom, and were now considering the form and direction which this additional effort should take.[97]

Some members of the Cabinet dissented from this line of reasoning in so far as they worried – bearing in mind that the Americans were accelerating their preparations for a major war which they calculated might occur in 1951 or 1952 – that German rearmament might bring such a war about, since the Russians could consider it a *casus belli* given their experience of German arms since 1914. Certainly they might be expected to tighten their grip on the satellite countries, which also feared Germany and had suffered in recent years from German occupation. But none of these objections were decisive in Britain. In France the prospect of German rearmament was a different matter. French opposition was based on a fear of Germany which outweighed any fear of the Soviet Union. Communists and Socialists opposed the idea within the Assembly, as was to be expected, but nobody voiced enthusiasm for the American plan within the French political establishment and this was a much bigger problem. This unbending opposition led to the Pleven plan for a European army as an alternative to the incorporation of West Germany into NATO. The Labour Government objected to the Pleven plan on two grounds – because of the delay it would cause to the creation of a unified force in NATO and because of its federal implications for Western Europe, even though Britain had no intention of joining such a European army and the French had no intention of making British participation a condition of its existence.[98] In October 1950 the Soviet Union proposed the demilitarisation of Germany as a step to reunification but this was treated as a propaganda stunt.

In the event it was only another twelve months before Labour was ejected from power in the general election of October 1951. Churchill's incoming administration, realising the disastrous scale of the projected defence expenditure, scaled it down. But in the meantime differences over foreign policy within the Labour Party, already evident before the Second World War ended,[99] had flared up when it was realised that the American demands of 1950 represented the price of success for the Government's foreign policy. Aneurin Bevan's resignation from the Cabinet was the dramatic signal. A period of exceptional bitterness in the internal politics of the Labour Party was begun, centring on foreign policy. The Second World War had already led to Anglo-American cooperation in the development of the nuclear bomb and in the sharing of intelligence. It also led to a remarkable deepening of international integration which locked Britain into a web of decision-making and policy-making structures, many of them dominated by the USA. These structures were intended to involve the USA in the defence of Europe and the management of global capitalism. The Bretton Woods system devised in 1944, created the International Monetary Fund, the World Bank and the dollar–gold standard. The USA as the largest economy in the world and the wealthiest nation essentially determined the policy of these institutions and their leading personnel. In 1947 a General Agreement on Tariffs and Trade (GATT), forerunner of the World Trade Organisation (WTO), was signed to oversee the progress to free trade. After the war central bank cooperation and coordination was revived through the operations of the Bank for International Settlements, originally created in 1930 in the context of the Young Plan for the rescheduling of German reparations. An Organisation for European

Economic Co-operation was created in 1948 to administer the Marshall Plan, becoming the Organisation for Economic Co-operation and Development (OECD) in 1961. Its brief was to promote free enterprise and free trade. As the provider of Marshall Aid, the USA was a major influence on OEEC policy even though it never belonged to the organisation. Similarly, the USA played a part in promoting European economic integration from this time. Militarily the defence of Western Europe led to the creation of permanent US bases in Britain itself as well as its neighbours. NATO, set up in 1949, developed an integrated military structure, under American leadership, and became a centre for coordinated planning and weapons procurement. Britain could claim a special relationship with the USA because it was the only American ally which played a world role alongside it, both militarily and financially. Though the aim had been a partnership the critics of this policy had warned of a dangerous dependency, even subordination, to US foreign policy goals if the policy was allowed to continue.

7 A party divided

The Korean War was in full swing when Labour lost the general election of October 1951. It was not until November 1964 – soon after the US administration of Lyndon Johnson announced 'retaliatory' air attacks on North Vietnam – that Labour was returned to power.[1] In the course of the intervening thirteen years foreign policy divided the party with as much acrimony as any domestic issue ever did. In 1952 *Problems of Foreign Policy* outsold other Labour pamphlets by as much as a factor of eight and the high levels of interest in such matters was ruefully acknowledged by Gaitskell in the second half of the decade. The Labour leader suggested that the malcontents, having little to complain about domestically, had transferred their fervour to international issues. Academic commentators have contradicted Gaitskell's reasoning by suggesting the opposite – that displaced resentment with the 'revisionist' thrust of Labour's domestic policy in the 1950s explains much of the passion over foreign policy.[2] The party was more than ever disunited around the ideology of socialism with all concerned imagining themselves belonging to the vanguard of 'a movement'. Virtually everyone in the party – a party overwhelmingly composed of war veterans in one way or another – now professed to believe in socialism but the fear of another world war hung over them. Discontent with the Attlee Government's record in international relations – especially in what was now called the Cold War – hardened in the course of 1950–1, as did the party's official support for NATO, the nuclear deterrent and US leadership in the war against Communism. Bevan's resignation from the Cabinet in April 1951 gave him the opportunity to complain that the Government was becoming dependent on the course of American foreign policy and his supporters made independence on this matter a prominent theme of their critique of the way the Atlantic alliance was developing.[3] Some of the critics denounced both of the power blocs as forms of imperialism. Nobody in the party leadership, however, saw the world in this light or favoured a 'third way' between the superpowers. The leadership had a record to defend and it was a record of standing against the spread of Soviet power and Communist revolution, alongside the USA. Most of the critics focused on attacking this orientation and some of them consistently gave the Soviet Union the benefit of doubt, while denying such reasoning in relation to the USA. One thing on which all were agreed was the world leadership role of Britain and the British Labour Party in particular. The self-styled 'greatest social democratic party in the world' was repeatedly told that it had to give moral and practical leadership to the world; depending on one's viewpoint the party was enjoined to lead the world for peace, standing up to Communism, disarmament, solving world hunger, or developing the Commonwealth as a free multiracial union founded upon equality.

The parliamentary leadership – which passed from Attlee to Gaitskell in December 1955 – took the view throughout these years that a system of collective security had been established by the formation of NATO, a purely defensive organisation. This implied a moral responsibility to contribute to the defence of the free world as well as a frank recognition of the essential role of the USA in making a reality of collective security against Soviet aggression. Without the support of the USA, it was some-times said, Britain would be unable to solve its own security problem – let alone the colonial problem, the German problem and the Chinese problem.[4] The critics, when not suspected of vulgar anti-Americanism or crypto-Communism, were accused of hypocrisy and bad faith. Bevan had belonged to the Cabinet which fashioned Britain's international alignments and obligations; other critics – such as Richard Crossman – had championed the Atlantic alliance in the House of Commons. For the party's front bench both were unreliable and unsound on foreign policy precisely because they lacked political principles. But even those who took this dim view of their opponents recognised that dissidence in the constituency labour parties ran deep and that it would be unwise for the leadership to rely on the bloc votes of the trade unions to guarantee the hegemony of Atlanticism within the party. In 1951 the divided Italian socialist party, currently following a pro-Moscow policy, suggested what might happen to Labour unless the Atlanticist argument was won at the party's grassroots.[5]

The leadership was unequivocal in blaming the Soviet Union for both the breakdown of the wartime alliance and the failure of the United Nations to live up to its promise. The Attlee Government, it was said, had sought cooperation with the USA and the Soviet Union in accordance with party policy.[6] It was the Soviet Union which rejected the generous offer of Marshall Aid and constructed the Iron Curtain. Its actions in Eastern Europe, as well as its sponsorship of North Korea, demonstrated its aggressive imperialist intent. It was the Soviet Union – not Britain or the USA – which had failed to disarm in 1945. Trade union leaders such as Tom Williamson of the National Union of General and Municipal Workers were as clear about that as the parliamentary leadership appeared to be. The NEC had asserted that 'The Soviet rulers make no secret of their lust for power. Their appetite is insatiable.'[7] The Soviet leaders had repeatedly demonstrated that they recognised no alternative 'between slave and enemy – neutrality is not a possible choice'.[8] This perspective not only endorsed the view that the Soviet state was ideologically driven and would only back down in the face of greater power but was also hostage to the US view that the choice for every state was either pro- or anti-Communist. Britain, on this reasoning, was provoked into rearmament because of the obstructive and aggressive attitude of Soviet diplomacy but no neutral geographical bloc could exist anywhere in Europe; the real Third Force 'must be a world-wide political alliance against totalitarianism wherever it is found'. The TUC justified rearmament on these grounds in 1951, following the lead of the Labour Government. Arthur Deakin, speaking as the fraternal delegate from the TUC in 1952, told the conference that there was no division within the unions – 'we stand for loyalty to Leadership all the time'.[9] In this view, the divisions over foreign policy were principally fuelled by the personal ambitions of Nye Bevan in his quest for the leadership of the party. This had spawned an illegitimate party within the party composed of Bevan's supporters. It was this group which supplied 'carping criticisms' of party policy to the left-wing journal *Tribune*. Deakin argued that such divisions weakened Labour's electoral prospects when what was needed was unity to effectively perform the functions of parliamentary opposition. For the critics no effective opposition to Conservative foreign policy was possible when the signs were already clear that a bipartisan policy had taken root. They wanted foreign policy to return to party politics. But a policy that was right under Labour, Attlee observed in 1951, did not become wrong just because a Conservative administration took it over. Both of the principal parties in British politics saw the USSR as the aggressor. Britain and America had made 'concession after concession', according to Philip Noel-Baker, 'while the communist armies have been rebuilt'. Refusing to stand up to aggression in Korea, in this view, would merely repeat the mistakes made at the time of the invasions of Manchuria and Abyssinia in the 1930s. August 1914 was no longer the key referent; Munich and appeasement had replaced it in the leadership's foreign policy rhetoric.

Yet even in the adverse circumstances of the Cold War Labour believed that a foreign policy based upon 'democratic socialism' was possible. Gaitskell identified its components in 1958, much as the party had done on earlier occasions.[10] It repudiated the doctrine of might is right and aimed for a world order based on international law; it denounced doctrines of racial superiority and affirmed the brotherhood of man; it asserted the right to self-government; and it believed in redistribution of wealth from the richer to the poorer countries.[11] Few of the critics of Labour's international policies complained that these goals were vague and insufficiently socialist. Most of the complaints doubted that the leadership was at all consistent or serious about their application – a criticism which was turned against the left on the grounds of its pro-Sovietism.

Foreign policy critics

Opponents of the PLP's foreign policy had argued since the early 1940s that the choice which faced Labour was between alignment with socialist and anti-imperialist movements or an American alliance that would help to defeat these very forces. The left-wing *Tribune* was sceptical about Bevin's foreign policy up to the summer of 1947 when the Marshall Aid programme was announced. In May of that year the *New Statesman* pamphlet *Keep Left* predicted that the USA would seek a system of forward defences against Communism around the globe and that anti-Communist regimes (in Spain, South Africa, Asia and South America) would be enlisted by dollar loans in the West's quest for collective security. Polarisation would create rival blocs and democracy would be squeezed out on both sides of the divide.[12] The same pamphlet argued that the Empire was 'a strategic anachronism'; Britain had become a European country whose prosperity and security depended on the 'rest of Europe'. But if this was a plea for a 'Third Force' foreign policy it did not survive the announcement of Marshall Aid which Michael Foot, one of the authors of *Keep Left*, described as an offer of a fresh start. If the Russians decided to contract out of it, he argued, they alone would be the architects of a divided Europe. Only a handful of prominent left-wingers such as Fenner Brockway argued that Marshall Aid was an expression of US interests and designed to exclude the Soviet Union.[13] By October 1947 – after the Soviet rejection of Marshall Aid and the launch of the Cominform – *Tribune* was aligned with the essentials of Bevin's foreign policy. It welcomed Bevin's 'Western Union' speech of 22 January 1948, supported Truman against Henry Wallace in the Presidential election campaign later in the year, and welcomed the formation of NATO. The Prague Coup of February 1948 and Stalin's measures to 'sovietize' Eastern Europe, which included the persecution of socialists and others who opposed steps to one-party dictatorship, clearly played a part in this conversion. Indeed *Tribune*'s condemnation and characterisation of the Soviet Union during 1948 and 1949 was all that Bevin might have wished. It warned after the Prague events that the

Communists 'cannot be appeased by any number of concessions'.[14] It applauded those Italian voters who chose 'a clericalist-dominated Coalition' rather than the Italian Communist Party.[15] Bevan himself contributed to the condemnation of Soviet repression in Eastern Europe.[16] The extent of the Labour left's change of attitudes is reflected in the fact that when NATO was formed in April 1949 only 6 MPs voted against the motion supporting the Treaty in the House of Commons – and only two of these – Tom Braddock and Konni Zilliacus – were Labour rather than Communist or crypto-Communist.

Even after June 1950 when the Korean War began – but before its consequences were known in terms of escalating defence costs, the prospect of chronic indebtedness to the USA and jeopardy of Labour's domestic reform programme – *Tribune* continued to focus on the Soviet threat, the dangers posed by its 'fifth column' – the Communist Parties – the ulterior motives of its phoney 'peace' and its 'Outlaw the Bomb' campaigns.[17] After the general election of November 1950 and especially when it became clear that the defence budget would double, the mood changed dramatically. Defence expenditure had been brought down from £7,500 million in 1945 to £750 million in 1948–9; in August 1950 the Cabinet approved a defence estimate of £950 million. If foreign policy had served the needs of social reform after the announcement of Marshall Aid, it had ceased to do so when the consequences of the Korean War were revealed. Resignations from the Cabinet were rumoured by the end of the year as the USA took the war over the Chinese border and pressurised the Government for further increases in spending. In the event Bevan, who publicly decried the received view that Stalin was preparing to attack Western Europe, resigned alongside Harold Wilson and John Freeman, ostensibly in revolt at the prescription charges proposed by the Chancellor, Hugh Gaitskell. Bevan made it abundantly clear in his resignation speech, however, that 'all this [was] because we have allowed ourselves to be dragged too far behind the wheels of American diplomacy'.[18] By July the *Tribune* pamphlet *One Way Only* was arguing that the Soviet threat was exaggerated and that the arms race missed the main development of the twentieth century – the growing demand for independence and equality in the colonies and semi-colonies, which the West should address as its main priority.

Bevan's complaint in 1951 was that Britain had followed the USA too closely. Taken at face value this was a plea for greater independence in the Anglo-American relationship, not for a break in the relationship altogether. But it is clear that many of those who wanted to follow Bevan as a leader went further than this in the debates on foreign policy which divided the Labour Party in the 1950s. This was an evolving situation after all. The meaning of NATO in say 1959, for example, might look different than in 1949 – in the light of a unified command structure, armed with nuclear missiles, under US control. The decisions to join NATO; to support the British army in Greece; to intervene militarily in Indochina, Indonesia, Malaya and Korea; to rearm and develop the atomic bomb were evidence in these quarters that Labour had made the wrong choices in the 1940s. The wrong choice was likewise taken by the USA in backing Chiang Kai-shek against the Communists in China and by Britain in the decision to support reactionaries in Greece. For many of the critics this was all of a piece with Anglo-American support for the restoration of colonialism in South East Asia. Evidence of the unsavoury consequences of Cold War polarisation continued to appear throughout the decade, whether it took the form of leniency towards former Nazis and beneficiaries of slave labour such as Alfred Krupp; or friendliness towards the Franco regime in Spain; support for anti-Communist dictators such as Syngman Rhee in South Korea; tolerance of the apartheid system in South Africa; the decision to rearm West Germany; the McCarthyite persecution of the American left; or the use of napalm against 'gooks' in Korea. As one delegate told the party conference in 1953:

> The Cold War is not, never has been and will not be always levelled, as it has been said to be levelled, against the Russian Government, the Russian peoples or the peoples behind the Iron Curtain: the Cold War which the Executive are asking us to subscribe to . . . is against the welfare of the people of this nation and the Commonwealth and against the welfare of the subject races throughout the world.[19]

In this view the Cold War was being driven by the ambitions of a 'crowd of reactionaries' who would damage the welfare services in Britain just as surely as they would damage the economic prospects of the subject peoples; their policies ensured that bombers and tanks would be exported rather than tractors and machine tools. Other speakers pointed to the Labour Executive's double standards. Genuine nationalism was acknowledged to exist in Tunisia and Algeria but not in Kenya, Malaya and Egypt where the Executive could only see terrorists and bandits. Rearmament was required to suppress opposition to imperialism, in the interests of Western control of natural resources. The 'free world' was already an alliance, it was said, of the advanced capitalist countries with right-wing dictatorships wherever dictatorship was convenient to maintain the status quo.[20] Opponents of Atlanticism denied the claims of collective security made by the defenders of NATO and pointed to the arms race and military alliances as evidence of insecurity and instability. US dominance of NATO increased these fears and reinforced the sense that British policy was in the hands of unaccountable and unreliable decision-makers. President Truman's apparent readiness to use the nuclear bomb in Korea – which Attlee was widely believed to have talked him out of – was the sort of incident which fuelled these fears, as was the actual use of napalm in that conflict; so was General MacArthur's readiness to take the Korean War into China and John Foster Dulles' preparedness to engage in nuclear brinkmanship.

The critics had always maintained that Britain's foreign policy commitments imperilled the health and future growth of the British economy, and therefore of British living standards. They were temporarily silenced when Marshall Aid was made available but resumed this line of attack when the Korean War put increased defence spending and welfare state economies back on the immediate agenda. Rearmament continued to feature in their critiques of Atlanticism throughout the 1950s. It was said to contribute heavily to the chronic balance of payments problem of the period, as did the scale of Britain's overseas role and its futile attempt to keep abreast of the most recent military technologies. In 1952 the party's experts estimated that the army's overseas commitments, involving eleven of its 22 divisions, included Korea, West Germany, multiple garrisons in the Middle East and the Far East, Austria and Trieste, together with garrisons in Gibraltar, Malta, Cyprus and the West Indies. The navy's and RAF's commitments were on a similar scale, though precise information was lacking, as indeed it was for that portion of the economy devoted to the armed forces.[21] The critics may have been surprised to learn that a Conservative Foreign Secretary agreed with at least part of their argument. In June 1952 Sir Anthony Eden thought that 'a choice of the utmost difficulty' faced the country – 'it would either sink to the level of a second-class power or have to sacrifice its standard of living to maintain its existing commitments'.[22] At a time of rationing people were not inclined to 'tighten their belts' any further. Growing consciousness concerning Britain's flagging productivity growth and, from the mid-1950s, its declining competitiveness in manufacturing, ensured that the defence bill was frequently cited as an unnecessary burden, as well as a contributing factor in Britain's dependency on the USA. It made the country dependent on US loans, undermined the possibility of an independent foreign policy and had even necessitated the export of conventional arms to offset the costs of British rearmament, as Harold Wilson pointed out in 1952.[23] Churchill's decision to cut the defence estimates promoted by Hugh Gaitskell was taken as an early vindication of this critique, made all the sweeter by the memory of the vituperation with which the press had greeted the original rebellion of 57 Labour MPs. But as early as 1951 some activists wanted to go further than merely scaling down defence spending and were calling for unilateral disarmament.[24] Many Labour activists were indignant that bipartisanship was emerging again in British foreign policy, while some members of the parliamentary party were prepared to admit that the days when a socialist foreign policy 'involved all-out opposition to capitalism' were over.[25]

Background sentiments

All-out opposition to capitalism at home was also increasingly difficult to maintain. The party leaders sought to keep in touch with the electoral and economic realities of full-employment Britain by steering clear of further public ownership and arguing for a Keynesian management of the mixed economy, a position broadly shared by the Conservative Party. The Labour left remained opposed to such 'revisionism' and still thought of socialism as a planned, largely state-owned, economy. Throughout the 1950s the perception of powerful industrial, technological and social advances in the Soviet Union influenced left-Labour thinking.[26] The left of the party in particular took a more optimistic view of what was happening to the Communist bloc in consequence of its socio-economic development. Bevan, who thought of himself as steering a middle course between the extremes of the Cold War, envisaged the totalitarian regimes succumbing to pressures for democratisation. This was a recurring theme of his contributions to *Tribune*, though it did not prevent him from denouncing the destruction of the non-Communist left in Eastern Europe or dismissing Communism as irrelevant in Western Europe, and thus earning the hatred of the British Communists.[27] His argument was that the economic growth and sociological changes which resulted from the success of planning called into existence an educated, urban population that would demand full political status. The same objective processes depended on political reform for their continuance and Bevan assumed the Kremlin leaders realised this. After Stalin's death in 1953, when there were signs of the Soviet regime liberalising, this position acquired a wider credence. The demand for summit negotiations with the Russians, taken up by Churchill as well as the Labour left, fed off the hope that a more reasonable collective leadership now existed in Moscow. Bevan's beliefs, however, were rooted in his conception of socialism as a system based on public ownership and centralised planning. Political democracy was the natural complement to the socialised economy just as capitalism was ultimately incompatible with majority rule.[28] There was a deductive logic at work here based on assumptions that many socialists found congenial. Empirically it was supported by the real economic and technological changes which the Soviet Union was undergoing in the 1950s – changes which persuaded many conservative observers of the potency of the planned economy.[29] Khrushchev's 'secret' speech, which was published in the West in March 1956, was taken as further evidence of de-Stalinisation. Bevan also saw signs of this process in the Poznan riots.[30] On the eve of the Soviet invasion of Hungary, Konni Zilliacus MP, welcoming the signs of de-Stalinisation, asserted that the challenge of Communism was social, rather than military. Even John Foster Dulles had admitted as much in Paris in December 1955.[31] The Soviet invasion of Hungary shattered this optimistic reading, but for many on the left the disillusion was only temporary.

By 1957 'the astounding surge of material progress' in the Soviet Union was symbolised by Sputnik and the theme of Russia's march of progress was taken up again in the pages of *Tribune*.[32] Bevan's last speech at a Labour annual conference, given in the autumn of 1959, shortly before his final illness, returned to his conviction that the real challenge came from the socio-economic advances of a Soviet system based on planning, not the might of its military. Some architects of Cold War policies in the West – Paul Nitze, Frank Roberts, George Kennan and Denis Healey among them – later admitted that the Soviet military threat to Western Europe was exaggerated, and to this extent conceded that there was something in the left-wing position.[33] Likewise left critics of Labour's front bench were right to insist that it was simply untrue to construe social revolutions around the world as manifestations of a Soviet conspiracy. Many were old-fashioned nationalist movements and anti-colonial campaigns and it was essential, according to the critics, that British Labour should be seen to take the side of victims of imperialism and landlordism, not that of its perpetrators. But it was also true that the left underestimated the determinate and enduring role of the totalitarian institutions of power, as Kennan said it did, as well as the irrationality, cruelty, and waste which the Soviet system entailed. Wishful thinking and ignorance explain these errors to some extent, but also an opposition to and hatred of capitalism which often pre-dated any love affair with the Soviet Union in the development of socialist convictions. It was, after all, a matter of belief (and experience) for many socialists that capitalism generated inequality, poverty, and war. Such people could not easily look upon the USA as a friend and the Soviet Union as an enemy. The USA had many virtues, but a commitment to socialism was not among them.

The Soviet Union's nationalised economy, on the other hand, as Bevan told the annual conference in 1959, was the source of dynamism; 'Our main case is and must remain that in a modern complex society it is impossible to get rational order by leaving things to private economic adventure. Therefore I am a Socialist. I believe in public ownership.'[34] A few months later Crosland wrote to Gaitskell to express his concern that the revisionists themselves should be ready to stress public ownership and planning, in view of the Soviet Union's impressive economic growth rates.[35] The Soviet lead in the space race so impressed the public in 1960 that polls showed 81 per cent of respondents in Britain, 74 per cent in France and 53 per cent in West Germany of the opinion that American technological and scientific superiority was coming to an end.[36] Richard Crossman took a similar view of the Soviet economic challenge, so did Harold Wilson. Both believed that the winning combination was political democracy and economic planning but that, as things stood, the Soviet system would supersede lethargic free enterprise.[37] Wilson and his advisors – economists such as Thomas Balogh and scientists like J. D. Bernal – continued to invoke the superiority of Soviet economic performance right up to the general election of 1964.

While the Soviet Union emerged from the war with credit for its disproportionate contribution to the war against the Nazis and a just claim for a friendly buffer zone in Eastern Europe in the eyes of many of the Labour left, it was not perceived in these quarters as an expansionist threat to the West. Mistrust of the USA, on the other hand, started with suspicion of its capitalist character. Anti-Americanism was a factor, then, in so far as the left thought of the USA as systemically reactionary (and the USSR as systemically progressive) but the extent of popular anti-Americanism in Britain was not as important as was feared in some official circles.[38] The Communists waged a sustained anti-American campaign in Britain, especially in the years 1948–53, and accrued no perceptible advantages from it, despite drawing from the well of established elite and middle-class prejudice against the objects of American mass culture.[39] There were undoubtedly matters of concern about the alliance with the USA, however, such as the arms race, American military installations in Britain and support for right-wing dictatorships abroad. But these were largely the concerns of the activists. In terms of popular attitudes all the evidence shows that twice as many people were anti-Soviet than pro-Soviet and more people were closer to the views of Labour's Atlanticists than they were to their Labour critics.[40]

Pro-American

The alliance with America was often defended by accusing its detractors of anti-Americanism, crypto-Communism and/or a failure to understand that the USA was no longer run by Wall Street, as Denis Healey put it at the Labour conference in 1951. On the eve of General Eisenhower's success in the presidential election of 1952 it was possible to point to two decades of Democratic control of the White House and the hegemony of the New Deal coalition. The USA was a prosperous, democratic country governed by a progressive movement for social reform. The return of the Republicans to the Presidency dented this image only slightly. Institutionalised racism and McCarthyism (both of which Labour officially deplored) undoubtedly provided propaganda ammunition to the left of the party but support for the Atlantic alliance did not require its advocates to like the USA, only to see that friendship with it was in Britain's interests. Some claimed that they arrived at this conclusion naturally and unselfconsciously.[41] It flowed from wartime cooperation, a shared culture and common experiences. There was continuity of policy in this stance stretching back to the war and beyond, just as there was in the deep suspicion of Soviet Russia. Veterans of the Attlee Governments had worked with the US, often secretly, on the Brussels Treaty and plans for a West European Union; in relation to Marshall Aid; on the matter of shared intelligence which was formalised in 1947; on the NATO project and the range of issues relating to military partnership (military bases for B-29 bombers, joint command structures, defence estimates, atomic bombs and so on); on a variety of economic problems, including the European Payments Union. The Labour leadership talked with a proprietorial defensiveness about NATO, the special relationship with the USA, nuclear deterrence theory, defence requirements and Commonwealth development because the Attlee Government had been the architect of many of these policies. They had been the objects of bipartisanship in foreign policy even as they came into being, as Bevin's opposite number, Anthony Eden, made clear from the Conservative Opposition benches. During the 1950s this framework was strengthened and Labour's front bench thus found itself defending the continuity of policy rather than seeking to change it.

In response to the Communist challenge the USA launched its own cultural war which Labour was inevitably drawn into. US economic aid to Europe already implied elements of cultural transfer. The State Department – with its 27 cultural centres called America Houses in West Germany – supplemented by the Economic Cooperation Administration for purposes of dispensing $12 billion under the Marshall Plan did what it could to bolster the Atlantic Community by promoting the American Way in models of business and society. The CIA spent $1 million to support anti-Communist parties in Italy during the 1948 election and interfered in the French media and trade unions (financing *Force Ouvrière*, for example, to destroy the Communist dockers' union in Marseilles). Polls conducted in Britain and France showed that people were aware of such meddling and throughout the 1950s the Americans were alarmed by evidence of significant neutralist sentiment, especially in France.[42] The Congress of Cultural Freedom (CCF) was set up in June 1950, secretly subsidised by the CIA (established in July 1947), and run by one of its agents Michael Josselson, for the purpose of attacking such neutralism and anti-Americanism by using the best left-of-centre intellectual talent available to it. The CIA recognised that the most effective enemies of the critics of Atlanticism were those with socialist credentials themselves (Arthur Schlesinger made this point at length in *The Vital Center* [1949]). The Information Research Department in Britain, set up by the Attlee Government in 1948, which counted the *New Statesman and Nation* among the feather-brains in need of treatment, took the same view. One of the most effective interventions of this approach was the collection of essays *The God That Failed* (1950), edited by that Labour veteran of psychological warfare Richard Crossman. The CCF financed dozens of front organisations, various publications – notably *Encounter* – and a host of artistic events. In the arts it fought Soviet 'socialist realism' and charges of Western cultural decadence by showing off the avant-garde – from abstract expressionism to jazz – in proof of the West's commitment to individualism, freedom of expression, and dynamic modernity.

Of course it was hampered from the start by McCarthyism, racism and the charge of US cultural and political conformity – criticisms which the American liberal left often made more eloquently than the USA's foreign detractors. Labour's Atlanticists often 'bent the stick the other way', by lauding the USA as a model society. Crosland notably had more to say about the USA in 1956 than any other country in his classic statement of social democratic revisionism, *The Future of Socialism*, in which even social democratic Sweden received fewer references. Strikingly, when discussing equality, Crosland compared class-ridden Britain, where status anxiety allegedly lay behind most resentments, with the 'fluid equal opportunity society' of the 'classless' USA, and its 'restless egalitarian ideology'.[43] In so doing Crosland echoed an older Labour literature, to which Harold Laski had contributed *The American Democracy* as recently as 1948, which extolled America's relative openness and classlessness. Of course the context had changed and the advent of the Eisenhower–Dulles partnership in 1952 had made it much more difficult to pretend that the USA was becoming social democratic. The goals of Atlanticism had to be actively promoted – by organisations such as the Friends of Atlantic Union, set up in 1952 by Hartley Shawcross with the support of Gaitskell, Tom Williamson and Sam Watson of the Durham miners. This was a very small piece in the larger Atlanticist organisational mosaic. The multifarious activities of the Congress of Cultural Freedom formed a bigger part of the picture. In August 1953 the United States Information Agency was also established to further what is now called the 'soft power' of American diplomacy by promoting various cultural events. Then there were various foundations financing lecture tours of the USA, doling out university fellowships, providing Fulbright scholarships, dispensing grants (like the Ford and Rockefeller foundations) and – like the Smith–Mundt scheme for world leaders – working in a general way to induct foreign opinion-formers into the US world-view.[44] Reflecting on his own first taste of America, financed at first-class rates by Smith–Mundt, Roy Jenkins concluded that it had been 'a brilliant piece of unforced propaganda by the United States'.[45] Between 1956 and 1959 the Ford Foundation spent \$4,250,000 on similar schemes in Britain which provided cash, consumption, prestige and contacts on a flattering scale, enabling recipients such as Healey and Crosland to make their contributions to the Alliance in lecture tours, journalism and broadcasts.[46] Many of the cash-dispensing independent foundations were penetrated by the CIA, as a Select Committee reported in 1976 when it found that of the 700 grants of over \$10,000 disbursed in the years 1963–6 by 164 foundations, at least 108 involved partial or complete CIA funding.[47] Enthusiasm for the USA did not depend on these subsidies, of course, and there is every reason to believe, as I have already observed, that the Labour leadership embraced the special relationship in what it saw as the national interest. The Labour leadership had been present at the creation, felt at ease with their New Deal counterparts and admired many aspects of American society. They were modernisers themselves, convinced Keynesians who wanted to jettison much of Labour's ideological baggage from the 1930s and bring the party up to the challenge of affluence. They not only shared the British political establishment's conviction that the USA could be influenced by Britain, as events were to reveal they were more convinced than many leading Tories that the 'special relationship' with the USA was beyond criticism. Still, the web of Anglo-American connections played a part in consolidating Atlanticism and campaigning for it and it would be wrong to discount the subtle pressures to conform exerted by flattery and the sense of power that came from sitting alongside the powerful on board the American gravy train.

Arthur Schlesinger held that Gaitskell was responsible for bringing about a 'new view of the United States' within the Labour Party.[48] But the praise might be extended to the whole 'revisionist' group who looked to Gaitskell for leadership. Healey, Crosland, Jenkins, Gaitskell and Rita Hinden attended CCF conferences, participated in its organisational structures and undertook foreign excursions at its expense. They aired their views in *Socialist Commentary*, *Encounter* and *New Leader* and, certainly in Healey's case, received, recycled and supplied information to the IRD.[49] In defending the special relationship they shared a vested interest in minimising Britain's relative weakness in the 'partnership', as Gaitskell privately acknowledged in 1952, because to admit it was to 'look much too like a satellite'.[50] Healey and Gaitskell were also founder-members of the Bilderberg Group, set up in 1952 to fight anti-Americanism by bringing members of the European governing and business elites together. This generated suspicion, not only because of the company they kept – the right-wing intriguer Prince Bernhardt of the Netherlands was another of its founders – but also because of its secrecy. Healey also pioneered strategic thinking on nuclear weapons – becoming friends with the likes of Henry Kissinger in the process – and obtained Ford Foundation money for his Institute of Strategic Studies.[51] The guilt by association which such activities entailed in Labour left circles was paid back in full by the Atlanticists – notoriously when the annual conference elected a raft of Bevanite candidates to the constituency section of the NEC in 1952 and Gaitskell 'explained' the result by asserting that as many as one-sixth of the delegates were Communists. Gaitskell was to conflate the Bevanites and Communists on other occasions, both publicly and privately.[52] His trade union allies – such as Arthur Deakin, Victor Tewson, Tom Williamson and Will Lawther – were similarly disposed. The emotionally charged, politically committed, and often acrimonious divisions over foreign policy which characterised the decade were not conducive to the cool appraisal of unfolding events. Doubts about the value of Britain's close relationship with the USA only began to surface in revisionist circles in the early 1960s when the Common Market emerged as an alternative pole of attraction to the USA for some members of Labour's centre-right (though not Gaitskell or Healey). Occasionally it could now be publicly admitted that Britain was too weak to influence the USA, too dependent on American nuclear technology and that it possessed more in common politically and culturally with its European neighbours. The pages of *Socialist Commentary* – unlike those of *Encounter* – could even complain of the American class system, the high levels of poverty, social inequality and racism in the USA, echoing arguments which Francis Williams deployed in *The American Invasion* (1962).[53] But even in the early 1960s this sort of criticism was a rarity and with the advent of the Kennedy administration it once again became expedient for politicians like Harold Wilson to contrast dynamic America with 'caste-ridden' Britain under the Tories.[54]

Third World and Commonwealth

From the moment Labour entered opposition both sides in the internal debate invoked the desperate condition of people in Africa, Asia and Latin America to support their arguments. The context was one of growing international hostility to colonialism, inevitably reflected in the UN. The party leadership almost annually talked of the urgent need to increase economic aid from the rich countries to one per cent of their

GDP. Meanwhile, the Conservative Government took up its predecessor's policy of opposing any trend within the UN which threatened to impose accountability to that body on the colonial powers.[55] Aid was explicitly linked to the task of preventing an alignment of the poorest countries of the world with the Soviet Union.[56] The critics complained that such a transfer of resources to the Third World[57] (as it would come to be known) simply would not happen if the arms race and the Cold War continued. The leadership claimed that progressive measures had been taken already to raise living standards in the colonies. They invoked legislation such as the Colonial Development and Welfare Act of 1945 and the Overseas Resources Act of 1948; they pointed to the work of the Colonial Development Board and the Overseas Food Corporation; and they promoted the economic aid proposals of the Colombo Plan, which was conceived at a meeting of British Commonwealth foreign ministers in 1950, as proof of Labour's commitment. In 1953 Labour was still persuaded that economic development of the colonies was a way of overcoming 'the dollar problem' and throughout the decade the Commonwealth was at the centre of its foreign economic policy. What was wanted, it argued, was more systematic exploitation, through a Sterling Area Development Plan, of those raw materials of the sterling area which would either earn dollars or obviate the need for Britain to spend them – such as oil, copper, lead, zinc, bauxite, chromite, cobalt and manganese.[58]

The leadership also insisted that the Attlee administrations had made significant advances in the promotion of cooperatives and trade unions in Britain's African colonies. The trade union effort continued throughout the 1950s, with the TUC 'assisting colonial trade unions to establish themselves', as one congratulatory resolution put it. But this interpretation was challenged by those who saw only class collaboration in the TUC's policies.[59] Certainly Vincent Tewson, the TUC's General Secretary (1946–60), accepted the official view of Britain's colonial role and was quick to spot extremism and 'unsuitable leadership' among colonial trade unionists, while stressing the 'common bond of British nationality' which bound 'responsible' trade unionists, irrespective of background, together. To these people he would stress that 'self-government is not a panacea'. Yet though the TUC held no 'magic wand' to help its colonial brothers, it was clear to Tewson that all constitutional change in the colonies since 1945 was evidence of 'progress'.[60] The trouble was that African union officials had a 'predilection for politics'.[61] This was something that was inevitable, it could be acknowledged, when – as in Kenya – the unions were the only legal organisations with which Africans could be associated. Likewise trade unionism and politics were 'inevitably and inextricably intermingled in the West Indies'. But this only underlined the dangers represented by weak or irresponsible leadership. 'Serious trouble' could quickly arise, as Communists and others took over.[62]

As the decade progressed Tewson complained bitterly of the Commonwealth's critics. Some of the big left-wing unions – the ETU and USDAW in particular, but even the NUM – forwarded resolutions denouncing colonial exploitation, demanding 'immediate withdrawal of all armed forces' and the institution of self-government, as 'the only way of saving the British Empire from disintegration and making possible a real commonwealth of nations'.[63] To Tewson's dismay the critics included the AFL–CIO and the ICFTU by the mid-1950s. These now joined the chorus demanding the elimination of colonialism, drawing attention to events in Cyprus and Algeria which, they argued, provided gratuitous fuel for the Communists.[64] In this context Tewson lamented the fact that 'it is widely assumed that the territorial enemy is the [British] Government and this assumption is fostered both by the ICFTU and by the Americans in their constant reiteration of the terms "anti-imperialism" and "anti-colonialism" . . . In theory, practice and experience we know more about the sound development of African trade unions than either the ICFTU or the Americans.'[65] By 1959, however, Tewson acknow-ledged that 'destructive influences within Africa have been greatly strengthened in the last few years' by such diverse influences as Radio Cairo, the Algerian 'rebellion', pan-African propaganda, and the bad impression created by apartheid in South Africa. All these, Tewson thought, 'contribute to a turning away from the white man'.

It was especially galling to hear fellow moderate trade unionists, such as those who led the AFL–CIO, complaining about the gifts to Communist agitation supplied by European colonialism. Tewson had been dedicated to rooting out Communism since the Cold War began. In fact the TUC added to its official role in the colonies on this issue in 1954, when it entered into regular tripartite meetings, at Oliver Lyttelton's instigation, with representatives of the Colonial Office and the Overseas Employers Federation (OEF). The Conservative Secretary of State for the Colonies could see the utility of involving the TUC in 'combating Soviet propaganda in the Colonies'.[66] The mission was soon adjusted to 'the exploring of the best means of tackling problems of industrial relations in Colonial territories', focusing on 'particular "crisis territories", most of them in Africa, as they became topical'. When the Kenyan Emergency began, for example, the TUC approached the Colonial Office with a proposal to help develop Kenyan unions.[67] When, in 1956, the Kenyan authorities found that the Kenyan Federation of Labour (KFL) was 'pursuing objects other than those declared in its application for regis-tration', activities that 'assumed the character of a political association' and which involved a breach of the Emergency Regulation (1956) forbidding nation-wide activities, Tewson successfully intervened to get the KFL to desist. Walter Hood, of the TUC's Colonial Section, helpfully stayed on for another 'several months' to supervise the KFL's adjustment.[68] The thrust of the TUC's contribution, throughout the decade, remained committed to nurturing 'responsible' trade unionism in the colonies and rooting out Communism, nationalist politics and other forms of subversion. By 1960, with many of the colonies now independent, the OEF was keen to involve the Foreign Office and the Commonwealth Relations Office in this work and expand the remit of the committee to consider 'the political and practical aspects of International Labour Office (ILO) Conferences', given 'the increasing impact of the ILO on the undeveloped areas and the increasing impact of the Communist bloc upon the ILO'.[69]

Both sides to the debate asserted that poverty bred discontent, racism and war. The TUC freely admitted, for example, that while 'terrorist' activities in Kenya were deplorable, solutions to the problems of land-hunger, the colour-bar and slum-dwelling had to be found 'if the Colony was to develop into a multi-racial society'. The party was officially committed to the view that the peoples of Asia were engaged in historic revolution. It claimed to support 'a world uprising of colonial peoples against the old imperialism', as *Challenge to Britain* expressed it in 1953.[70] The Labour Government had recognised the People's Republic of China soon after it came into existence and the party criticised the USA for not doing the same, instead clinging to the pretence that Formosa/Taiwan legitimately represented the Chinese nation inside the UN. Attlee assured the party that the government of China embodied 'the national revolt of China' and was not to be confused with the governments of the satellite states of Eastern Europe. In 1954 he admitted that 'you can see that same spirit in Indo-China', an admission that came in the wake of the Geneva Accords of July which had partitioned the country and provided for free elections (which never took place). He told the conference that this national spirit could be seen 'throughout the East'. It was necessary 'to persuade the colonial peoples that they can fulfil their aspirations in co-operation with the West'. This would involve massive investments in developing food and raw material resources and programmes to eradicate the 'causes of misery'. The party was content to repeat its declaration of 1947, recently restated by the Conservative Colonial Secretary, that:

> The central purpose of British Colonial policy is simple. It is to guide the Colonial territories to responsible self-government within the Commonwealth under conditions that ensure to the people concerned both a fair standard of living and freedom of oppression from any quarter.[71]

But elements on the left of the party were not afraid to question the party leadership's anti-imperialist credentials – seeing the evidence in Britain's continuing military role in the Middle East after the war (as in Egypt) and in the exploitation of Africa (by 'living off other people's dollars', as one conference delegate put it) during the period of the Labour Governments. The wars in Malaya, Korea and Indochina – all depicted as Soviet-inspired by their Labour supporters – were seen on the left as Western capitalist aggressions designed to destroy legitimate nationalist movements. If the Communist insurgents of Malaya were so unrepresentative, one delegate asked the 1952 conference, why were half a million Malayans incarcerated in so-called resettlement camps, why was collective punishment employed and chemical warfare and why was the war taking so long to finish; was not the conflict really about British control of Malaya's tin, rubber and mineral wealth and the dollars it supplied to the sterling area?[72] Three years later the Malayan Labour Party made representations to the NEC complaining that under the Emergency Regulations 7,000 people had been detained for up to two years on suspicion and that it was 'well nigh impossible under this prevailing cloud of suspicion for any growth of legitimate political activity . . . among genuine Malayan nationalists'.[73] How would the skills for future self-government be developed, who were the people who would lead the newly independent nations, what was the agency (or agencies) of change and progress in the colonies – other than the drafters of constitutional documents in Whitehall?

The leadership itself was wont to invoke the Commonwealth as Britain's key global responsibility – at once the vehicle for Britain's moderating influence upon world events, source of Britain's economic independence and prosperity and proof of its multi-racial cooperative commitment and anti-imperialist purpose. It pointed to the constitution-making activities of the Attlee Governments, as well as withdrawal from the Indian subcontinent, as evidence of steps towards genuine partnership. Withdrawal from the African Crown Colonies was still depicted as a childish fantasy and support for it was said to reveal more about the irresponsibility of the (domestic and colonial) extreme left than the realities of colonial development. The maintenance and economic development of the Commonwealth, the close individual links of 'every single member of the Commonwealth', as Patrick Gordon Walker expressed it in 1952, depended on the alliance with the USA. Thus utilising the special relationship, Britain's own high standards in the Commonwealth were expected to win it friends in the Third World generally, while the need to win friends among Third World nationalists was to act as an additional incentive to reach those standards within the Commonwealth. Institutionalised racism in Kenya, Tanzania and

Southern Rhodesia – to take some obvious examples – posed a public relations problem for this vision, as did apartheid South Africa's membership of the Commonwealth. The South African regime justified itself to the world in the common language of anti-Communism and was left to get on with apartheid by the USA and Britain until the Sharpeville massacre in 1960. Cold War alliances everywhere were apt to take on the appearance of a 'white man's club' like the ANZUS Pact which came into force in 1952.[74] The hasty creation of SEATO in 1954, in response to the French defeat in Vietnam, failed to dispel this impression (and prompted Bevan's resignation from the Shadow Cabinet). All the main countries of Asia – India, Indonesia, Malaysia and China – were outside the organisation and viewed it as an instrument of power politics imposed on the region by the USA with the intention of destroying national liberation movements under Communist leadership in South East Asia. Certainly, this was the dominant perception expressed at the Bandung Conference of neutralist countries in 1955. By this time Communist insurgencies in Malaya and the Philippines had been defeated, though similar movements continued sporadically in Burma and Laos. More important was the growth of neutralist feeling such as that represented by Nehru in India and Sukarno in Indonesia. Indonesia had a growing Communist Party which won almost a quarter of the vote in the 1955 election. Sukarno himself was militantly anti-imperialist and a leader of the non-aligned movement which the Bandung Conference came to symbolise. British and French policy could live with neutralism as a way of dealing with lost causes such as Laos, Cambodia and Vietnam but the Americans looked upon it as another way of nurturing the Communist problem. The USA was therefore determined to create a pro-Western, national Government in South Vietnam. Open force and covert operations would be used when necessary, as left-wing commentators on Vietnam observed in the pages of *Tribune* throughout the decade. SEATO, with Britain as a charter member, was thus committed to the 'defence' of countries like Vietnam from Communism. Covert operations initially had a large part to play in this, in the wake of the French defeat in Indochina, and spread throughout the region from Singapore to Laos and Indonesia.[75] France and Britain were more resistant, however, to US pressure for open military intervention in the region.

Labour's vision of the social revolution in Asia and of the need to come to terms with nationalism was a commonplace among policy-makers on both sides of the Atlantic during the 1950s and can be traced back to pre-war discussions in Britain itself. The spread of nationalism to Africa, for example, was anticipated by Lord Hailey and officials in the Colonial Office in the 1930s. Labour's own flurry of constitution making in Africa after 1945 was one aspect of the attempt to manage the process – India, Pakistan and Palestine were others. Nationalism came in many varieties and could not always be managed. It was often dismissed as the work of Communists, deracinated agitators and half-educated wreckers. To talk of using it as a buffer against Communism – as almost everyone did in the 1950s – was at best superficial. Western policy throughout the decade was often unable to distinguish nationalism from Communism in the Middle East and South East Asia or to refrain from interpreting local events through the prism of the Cold War.[76] But it could not be denied that most Third World countries were experiencing rapid population growth and urbanisation. Aspirations for rapid economic growth and modernisation sponsored by the state appealed in this context, at a time when the rhetoric and practice of state-directed planning was prominent in all industrialised economies. British policy, however, was caught in a net of contradictions. As Bevin discovered, it could not afford to take the lead in the modernisation of whole regions such as the Middle East and Africa, where it wanted to play the Great Power role. As the imperial Power Britain was inevitably saddled with a negative image which could even deteriorate. After 1948 'the prevalent opinion' in the Arab countries, to take an obvious example of this deterioration in practice, was that British policy had allowed Zionism to triumph in Palestine.[77] Britain was further disadvantaged by its long-held imperial role, now widely disfavoured, as illustrated by sustained Egyptian intransigence over renewal of the treaty of 1936 and the refusal of Iraq to renegotiate the treaty of 1930.

In Opposition Labour recognised some of these disabilities.[78] Though Britain was 'the only foreign power directly involved in protecting the Middle East from aggression', it argued, nationalism – 'the one political feeling easily aroused' in the region – 'usually means violent hatred of Britain'. The Attlee Governments had, it was acknowledged, failed 'in laying firm foundations for future policy'. Yet 'twentieth-century forces' were visibly changing the political landscape of the Middle East by the early 1950s. The party's experts on international issues noted that 'Communist opinion is already considerable in Persia and growing in Egypt, Syria and Lebanon'. The task ahead was to meet nationalism by assuring the states of the region equality in arrangements for Middle Eastern defence. This was the 'imperialism by treaty' approach pursued since the end of the Second World War. Beyond that some means had to be found for raising living standards, but the party was no clearer about how this could be achieved in 1952 than Bevin had been years earlier. The 'corrupt and incompetent' governments of the region were just as likely to spend foreign aid in the casinos of Monte Carlo as use them for development projects. The 'only exception' to this general picture that Labour could see was the state of Israel, where an industrious, highly intelligent people was led by 'men of outstanding ability' with close personal ties to the West (indeed, 'many of them served their apprenticeship in the ranks of the British Labour Party'). The party's policy-makers admitted there was also Turkey – 'a dictatorship which is developing peacefully into a democracy' – recently admitted to the Atlantic Pact and now considered a European power.

Though British troops in Egypt were withdrawn to the Canal Zone, serious disturbances in 1951 and 1952 testified to the strength of opposition to the continued military occupation. The events of 1952 provided the opportunity for the overthrow of the King and the installation of a Free Officers' regime in which Abdul Nasser emerged as the key figure. Egypt enacted measures of land reform which helped to destroy the old power bloc. Similar moves were made by modernisers in Syria. The state was becoming more active in educational reform throughout the region in the 1950s. Literacy levels rose and access to the mass media of newspapers, radio and cinema increased dramatically. Workers' organisations developed across the region – trade unions, socialist, Ba'athist, and Communist parties in countries such as Egypt, Iran, Iraq, Syria, Lebanon and Jordan. The educated elite embraced a modern Islam that could coexist with modernity, one that was 'rational, humane, democratic and devoted to economic progress'.[79] At the same time the fundamentalist religious teachings of organisations like the Muslim Brotherhood also took root in Egypt and Syria. But much more important were the great drivers of collectivism. Were these the political currents which the British Government and 'the West' would seek to nurture? It would be very difficult to achieve even if such an objective had been consistently pursued. The nationalist movements arose in opposition to imperialism. On the world stage they identified with and helped to shape the idea of the 'Third World', whether acting in the UN or as 'nonaligned' countries. The appeal of socialism ('Arab socialism', 'African socialism' etc.) was as likely to draw them into the Soviet orbit as that of the West, so too the drive to raise living standards. 'Nasserism' was the name best associated with these changes, developing as a language of reformist Islam at the service of modernisation, Arab nationalism and unity.

The British position in the Middle East – as elsewhere in the Third World – depended on traditionalist and reactionary elements, often by virtue of the 'imperialism by treaty' I have already referred to; thus the protectorates of the Persian Gulf such as Aden, Bahrain, Oman, and the Trucial States of Abu Dhabi, Dubai, Ras al-Khaimah, Fujairah, Sharjah, Ajman, and Umm al Qaiwain. The military base at Aden was a launching pad for intervention in Kuwait – another dependency with which Britain had signed a defence treaty – to protect oil supplies. Britain also cultivated Iraq under Nuri el-Sa'id and Jordan under the Hashemite monarchy, sending troops to the latter in 1958. It also constructed, with Labour support, the Baghdad Pact with Turkey and Iraq in 1955, by which time Nasser had long been identified in London as a rogue element with ambitions to establish revolutionary regimes throughout the region but especially in Iraq, Jordan, Libya and Saudi Arabia. Britain could not rely on the USA to underpin its Middle Eastern position. Washington fancied itself as a friend of the new nationalist movements, which were often anti-British, and wanted to keep them out of the Soviet orbit. This was never a consistent policy and could not be, given the Americans' tendency to regard neutralism in the Cold War as tantamount to pro-Sovietism and evidence of Communist infiltration. But if the British expected a simple *quid pro quo* in the Middle East for British support in Korea they were mistaken.[80] Eden tried and failed to get US support for Britain as he negotiated for an acceptable treaty with Egypt to replace that of 1936. The Americans were already friendly with elements in the Egyptian army opposed to what they saw as the British puppet-state in Cairo and saw the need to get the British out as quickly as possible.[81] Nasser and his co-thinkers were wooed before and after the military coup of 1952 and while the CIA established close links with the Free Officers group, MI6 lost its covert connections as the old regime went under.[82] Nasser, it was hoped in Washington, was a moderniser who would fight Communism as well as Islamic fundamentalism and establish Egypt as an ally of the West. The USA had already shown, however, that it was perfectly prepared to overthrow nationalists when they refused to play according to these rules. It was the USA which sponsored the coup which removed Mussadiq in Iran in 1953, replacing a nationalist nuisance with a pliable king. Britain's Egyptian problems simply coincided with an American effort to build alliances in the Middle East – including negotiations with Iraq, Pakistan and Turkey for a Northern Tier defence pact – perhaps leading to a US hegemony in the region that might replace Britain altogether. British operations were often in the way. Dulles complained to Eden that while the USA was keen to 'sponsor' nationalism as a way of beating the Soviets at their own game, and also in accordance with the USA's 'historic tradition', the Americans were often 'restrained from doing so by a desire to cooperate with Britain and France in Asia, in North Africa and in the Near and Middle East'.[83] In other words, the Anglo-American association did not always help with the cultivation of friendly nationalists and it was in any case unwise to present a united front to the Arab world that would only smack of imperialism. But any suggestion of a conflict of interests within the special relationship was taboo on Labour's front bench and it is arguable that the world saw the relationship in the same simplistic way as Labour. Since, in fact, Britain and the USA were on the same side in the Cold War and both supported

Israel, anti-imperialist sentiment in the Middle East, combining with grievances over Palestine and a rising nationalist sentiment, provided an ideological cocktail for neutralism in the Cold War, if not actual alignment with the Soviet Union.

That outcome was arguably made more likely by the impressive number of CIA covert operations in the Middle East recorded after the overthrow of Mussadiq, building on the work done during the Second World War by its forerunner, the Office of Strategic Services.[84] Syria was a particularly fertile field of operations. In 1948 the CIA had a hand in the overthrow of President Shukri Quwatly, under whose nationalist regime the largest Communist Party in the Arab world was allowed to prosper. The succeeding military regime promptly imprisoned hundreds of Communists. Two further coups produced the military government of Adib Shishkali who allowed the CIA to train his own security forces. When he too was overthrown, the Agency worked to topple the Ba'athist government which followed. The assassination of Colonel Adnan Maliki in 1955 cut short the blossoming relationship between Syria and Nasser's Egypt but also let loose a wave of anti-Americanism in Damascus which produced another unwanted administration seeking Soviet assistance. Britain and the USA now conspired to remove it. The Suez Crisis diverted attention and delayed proceedings, however, until 1957 when Syrian intelligence intervened and expelled some of the plotters from the country. The litany of covert interventions and unintended consequences chalked up in Syria was repeated in Iraq after 1958. Once again 'leftist' regimes, such as that of Abdel Qassim in 1963, were forcibly removed with CIA assistance only to create further violent turbulence and uncertainty – this phase concluding only when Saddam Hussein instituted his personal dictatorship. Somehow all of this was designed to produce allies for the West. But while the USA was engaged in finding friends in the Third World, British Labour was boasting that it already had them in abundance.

West European integration

The Labour leadership made the conventional mistake of assuming that the Commonwealth was the best basis for Britain's economic prosperity in the 1950s. Prior commitment to the world political role informed this analysis and screened out empirical evidence which contradicted the ruling assumptions, even when such evidence accumulated as it did in the late 1950s. The party had no objection to the steps being taken towards a federal Europe but objected to British participation. Few could follow Healey in arguing that 'the maintenance of Britain as a world power is a precondition of a socialist foreign policy'.[85] But it was commonplace to talk, as Dalton talked in 1951, of the danger of 'reactionary elements' dominating any supranational authority and preventing socialist measures in Britain and this became a settled (though not unanimous) view on the left of the party until the 1980s. Initially it was convenient to stress the socialist credentials and purposes of the party, as much as the global interests of Britain, as incompatible with the American enthusiasm for European integration.[86] Socialism was 'indispensable' in democracy's ideological battle with Communism, so nothing should be done to impair its chances in Britain. But the party leadership was also perfectly frank in claiming that Britain was not just another European country. It was the 'nerve-centre' of a world-wide Commonwealth. Its people had more in common 'in every respect' with the people of the Dominions than with Europeans. The economies of the Commonwealth, moreover, were complementary with Britain's 'to a degree which those of Western Europe could never equal'. The sterling area represented the largest multilateral trading area in the world and was 'a vital British interest'. Labour had transformed 'four hundred millions of Britain's Asian subjects into friends and equal partners', building a bridge between East and West and between white and coloured people. The Commonwealth 'now represents the nucleus of a potential world society based on free cooperation' and could become the basis for the unification of all non-Communist peoples 'into a single system which is both economically stable and politically secure'. Since 'the battle for Europe could well be lost in Asia' the political value of the Commonwealth was self-evident. But Labour was also adamant that the construction of 'an organic unity throughout the whole of the non-Communist world' could not be achieved without the USA.[87] The prospectus, then, was for an Anglo-American partnership in which Britain would employ its global assets for the mutual struggle against Communism.

On a less grandiose level the party also found reasons to doubt the economic benefits of a supra-national European unity, the feasibility and democratic credentials of the supra-national project, the wisdom of its reliance on market forces, the political stability of the participants, and the appropriateness of the project for surmounting such pressing practical problems as the dollar gap. Britain's world-role also raised obvious practical issues in 1951–2. Could the loose association of the Commonwealth be tightened institutionally? Should the cultivation of good relations with black Africa change Britain's hitherto lenient stance on apartheid South Africa? Could future economic aid to the undeveloped economies do better than the failing Colombo Plan? What was to be done about the fact that Pakistan was showing a tendency to team up with the Arab countries against Britain in the Middle East or the fact that India, Burma and Indonesia were well disposed towards Communist China? What exactly were Britain's 'vital interests' in the Middle East and what was the best way to guarantee them, bearing in mind that Britain's power 'is now much reduced'? What was to be Labour's attitude to corruption in 'the Arab ruling cliques'? What plans did it have for the economic and political development of the Arab countries? This is just a sample of the 'Questions of International Policy' which Morgan Phillips, the party's secretary, asked the NEC to consider at the beginning of the 1950s.[88]

Such questions were not allowed to qualify public support for the 'revolution in British foreign policy' which the Attlee Governments had carried out in 'adjusting Britain's international position to the political and economic changes of the atomic age'.[89] Though nationalism was seen to be spreading to Africa, it was asserted that under a Labour Government 'economic development in the Commonwealth [had] proceeded many times faster than before the Second World War – to the mutual benefit of all concerned'. Though there was evidence that the USA 'was becoming less tolerant of foreign advice' the Commonwealth itself 'could not survive a break between Britain and America'. British commitments had to be brought into alignment with both its physical strength to sustain them and with the fact that the world was coming to realise the limitations of this strength. This was one of the reasons why 'many of the Labour Party's most important objectives in world affairs depend on America assuming, not fewer responsibilities than she has already, but more': 'The problem for Britain may be summed up as follows: How can we ensure that America plays an increasing part in world affairs without losing our own influence and even sacrificing vital British interests?'[90]

This was a reason why 'the methods adopted to create European unity must serve above all to achieve solidarity in the face of Soviet expansionism'.[91] This position only began to change in 1960–1, when it became clear that the economies of the six countries belonging to the Common Market were growing faster than Britain's and that living standards were catching up with, 'even overtaking', Britain's. Whether Britain joined the Common Market or not, faster economic growth had become essential to it.[92]

It continued to be stressed, however, that Britain was a world power enjoying a unique role both as the centre of a Commonwealth and in the special relationship with the USA. But it was more apparent in 1961 – after a decade of relative decline – that the world political role depended on a strong economy. The question, for some, was whether Britain could obtain one on its present basis. Even in 1961, however, political considerations loomed larger for most of the Labour Party and these argued against membership, either on socialist or Great Power grounds. The Finance and Economic Policy sub-committee of the NEC, for example, admitted that 'the balance of economic advantage . . . probably lies in joining the Six' – it was not especially clear – but political considerations pointed the other way. Economic advisors such as Thomas Balogh and Nicholas Kaldor were not shy to question either of these arguments. Balogh dismissed the special relationship and the Commonwealth as mere sentimentality and favoured membership, but only as a last resort 'when all else fails'.[93] Kaldor doubted whether membership would jolt Britain into economic efficiency and dynamism but was certain that integration with the Six would reduce Britain's role in world affairs.[94]

Gaitskell, nevertheless, was still able to unite left and right of the party behind an anti-Common Market stance in 1962, focusing on the sentimental side of the world role – the Commonwealth – as Dalton had done ten years earlier. Some of the Gaitskellites had always been more concerned to defend the Atlantic alliance than to think very much about the Commonwealth as an economic asset – but emphasising the virtues of the Commonwealth was one of the devices they employed to achieve their objective. For such people as Denis Healey European federation fuelled the idea that Europe 'could somehow contract out of the world struggle', as he put it in 1951. In 1962 it implied the desire to stabilise 'the unnatural post-war status quo in Europe and to render it more permanent', while Britain's entry 'might assume the same obstructive role in relation to the USA's demand for a global free trade area as France adopted towards Britain on the European Free Trade Association'. It might also provoke, Healey feared, 'a major political and economic split in the West'.[95] It never mattered that the USA itself favoured Britain's participation. The American Ambassador in London found Healey 'genial and calm' in March 1964 and reported that 'he only showed emotion when he referred to the prospects of European unity', commenting that 'his anxiety to prove that unity would never happen seemed to reflect special concern'. He advised that Healey's education on this matter would accelerate after Labour came to power and he came 'up against the reality of German desires'.[96] The real difference by then was that there were more people in the PLP who saw through the rationale for the world role based on the Commonwealth, though not enough to make an immediate difference.

German rearmament

Ten years earlier the European unification debate that mattered was all about defence. The Korean War convinced the US administration in 1950, as we saw in the previous chapter, that West Germany had to be rearmed. Strong objections to this proposal in Europe led to a French counter-proposal to bring West Germany into a European Defence Community

(EDC) which would integrate the armed forces of the partners in the recently formed European Coal and Steel Community. This had the effect of calming fears and tempers in the Labour Party for a while. It allowed the leadership to argue that while it favoured 'the construction of an international system of collective security within which German forces could serve without danger to their neighbours', it first of all wanted French rearmament and a Four Power conference (USA, Soviet Union, Britain and France) to settle the question of German reunification after free elections had been held in both parts of the country. A Soviet offer to permit German reunification – if the Oder–Niesse frontier was taken as final and a united Germany was made neutral – was put in March 1952 and rejected by Adenauer who demanded free elections in East Germany. Adenauer's foreign policy worried much of the Labour Party. West Germany continued to be seen as a haven for former Nazis and war criminals throughout the 1950s. It was already 'the strongest single continental power and was beginning to compete effectively in exports with Britain, both in Europe and overseas'.[97] Under Adenauer's leadership it was staunchly right-wing, pro-American and anti-Soviet. Its foreign policy was committed to the restoration of Germany's 1937 frontiers, which meant refusal to accept the current Polish frontier, let alone the legitimacy of East Germany.[98] West Germany thus had 'no interest in the survival of the present status quo'. Labour also had problems with the German social democrats (SPD) whose leader, Kurt Schumacher, had opposed some of the Labour Government's policies in occupied Germany.[99] Even after Schumacher's death the SPD continued to oppose EDC and any system of collective security involving West Germany, chiefly on the grounds that it would obstruct reunification.[100] It too stood for the frontiers of 1937. Four-Power negotiations preparatory to reunification, the SPD argued, would be scuppered for ever if the provisional Federal Republic was transformed by military alliances into something permanent and irrevocable.[101] Attlee tried to placate critics of German rearmament by insisting that it would not happen unless post-war boundaries were accepted, Germany remained nuclear free and East–West issues were subject to negotiations. The 1952 annual conference was told that there was no need to vote on this issue because in the Executive's view 'conditions do not yet exist in which German rearmament can be safely undertaken'. This reassurance did not prevent delegates objecting to the rearmament of 'Nazi Germany' on principle and expressing suspicions of the 'reactionary' Adenauer Government and fears of a revived German militarism.[102] The alliance with the USA, it was argued, had forced Labour's leaders to accept the principle of German rearmament as early as December 1950. In 1953 the Executive said that there should be no German rearmament until further talks had been given the chance to secure the peaceful reunification of the country. But even though Attlee's defence of this position was careful to observe that an unarmed Germany was an altogether unrealistic option, Denis Healey complained that in supporting the idea of a summit the party was merely following the lead taken by the Prime Minister, Winston Churchill, and ignoring the fact that Labour had agreed to German rearmament when in power in 1950 and 1951.

Although the EDC Treaty was signed in May 1952 the French National Assembly refused to ratify it and thus killed the project in August 1954. Before this outcome was known, however, Harold Wilson had moved a resolution opposing rearmament at a meeting of the PLP in February 1954 (losing 111 votes to 109). West Germany's accession to NATO in September only served to strengthen Adenauer's conviction that reunification must come before there could be any détente with the Soviet Union. Labour argued the reverse – détente and acceptance of the Oder–Neisse line as the first steps in a process that might lead to reunification. The Conservative Government now proposed the modification and completion of Western European Union (WEU), which the Brussels Treaty of 1948 had provided for shortly before the creation of NATO.[103] In October 1954 WEU was revived and amended to incorporate West Germany (and Italy) into Western defence. These decisions, following quickly on the failure of the Four-Power conference on German reunification at Geneva in February, set the scene for the angry Labour conference debate about German rearmament later that year. Attlee explained that it was all about integrating 'Germany' with the West; later in the same meandering speech, he implied that this entailed arming West Germany. Opponents of this project pointed out that the German Social Democratic Party opposed rearmament and even the Labour Executive had not had the courage to openly support the proposal. Some unions had already registered almost unanimous opposition at their own conferences, no doubt informed by the fact that the Labour leadership itself had made German reunification a precondition for any rearmament of Germany and this prospect had been scotched at Geneva. George Brown MP frankly asserted that an armed West Germany was necessary when 'there is a vast, well-armed military power coming down very near to our shores'. Others observed that 'Russia' would never allow free elections in East Germany – an uprising there had been suppressed as recently as June 1953. West German rearmament could not be prevented by the Labour Party or the British government, nor could anyone indefinitely commit the occupation forces necessary to keep it disarmed. Denis Healey invoked Tito's support for German rearmament and tried to suggest that it would be a step towards international disarmament. Somehow the government of Mendès-France – the best in France since the war, he said – depended on it and would fall if it did not go ahead. The battle of Dien Bien Phu, signalling the end of French occupation of Vietnam, had already taken place but Healey's French friends were about to begin another colonial war in Algeria.

Opponents of West German rearmament feared that the Russians would retaliate by further militarising Eastern Europe (the Warsaw Pact and Adenauer's intention to build up the *Bundeswehr* were both announced in May 1955). The pacifist leanings of younger Germans would be betrayed. The possibility of German reunification would be quashed because the Russians would fear that the whole of it would end up in a Western power bloc and the American military bases would creep forward to the Polish border. They wanted to know why an invasion of unarmed West Germany had not happened in the nine years since the war but was more likely to happen now if West Germany remained unarmed. The vote which ended the German rearmament debate in 1954 gave the Executive a majority of only 250,000 votes out of the 6,250,000 cast. But the issue returned in 1955 when delegates quoted Erich Ollenhauer, the leader of the West German social democrats, to the effect that West German rearmament obstructed German reunification. In 1956 conference was urged to demand the progressive withdrawal of NATO and Soviet forces from Germany. After the Soviet invasion of Hungary the Labour leadership began to argue for a neutral belt in Central Europe comprising both Germanies, Czechoslovakia, Hungary and Poland.[104] A *modus vivendi* would be created by the withdrawal of all foreign forces from the zone. The party was united in its opposition to a West German nuclear arms capability and gave qualified support to the Rapacki Plan for a nuclear-free zone in Central Europe. By the 1961 annual conference the leadership was calling for de facto recognition of East Germany which could now be seen as a contribution to resolving the dispute over Berlin which had led to construction of the Berlin Wall in August.

The bomb

Before the end of 1945 dispassionate analysis of the implications of atomic weaponry had already concluded that the prospects for future control were grim.[105] The capacity would soon exist to 'dislocate beyond hope of recovery the political and economic framework of our lives'. Proliferation of nuclear weapons was to be expected and even an equal balance of power, coupled with the certainty of effective retaliation, was not proof against 'over-confident risk-takers', let alone those 'revolutionary nihilists' who regarded destruction as the necessary prelude to any lasting improvement. The Hitler regime had shown that such forces could capture whole societies. All the logical safeguards against nuclear warfare were flawed and even if any of them were to work in the short-term political liberty was likely to suffer as the power of the state grew. In the immediate aftermath of the war observers talked of a certain numbing of the popular mind in relation to atomic weaponry, which future international crises were confidently expected to change. The course of events did not confound these expectations. The Soviet Union acquired its own bomb ahead of schedule in 1949. The USA successfully tested a hydrogen bomb in November 1952 and the British responded by planning for the manufacture of their own.

It was a Labour Government which had decided to produce a British nuclear bomb so it was fitting that the party's 'Bevinite' wing should also produce the first socialist 'defence intellectual', modelled on the American prototype, whose first cohort was led by men such as Hans Morgenthau, Bernard Brodie, Reinhold Niebuhr, John Herz and Henry Kissinger. Denis Healey's maiden speech in 1952 was a defence of German rearmament. In the same year he argued that Hobbes' *Leviathan* was a better guide to international relations than *Fabian Essays*. His self-styled 'realism' enabled Healey to develop the expertise required to sell nuclear war to the public as a thinkable proposition. This ideological spadework began by nurturing a fear and loathing of the enemy, a process in which Healey had had a hand since 1946 and to which he continued to make contributions throughout the 1950s. The Soviet state was thus depicted as an ideologically driven expansionist force intent on war. There was no distinction between this state and the Communist Parties, which were wholly subservient to Moscow and dominated by 'inhuman' types on the lookout for local wars, as in Indochina, within the 'thermonuclear stalemate'.[106] Sharing the general incomprehension among American strategists about what was actually happening in Vietnam, like them Healey looked for an answer to the Communist threat in 'tactical' nuclear weapons. These were supposed to be the sort of nuclear weapons that could actually be used – unlike their 'strategic' counterparts which threatened mutually assured destruction. Whether they actually existed was less important than believing in them. In the first place, as Healey argued in 1956:

> It is essential and urgent to establish a distinction between the use of the precise atomic weapons which are ideally suited to land defence and the strategic use of indiscriminate weapons of mass destruction like the hydrogen bomb which are primarily suited for attack on centres of population with hazards of 'fall-out' and atmospheric contamination which tactical weapons do not present. There are obvious difficulties in establishing a distinction either in weapons or in targets which would break down in war; but unless such a

distinction can be made convincing it will be increasingly hard to justify Western expenditure on land forces for European defence at all.[107]

The difficulties were overcome through the labours of Brodie, Kissinger, Edward Teller and Robert Osgood. 'Limited' or 'tactical' nuclear warfare became the antidote to Soviet preponderance in conventional weapons in Europe and the presumed reluctance of the USA to commit nuclear suicide by responding to a Soviet attack in, say, West Germany, by a resort to its 'strategic' arsenal. Healey adopted 'limited' nuclear warfare as his own. To deter the Russians it was necessary to persuade them that the West had 'tactical' atom bombs ready for use against the Red Army. Nobody could explain how West Germany would escape extinction in this scenario or why the Russians would refrain from using their own tactical weapons or indeed, why there would not be 'escalation' to mutually assured destruction. Healey's answer to the last problem in 1957 was that:

> once the West is seen to believe in the general *possibility* of limiting nuclear warfare any residual uncertainty about the feasibility of maintaining the limitations in practice would simply add to the deterrent. If Russia once believes the West has both the capacity and the will to meet local aggression by limited nuclear war, she would avoid any risk of putting Western will-power to the test.[108]

This was the reasoning which inspired *Dr Strangelove*. The Russians would allow NATO to use atomic bombs without retaliation, according to Healey, for fear of the situation getting out of control. In fact the 'precise' weapons did not exist, the other side perceived the doctrine of 'limited' nuclear war as more threatening than the 'thermonuclear stalemate' which Healey deplored, and there was no reason to believe in the sort of perverse collaboration between the belligerents which Healey and Kissinger hoped for. West Germany also stood in danger of radioactive incineration. In 1958 Healey argued that the very fact that any tactical nuclear war would be fought in Europe gave America's European allies a strong case to demand their own tactical nuclear weapons. Healey thus wanted proliferation of nuclear weapons 'because the only way of making limited atomic warfare a certain response to a Soviet attack is to give the capacity for initiating it to the country which is threatened by attack'.[109] As the science (and technology) of nuclear weapons strategy evolved some of these emphases changed but if Healey's friend Henry Kissinger can be believed tactical nuclear weapons remained relevant well into the 1960s. At the end of that decade

Kissinger, who was on his way with President Nixon to talks with Soviet leaders in Paris, spoke to Healey, then Defence Secretary, in London, and was advised that they should tell the Russians of NATO's readiness to use tactical nuclear weapons and risk a full strategic exchange in any future conflict. Kissinger records that he found this advice evidence of backward thinking and of double-standards since early resort to nuclear weapons would never be advocated by people whose own country would be directly affected. Lord Mountbatten found evidence of 'primitive reactionary thinking' when Healey repeated the advice publicly in a magazine interview later that year.[110]

Supporters of the main lines of Cold War foreign policy had always boasted of the calm, restraint and reason which Britain's participation in the Western alliance had allowed it to bring to the table. Labour had special credentials in this respect, having already 'prevented a war on China' under Attlee's leadership, as one trade unionist gave voice to the legend in 1952. In 1953 the Executive stood for the resumption of 'summit' talks with the Soviet Union in the form of a Four-Power conference. The death of Stalin in March of that year and the signing of an armistice in the Korean War in July had generated some optimism about the prospects for agreement on 'outstanding issues'. When Attlee moved the resolution on foreign and Commonwealth policy at Labour's 1953 conference delegates were invited to support this stance. But while warm words were used in the Executive's statement about 'general disarmament' through the UN and the commitment of the Commonwealth to 'genuine partnership', 'racial equality' and 'responsible self-government', the party was also invited to support the necessary 'repression of the Mau Mau' in Kenya, continued NATO membership, and a defence programme adequate to the tasks set for British foreign policy. Kenya excited little interest in the debate that followed, though Reg Prentice's remarks about the land theft and undemocracy practised in Southern Rhodesia were just as applicable there, as many Labour Party members had been told ever since the 1920s. It was also observed from the floor of the conference that democracy was absent in gerrymandered Northern Ireland on Britain's doorstep. Britain itself was occupied by US troops subject to special legal provisions in the Visiting Forces Act, which ought to be repealed. Britain's ally, the USA, was giving financial support to Chiang Kai-shek and General Franco and generally backed the landlords in countries where the main social problem could be expressed as 'how do we get rid of the landlords?' As the conference met it was announced that the USA had given the French £137 million to assist their war effort in Indochina. The conference was also told by Geoffrey Bing MP that Chiang-Kai-shek's forces were using northern Burma to make military incursions into the People's Republic of China.

Other delegates complained of the ongoing repression in Franco's Spain against opposition forces which Labour had supported during the civil war. But the conclusion in 1953 of the American–Spanish military agreement would seem to have transformed Franco into a friend of the free world, even though socialism was a 'heinous crime' in that country. Meanwhile, as John Burns of the Fire Brigades Union pointed out, the USA had established military bases in 43 countries 'ringed round the Soviet Union'.

Some of these bases, the delegates were told, possessed atom bombs. It should be a matter of unease, according to Burns, that Britain was locked into a military alliance – NATO – which had 'a permanent command, permanent manoeuvres, [and] arms standardisation under American control and American supervision'. Konni Zilliacus, one of the six Labour MPs who voted against the NATO treaty in 1949, raised the matter of military bases again at the 1956 annual conference, arguing that rights to such bases, including the traditional fortress territories of the British Commonwealth, should be recognised only if they formed part of the UN world security system. Their occupation, he argued, would have to be 'negotiated without imposing limits on the political freedom and aspirations of the local population' – a condition clearly not satisfied by many, if not most, of them as the contemporary crisis in Cyprus illustrated. By now party activists had been made aware of hydrogen bombs which were tested by both superpowers in 1953 and 1954. The leadership knew that it had to resist a growing feeling within the party for unilateral renunciation of nuclear weapons by Britain. Bevan was seen as a leader in the critique of defence and foreign policy because of a series of dramatic interventions in 1954 and 1955, though with hindsight they now look like manoeuvrings for the leadership succession. He resigned from the Shadow Cabinet as a protest against the formation of the South East Asia Treaty Organisation (SEATO) in September 1954 after openly criticising Attlee's support for this US initiative in the House of Commons. Another challenge to Attlee in the House came in March 1955 when Bevan invited him to deny that Labour supported the Conservative Government's commitment to first use of nuclear weapons. He then led a bloc of 57 Labour MPs in abstaining from the vote on a Labour amendment – a crime which led to withdrawal of the Whip and only narrow escape from expulsion from the party. In May Britain tested its own hydrogen bomb, the same month in which the Conservative Party was returned to power with an increased majority. That autumn the leadership re-emphasised the case for multilateral disarmament but was faced by an Opposition which doubted the deterrent effect of the British nuclear bomb and the good sense of the military commanders entrusted with it. Nor did the Opposition believe that the British bomb enhanced

Britain's negotiating hand with its major ally or protected it from the much bigger Soviet arsenal. The balance of power was inherently unstable; yet here was a weapon of genocide, according to the critics, ready to go off at a moment's notice. The cost of the nuclear programme was ruinous, the cost of using nuclear weapons would be centuries of radioactivity, perhaps the extinction of life on earth. It was the leadership's view, however, that Britain needed its own bomb precisely to avoid a dangerous dependency on any other country and to count as a force for peace.

Denis Healey was one of the consistent voices raised against the critics. He warned that even under Khrushchev the Soviet Union did not share Britain's 'basic aims in world affairs'; namely the rule of law, as expressed through the UN, and anti-imperialism, as shown by Labour's efforts to get 'a completely new system of cooperation' based on free consent. Noel-Baker, supporting this line, contrasted Labour's policy with that of the Conservative Government which spent £1,500 million annually on armaments and £2 million on the UN, the ILO and all of its other agencies. It sent the Chancellor, the Foreign and Defence secretaries to NATO, he said, but entrusted 'a bunch of junior clerks' with disarmament and the UN. Labour's priorities were different. But this seemed like self-righteous hypocrisy and illusion to other sections of the party, conscious that it was a Labour Government which started rearmament and initiated the nuclear weapons programme and that for every Poznan there was a Nicosia. Peaceful coexistence and non-interference with the affairs of other people were not best served by the Dulles doctrine of anti-Communist intervention.

But it was at Brighton in 1957 that the party was forced to confront the developing case for unilateral disarmament, almost one-third of the resolutions submitted to the annual conference that year having been concerned with 'the bomb'. The immediate stimulus came from the testing of a British hydrogen bomb in the Pacific and Duncan Sandys' White Paper on defence which apparently committed Britain to a policy of massive nuclear deterrence. The White Paper made much of the costs of conventional defence, estimating that it had absorbed an annual average of 10 per cent of Britain's GNP over the previous five years, placing a heavy burden of the balance of payments and utilising some 7 per cent of available manpower.[111] By now Bevan had been the Shadow Foreign Secretary for 12 months, his reconciliation with the leadership having begun after his main rival, Hugh Gaitskell, was elected leader in December 1955. Gaitskell saw merit in promoting Bevan after the latter's performances in the Commons' foreign policy debates surrounding the Suez and Hungarian crises. Bevan was a keen supporter of multilateral disarmament, though his rhetoric had often made him sound otherwise and up to the moment he wound up the debate at the Brighton conference his supporters were not sure what he would say. But the Labour leadership had already given its support to the general objectives of the Government's Defence White Paper which seemed to be saying that nuclear deterrence based on the threat of overwhelming retaliation was the cost-effective solution to Britain's problems. The Conservatives also announced their intention to end conscription, a policy Labour supported. If, as the nuclear strategists reasoned, the US was less and less likely to run the risk of its own extinction in the defence of Western Europe, the Europeans needed their own independent nuclear deterrent to persuade the Russians that the threat was real. The reliance on nuclear weapons was thus growing in the light of such considerations and served to heighten the sense of insecurity in an age dangerously dependent on the deductive logic of the nuclear strategists, their questionable and shifting assumptions and the runaway technology on which it was all based. The successful launch of Sputnik on 4 October underlined the point by opening a debate on inter-continental missile attacks.

At the annual conference in 1957 Frank Cousins, the left-wing president of the mighty TGWU, reported that his own union had approved by acclamation a resolution dissociating Britain from the testing, use, or manufacture of the H-bomb. John Strachey suggested that without the bomb Britain would become 'the wholly dependent satellite of the United States . . . It would make a future Labour Foreign Secretary unable even to consider policies which were not approved by the State Department in Washington.' This was more or less the line taken by Bevan. Unilateral disarmament would mean renunciation of all the international 'arrangements' and 'facilities' which Britain was connected to. It would send a British Foreign Secretary 'naked into the conference chamber' for the sake of 'an emotional spasm' and make it impossible for Britain to exercise influence on the policies of the superpowers. For all the cries of 'betrayal' which greeted Bevan's successful quashing of unilateralism, the critics had overlooked Bevan's consistent optimism concerning the future evolution of the Soviet Union and his fidelity to its own stance on (multilateral) disarmament. When the Soviet Union offered a test ban at the beginning of 1958 Bevan was quick to acclaim it and the Labour Party followed suit in proposing a unilateral test ban for Britain. Britain, the USA and the Soviet Union entered negotiations for a comprehensive test ban that year.

The unilateral disarmament argument would not go away however, despite the fact that opinion polls showed a large majority of 75–80 per cent of the public against any such action in the critical years 1958–61.[112] Following Bevan's break with *Tribune* the first step towards the formation of a campaign for nuclear disarmament was taken when J. B. Priestley criticised Bevan's conference speech in the pages of the *New Statesman*.[113] CND was officially launched in January 1958 in response to the support which Priestley received, with Bertrand Russell as president and a host of well-known intellectuals as founder members (Russell was now talking of the USA as a 'police state', thus renouncing his initial support for Atlanticism in spectacular style).[114] But the appeal of its case was clearly not confined to the young or the intelligentsia. At the 1958 annual conference at Scarborough the unilateralist position was presented by a leader of the Fire Brigades Union, representing the unanimous opinion of his union's conference. He wanted to know why Labour opposed nuclear proliferation if it really believed in the deterrent value of the bomb and its persuasive powers in international diplomacy. Surely what was good for Britain was good for every other state, or would be seen that way? He also pointed to current NATO assumptions concerning the viability of using 'tactical' nuclear weapons in battlefield conditions, though the bombs concerned were substantially more powerful than the Hiroshima bomb. The conference was also told that Britain had recently signed away land in Britain itself for missile bases, as well as in the Bahamas, Cocos Islands, at St Lucia and the Ascensions. The feeling among CND supporters was that the most likely cause of the incineration of the British Isles was a war between the USA and the Soviet Union in which Britain would figure only as a target. Quite apart from disarmament the conference was asked to support a call for opposition to any missile bases in Britain and the end of routine US patrols carrying atomic weapons across British air space. Britain had become 'a United States nuclear aircraft carrier'. A third resolution informed the conference that the Conservative Government's Defence White Paper committed Britain to first use of the hydrogen bomb in the event of war. Some speakers in the debate admitted to a moral rejection of war *per se* but increasingly the unilateralists announced that they had never been pacifists, they simply saw through the logic of those who defended British atomic weapons. There was no evidence whatever, Peggy Duff observed, that possession of these bombs had done anything to enhance Britain's persuasiveness in relation to the USA's policy in the Far East and there was no reason to believe that a Labour Government would have found the bomb useful in deterring the Soviet invasion of Hungary.

Emrys Hughes MP also put the case against NATO which he described as an American-dominated organisation involving immense expenditure by Britain and its support for a nuclear weapons strategy. Against this mounting criticism the leadership argued that a policy of unilateral disarmament would prevent Labour from ever gaining office again, as there was no evidence of its electoral appeal. Gaitskell also denied that it would lead to other countries renouncing nuclear weapons. All Britain would be doing in renouncing the bomb would be sheltering behind the American deterrent – though this was precisely what most NATO members were already doing. If Britain left NATO, Gaitskell warned, the USA would either adopt an isolationist policy or promote 'Germany' as the leading power in Western Europe. Either way Britain would lose the influence it exerted as 'America's strongest and closest ally'. The NEC's 'ad hoc committee on disarmament', however, considered proposals in 1959 which went beyond Gaitskell's thinking, by observing that opposition to unilateralism did not commit the party to go on producing nuclear weapons or supporting the current defence priorities which relied on them.[115] It was possible to imagine 'a solemn agreement' under which every nation in the world would renounce nuclear weapons except the USA and the USSR. This would in no way affect support for NATO or the US bases in Britain. By the summer of 1960 the whole question was thrown open again by the Government's decision to abandon the Blue Streak missile, the basis for Britain's independent deterrent. In a speech at Leeds Gaitskell admitted that it was unlikely that Britain could ever again produce its own rockets, while buying them from the USA could become an expensive and precarious form of dependency. This left two other possibilities – sharing weapons or leaving the USA to supply and control them all for Western defence.[116] This raised the question of political control of nuclear weapons within NATO, as did current attempts by France and Germany to acquire weapons of their own. The reality was that the Western strategic nuclear deterrent would remain wholly in the hands of the Americans and Britain's 'tactical' weapons were already wholly supplied by the USA. By the annual conference of 1960, then, Gaitskell and his co-thinkers recognised that Britain could not afford to be an independent nuclear power and its future role in the 'nuclear club' was more uncertain than ever before.

Sam Watson, opening the foreign policy and defence debate at the 1960 annual conference, was aware that victory for unilateralism was probable. Enough of the big trade unions were converted to CND's case to ensure its success that year. But he warned that the Scarborough conference would only obtain a 'Pyrrhic victory' because the final arbiters – the electorate – would settle the future of the party; in fact it already had, by giving the Conservative Government an increased parliamentary majority twelve months earlier. This was Labour's third consecutive defeat and it generated a flurry of activity designed to further dissociate the party from out of date ideas – all of them identified with the left of the organisation, as unilateralism was. There were no new arguments, however, in Watson's repertoire on the bomb, but the Government's cancellation of the Blue Streak weapons' system was formally acknowledged to mean dependence on the USA for 'the West's strategic deterrent' at a time, he said, when NATO's dependence on nuclear weapons had become 'dangerous'.[117] These remarks were not likely to dent the arguments of the unilateralists. It had been part of Gaitskell's defence of the British hydrogen bomb that it gave the country independence. That independence was now gone. The dangerous and cowardly reliance on the USA which the Front Bench had previously deplored as a morally bankrupt consequence of unilateralism became party policy in the wake of the Conservative Government's decision to purchase Skybolt air-launched missiles from the USA.

Michael Foot thus seized upon the cancellation of Blue Streak and its consequences in the 1960 debate at annual conference:

> If you tie up the whole of your military machine with that of a much greater military power and become dependent on them for the supply of essential weapons, then you lose a part of your independence and you lose a great deal of influence. I do not have to persuade Hugh Gaitskell about that, because that is the reason why, up to a few months ago, he was saying that we must have our own bomb.

Both the AEU and the TGWU had forwarded resolutions which not only rejected nuclear weapons and the presence of US bases in Britain, but made clear their disillusionment with NATO. Nearly 80 constituency resolutions were withdrawn in favour of these statements of their case. Frank Cousins specifically called attention, in presenting the TGWU resolution, to the effective autonomy of NATO decision-making, which rendered nugatory any talk of political control over that organisation by a British Government. NATO had just installed 45 Jupiter missiles in Italy and Turkey, firmly under the control of the American General Norstadt. It was now a fourth strategic H-bomb power, rather than the defensive shield originally intended. Control of policy was firmly in the hands of the military. When a state of alert was declared by the US Secretary of State for Defence, as had happened that year, Cousins pointed out, planes with atomic weapons took off from USAF bases at Brize Norton and Lakenheath without so much as a telephone call to the British Government. De Gaulle's decision to ban US nuclear missiles from France in 1959 showed what could be done (though it was not until 1966 that French sovereignty was completely restored with the removal of all foreign troops). The conference did not yet realise that de Gaulle's 1959 decision led to the redeployment of the squadrons concerned to Britain and West Germany, but delegates were already complaining of the 'conspiracy of silence' about the American bases in Britain.[118] More important, the unilateralists had called the leadership's bluff over NATO;

the nuclear arms race had turned that organisation into a source of danger rather than security. There was also a feeling in the air, which the French decision probably strengthened, that there was more influence to be had in international politics outside of the Western alliance. India, which had refused to join SEATO, was one of a number of non-aligned states giving credence to the idea of a 'positive neutralism', a third way that was critical of both blocs in the Cold War and actively concerned to promote peace and decolonisation.[119] Some of the critics tied these policies to a call for planned international trade with the Commonwealth and the socialist bloc (which was presumed to be a source of economic dynamism). Since the Bandung Conference – at which Nehru made an eloquent speech for independence from both blocs – sentiment in favour of non-alignment had grown inside the Labour Party. But when the conference supported the unilateralists the verdict was more of a negative judgement on Western strategy than a positive commitment to something else.

The decisive majorities had been slim – well under half a million votes from a total of six and a half million cast – and the unilateralist position was overturned the following year after a well-financed Campaign for Democratic Socialism was launched within the party to uphold the Gaitskellite position. But the blows to Britain's independent nuclear strategy which the failure of Blue Streak represented were dramatised again in 1962 when the USA cancelled its replacement, Skybolt. In the event Harold Macmillan returned from a meeting at Nassau with President Kennedy in December 1962 with an agreement that the USA would supply Britain with Polaris, the submarine-launched missile system. Meanwhile US nuclear capabilities were advancing at such a rate that it became increasingly obvious that the cost of keeping up was both prohibitive and pointless. It was difficult to imagine any plausible scenario in which Britain would be engaged in nuclear war with the Soviet Union on its own and it was doubtful that Britain exercised any influence on the USA as a result of possessing the bomb. Why not simply rely on the US deterrent as, say, Italy and West Germany already did? In practice Britain already waited upon American decision-making. The Cuban missile crisis of September 1962, when the world seemed to be on the brink of a nuclear disaster, was handled without a British contribution. The Blue Streak–Skybolt fiasco enabled the USA to extract a base at Holy Loch for its nuclear submarines even before Macmillan secured Polaris missiles. Key members of the American administration such as Robert MacNamara were also coming to the conclusion that British possession of nuclear weapons was unhelpful. They did not contribute very much to Western defence but they could serve to stimulate the search for independent nuclear deterrents in other countries while providing a rationale for cuts in conventional defence spending which the Americans were opposed to. Doubts of this sort had grown in Washington since de Gaulle launched France down the road of nuclear deterrence after 1958. De Gaulle reasoned that while the US deterrent was unreliable as a protection for Europeans, the growing American taste for war around the globe could drag Europeans into a nuclear conflict they did not want.[120] The Americans were also confronted by the Adenauer Government's demand that West Germany be accorded a nuclear weapons role. Some sort of NATO nuclear force began to recommend itself to the Eisenhower administration. Under Kennedy this became known as the Multilateral Force (MLF), an idea with more advocates in the State Department than the Pentagon. It involved an internationally manned fleet of surface or submarine ships under NATO or SACEUR command. It was evident that the Germans were more enthusiastic about this proposal than the Americans and in 1965 the British sought to quash it altogether by countering with an Atlantic Nuclear Force (ANF) composed of an equal number of British and American Polaris submarines and a mixed-manned surface fleet. The details need not detain us because nothing came of either proposal. The point, rather, is to supply a context for Labour's musings upon nuclear deterrence in the late 1950s.

By now the Labour Party accepted that Britain had no independent nuclear deterrent and such weapons as it obtained from the USA added little to its standing or defence. A Partial Test Ban Treaty – banning tests in the atmosphere, under water or in space – was concluded by Britain, the USA and the Soviet Union in August 1963. CND was visibly in decline, perhaps because many of its adherents believed that the nuclear weapons issue was coming under control. By this time Harold Wilson had become leader of the Labour Party following Gaitskell's untimely death. When Labour's manifesto for the November 1964 general election was published Polaris was dismissed as adding nothing to British defence. Indeed the British bomb was found generally wanting – it was neither British, nor independent, nor much of a deterrent. The sensible alternative was to strengthen conventional forces and place all of NATO's nuclear weapons 'under effective political control so that all the partners in the Alliance have a proper share in their deployment and control'.[121] Many of Wilson's speeches of this time gave the appearance of Labour having woken up to the fact that Britain was a medium-size state, grown weary of trying to 'punch above its weight' in matters of defence and foreign policy.

Suez crisis

The party's generally supportive attitude towards the Israeli state from 1948 was conditioned by the perception – promoted by Poale Zion but widely accepted in any case among socialists and trade unionists – of its democratic, trade union, cooperative and socialist credentials in a region supposed to be lacking these qualities. Since the *War Aims Memorandum* of 1918 Labour had supported the right of the Jews to found a homeland in Palestine. In the early 1950s the Israel–Palestine problem was mentioned often enough but never excited much interest at Labour Party conferences, even though the danger of war in the Middle East was frequently recognised. The plight of the Palestinian refugees received no mention in the report, drafted by Sam Watson and Alice Bacon in January 1950, which recommended British recognition of Israel and this issue was given no serious attention until 1973.[122] At Margate in 1953 it had been content to express 'deep satisfaction' at the constructive work of Israel – described as 'a stronghold of social democracy in the Middle East'. The 'serious incidents' on Israel's borders were attributed to the failure of the Arab states to reach a final settlement. A delegate to the annual conference in 1955 could quote King Ibn Saud of feudal Saudi Arabia to the effect that he was prepared to sacrifice the lives of 10 million Arabs to wipe Israel off the face of the earth.[123] That year Labour complained of British arms sales which put Israel at a disadvantage and demanded a military pact with Israel to offset the imbalance caused by the Baghdad Pact.[124] In fact the Israeli Defence Force was already bigger, better equipped and better led than its rivals in the region. Soviet friendship with Abdul Nasser was also noted, however, and this only served to emphasise the image of the Israeli David surrounded, alone and threatened by a potential Arab Goliath. Sam Watson, speaking for the Executive, frankly admitted that the main issue in the world was now the Middle East because that was where 60 per cent of the world's oil reserves lay and the world needed oil. But there was a second reason for its importance:

> there is a socialist state growing up in the Middle East, and that socialist state contains within itself some of the finest creative impulses mankind has ever seen. If you want idealism go to the Negev and see the young men and women, some of them only 16 years old, making grass grow where it has never grown before. Go out and watch men who are giving up every possibility of high position, without thought of self or reward, and dedicating themselves to turning sand into soil. Go out and watch the greatest trade union organisation the world has ever seen – Histraduth – which owns and controls one-third of Israel's economy and assists private enterprise by loaning money to develop other forms of control in industry . . .
>
> The state of Israel is a beacon light in the Middle East. Here, right on the verge of poverty and in the face of terrific exploitation, is a

social experiment going on the like of which we have not seen before. If it be right that we should, as we have been told, defend the spirit of socialism, I would say if you desert these people in the Middle East you will bring the greatest victory to reactionism.[125]

Nobody in the Labour Party was proposing to desert Israel. Watson's description of Israel was shared by virtually all those in the party who thought about it. Labour's policy in 1955 was to seek a defence pact with Israel – a deputation of the NEC interviewed the Foreign Secretary for this purpose in April 1955. Nasser, the Egyptian President, claimed to stand for 'Arab socialism', but nobody in the party took this claim seriously even though Nasser had confiscated land from a small number of big landowners and favoured the economic modernisation of his country.[126] The problem was that Nasser had emerged as the strongman of Egypt in 1954 following the Free Officers Movement *coup* in 1952 against King Farouk. By this time Britain had agreed to withdraw all troops from the Canal Zone by June 1956. Nasser conceded the demand that British troops would return in the event of a conflict involving an outside (that is, Soviet) power but he was already emerging as a 'problem' in his own right. He was the only candidate in the presidential elections of 1956 and had announced his intention of liberating Palestine. Gaitskell was clear in his own mind that Nasser planned the 'extermination' of Israel.[127] A peace settlement over Israel was now seen to be 'an impossibility' because of this attitude. Israel was endangered, but Western policy had armed its enemies. Labour complained that the Western powers had perversely 'embarked upon a policy of unilateral Arab rearmament', while guaranteeing the security (by the Baghdad Pact) of much of the Arab Middle East, including Egypt itself. Looked at this way, bearing in mind that Nasser had also inherited one of the greatest military bases in the world after the withdrawal of the British, the policies were indeed difficult to understand.

In reality it was not at all obvious that any of these security pacts with the Arab states commanded any support beyond (the often temporary) elites holding state power. In part this was because their purpose was anti-Soviet rather than anti-Israel. Nasser, who did have popular support, was seen as a problem by Britain because he was stirring up pan-Arab feeling and was disposed to play off the two sides in the Cold War. This obviously ran counter to British (and American) efforts to stitch up the whole of the Middle East in anti-Soviet defence pacts. This strategy was undermined when the Egyptians revealed they had negotiated an arms deal with the Soviet Union in September 1955. During the course of 1956 Nasser's subversive hand was seen behind Jordan's dismissal of the British commander of its army and attempts to stir up trouble in

Saudi Arabia and the Persian Gulf. The Egyptian dictator also established diplomatic relations with China and Egypt's relations with the Soviet Union grew warmer as Nasser sought funding for the Aswan Dam project, which the USA publicly pulled out of in July. Before the end of the month Nasser nationalised the Suez Canal Company (owned largely by Britain and France). At the beginning of August Labour agreed with the Conservative Government that this action was illegitimate. Gaitskell told the House of Commons that the threat Nasser posed was 'exactly the same as that we encountered from Mussolini and Hitler'.[128] Nye Bevan supported this interpretation in the House of Commons and on another occasion compared Nasser to Ali Baba and the forty thieves.[129] Bevan's supporters at *Tribune* disagreed, defending Nasser's right to expropriate the company. The official line, however, was that this act of banditry should be opposed – by force, if necessary, but only with the agreement of the United Nations – because the Suez Canal was too important to be controlled by a single state and should be internationalised.

During the summer of 1956 the USA made plain its opposition to an Anglo-French invasion of Egypt while the Labour Opposition in Parliament demanded that the dispute be referred to the Security Council. The Prime Minister, Anthony Eden, told the House of Commons on 2 August that he had sent troops to the region. Gaitskell reminded him of the necessity to avoid any breach of international law or any action 'contrary to the public opinion of the world'. Every national newspaper carried the story the following day that Eden planned to issue an ultimatum backed by a threat of war. The Labour line was that as members of the UN Britain 'had always avoided action in breach of international law'. This argument became adamant in the course of the crisis. As Gaitskell said, one could not 'pick and choose' in the Charter of the UN; one had to accept the whole of it. This was repeated fiercely in response to every sign that Eden was planning to unleash war on Egypt, with Labour's Front Bench emphasising US support for its position. In fact Eden was secretly colluding with the French and Israelis to overthrow Nasser by armed action. The party's annual conference, meeting at Blackpool in September, congratulated the PLP for 'preventing the Tories from committing, as yet, the aggression they are still aching to unleash on the Middle East'. All were agreed that 'there can never be any set of circumstances in which it would be to the advantage of Britain to act outside or against the letter and spirit of the Charter of the United Nations'.[130] There could be no illusions about Nasser, a man who ruled by decree and wasted millions of pounds on arms, but his popular base in Egypt could not be denied. Nor could the fact that Britain had supplied much of this weaponry, including Centurion tanks, while denying them to Israel, as a delegate from Poale Zion argued. Other speakers in the debate demanded that Israel be armed, attributing the 'war psychosis' in that country to feelings of insecurity. The Middle East was 'a cauldron of venom and hatred', according to James Callaghan MP, and it would be very unwise to take any side other than the side of peace. Israel, he asserted, stood for peace. But the region was pregnant with future crises unless a long-term policy could be devised, informed by the fact that 'in conjunction ... with the Americans, we have got the oil in Iraq and Kuwait, the trucial states, and in Saudi Arabia and the Lebanon'.[131] This might mean ensuring that the states concerned received a fair return on their oil resources. Patrick Gordon Walker added that this strategy, which could tolerate the nationalisation of oil, would come to terms with 'genuine nationalism' in the Middle East while cutting the ground from under Nasser's feet.

Gaitskell's conduct during the Suez Crisis was undoubtedly informed by the displeasure of the US State Department with Eden's policy. In September the *Guardian* reported Washington's perception that Britain would simply use the UN to demonstrate Egypt's refusal to accept a negotiated settlement so that the way would be opened for war. This approach, as Gaitskell reported to the party's annual conference, found no favour in the US administration. 'We cannot have this Government treating the United Nations as a formality', Gaitskell insisted. The high moral tone of the Labour leader throughout the crisis was widely praised, even though he had spoken of Nasser in the same exaggerated terms (invoking Hitler for comparison) as Eden when the crisis began. But was this the reason Gaitskell courageously broke with protocol and continued to criticise Government policy even after the deployment of British troops on 31 October (when public opinion swung in favour of Eden), or was his strength derived from knowledge that the 'special relationship' had been damaged? Gaitskell certainly did not use the Suez crisis to reflect critically on the broader picture of British and American interventions in the Middle East, though his case for legality and legitimacy was applicable to it, and implicitly critical of it. Reflecting on the Suez crisis Bevan argued in 1958 that war was obsolete as a means for achieving political and economic goals in the world. The Middle East was supposed to illustrate this point perfectly in that it was obvious that war could not supply the West with oil and the peace of the region would not be secure until the problem of the Palestinian refugees had been solved. The refugee camps were 'breeding grounds for discontent', according to Bevan, because there did not exist in the world 'such a concentration of mass misery as is to be found in those camps'. He might have added that in the aftermath of the Suez crisis Nasser's standing among Arab peoples had risen to new heights of prestige, causing or fastening upon internal divisions in other Middle Eastern states. Power struggles in Syria, Iraq and Lebanon in 1958 were related to the Egyptian bid for leadership in the region and British interests in Aden and Yemen were affected by the same process. Many of the political and military responses of Britain and the USA seemed only to stimulate new demands they could not accept.

The USA opposed armed action because it interfered with its own careful diplomacy in the Middle East and covert planning in Syria which was well advanced before the Israeli invasion of Egypt disrupted it.[132] Preparations for a coup were subsequently foiled. In 1958 the pro-British regime in Iraq was overthrown by the army. Iraq withdrew from the Baghdad Pact (the organisation thereafter being known as CENTO, Central Treaty Organisation). Anglo-American covert operations in Jordan and Lebanon were followed up in the same year by armed intervention. By September Labour's NEC had received 41 resolutions condemning British and American intervention in the Middle East; a further 21 resolutions added that the party should 'run a 'Suez-type campaign' to bring about the withdrawal of troops; 20 more resolutions stressed the role of the UN and summit talks in finding solutions in the Middle East; another 20 variously opposed Western intervention in Iraq and demanded that the party developed a more positive Middle Eastern policy.[133] Labour's NEC finally set up a Middle Eastern working party in November 1958, joining those which already existed on European Cooperation, Defence and Disarmament. The party needed to think more about the region than it had hitherto. Nasser's influence was growing as symbolised by the announcement that Egypt and Syria constituted a United Arab Republic. Yet the British continued with their policy of propping up the sheikhdoms and monarchies, ignoring the advice of those who argued that there was no visible enemy to fight in the region and that therefore an interventionist policy was redundant and even counter-productive. Policy was supposedly informed by the perceived need to block Soviet influence and that of Nasser while protecting oil supplies. But there were also Foreign Office voices which stressed that oil was a wider Western strategic interest and that Britain damaged itself by taking sides in inter-Arab disputes and by aligning itself against nationalism in the region beyond the Gulf.[134]

At the end of the year Labour's thinking began to reflect, albeit in a veiled way, some of these problems. The 'fabulous wealth of feudal rulers' was contrasted with mass poverty in the Middle East and the fact that 'the West' had bolstered such regimes and had failed to recognise the emergence of new social forces.[135] The Tories were blamed for this failure and the military intervention in Jordan in 1958 was cited as an example of it. Bevan claimed in the House of Commons on 30 October that nationalism was to be distinguished from pan-Arabism under

Egyptian hegemony, which most of the Arab world rejected. The West could 'come to terms' with nationalism, he said, reflecting the somewhat abstract conventional wisdom of policy-makers at the time. Labour also deemed it essential that the Great Powers did 'not seek military allies to foster the formation of military blocs among the States of the Middle East'. But this was precisely what they had been doing and continued to seek. The British, for example, could not resist attempting to build up the new Iraqi regime as a counterweight to Nasser and approved arms sales at the end of 1959 when the regime suppressed local Communists. The 'Eisenhower Doctrine' – the US commitment to protect pro-Western regimes in the region announced in January 1957 (in formal recognition of Britain's eclipse since Suez) – was aimed at international Communism, rather than Nasserism per se, though it was obvious enough that Nasser's behaviour would determine whether he was 'controlled by international Communism' in the eyes of Washington. In any event it made a nonsense of Labour's claim that the 'United States has never claimed a direct strategic interest in the area'.[136] This claim employed the false assumption that the USA could live with Nasser's neutralism, as recently expressed following his 1958 visit to Moscow. Nasser displayed anti-Communist credentials at home often enough for the USA under both Eisenhower and Kennedy to persist in its efforts to court him. But it was perfectly apparent that the purpose of this effort was to wean him away from neutralism and there was no sign that either Britain or the USA was reconsidering its general orientation in the region. Thus when, in 1961, Iraq threatened to annex Kuwait (which supplied half of all British oil imports after 1957) it was stopped from doing so by the biggest British mobilisation since Suez, which enjoyed US support. In the same year, however, Norman Brook, Macmillan's Cabinet Secretary, repeated doubts about both the wisdom and the practicality of Britain's Middle Eastern role which, he said, amounted to 'propping up . . . reactionary regimes'.[137] That policy nevertheless continued and there was rejoicing when Syria left the UAR after a military coup in Damascus in September 1961 on the grounds that it dealt a blow to Nasserism. From the autumn of 1962 civil war in Yemen provided an opportunity for intervention by both Nasser – backing the army pledged to modernisation – and Saudi Arabia and Britain, which supported the royal family. Britain also supplied the Saudis with arms and military training to forestall the emergence of Nasserite tendencies in their own armed forces. Large-scale military operations in Aden and near the Yemen frontier continued to rage just months before the 1964 general election, when Labour was next returned to power, by which time Nasser had emerged as a sponsor of the PLO and the insurgency in Aden.

Kenya

Gaitskell's promise that 'you can rely on us in the Parliamentary Party to be ever vigilant in favour of peace and settlement in the Middle East' had some basis in fact during the course of 1956. But vigilance was not a characteristic of its role during the Kenyan Emergency (1952–60). Labour's colonial policy in the mid-1950s allegedly expressed a 'steadily growing interest in colonial affairs' within the party and the trade unions. It committed Labour to the vision of 'the plural society', the creation of tolerant, multi-racial democracies where there was currently racial segregation and minority rule.[138] For this reason, Labour stood for the maintenance of British authority in the colonies 'until the basis of political democracy is satisfactorily established'. This perspective continued to talk of the economic, educational, welfare and institutional developments necessary for future self-government. But there was no suggestion that this was incompatible with the Conservative Government's aim of creating 'multiracial' societies in much of East and Central Africa based on partnerships between the various ethnic groups under the white leadership which was deemed necessary for progress. If there was anything distinctive it was the suggestion that the growth of 'free' trade unionism and cooperatives was Labour's specific contribution to this process.[139] In East and Central Africa the political, social and economic progress of the black African populations was so slow that many more decades would have to pass before majority rule could be envisaged. The Labour leadership's critics wanted to know why it had not declared apartheid to be inconsistent with South Africa's membership of the Commonwealth or why it continued to deny claims for the redistribution of land in Kenya, while continuing to claim its fidelity to the principle of 'native paramountcy'.[140] They sometimes referred to the reality of economic exploitation behind the veil of economic aid and to the repression of political activism which accompanied the talk of future democratic self-government.[141] It was also observed that the British Government adopted a stance of neutrality on apartheid whenever it came before the UN. There were suggestions that South Africa's anti-Communist credentials had something to do with this. Later the Simonstown Agreement (1955) and Britain's fly-over rights would become known, revealing that Britain sold arms to South Africa in return for the use of the Simonstown naval base – an agreement which survived until 1975. This was then added to the list of hypocrisies publicised by marginal organisations of the Labour left such as Fenner Brockway's Movement for Colonial Freedom, formed in April 1954 to promote decolonisation.[142] The evidence of brute *realpolitik* behind the verbal screen of 'the plural society' was already copious when the phrase was coined, as was the pervasiveness of racism. 'The colour bar' existed in many parts of the British Commonwealth. Indeed critics pointed out that it could be found in Britain itself – Brockway's Racial Discrimination Bill, seeking to outlaw racial discrimination in all public institutions, was making its way to parliamentary defeat as 'the plural society' document was being debated.

Racism in Britain and racism in the British colonies were never separate issues but they were given direct mutual support during the Mau Mau rebellion in Kenya. Labour supported the war against Mau Mau, when the Emergency was declared in October 1952, while the press in Britain began its lurid campaign of demonisation of the insurgents. Yet behind the scenes officials in the Colonial Office were sceptically concerned from the outset that the Kenyan Legislative Council viewed the matter exclusively as a law and order issue and saw no need for 'positive policies'.[143] Brockway wrote to Oliver Lyttelton, the Colonial Secretary, as early as September 1952 to complain that the Emergency suspended elementary human rights and was inconsistent with Britain's declared policy of preparing the colony for democratic freedom. He reminded Lyttelton that the linked problems of poverty, unemployment and land hunger among the Kikuyu had grown worse since 1945.[144] The Governor, Sir Evelyn Baring, argued the contrary in October, by informing Lyttelton that Mau Mau was comprised of 'fanatical nationalists' (5 per cent), 'thugs' (20 per cent) and those they intimidated (75 per cent). Yet he feared civil war, blaming Jomo Kenyatta, even though the leader of the Kenyan African Union had denounced Mau Mau to a meeting of 30,000 Kikuyu the previous August.[145] Between October 1952 and December 1953, it was estimated by the authorities that 153,398 Kenyans were arrested, 23,204 imprisoned and 150 executed; a further 92 died in custody, reportedly from natural causes.[146] By this time Lyttelton was already receiving complaints and evidence of beatings and murders of Mau Mau suspects.[147] The policy of minimising or ignoring such evidence persisted after the appointment of his successor, Lennox-Boyd, a man who turned a blind eye to copious evidence of British brutality in the colony and stonewalled all attempts to expose the truth. Meanwhile the entire press corps gave sensational coverage to the black savagery of Mau Mau ensuring that it entered the popular imagination as a manifestation of the primitive backwardness of Africa.

From 1953, however, critics of the Emergency, such as Fenner Brockway and Barbara Castle, complained of mass detentions without trial and the floggings and hangings which accompanied them.[148] Brockway also drew attention to collective punishments (also employed in Malaysia), observing that these had been universally condemned when practised by the Nazis; 'now only a few voices are raised in protest', he told the House of Commons. The ILO had also made the damning equation of forced communal labour as akin to enslavement.[149] Further complaints in 1954 were prompted by the outbreak of typhoid at Manyani camp which was holding 16,000 detainees – well beyond its theoretical capacity. Barbara Castle reported in *Tribune* (30 September 1955) that a police state existed in Kenya in which 'the murder and torture of Africans goes unpunished'; at last, she said, 'the Labour Party has declared war on this state of affairs'. By this time Castle's own research into the legal records had 'revealed a picture of behaviour so horrifying that one could not imagine it happening in a British colony', as she later wrote in her memoirs.[150] But this was part of the problem; if a critic like Castle could not imagine such repression in a British colony, it is less surprising that the more complacent members of her own party seemed unmoved by the evidence she and others had uncovered. The Labour Party had not declared war on the Government, contrary to her assertion. Real concern in the PLP was confined to a handful of its backbenchers of whom Castle and Brockway were the most tenacious. Castle visited Kenya in November 1955 and publicised her damning findings of abuse and torture in the *Daily Mirror*, as well as the small circulation left-wing journals.

The following year a former rehabilitation officer who had worked in the Kenyan camps, Eileen Fletcher, published a three-part series in the Quaker journal *Peace News* under the heading 'Kenya's Concentration Camps – an Eyewitness Account'.[151] This revealed, *inter alia*, the detention of juveniles under life sentences, sexual abuse of detainees, malnourishment and insanitary conditions. Nye Bevan was among the Labour MPs who demanded an investigation in the House of Commons. By 1956 there was enough evidence of brutality in Kenya for the Labour conference to carry a motion supporting his call for a judicial enquiry, but no members of the Executive or of the parliamentary leadership spoke in the debate other than to say that it had already called for this measure in 1955. Some delegates complained that far too little publicity had been given to the evidence which exposed the repression in Kenya, such as the fact that at least 27,000 people had been detained in camps and prisons, most of them without the chance to defend themselves in court. The point was made to apply to the British colonies in general, the lack of information making it difficult, as Jennie Lee observed, for British citizens to judge the truth or falsehood of statements made about them. The implication was that Labour's front bench should supply authoritative publicity about what was happening. Lee added that the whole relationship of the Colonial Office to Parliament should be examined and reformed to ensure more transparency. But Labour's criticisms of Government policy in the concurrent crisis in Cyprus, where the British refused even to concede the principle of self-determination to the nationalists, showed that more could be done under current circumstances if the Front Bench put its weight behind complaints of brutality. The record shows that making such efforts could not always be relied upon. British military intervention in 1953 had deposed the democratically elected government of Cheddi Jagan's People's Progressive Party on the grounds of its (spurious) Communist leanings.[152] Labour had supported this action in the House of Commons and so the event generated no public controversy within the Labour Party, or the country, at the time – though subsequent instalments ensured that the episode was occasionally mentioned in the years that followed.[153] Similarly, one delegate observed, that for all the talk of economic aid and assistance to the colonies, it was not generally understood that the colonial contribution to the sterling balances in the period 1951–6 was double the amount of money which flowed in the opposite direction.[154] This too was evidence which the Labour front bench was seemingly not keen to publicise – perhaps because similarly embarrassing disproportions had applied under the last Labour Government. Over Kenya too, it would seem that the Labour leadership was likewise too close to Government policy to perform an effective opposition

Some Labour activists speaking at the 1956 annual conference wanted a general British withdrawal from the colonies, pointing to an ongoing general policy of repression in response to major labour disputes in Northern Rhodesia, Kenya, Sierra Leone and Nyasaland over the previous twelve months. The argument was that British police and military forces were necessarily implicated in these events, rendering talk of future independence and preparations for self-government worthless. More allegations of widespread torture in Kenya were published by a former police and rehabilitation officer, Captain Philip Meldon, in January 1957. These 'effusions', as an official in the Colonial Office described them, told of 'irregularities' in the detention camps amounting to torture.[155] Meldon's allegations were publicised by *Peace News*, *Reynolds News* and MPs like Castle and Brockway. Lennox-Boyd, faced with mounting pressure for a public inquiry, finally decided that he needed positive evidence on Kenya and so appointed a delegation of the Commonwealth Parliamentary Association (CPA) comprised of three Labour MPs and four Conservatives. The CPA's positive report, following its three-day trip, was published in July 1957. Austen Albu MP and Bernard Braine MP found an 'atmosphere of energy and purpose in Kenya and a search for effective methods of overcoming the country's difficulties'.[156] In Kenya itself the repression was actually intensified and the squalid reality continued to surface until the end of the decade, despite the Government's success in preventing an independent enquiry. Elkins observes that the 'leaders of the Labour Party, men like Hugh Gaitskell and Harold Wilson, were never front and center in the campaign against the Conservative Government's actions in Kenya . . . the Labour MPs leading the charge, with the exception of Aneurin Bevan, were relative lightweights . . . no one in the leadership of the party really wanted to rock the boat over Mau Mau'.[157] Yet these were the people dedicated to 'the plural society' and Kenya had always been a conspicuous example of its opposite.

During the Kenyan Emergency, which officially ended in 1960, about 160,000 Kenyans entered the mass detention camps with which the British set out to defeat the largely Kikuyu revolt known as Mau Mau. Land theft, a long-term grievance of the Kikuyu, had accelerated between the opening of the Second World War and the end of Attlee's Labour Government, when the white settler population doubled. Drawing on their experience of suppressing the insurgency in Malaysia the British forcibly removed over one million Kikuyu from their villages and put them behind barbed wire, where they were forced to build their own huts. A network of detention and hard-labour camps was created alongside the new 'settlements', known as the Pipeline. Torture (maiming, castrating, raping etc.) and hard labour characterised the 're-education' of many of those who went through the Pipeline in over 100 camps. At its height over 80,000 Kenyans were held without trial, though as many as 320,000 people experienced detention at one time or another. Over 1,000 Africans were hanged, more than double the number of executions which the French authorities carried out against convicted terrorists in Algeria during another colonial war which the British were inclined to regard as evidence of (greater) French brutality and ineptitude. About 20,000 Mau Mau rebels were killed in combat and as many as 130,000 Kikuyu lost their lives all told if census projections are a reliable guide, as Elkins' study argues they are. Even if Elkins' estimates are wrong it was quite an achievement for the Conservative Government in Britain to minimise, if not actually to suppress completely, the truth about the repression in Kenya. For this the Labour parliamentary leadership, the official Opposition, must bear some of the responsibility. Nor was the violence in Britain's African colonies confined to Kenya.

Nyasaland also witnessed a widespread revolt – in this case against its planned merger into the Central African Federation, in which the white minority of Rhodesia expected to dominate. A state of emergency was declared in 1959 which only exacerbated the disorder, as the report of the Devlin Commission revealed later in the year. The 'police state' (Devlin's description) which the Governor had created in order to suppress the supposedly small minority of malcontents was exposed by the report which documented the reality of widespread opposition to the proposed Federation. The Devlin Report was a rare window into the true state of play in some of Britain's overseas territories. But Jennie Lee's concern that Parliament was not kept well informed about such dependencies is also relevant to this and other conflicts of the decade. It is doubtful that many MPs were well informed about such matters because the Government of the day was often ignorant itself about local conditions and popular grievances. Then there were the covert operations and quiet police actions which were taken without parliamentary or press discussion. It is doubtful, for example, that many MPs knew that the RAF and Special Air Services were involved in suppressing a 'rebellion' in the Jebel Akhdar region of Muscat and Oman in 1958. Though questions were asked in the House of Commons in November, there was no clamour raised against the RAF's sustained aerial campaign, which involved as many as 1,635 sorties and thousands of fragmentation bombs.[158] It is also doubtful that many Labour MPs were familiar with the fact that British money and protection had sustained the sultanate since 1871 and continued to do so until its overthrow in 1970. As late as 1967, when oil production began, over half the state revenue was still composed of British money. Illiteracy stood at 95 per cent and infant mortality at 75 per cent in the late 1960s and malnutrition and disease were still widespread when the British finally withdrew.[159]

The Labour Opposition actually lagged behind Macmillan's Conservative Government in thinking about decolonisation and reorientating British policy towards membership of the Common Market. The French under de Gaulle had set the pace for both by signing the Treaty of Rome in March 1957, which created the Common Market, and by announcing a referendum to decide the future of all of their twelve African colonies in September 1958. With the exception of Guinea all voted for continuing association with France but in 1960 they too became independent states along with Cameroon and Togo, which France administered under a UN mandate. Macmillan's own calculations were influenced by these events, as well as the evidence of the unrest in the African colonies which we have already alluded to. Part of his public rationale for a speedy advance to decolonisation was the fear that Communism would emerge the victor if Britain continued to respond to nationalism with repression. The upshot was that Sierra Leone, Tanzania (both 1961), Uganda (1962), Kenya and Zanzibar (1963), Northern Rhodesia and Nyasaland (1964) were rushed to independence. It cannot be said that British rule had prepared the black majority for self-government in any of these dependencies. In the case of Southern Rhodesia, internally self-governing since 1923, the 220,000 Europeans exercised a monopoly of power whose only concession to the black majority, as late as 1961, was to enfranchise 1 per cent of them. To extract that concession the Conservative Government in Britain relinquished its surviving powers to intervene legislatively on behalf of the black majority, in the face of near-unanimous UN opposition.[160] Yet Chief Justice Tredgold had described Southern Rhodesia as a 'police state' only a year earlier, as it added even more repressive laws to the statute book to outlaw nationalist activities.[161] When Labour returned to power it inherited the Rhodesian problem, as well as the decolonisation dynamic begun by Macmillan. But it was no clearer than the Conservatives about the future basis of British foreign policy. In de Gaulle's view Britain's application for membership of the Common Market in 1961 had not prepared Britain for a life outside the special relationship with the USA; the application was vetoed in 1963.

8   The last pretence

The Defence White Paper of 1960 surveyed Britain's commitments to NATO, SEATO and CENTO entailing obligations in West Germany, Malta, Cyprus, Libya, Aden and the Persian Gulf, Singapore, Malaya, Hong Kong, the West Indies and West Africa, as well as the maintenance of 'detached units' in Australia, Borneo, India, the Middle East, Canada and South Africa. A total service manpower of 700,000 in 1957 was supposed to be shrinking to a targeted 400,000 in 1962, but even if this goal was realised Britain's defence burden would still remain larger than any other member of NATO with the exception of the USA. The Defence Estimates for 1960–1 stood at £1,629,830,000, but were rising.[1] They would continue to do so if only because a large proportion of the spending serviced commitments that could not be curtailed at short notice. An example was SEATO – originally sold as a temporary expedient designed to 'stabilise' South East Asia following French withdrawal from Indochina. In Laos military intervention by SEATO was considered in the struggle to determine whether the country adopted a pro-Western or neutralist foreign policy. US aid poured in after 1954 to discourage neutralism and America's closest ally in the region, Thailand, favoured armed action to destroy the Communist Pathet Lao. This course was eventually rejected by the British because it was unlikely to result in anything more than a stalemate – when there was 'every likelihood of defeat' – unless tactical nuclear weapons were used.[2] British involvement in CENTO derived from its history of intervention in and occupation of the Middle East, most recently demonstrated by the mobilisation which followed when the military regime in Iraq asserted its right to absorb Kuwait in 1961. British forces in Cyprus, Aden and Bahrain were maintained for precisely such interventions, as the suppression of the revolt in Oman also illustrated. Before reluctantly conceding independence to Cyprus in August 1960, the Conservative Government in London successfully negotiated for the retention of two 'sovereign areas', constituting a total of 122 square miles, to be used as military bases, subject to expansion as and when Britain required.[3] The island's strategic significance included extensive signals intelligence sites. Neither Britain, nor the USA, would allow these to be lost.[4]

Another example was the commitment to Singapore and Malaysia where the British were hoping to create a Greater Malaysian Federation (launched in September 1963), embracing the peninsula and the populations of North Borneo, Brunei and Sarawak, as well as Singapore – even though it was recognised that there was resistance to the administration of the Malays among all the minority peoples concerned.[5] The plan – which Britain promoted in the interests of regional security – led to 'Confrontation' (1962–6) with Sukarno's Indonesia, which opposed it as a machination of British imperialism. Indonesia orchestrated armed action in Sarawak, Brunei and along the border of North Borneo when it became clear that the federation would go ahead whatever the results of a promised referendum on the future of the disputed territories. The Philippines also broke off diplomatic relations with Malaysia over the incorporation of North Borneo. As Confrontation developed British and American hopes centred increasingly on the prospects for Sukarno's downfall in Indonesia and his replacement by pro-Western elements in the army. The Sukarno regime relied on the support of the Indonesian Communist Party, as well as the army, and his external allies included China, North Korea and the Soviet Union. Experts on the region, such as Lord Selkirk, High Commissioner of Singapore, agreed that Chinese expansionism threatened the region more than any other factor. Communist insurgency in Laos was seen as evidence of this. Confrontation with Indonesia was thus an unwelcome distraction from this central antagonism, at a time when the USA continued to supply the Sukarno regime with aid – above all, military aid.[6] The Sukarno problem was worsening when Labour returned to Government in October 1964 (by which time Britain deployed around 55,000 armed service personnel in the area) and the Cabinet was told that 'the principal factor in weakening Confrontation – [despite the scale of the British military commitment] – was the level of unrest in Indonesia'.[7] In short Confrontation would end when Sukarno's regime came to an end.

A similar British scheme, attended by similar problems, was applied in southern Arabia. The Southern Arabian Federation was an attempt to rationalise British commitments in the area by uniting the port of Aden with protected territories in its hinterland. Armed conflict was raging in Yemen and Aden when Labour returned to power. But Labour shared the Conservative Government's commitment to the region even though both parties recognised that it had become immensely more complicated as Britain's ability to influence events continued to diminish. Labour saw that 'the pace of change' in the Middle East was accelerating, that 'major upheavals' had taken place in every part of it and that more were in prospect.[8] The British position, it could be acknowledged, depended on 'treaties negotiated under somewhat doubtful circumstances at the end of the nineteenth century', providing a complex of bases necessary to protect the flow of oil, but saddling Britain with the reputation of an unrepentant colonial power in league with 'every reactionary in the . . . area'.[9] Anti-colonialism remained a potent sentiment in a region where solidarity had grown on the basis of an Arab and Muslim identity. Israel was perceived as a denial of Arab rights and a creature of imperialism. The Arab states could be expected to shun Western advice for all these reasons and turn to Russia or – more likely – the UN (when they turned to any outside force). Their destinies were still determined by small groups, rather than the people, and by Nasserite groups in particular, though Ba'athist and 'Young Nasserite' alternatives existed. A future war with Israel could not be ruled out and conflicts over resources such as water were predicted. Labour's sympathies remained with Israel and it could see that British dependency on the most backward part of the Middle East in respect of both oil (Kuwait, Saudi Arabia) and military bases constituted further handicaps in dealings with the Arabs. It was advised that the solution was to safeguard oil supplies through commercial arrangements rather than the threat of force and adopt deadlines for termination of the 'anachronistic treaties', thus withdrawing protection from reactionary statelets in the region.[10]

Then there was the Commonwealth, legacy of Empire, but increasingly led by its non-white majority. This was another concern for London with the prospect of an agenda increasingly of others' choosing and Britain becoming an 'Aunt Sally' for the grievances of countries which the British themselves had little empathy for.[11] In January 1964 British intervention quashed military rebellions in Kenya and Tanganyika. A few months later the Cabinet was worried that Zanzibar was falling under the influence of the Soviet Union.[12] In the division of labour with the USA in the policing of the world sub-Saharan Africa, like the Middle East, was a British responsibility, and the interventions in Kenya and Tanganyika would be invoked as evidence of its fulfilment. But Southern Rhodesia told a different story, as its leaders informed Britain that they did not recognise its right to interfere in its affairs and other signals of the intention of the white minority to permanently block majority rule were received after December 1961. The formation of a new political party in 1962 – the Rhodesian Front – and its sweeping election victory at the end of the year were clear indications of trouble to come. Labour was advised in June 1963 that 'multi-racialism in Africa', its decade-old policy, was dead because many Europeans and Africans did not want to live on the basis of racial equality; 'the only question is how long it will take the bulk of the European population to leave'.[13] Provided there was a British intention to use force, a declaration of independence in Rhodesia could be avoided in this view and the rights of the black majority eventually upheld. When Ian Smith became Prime Minister in April 1964 on a prospectus of independence a collision with Britain became inevitable.

Doubts about the significance of the Commonwealth as a political and economic asset were not allowed to influence Labour Party policy, which remained firmly wedded to the old orthodoxy.[14] Any such doubts were eclipsed by hostility towards the Common Market. Wilson's appointment as Shadow Foreign Secretary in 1961 coincided with Harold Macmillan's attempt to take Britain into the European Economic Community (EEC). This gave him an opportunity to enhance his left-wing credentials by denouncing the Common Market as 'an arid, sterile and tight trading and defensive bloc against the East'.[15] This was the language of left-wing (and Communist) opposition to the EEC, unlike Gaitskell's equally hostile rhetoric, as delivered to the party conference in 1962, which invoked the kith-and-kin ties of the Commonwealth and the defence of a national independence symbolised by 'one thousand years of history'. The fifth congress of socialist parties of the member countries in November 1962 left Labour observers clear that the objective of the continental left was 'a democratically controlled Federal Europe'. A much stronger executive was desired which would extend political union to cover defence and foreign policy, while enabling economic planning of the sort the left preferred.[16] 'We must tell our British friends', said Georges Brutelle of the Section Française de l'Internationale Ouvrière (SFIO), 'if they only want inter-governmental cooperation, then there is no place for them. Each nation must accept common policies in every field.' The 'programme for common action' adopted by the congress amounted to a United States of Europe. But it would be based on a mixed economy, liberal democracy and alignment with NATO. Labour was also assured that 'the implementation of the European Community creates no obstacle whatever to the achievement of socialist aims. The majority of the political and democratic forces of the European Community recognise that the creation of a vast economic unit implies the need for Community economic planning based on national economic plans.'[17] The nationalisation of fuel and power in Italy was said to be a clear illustration of the fact that the Paris and Rome treaties were neutral as regards types of ownership, while providing a stronger commitment to workers' rights such as equal pay. The Community had also witnessed a 21 per cent growth of its GDP in its first five years compared to the UK's 12 per cent over the same period. Under Wilson's leadership, however, there was no evidence until the second half of 1966 that Labour was really interested in the Common Market. The favoured perspective was the old one reinvigorated by the prospect of faster economic growth by virtue of domestic planning. For all those who disliked the idea of a federal Europe it was convenient to ignore the assurances of the continental left that membership would be no impediment to socialist planning.

While Labour talked about the need for negotiation about the all-important terms of entry to the Common Market, whenever the occasion demanded, British foreign policy was still informed by the belief that Britain could help to maintain the peace of the world and contribute to 'the creation of conditions in which this over-populated island can maintain prosperity and its influence'.[18] There was no dissent from this mission on the Labour Front Bench. But even those at the heart of Government reflected on the problems of this policy, chief of which was 'the result . . . that we are stretched to a point where our strength might snap under the strain, and indeed our present position would be highly perilous were it not for our basic dependence on the USA'.[19] In South East Asia, for example, beset by broken lines of communication and a greater need for local consent than used to be the case, it seemed obvious to Lord Selkirk that 'the only long-term effective answer to Communist China is nationalism, coupled with a recognition by each state that it has an obligation to defend its own territory'. This was an idea more readily recognised in Washington, he believed, than formerly. It followed that 'we must clearly do everything we can to promote nationalism as a counter to communism and avoid policies (especially those with an imperialistic flavour) which may lead nationalists and communists to join forces against us':

> In these circumstances to pursue a defence policy for purposes which cannot be identified with the interests of the area and may even be contrary to the wishes of its inhabitants is both militarily hazardous and politically unwise. Our object must rather be to identify our presence in South East Asia with the national aspirations of the area, and at the same time play down and eventually obliterate the concept either that the United Kingdom has a distinctive interest apart from those of the countries in the area or that the United Kingdom proposes to continue to maintain the defence of the countries and stability of the area regardless of the individual policies of the countries concerned.[20]

The fact that countries such as India and Malaysia refused to join SEATO, however, ensured that it would continue to be regarded as 'a white man's club' and a device of imperialism. Selkirk doubted that SEATO would be able to survive for long unless it became more closely associated with the peoples of the region. He advocated a gradual 'redefinition', that is reduction, of Britain's role in the organisation, emphasising the need to avoid giving the impression that this was what was contemplated. Meanwhile other countries – Australia, New Zealand, Thailand and the Philippines – would have to assume more of the responsibility for policing their own area. The plan would 'need a good deal of explanation to the United States of America' which was increasing its involvement in Indochina. It was already clear to the British that the corrupt regime of Ngo Dinh Diem in Vietnam, under strong attack from the Vietcong by early 1961, lacked support even within the middle class and the army.[21] The USA was demanding a British commitment to Indochina as it decided, against British judgement, to increase its own 'military advisers' to South Vietnam. The Thompson Mission originated from these discussions, though the Cabinet never discussed it. Drawing on British techniques used in the Malaysian emergency the mission advised the creation of strategic hamlets in the Mekong Delta, though the actual implementation of this policy followed none of Thompson's advice concerning the modest pace of the programme or careful attention to the maintenance of social structures. The USA had in any case used similar techniques to defeat the Huk insurgency in the Philippines. Diem was overthrown in a military coup in November 1963 and the programme collapsed in the months that followed. Britain drew back from any further involvement as it was already clear that a military 'solution' in Vietnam was extremely unlikely. But while de Gaulle openly favoured an American withdrawal, the British did not. The incoming Labour Government inherited the contradictions of Britain's position on Vietnam and took them to new heights as 'impartial' co-chair with the USSR of the Geneva Conference of 1954 and close ally of the USA, committed to the 'defence' of Vietnam from Communism, yet convinced that the war would achieve nothing.[22]

Getting the Americans to see the advantage of building up nationalism as a buffer to Communism was a minor impediment – if it was any sort of problem – compared to the problem of building up reliable states in the region which shared Western conceptions of their interests. Could this be done in a way which identified such states with the peoples they were supposed to represent, or was this ruled out by the very fact of Western interference? Covert assistance to reliable elements, combined with arms sales, military training, and economic aid – coupled with covert interventions to undermine and destroy unreliable elements – normally amounted to support for the authoritarian right and dictatorship, and the destruction of movements of the left. When Communists were associated with the latter, as in Vietnam, extensive violence was seen as legitimate in Washington and London, even when the Communists could plausibly claim to represent the nation. The more subtle thinkers, like Selkirk, placed no real objections to this logic, and their vision of the way forward assumed, like those around them, that Britain would continue to play its world role for the foreseeable future. Labour was caught in the same trap.

This perspective forced successive governments to resist the logic of decline, though the economic problem was continually present in discussions concerning defence and overseas commitments, as it had been since 1945.[23] If Britain trimmed such commitments according to its reduced circumstances and changed interests, it ran the risk of losing prestige and influence – two commodities which were as prized in London as they were difficult to substantiate. Influence was especially elusive in the case of the 'special relationship' with the USA, which officials believed in fervently while admitting that it would cease to exist if anyone tried to institutionalise it. Even mentioning the special relationship in public was unwise, lest it disappear altogether. Yet it was this unmentionable relationship which was said to allow Britain to 'exercise greater influence than our friends and rivals in all the major political, defence and economics issues of our time'.[24] One thing that was palpable about the special relationship was that Britain had to perform a world role if it wanted to be treated any differently than other medium-sized countries such as West Germany. 'Punching above its weight' was the British aspiration. Spending above the average was the British reality. Britain's world role gave it a place in a division of labour in which there was only one other participant – the USA. This was special and gave the two states a similar perspective in organisations such as NATO, the UN, and the various international financial and trade organisations. Any doubts about the degree of extra influence this gave the British in Washington were apt to be suppressed.[25] Britain was obviously much weaker than the USA but could derive no benefit from adopting independent policies 'for their own sake', like the French.

Trimming the defence budget might mean losing influence in Washington. Trimming might also provoke alien elements to occupy any vacuums thus created. The Chinese were favourites for this role in South and South East Asia and Africa in the early 1960s, according to British and American estimates, unless the West was successful in encouraging nationalism and avoiding its enmity in key countries such as the Philippines, Indonesia and the like. British and American political and military intervention, however, was just as likely to stir the wrath of nationalism and push it towards Communism, as in China and Vietnam. Greater Malaysia was an attempt to enlist local interests in the West's security plans while allowing the scaling-down of British defence expenditures in the region, but it had provoked nationalisms elsewhere in South Asia. An Anglo-Malayan Defence Agreement was secured as an element in the transition, while the British also sought 'burden sharing' in the region by enlisting the support of the USA, Australia and New Zealand.[26] The pace of such readjustments was painfully slow compared to the speed with which the British economy failed to keep up with demands made upon it.

By the summer of 1964 the latest figures for public expenditure had shown, in the words of officials, 'a grave deterioration'.[27]Assuming an unlikely economic growth rate of 4 per cent, sustained over four years, taxes would have to rise by £100 million annually up to 1968–9 and by twice that amount if the growth rate of the last few years was repeated. The balance of payments was a particular cause for concern, as it had been for many years. The Cabinet was told:

> The conclusion is inescapable that to maintain the health of our economy over the next few years we shall have to make substantial changes in the use of our resources. The commitment of so much of our manpower and our foreign resources to defence purposes is only one example of a load that the economy cannot indefinitely carry. We have not thought it right as a Government up to now to make fundamental changes in defence policy to meet the financial realities although we have recognised that this would have to be done in due course. We must point out to our colleagues that time for doing so is rapidly approaching.[28]

It was a familiar story to those concerned. Most of them knew that Selwyn Lloyd had proposed cuts to overseas expenditure in June 1961 even if it meant a reduction in Britain's NATO contribution and worldwide commitments. The balance of payments had been heavily in deficit since mid-1959 and was supposed to be 'alarming to put it mildly' by 1961 as external reserves declined rapidly and 'the pressures on the economy both from within and without [became] increasingly dangerous'.[29]

Wilson

Under Harold Wilson's leadership the Labour Party seemed altogether more radical than it had been under Gaitskell, even on matters of defence and foreign policy. Wilson had openly admitted that Britain no longer possessed an independent nuclear deterrent before the dramatic Scarborough conference of 1960 and up to and including the manifesto of 1964 there was talk of a fundamental review of defence expenditure, giving greater weight to conventional forces and renegotiation of the Nassau agreement to purchase Polaris.[30] The Conservatives reinforced this image of Wilson's radicalism, with Alec Douglas-Home warning that Labour would scrap nuclear weapons if elected. Other observers noted that orders for missile purchases had been 'deliberately placed prematurely' to forestall such an outcome.[31] But Wilson's derision at the idea of an 'independent deterrent' had always obscured the range of conclusions that might be deduced from this fact and his language was careful to add to that obscurity. The Cuban missile crisis in October 1962 frightened the world and Wilson's public observations reproached the USA as much as the Soviet Union. On taking over the leadership of the party in February 1963 he nevertheless affirmed his faith in the Western deterrent, while pouring scorn on Britain's independent contribution to it. *Let's Go With Labour* (1964) suggested that Polaris would either be scrapped or pooled in some undefined way as part of NATO's forces. Nuclear weapons were no longer as controversial as they had been at the height of the CND agitation. Wilson's main emphasis, which won the enthusiastic support of all sides of the party, was on the need for a radical modernisation of Britain at a time of widely perceived stagnation and lack of direction. To this debate Wilson brought a zeal and verbal panache which persuaded the left to suspend its disbelief in a way which Gaitskell's presentation of the same policies had failed to achieve. Wilson's stress on a future of purposeful planning and the need to dispense with patronage, amateurism and nepotism in British industry and society raised expectations of structural and cultural change forged in 'the white heat of the technological revolution'.

Wilson flew to Washington in March 1963 to meet J. F. Kennedy and to assure his administration of Labour's soundness on foreign and defence policy. In the autumn of that year he visited Moscow and alarmed the Americans by speaking out against German possession of nuclear weapons. Since the Eisenhower administration, as we saw in the last chapter, the USA had considered various plans for sharing nuclear weapons in order, so it was said, to meet German aspirations and European anxieties over decision-making in NATO. By May 1963 this process had produced the idea of a Multilateral Force (MLF) involving mixed-manned ships armed with Polaris. The idea did not appeal to the French or either of the main political parties in Britain, and though Wilson's public utterances on the subject were few and vague, the suggestion of 'pooling' Britain's nuclear weapons was allowed to give an impression of new thinking on nuclear weapons. British policy – Tory and Labour – was actually to kill the idea of a shared European capability at the first opportunity.[32]

Two days after Kennedy's assassination, in November 1963, Wilson's conversation with a Foreign Office official who accompanied him on an overseas trip was made the subject of an official report.[33] According to the report, Wilson had already decided that in the event of a Labour Government James Callaghan would become Chancellor, Douglas Jay would head the Board of Trade, and George Brown, assisted by Sir Eric Roll as Permanent Secretary, would take over the running of a new planning ministry. The fact that these appointments were made eleven months later adds credence to the report as a whole, much of which is concerned with Wilson's views on foreign and defence policy. The Labour leader, who had served in the Attlee Governments as President of the Board of Trade, observed that Bevin 'had run foreign affairs and had been a prisoner of his civil servants, his anti-semitism and above all of his rigid anti-Soviet views'. It was less clear what Wilson's own views were on matters such as the British independent deterrent. He gave the impression that if Polaris had been a British missile he would have no objection to it. He would have supported a successful Blue Streak and wished that it had not been abandoned. He excluded the possibility of a 'nuclear Suez' – Britain would never fight the Soviet Union on its own. He deduced from this assumption that 'the deterrent was a form of blackmail of the Americans. As such it [a British nuclear arsenal] made no sense if our deterrent in fact depended on American weapons.' Wilson apparently did not believe that possession of nuclear weapons made any difference to Britain's international standing – economic strength and powerful conventional forces were just as important, though Britain had struggled to maintain this combination since 1945. Nor did he believe the American story according to which Germany demanded a nuclear weapons role. Wilson did not rule out a bipartisan approach to defence with the Conservative Party. On Europe he was opposed to any form of supranationalism, other than a facade behind which stood the reality of British independence. He thought that Commonwealth trade could be built up and serve as an adequate substitute for the Common Market, but agreed with his interlocutor that 'his [Wilson's] policy of isolation depended on the Six falling apart or at least not getting closer'. In the end, concluded the observer, 'it was very difficult to be sure what Wilson's real views on policy were . . . It was also difficult to disentangle what he found politically expedient from what he thought right.' This 'preface' to Wilson's Prime Ministership, it transpired, could also serve as his epitaph.

Labour won the election with just 44 per cent of the votes cast – the smallest proportion of any majority government since 1922. Its parliamentary majority over all other parties amounted to only four seats until the Government was re-elected in March 1966. By that time, however, the benefits of an increased parliamentary majority were somewhat offset by the loss of goodwill for the Government within the party both inside and outside Parliament. Between October 1964 and February 1965 the

Labour administration was beset by economic problems associated with speculation against the value of sterling and the related balance of payments deficit which it inherited from the previous administration. Bouts of speculation recurred in May 1965 and again in July 1966. The Government's response to this problem relied on deflationary measures which threw its domestic reform programme into doubt. But in October 1967 the problem returned and the process was begun which led to the devaluation of sterling the following November. The life of both Labour Governments between 1964 and 1970 was thus characterised by crisis management of an economy afflicted by chronic balance of payments problems and the inevitable accompanying speculation against sterling.[34] It is fair to say that all shades of opinion in the Labour Party were disappointed that the National Plan, in which so much hope of improved economic performance was invested, was effectively sabotaged by the deflationary measures which the Government employed to save sterling's role as a reserve currency. Certainly Labour's belief that it had the policies to stimulate economic growth were gone after devaluation.

Wilson entered office hoping that Britain would be able to play an independent role mediating between the superpowers. He subscribed to the conventional foreign and defence doctrines according to which Britain was required to play a world role in partnership with the USA and maintain NATO against its critics (who currently counted de Gaulle among their active number). But if he wanted to avoid too close an association with the USA, as has been suggested, he was stuck with the conundrum of how to reconcile these conflicting ambitions with Britain's accelerating relative decline as an economic power.[35] There was every indication that there would be no new thinking on these foreign and defence policy issues. In common with most of his predecessors the new Prime Minister was keen to be his own Foreign Secretary, ensuring that the man who actually carried this title would be drawn from the ranks of the grey and pliable.[36] Wilson's first Cabinet gave all the key economic, defence and foreign policy positions to members of the party's right and these people – Wilson himself, Callaghan, Brown and Jay on economic issues; the first three plus Healey and the Foreign Secretary (Gordon Walker, then Michael Stewart) on foreign and defence issues – made policy outside the Cabinet and sometimes without even consulting it.[37] Despite this centralisation of decision-making, and the accompanying secrecy, critics of the Government's policy could see some of the connections between economic policy and foreign and defence issues, just as they had under Conservative governments. Indeed, it had long been argued on the left that a vicious circle had been created. The critics reasoned that the real priorities of British governments since the war were maintenance of Britain's world role and defence of the value of sterling. By the early 1950s the burden of this world role, according to critics, contributed to a chronic balance of payments problem, a major strain on Britain's resources, including manpower, and a lower standard of living than might otherwise be afforded.[38] They might even agree that these commitments placed Britain in a position of unhealthy dependence on, if not subordination to, the USA.[39] Thus it was not difficult to see in 1964 that if Labour was determined to preserve the value of the pound the Government required US financial support. But in order to obtain such support, it could be reasoned, Britain had to maintain its role East of Suez, thus feeding one of the causes of the chronic balance of payments problem and the financial speculation which accompanied it.[40] What the critics could not see, of course, was the detail of Harold Wilson's relationship with the administration of President Johnson.

Well before British Government papers were released under the 30 Years Act US sources unsurprisingly showed that ministers spent much of their time communicating with members of the US administration in policy formulation.[41] But Ponting's examination of these sources led him to conclude that 'the overwhelming impression of the first few months of the new government is that it actively sought to increase British dependence on the United States and develop its relationship with the American administration into the central pillar of its policy in the strategic, foreign, defence and economic fields'.[42] Changes in these areas – whether affecting the bank rate, the budget, public spending or policy concerning Rhodesia, confrontation with Indonesia, British Guiana, and other areas of foreign affairs and defence – were invariably made only after consultation with the Americans. In fact continuity with the previous Conservative Government characterised most of the relevant considerations in respect of these issues. A rethink of the structures in which UK overseas policy operated was never formulated, even though Wilson himself had given the impression on occasions of a radical intent. Such generalised sloganising was notable for having persuaded virtually the whole of the Labour left that something radical was in the offing and CND supporters, such as the war correspondent James Cameron, could point to campaign pledges of this sort as evidence for new departures in foreign and defence policy. In the event, the Foreign Secretary visited Washington days after the new Government was formed to emphasise, so Dean Rusk informed Johnson, that 'the United Kingdom does not plan any radical foreign policy initiatives embarrassing to the United States'.[43]

In fact Wilson, though acutely conscious of growing defence costs and Britain's financial problems, was quite openly committed to Britain's world role in defence and financial matters. This meant maintenance of the sterling exchange rate as well as the 'East of Suez' presence in the

Middle East, Persian Gulf and Malaysia. But even under the previous Conservative administration the need to find economies in defence spending had been acknowledged and the question had already been raised that further cuts implied policy changes such as withdrawal from South East Asia.[44] Within weeks of the general election Wilson arranged for discussions on defence policy at Chequers. According to a briefing paper prepared by officials, the salient points for discussion included the steep rise in total expenditure from £1,596 million in 1960–1 to an estimated £2,141 million in 1965–6, rising to £2,400 million in 1969–70. The balance of payments burden was underlined by the fact that direct overseas expenditure in defence and related matters was 'at least as large as what we believe to be the "hard core" of the balance of payments problem', that is £300 million.[45] But there was also the unseen burden of the skilled manpower and technological resources employed by defence industries, amounting to one-fifth of the qualified scientists and technologists engaged on research and development, and the fact that 40 per cent of all R&D expenditure was consumed by defence. It was thus decided that in five and ten years' time the defence budget would not exceed £2,000 million at 1964 prices, enabling defence spending to fall to 6 per cent, then to 5 per cent, of estimated GNP. This target figure necessarily posed the question of which interests and commitments Britain was prepared to curtail or abandon – if any – and the question of which capabilities should be reduced or eliminated. The assumption that interests and obligations were fixed and indefinite, which had informed previous discussions, was thus questioned from the outset, but just as quickly restored to the subsequent discussions. Instead the focus, for both political and economic reasons, was the belief that it would not be possible to maintain the current scale of commitments either in the Far East or in the Middle East and that even Britain's military commitment in Europe (where Soviet aggression seemed very unlikely) might have to be reduced.[46]

Yet alongside this apparently radical thought some old assumptions were reiterated:

> Since the end of the war we have managed to continue to exercise a degree of power and influence throughout the world which has been greater than our relative military and economic strength actually justify; and the mere fact of our military presence in several of the key areas of the world has made some contribution, however unquantifiable it may be, to this achievement.[47]

Ministers were warned that while the world role could do 'grave damage to the economy', any reduction could 'endanger our political and economic independence'. Other policies lauded for their purchase of 'influence' – arms sales, capital aid, technical assistance, diplomacy, cultural services and the like – did not constitute a satisfactory alternative in this view. Thus if Britain were to withdraw from Singapore and Aden, an alternative military presence in these areas would be required 'to protect our interests and discharge our commitments in those areas'.

An order of priority of overseas commitments was sketched out for the Chequers meeting by the Long-term Study Group established by the Cabinet Secretary Burke Trend in May 1964. The 'political cohesion' of Western Europe was said to be of 'paramount importance' and so no cuts could be envisaged there. Britain's dependence on Middle Eastern oil (and regional holders of sterling balances such as Kuwait) made Aden second in importance, though it was admitted that 'sharp differences of opinion' existed over the commercial significance of the military presence. But on this reasoning Singapore was of least economic signifi-cance and would represent a waning asset, assuming the confrontation with Indonesia was overcome and the region was won for 'political neutralism'. Here was also an opportunity for 'sharing the burden' with the USA, Australia and New Zealand. Such thinking was questioned by those who argued that South East Asia, despite its insignificant economic importance, was faced with the danger of 'absorption by Communism'. This had to be stopped and Britain had to continue with its role in the region in order to remain the USA's principal partner. Nationalism might be nurtured as a barrier to Communism, but military measures would remain essential; the military defeat of the West – perhaps in Vietnam – had to be avoided if long-term objectives were to be realised.[48]

In Cabinet, just before the Chequers meeting, Wilson said there was no longer a risk of war in Europe, as long as NATO solidarity held. He also argued that future developments in nuclear technology would make it too costly for the UK to remain an independent nuclear player over the next ten years. Maintenance of the world role was, however, essential for the foreseeable future.[49] The Cabinet was nevertheless informed that the Polaris system was cost effective and at Chequers – after Denis Healey disposed of the objections of George Wigg and Lord Chalfont – it was decided to go ahead with the programme.[50] Wilson's doubts about the wisdom of trying to keep up with technological change in such weapons were later confirmed, however. For when the system became operational in 1968 Polaris was immediately threatened by obsolescence owing to the development of anti-ballistic missiles (ABMs). The effective riposte to ABMs took the form of multiple independently targeted re-entry vehicles (MIRVs) which Britain did not possess. In June 1967 Wilson told parliament that the Government would not purchase Poseidon missiles to keep up with this technological change. The succeeding

Conservative Government, however, opted for an appropriate modernisation of Polaris but the decision to invest in this so-called Chevaline project was actually taken by the next Labour Government at an eventual cost of £1,000 million.

At Chequers Wilson's argument that there was little prospect of war in Europe encouraged the view among Ministers that the East of Suez role was actually more important in demonstrating Britain's unique contribution to Western defence. Much of the discussion was thus concerned with the presentation of the Government's reasoning on the future shape of its world role to the USA. Wilson wanted negotiations over the Atlantic Nuclear Force (ANF) 'on the basis that we would maintain our present nuclear capability unless and until this could be replaced by something more satisfactory in the form of joint control'. By this device the issue of the future of the British nuclear deterrent was side-stepped by the suggestion that its future role was somehow to be collective, though no one knew how this would work in practice. The Prime Minister was able to refer to Britain's 'inter-dependent deterrent' in a speech to the House of Commons.[51] In Cabinet Wilson also misleadingly implied that the decisions to develop Polaris had reached such an advanced stage that the Government was faced with a *fait accompli*.[52] Two of the five Polaris submarines were already at an advanced stage of development. Polaris would be committed to the joint NATO force on the basis of four such submarines.[53] The ANF, it was said, also constituted a possible bargaining counter in Britain's attempt to reduce its world role. It might also answer the need of non-nuclear members of NATO to exercise greater influence on nuclear planning, policy and strategy and encourage the non-proliferation of nuclear weapons, though France was expected to see it as another sign of Britain's Atlantic bias. It would involve, proportionately, a bigger British contribution than the MLF and thus increase Britain's relative status while diminishing Germany's (to zero in terms of the nuclear trigger). This was another of its advantages according to Wilson. The political and technical/operational control of the ANF was, however, yet to be resolved. The real function of the ANF proposal was to kill the MLF idea. The USA might insist upon the MLF but whether it did or it did not there were many questions to be considered. Should Britain abandon its independent deterrent and, if so, would it be able to exercise real decision-making power within the MLF or ANF or, failing this, ensure that the USA remained committed to the nuclear defence of Europe and Britain itself? Britain might try to bargain with the USA, trading its ANF commitment for a reduction of the defence burden overall. Western Europe's dependence on Middle Eastern oil was as big as Britain's, it was pointed out, but 'it contributes nothing towards the expenditure which we incur, at Aden and elsewhere, in protecting the Gulf'; there was a possibility for burden sharing here though Britain's commitments in the region were largely the result of treaties which could not be discarded lightly or abruptly. The best bet, it seemed, was to promote the ANF and demand compensating defence expenditure reductions elsewhere. Ministers were also advised to launch a sophisticated cost–benefit study of current and projected overseas commitments.

The only clear commitment to emerge from these meetings was that defence spending had to be curbed because of its damage to the balance of payments and the productive resources of the country. In November 1964 Healey, the Defence Minister, informed the House of Commons that 'we must be prepared to reduce the calls on our military resources' and eliminate commitments 'which have no justification in modern terms'. He also warned that the rising costs of commitments considered indispensable to 'our national security or to the peace and stability of the world' made even this burden too great to bear alone.[54] Britain was spending more on her defence than any country of her size and wealth, Healey observed, while France and Germany, spending only a little less, largely confined themselves to defending their own territory. The only other country playing a world role – the USA – spent ten times as much as Britain. By 25 November Wilson was repeating this telling comparison when he informed the Cabinet what had been agreed at Chequers and what he proposed to tell Washington in a week's time.[55] The first conclusion of the Chequers meeting was that the proposed ANF would include Britain's strategic forces, the Polaris submarines, while V-bombers – now obsolete for nuclear purposes – would be retained for the Middle East and Far East without affecting 'the basic principle of our proposal to abandon our independent nuclear deterrent'. (George Ball, the US Under-Secretary of State, assured Wilson that the Americans would view sympathetically the indication that Britain would seek to phase out its national capacity for nuclear war.)[56] Britain would also endeavour to obtain a veto over the use of nuclear weapons by the ANF and, failing this, insist that the USA retained such a veto. It would also seek to extend its 'influence' on the control of US weapons outside of NATO and ensure that non-nuclear powers stayed non-nuclear. 'The main recompense' for British contribution to the ANF would be some relief from burdens in Europe so that the rest of the overseas role did not involve unsustainable aggregate costs and could carry on as before. In this way the Labour Government proposed to maintain Britain's world role while sticking to its defence budget target of £2,000 million. The cost in foreign exchange of keeping 51,000 British troops in West Germany was one of the items which Labour, following Conservative precedent, looked to for economies by increasing the German share of the cost.

This had now to be sold to the USA. Wilson was advised to impart his 'view of the world scene as a whole' to Johnson because it was only by 'worldwide collaboration that we shall preserve, unspoken, the "special relationship"'. The shape of the world, as seen from London, he was told, included stalemate in Europe, but also 'Britain and the US in trouble in Malaysia and Indochina, Aden and Libya, Cuba and British Guiana'. The Soviet Union and China were vying for political influence in the Third World and there was 'the danger of North–South conflict, with poverty tending to divide the world on racial lines'. In this context it was 'manifest nonsense to pile up ever more sophisticated arms for a war which can never be fought . . . It is time the West realised that it has in fact won the battle for Europe.' NATO did not have a war to fight and this was the real reason why France could pursue 'rogue elephant policies' in relation to it. Wilson scribbled 'this is the best sense I have seen yet on this' across the memorandum, just days before he left for the USA.[57] His discussions in Washington served to cement the Government's commitment to the world role. Accompanied by the Foreign Secretary, Patrick Gordon Walker, and Denis Healey, it was the latter who supplied the Americans with a general survey of the problems confronting Britain in the field of defence, leading to the conclusion that:

> The only practicable way of achieving cuts was by reviewing our equipment programme in the context of a judgement of priorities between the three main roles which we undertook – our nuclear deterrent, our presence on the continent of Europe in support of NATO, and our world-wide deployment outside the NATO area. The general view of the Cabinet had been that we should give the highest priority to the third of these.[58]

Healey listed as the main reasons for this priority, 'our moral obligations as senior members of the Commonwealth', treaty obligations to SEATO and CENTO, the positive contribution Britain could make 'almost alone' between Suez and Singapore to the preservation of stability, and finally, the very small danger of a war in Europe. Rapid British action, he said, had prevented East Africa becoming another Congo and greater dangers to peace continued to exist outside Europe.[59] Healey also expressed the UK's desire to solve the nuclear problems of NATO by 'committing the whole of our strategic power to the alliance for its duration'; to forgo the right of independent withdrawal inherent in the Nassau Statement; and to accept that Germany should have parity in respect of powers of control and veto over these nuclear arms. Healey reported that weapons procurement policy would be guided by the assumption that fighting was more likely to take place outside of Europe. The British Government would also take account of the respective roles of Britain and the USA in different parts of the world. He asked:

> Could not our two countries cooperate in the provision of logistic support and in the development and procurement of weapons? The United Kingdom might perhaps find that it could cover 95 per cent of likely contingencies with a given level of sophistication in weapons systems . . . We wondered whether it might be possible for the Americans to cover this outstanding 5 per cent of contingencies.[60]

Dean Rusk, US Secretary of State, 'urged the British Government to give full weight to the role of Britain as a world Power beyond the NATO area'. In doing so he repeated Healey's view of Britain's obligations, adding 'that of all America's allies she was the most committed to those concepts to which the American people were themselves most fundamentally committed'. The US Administration 'would look with the greatest concern on any plan for a deliberate withdrawal of British influence from any part of the world'. British Guiana,[61] East Africa, Cyprus and Malaysia 'formed a pattern of major contributions to the defence of the free world'. He then stressed the cost of the USA's contribution in money and lives – $600 billion and 160,000 casualties in the seventeen years 1947 to 1964. 'This had been a deliberate decision, but the contributions of others had helped the Administration in leading the American people. Thus Britain's world role was important to America as well as to herself.' Rusk seems to have been saying that it was a matter of legitimation – the legitimation of America's interventions abroad – as well as a question of burden sharing. If so it was certainly a salient issue. The USA had expanded its military advisors in Vietnam to 17,000 before Kennedy's assassination. Since the Gulf of Tonkin incident in August 1964 Congress had authorised President Johnson to take 'all necessary measures'. Days before the British delegation arrived in Washington Johnson met with Rusk, Robert McNamara, his Defence Secretary, and others (on 1 December) to prepare a two-phase bombing campaign over North Vietnam. Three months later the first official combat troops from the USA landed in Vietnam.

At the meeting of 7 December McNamara informed the Labour Ministers that 'he did not think that Britain could achieve any substantial reductions of manpower – the United States already had twice as many men under arms as their allies and the American people would not approve a world-wide deployment of American military power unless other countries made some contribution. Britain must, therefore, maintain her military strength at least at its present size.' That included Britain's contribution to NATO. In McNamara's opinion the only real solution for Britain lay in the area of weapons procurement. Japanese and German prosperity showed that an arms industry was not essential to a modern economy. Britain could buy its weapons from the USA. 'What the United States most required from Britain was the maintenance of the British policy of playing a world Power role.' The British side ignored McNamara's invitation to give up its arms export industry, but Healey ventured the opinion 'that another out-moded concept was to regard military forces world-wide as essential barriers against Communism' and that it was wrong to extrapolate from past history and suppose that withdrawal from Singapore and Aden would mean their loss. These observations – implicitly questioning the vacuum theory, as well as US policy in Vietnam – were also ignored, President Johnson having publicly endorsed the vacuum/'Domino Theory' as recently as March of that year, not to mention the decision to step up military intervention in Vietnam. The discussion turned to the pros and cons of the US and British proposals for, respectively, an MLF and an ANF. It would take another two years before both proposals were finally killed off.

When Wilson and Johnson joined the group Rusk reiterated the importance of the British world role. Johnson added 'that there were other places where a United Kingdom military presence, on however limited a scale, might have a significant effect. A few soldiers in British uniforms in South Vietnam, for example, would have a great psychological and political significance.' Wilson answered this invitation by invoking Britain's co-chairmanship (with the Soviet Union) of the Geneva Conference of 1954 – the hitherto ineffectual custodian of the Accords of that year – and the difficulty which this role, should it be activated by US action in Vietnam, would create if Britain was directly involved in the military conflict. As things stood, he reminded the President, Britain had 'faced exactly the same problem' in Malaysia and was already making a contribution to the American effort in the shape of the Thompson mission,[62] by training Vietnamese troops in jungle warfare techniques in Malaysian schools and by providing police in Saigon. Britain also supplied signals intelligence, arms, port facilities in Hong Kong and various maintenance facilities. In 1966 Labour provided additional assistance by formalising an agreement that the Indian Ocean islands of Diego Garcia would be made available as an American military base East of Suez; two thousand of their inhabitants would be removed to Mauritius.[63] No one in the Labour Government argued for British troops in Vietnam, but Ministers who referred to the war in public were careful to avoid criticism of American policy, when they were unable to support it. Wilson has been lauded in recent years for refusing to commit British troops to Vietnam but when he reported to Cabinet on his discussions with Johnson he argued that the Americans had not really expected him to make this commitment.[64]

British and American interests coincided perfectly when it came to management of the Bretton Woods system. Financial speculation against the pound, should it succeed, would only turn attention to the dollar. The US economy, like Britain's, suffered from a worsening balance of payments problem. Unlike Britain, US public expenditure grew rapidly as the war in Vietnam developed and Johnson embarked on expensive welfare reforms at home. Both were financed by borrowing rather than increased taxation. Wilson, who was opposed to devaluation for political as well as economic reasons, knew that he had American support for this stance from the moment he entered office.[65] Whether he entered into a formal agreement with President Johnson in order to obtain support for the pound is the subject of some controversy. But most studies are agreed that Wilson was in any case committed to the essentials of the *quid pro quo* – maintenance of a British role East of Suez and maintenance of sterling at $2.80.[66]

Continuous defence review

The defence White Paper of February 1965 repeated the hope that expenditure cuts could be made in Britain's European commitments while it continued with the East of Suez role. But a major defence review was still underway and debate returned to the question of how best to disengage from the Far East. The problem of confrontation with Indonesia continued to inform these discussions. It was thought that a quick resolution of this conflict would ease the way to scaling down the British commitment in Singapore. Ministers were consistently advised that the British presence in Singapore was the least relevant overseas base to Britain's material interests, but also that the economic need to get out of the Far East had to be balanced against the political desirability of retaining a military presence.[67] The best long-run solution continued to be seen as 'the neutralisation of South East Asia in a form which would enable local nationalism to present a barrier to the spread of Chinese Communism', with a British military presence removed to Australia – a proposal first raised by Macmillan's government. Meanwhile both the Prime Ministers of Malaysia and Singapore wanted the British military to remain in place. Ending the confrontation with Sukarno's Indonesia was thus the key to an orderly withdrawal, future stability and continued 'influence' in the region. An understanding between President Johnson and Wilson's Conservative predecessor, Alec Douglas-Home, in February 1964 determined that Britain and the USA would support each other over Confrontation and Vietnam.[68] Both sides expected this arrangement to continue, Sukarno having graduated to a major problem because of his support for North Vietnam and his increasingly friendly relations with China. In January 1965 he pulled Indonesia out of the UN, while his relations with the PKI grew warmer. American advice was firmly against a British initiation of negotiations with Sukarno on the grounds that this would be regarded as a sign of weakness.

The US Under Secretary of State, George Ball, met Wilson in September 1965 to stress that a reduction of the UK commitment to South East Asia would be inopportune at a moment of increasing US commitments in Vietnam. Wilson assured him that the ongoing defence review would not entail 'a policy of scuttle' and that he had personally stressed 'the danger of a vacuum if we were to evacuate Singapore'.[69] Ball argued that Britain needed 'to treat the financial, defence and foreign policy aspects of the US/UK [relationship] as a totality', adding that the US view was that 'the international monetary problem and the future of sterling were essentially linked to the problem of the UK's defence responsibilities'. Indeed UK participation in Vietnam was required 'if the US was not to appear to be dominating the world by trying to become "another Rome"'.[70] There was now the added complication that Singapore had just left the Malaysian Federation, which had only been launched two years earlier. The Foreign Office's judgement was that the separation of Singapore had weakened both British tenure in the region and its position relative to Confrontation. The US remained adamant, however, that a voluntary withdrawal of the military presence from Singapore by 1970 was 'unthinkable' and British intentions to end Confrontation by negotiation 'would only lead to the weakening of our position in Singapore and thus of the whole area'.[71] These points were reiterated in the course of Quadripartite talks with the governments of the USA, Australia and New Zealand and then put before the Cabinet.[72]

The British perspective thus far envisaged a continuing role in the defence of the Far East even after 1970, by which time it was anticipated that Confrontation would be over and Britain would no longer be able to count on the use of the Singapore base. Reduced facilities and forces would be based in north-west Australia. The other governments took the view that both the Malaysian and the Singapore governments would want Britain to remain in place. They also insisted that there was 'no substitute for Singapore as a base for Western defence operations in the area east of the Indian ocean'. As for Indonesia and Confrontation, the advice to Britain was that it should 'wait and see'; the other governments suggested 'that internal developments in Indonesia, e.g. Sukarno's death, could cause military confrontation to fade away sooner than had been expected'.[73] Further reflection on these meetings testified to the 'violence of their reaction at any suggestion that we should "pull out of the Far East", still more that we should take any initiative to end confrontation':

The last pretence 265

we could not insist on making an early move to end confrontation without causing grave offence to our allies and prejudicing the prospect of their future collaboration. (This is particularly relevant to the United States attitude in relation to support for sterling.)[74]

The reference to Sukarno's health reflected the fact that he collapsed in public in August 1965 and was secretly diagnosed with kidney disease. Western intelligence was also extremely active in preparing the way for his downfall. President Johnson had withheld economic aid from December 1963 but continued to supply military aid to anti-Sukarno elements in the Indonesian army, many of whose leaders were US trained. At the end of September 1965 the 'wait and see' advice was vindicated. A supposed coup provided the immediate pretext for a military onslaught against the Indonesian Communist Party. By 1966 half a million Indonesians had been murdered and Sukarno had handed over executive power to General Suharto. In January of that year Dean Rusk told Healey and Stewart that if the army took over in Indonesia it 'would take a more moderate and constructive course' than Sukarno had.[75] He was well informed. In May confrontation was formally ended. Sukarno was placed under house arrest and the largest Communist Party outside China and the Soviet Union had been destroyed. Indonesia's ties with China were broken and it rejoined the UN. British and American support for the overthrow of Sukarno involved covert actions according to some analysts.[76] While there is no evidence of direct involvement in the coup, nor is there evidence of a PKI attempt to seize power – this was the pretext for the military takeover and the mass killing of Communists.[77] During the repression Britain and the USA supported the army – with the US supplying arms as well as propaganda and lists of Communists for elimination – but was advised from within Indonesia to do so in a low-profile way to avoid stirring anti-imperialist sentiments in the country.

In December 1965 the defence review was discussed at a meeting in the White House which Wilson attended with President Johnson, George Ball and McGeorge Bundy. The main issue to be resolved was how the British might contract their defence commitment while maintaining the world role. Among the options mentioned – in a spirit of interdependence with the USA – was the possibility of employing a little more of British resources in the Middle East and Africa '(where the Rhodesian crisis made us peculiarly alive to the dangers of Chinese penetration[!])', and a little less in the Far East.[78] This could involve deploying Polaris submarines in the area East of Suez, 'provided that they were "internationalised" by one means or another', though Wilson was unable to define what this meant beyond some sort of four-power defence grouping. Wilson also talked of abandoning one of the bases in Cyprus, withdrawal from Malta and Libya, and, eventually, of leaving Aden while reinforcing Britain's position in the Persian Gulf. Apropos the latter he said 'it had been right to establish, in cooperation with the United States, the new Island bases in the Indian Ocean' – a reference to Diego Garcia – and reported that the 'excessive demands of the Mauritians for compensation had been successfully resisted'. Forces would be maintained in Bahrain and Masirah with an eye on the defence of Kuwait (from Iraq) and Iran, where the Shah might possibly reorient towards 'Russia'. The Far East continued to present difficulties. Wilson said that it still made sense to plan for 'an alternative posture' in the region, involving the building up of Indonesia 'to contain Chinese expansionism' and a resolution of the tension between Malaysia and Singapore and the confrontation with Indonesia.

Bundy stressed the priority of politico-strategic considerations over mere affordability on the question of the East of Suez policy. McNamara, who had made plain to Callaghan in June that any diminution of Britain's defence commitments would place the whole Anglo-American relation-ship in jeopardy,[79] in effect stressed the old issue of legitimacy. From a purely military point of view the USA could provide the defence of South East Asia on its own, 'they certainly could not do so politically'. Wilson thought that some of these issues would become clearer when the role of Indonesia as a buffer to Chinese expansionism was less ambiguous. McNamara agreed but observed that this would still leave a problem to the south-east and south-west of the archipelago. He attached a higher priority to the British presence in Asia than in Europe and believed 'that the United States could materially help . . . with the problem of foreign exchange costs in Europe'. Bundy argued that Singapore could be regarded as the key point in the containment of Chinese expansion, while Wilson offered a division of labour which would see Britain focusing on Africa in this task, while the US would assume primary responsibility for Asia. Wilson added that the Simonstown base in South Africa would be retained 'for use in an emergency' and forces would remain in British Guiana and the Caribbean, Gibraltar and Cyprus. Her Majesty's Govern-ment had not yet taken final decisions but would welcome US views on priorities, given the £2,000 million defence budget.

Further economies, bigger doubts

The defence review discussions reported in February 1966 that defence spending was half way towards the £2,000 million target figure set in November 1964, but that this progress had not reduced 'the excessive cost of defence in foreign exchange'. Nor had it addressed the overstretch of military resources.[80] It was thus agreed that further cuts in expenditure to within £50 million of the target figure would be implemented. Britain would withdraw from the Aden base 'and disengage ourselves until we have reached the hard core of our obligations to CENTO and States in the Persian Gulf'. But it would stay in Singapore, assuming it was not forced out by the locals and was not engaged in a larger conflict with Indonesia. It was already possible, despite these uncertainties, to envisage the nations East of Suez providing for their own defence against Communism because things were going so well in Indonesia. This, as Rusk pointed out in January 1966, was better than a 'white man's club' and better, as Denis Healey observed, than reliance on SEATO whose doubtful utility was illustrated by the fact that Pakistan belonged to it.[81] The defence White Paper, published on 23 February, duly announced that withdrawal from Aden was expected in 1968 and reductions in Far Eastern commitments would be implemented once confrontation was over. It was also announced that there would be no spending on a new aircraft carrier and that the order for the American F-111 fighter plane would only be maintained at a reduced level. A 'quite unnecessary provocation' was however deleted from the published version. Chapter 1 of the White Paper, written by Healey, had 'contained a flaming apologia for Britain's role in NATO as the chief apostle of a return to massive nuclear retaliation'. The Foreign Secretary, while not challenging the doctrine or the strategy, successfully led the charge against its inclusion.[82]

The need for further economies was underlined later in the year when the seamen's strike disrupted exports and there was more speculation against sterling. The question of devaluation returned, with more Ministers now favouring this option. According to Barbara Castle, the excitable George Brown declared that 'We've got to break with America, devalue and go into Europe'.[83] The leader of the Opposition, Edward Heath, might have been able to identify with this argument himself. Castle and Richard Crossman were already convinced that the world role was an unnecessary burden, so too was its former custodian, Lord Gladwyn (Gladwyn Jebb), and the Conservative defence spokeman, Enoch Powell, as well as the Government's left-wing critics.[84] Wilson was obliged to mount a lengthy defence of his policies at a meeting of the PLP in response to critics such as Christopher Mayhew who wanted an end to the world role.[85] The speech Wilson gave is of interest in revealing the grandiose perception of the British contribution which Wilson subscribed to. His Rhodesian policy, for example, had prevented the UN and the world splitting down 'the greatest and most dangerous divide you can have in this century' – race; it would not have been possible but for Cyprus and Aden and the staging posts – 'the key to power' – which they afforded. More were needed, not less. There had been four other interventions in East Africa in early 1965 to illustrate the same point. There was also the need to contribute to the defence of Australia and New Zealand. To 'pull out of all influence in Asia' was to leave the field to China, the United States and the Soviet Union. Wilson could not believe that Britain had nothing to contribute, when to contract out was 'the surest prescription for a nuclear holocaust that [he] could think of'. It was the same in Africa. 'Is it really argued that we have no role there? If we abdicate responsibility who will exercise that role – America can't.' Nor could other European powers. Again the field would be left to Russia and China, perhaps South Africa or an 'inward-looking African nationalism'. Then there was India; 'does anyone think that India wants us to leave her to become a cockpit forced to choose between Russia and America to protect them against China?' Britain's presence in Asia, Wilson believed, prevented India from having to 'go nuclear herself' and helped to 'prevent polarisation'. Britain, fortunately, had a role in influencing America and it was precisely for this reason that the Russians listened to her. Indeed 'the Americans have repeated time after time their willingness to accept any initiative we take' as they had in 1965.[86]

A Cabinet majority had already been found to support more deflationary measures and a wage freeze before this peroration was delivered. The pressure to find more savings on defence was nevertheless strengthened by the deteriorating economic situation, prompting another defence review. The end of Confrontation in August also removed an obstacle to withdrawal from the Far East, yet when the defence White Paper was published in February 1967 there was no basic change of policy and over sixty backbenchers registered their disapproval by abstaining in the vote. By July, however, evidence of the continuing pressure to reduce commitments was made public in a supplementary White Paper, which said that the British military presence in the Persian Gulf would end by the mid-1970s, while military personnel in the Far East would be halved by 1971. Some members of the Cabinet concluded that the world role was finished.[87] The decision to re-apply for membership of the Common Market, formally put in May, was taken in some quarters as evidence of the same reorientation and in some respects it undoubtedly was. Shortly after taking office in October 1964 the Defence and Overseas Policy Committee considered Europe in the context of 'British Interests and Commitments Overseas'.[88] It was plain then, as it had been in the late 1940s, that there was danger for Britain if it allowed itself to become isolated from the process of European integration. The big change since the earlier discussions was that the Common Market was becoming one of the main political and economic power centres in the world, something that could only be imagined when the prospect of European integration was first raised. The Commonwealth, meanwhile, was turning into a nuisance. The economic consequences of remaining aloof from Europe could be just as damaging as the exclusion from world political decision-making which renunciation of the world role had always meant for its advocates. Nevertheless, in the absence of convincing economic arguments in favour of entry, it was the danger of Britain's future political weakness in world affairs which inspired Michael Stewart and George Brown to look favourably on membership during the period of the first Wilson Government.[89] The USA itself continued to attach great importance to Britain's full involvement with its European neighbours, as it had done since 1948. What is perhaps surprising is that there was no real pressure from inside the Wilson Cabinet to renew Macmillan's first application to join in the period up to March 1966. The Prime Minister still believed in these first two years that the Commonwealth connection supported 'our claim to be sharing the global responsibilities of the US more than any of her Western partners' especially in the Far and Middle East – and most of his Cabinet agreed with him. By the middle of 1966, however, the persistence of economic and financial problems strengthened the case of those who wanted to retreat from these global commitments. The chronic need for defence economies questioned the viability of the world role on the old basis even in the eyes of its supporters, who now looked to Europe as the base for British influence in the world.

Wilson had already come round to the idea of applying for membership when he convened a Chequers meeting in October 1966 to discuss the matter and announce his intention of touring the European capitals with George Brown to sound out opinion among the Six. It was during this tour, begun in January, that he realised he would have to drop all reference to conditions if the British application was to be taken seriously. The Cabinet approved this approach in April 1967 and the application was made in May. Wilson occasionally stressed to his colleagues that membership was now vital if Britain was to retain its political independence in the world, but it is difficult to see how this could be disentangled from considerations of Britain's continuing relative economic decline and the diminishing economic and political significance of the Commonwealth. Britain's economic weaknesses were indisputable and the wonder was only that the Government had persisted with the world role for as long as it had. But a Government so committed to faster economic growth and so unsuccessful at achieving it was bound to be impressed with the superior economic performance of the Common Market countries. The Department of Economic Affairs had joined the Foreign Office in agitating for 'a declaration of intent' to join in October 1966 and Wilson himself became more favourable after the financial crisis of July 1966.[90] Even opponents of entry like Crossman saw advantages if it severed the special relationship and led to withdrawal from the world role, such was their conviction that these burdens held Britain back. They also linked it with the devaluation of sterling, something which they thought necessary to escape from the cycle of sterling crises and deflationary budgets. Support for entry by 1967 was also strong in the press, all three main political parties, business organisations such as the CBI, the TUC, and public opinion. Foreign policy considerations were at least as important as the economic arguments, but in the end the two were inextricably connected. Britain could no longer expect the USA to regard it as a special partner if it was unable to perform either the traditional world role or a new role within the counsels of the Common Market.

Arab–Israeli dispute

Labour inherited problems associated with the scheme to create a Federation of South Arabia inaugurated by the Macmillan Government and into which Aden had been shoe-horned in 1963. It was intended as a device for consolidating the rule of various tribal leaders who looked kindly on the British military presence. But it was widely opposed for the same reasons by nationalist forces unimpressed by Britain's declared policy of withdrawal by 1968, subject to retention of the military base and the unpopular federal government. An insurgency began which overlapped with the civil war raging in neighbouring Yemen. Labour persisted with Conservative policies until the decision to withdraw was publicised in the defence White Paper of 1966. By this time the wisdom of Britain's close association with traditional rulers in the region had been questioned in Whitehall for some time and it was unclear what economic interests were served by the continuing military presence, despite reliance on Kuwait for two-thirds of its oil imports. Nor was it obvious that British military power in the Middle East could be militarily effective – Suez had cast doubts on this since 1956.

Michael Stewart's lengthy reflections on Britain's interventions in the Arab–Israeli dispute, which he despatched to British ambassadors and representatives throughout the Middle East (and in Paris, Washington and New York) in March 1966, was informed by these growing doubts. Britain's declared policy of impartiality, he said, actually favoured Israel because it stood for maintenance of the status quo. It seemed paradoxical, then, that this meant that the UK was often negative towards Israel in public. But this was easily explained because in common with the USA, Britain was merely saying to Israel, in effect:

> We see no prospect that the Arabs will be willing to make peace on terms which you can accept in the foreseeable future, or any means

of compelling them to. You must be realistic about the strength of Arab feeling on this. You must also recognise that it is important to Western interests – which are extremely important to your own survival – for us to maintain tolerable relations and some influence with the Arabs. You must not, therefore, expect us to take sides, or to appear to take sides, with you against the Arabs. For our part, we will see that you are able to acquire weapons for your defence; and, as you know, the Arabs are well aware that they cannot attempt to destroy Israel without taking on the United States Sixth Fleet. In return, we expect you to cooperate in preventing the dispute from coming to the boil, by acting with restraint, and by maintaining a reasonable relationship with the United Nations so that, if you have to be helped, it can be done under the United Nations cover. We understand the difficulties of your position, but, by the law of possession, the preservation of the status quo works markedly in your favour.[91]

To the Arabs the message was shorter. They had lost a diplomatic war, a military war and a cold war. Eventually they would have to accept that there was no prospect of any substantial concessions from Israel. They would have to swallow their pride and accept the status quo (perhaps taking American compensation for the refugees). According to Stewart, the Arabs were resigned to, though resentful of, this situation – hence Britain avoided mentioning it as much as possible. Israeli diplomacy, by contrast, was active and generated more occasions (such as in punitive retaliatory actions) for having to say 'no' in order to protect British interests. These interests included relations with friendly Arab states and the British military bases in the region. British association with Israel, if it were too close, would jeopardise these interests. Disengagement from the Arab–Israeli dispute was not an option, but since the USA was now the major Western military power in the region, Stewart thought there was scope for 'cautiously feeling our way towards the exit' by emphasising the authority of the UN, rather than any special British responsibility or the possibility of any British initiatives to mediate between the contending parties. The relevant context for Stewart's reflections was the chronic border conflict between Israel and Syria and Jordan. One of these incidents, in November 1966, confirmed Stewart's worst fears when the Israeli Defence Force attacked a Jordanian village and thereby jeopardised all the years of Anglo-American diplomacy in supporting King Hussein of Jordan, a man who was hated in parts of the Arab world for his lack of militancy against Israel.

Six months after Stewart composed his analysis, Abdul Nasser – bound to Syria by a military alliance of 1966 and still pan-Arabist in aspiration

– stepped up his fulminations against 'Arab reactionaries', whom he linked to British and American imperialism. As Hourani points out, 'Throughout the 1960s the public life of the Arab countries continued to be dominated by this idea of a socialist, neutralist, form of Arab nationalism, with 'Abd al-Nasir as its leader and symbol.'[92] This was the context in which Nasser continued to depict Israel as an expression of Western imperialism in the Middle East, just as, he said, the overthrow of Sukarno had been an expression of it in Indonesia. On 23 May 1967 Nasser closed the Straits of Tiran to Israeli shipping, cutting off its trade route to Asia and Iranian oil. That night the Foreign Office received a telegram from Washington emphasising that the USA did not want to interpose itself alone in order to prevent war.[93] On 30 May Jordan joined the military alliance of Egypt and Syria, though Nasser had denounced King Hussein as an imperialist lackey just days earlier. The Egyptian leader declared that the basic objective of the allies was the destruction of Israel. In the days that followed, the Foreign Office PUS, Gore-Booth, worried that the Soviet Union had now 'acquired a position of major influence' at the expense of Israel and the West. It had achieved this by arming Nasser and Syria. Any steps taken by the West would now be depicted as anti-Arab. Gore-Booth thought 'it is quite arguable that it is in the real interests of the Israelis, if they are to survive, to draw the logical conclusion that their only hope of survival is to break out and take on the Arabs'.[94] In the meantime Britain would need to stress UN mediation, though the latter's failure in respect of the problem created by Nasser, according to Gore-Booth, raised the issue of whether Britain should tolerate 'constant harassment on secondary issues' from the UN in the future.

Wilson was worried by American expectations that Britain would take the lead in the formation of a maritime force to keep the Straits of Tiran open. Eugene Rostow, Johnson's Under Secretary of State, had informed the British that the Vietnam commitment precluded US leadership in the region.[95] Had not the British, in any case, played-up the division of labour with the USA in the exercise of the world role, with the US focusing on South East Asia? But British thinking also continued to stress the desirability of increasing their distance from the Middle East conflict – Kuwaiti threats to stop the flow of oil if Britain engaged in any acts which they interpreted as hostile to Arab interests were a reminder of the need to project an image of impartiality.[96] Days later the British problem was solved when Israel attacked Egypt and routed its enemies in the space of six days. In July the Cabinet considered a memorandum from the Foreign Secretary, in the wake of this crisis, which repeated his analysis of British economic interests in the Middle East – oil, the Suez Canal, trade and 'large sterling balances'. It repeated his contention that Britain was unable to influence events in the area and 'should seek to disengage' as far as possible from a problem whose resolution, if it ever came, would leave both sides unhappy. In discussion the view was also expressed that Britain's military presence in the region was 'of no value to our economic interests and that this presence should be withdrawn as quickly as possible'.[97]

Towards devaluation

Short though the Arab–Israeli war was it contributed to renewed speculation against sterling and highlighted Britain's dependency on Middle Eastern (Kuwaiti) oil. Britain's application to join the Common Market had already reinforced the view in financial markets that devaluation was at some point inevitable, even though the Government ruled it out. The long-standing American support for Britain's membership may also have weakened US opposition to devaluation, in the wake of the British decision.[98] A dock strike in October eliminated any prospect that the balance of payments would improve sufficiently to calm the markets. Support for devaluation could now be found in the Treasury. But Wilson sought a meeting with Johnson to obtain massive financial support precisely to avoid this outcome. When the beleaguered President – faced with escalating war, rising costs and growing political opposition – failed to respond positively to these pleas for help, devaluation moved closer. Wilson told Callaghan on 6 November that devaluation would be a political and economic 'disaster' if other countries were to do the same. If there had been more time he would have preferred to float the pound, the option preferred in Cabinet by Barbara Castle. A week later he was much more upbeat about it, telling Crossman that devaluation was a positive development, rather than something the Government had to be resigned to. It would lead to the desirable end of the sterling area and Britain's remaining imperial commitments, paving the way to 'really major defence cuts', such as scrapping the F-111, withdrawal from the Middle East and termination of Britain's nuclear deterrent. It would strengthen Britain's bid, still under review, to join the Common Market. Support in the region of $3 billion would be required to relieve the burden on sterling and Wilson advised Crossman that there was no prospect of this except on politically unacceptable terms.[99] The next day Operation Patriarch was launched to consider the details of devaluation. Brown doubted that a devaluation to $2.40 (14.3 per cent) would be enough. He wanted it to be a signal to 'tell the world we are going to deal with industrial anarchy'. He did not want the proposed deflationary package that would accompany devaluation, observing that it was bigger than the deflation of 1966 and would bite even harder in the context created by the earlier measures.[100] On 16 November the Cabinet was informed of the decision to devalue. Barbara Castle records being told that 'only in this way could Britain retain its independence'.[101] Wilson's telegram to President Johnson, the next day, blamed the current crisis on industrial strikes, but also mentioned the impact of the Six Day War and the activities of speculators. He said that the new rate had been chosen to cause minimal disturbance to the dollar. Again the mood was optimistic:

> Each of us, I suppose, must at times have suffered the misery of the abscess which breaks out, is temporarily healed, then breaks out again. Each of us has shrunk from having the tooth pulled out. But when we finally decide to do so, the feeling of relief is not simply an illusion. The removal of a certain poison from the system purges the whole system itself.[102]

Wilson had wanted to meet Johnson before devaluation but had been advised by Rusk that a telephone call would suffice. In the draft of an unsent letter which referred to decisions of a 'very fundamental character' Wilson began by saying 'I do not of course expect you to change policies on Vietnam', a superfluous point, perhaps, though the Washington embassy was briefing Johnson to the effect that Labour was under 'intense pressure to dissociate HMG from the USA and to demand immediate cessation of the bombing'.[103]

The USA's reaction to devaluation was muted. In Germany it was welcomed on the grounds of a supposed signal of determination to solve 'the English disease' and strengthen Britain's case for Common Market entry. But German comment also saw persistent weaknesses in the quality of British management, low productivity and structural problems in the economy. In France, especially Gaullist circles, there was disappointment as well as *schadenfreude*. French policy had sought to hoard gold since 1965. Britain, in this view, had apparently missed a great chance to assert real independence from the USA. It put the USA first by not coordinating a general devaluation of the major economies which would have exposed the over-valuation of the dollar and isolated it.[104] The British embassy in Paris was informed that the French were disappointed to see that Britain had not renounced its special relationship with the USA. The CIA came to a similar conclusion, deducing that sterling would remain a reserve currency and the special relationship remained intact.[105] On 27 November de Gaulle once more vetoed Britain's application to join the EEC. Meanwhile, the price of gold, which had been rising since mid-September, continued its upward turn – a clear sign of low confidence in the current value of the dollar. Financial turmoil would continue until the end of March 1968, when the USA abandoned its commitment (except to the

Central Banks) to supply gold at $35 an ounce and the Labour Government introduced the biggest tax increases in British economic history.

Shortly after the Cabinet took the decision to devalue it approved a further £100 million of defence cuts, but Callaghan's successor as Chancellor, Roy Jenkins – the strongest advocate of the Common Market in the Government – immediately began work on further economies. By the end of the year Jenkins had sought agreement on withdrawal from South East Asia by 1971 and the Persian Gulf by 1968–9. In January 1968 the Cabinet also agreed to cancel the F-111 fighter plane – a decision informed by the $725 million foreign exchange deficit which emerged when the proposed expenditures were compared to the cost of maintaining US forces in Britain over the coming 12-year period. Brown, Healey, Callaghan and Stewart opposed the cancellation in Cabinet with Brown warning that it might signal the end of 'cooperation between the United States and ourselves'.[106] President Johnson repeated this threat to Wilson.[107] The American administration and Britain's allies in the Far East also continued to lobby against withdrawal from East of Suez but when the dollar was hit by speculation in March, sterling needed further support from the central bankers pending withdrawal from its role as a bankers' currency. De Gaulle's veto of the British application on 27 November reflected his conviction that Britain was still too close to the USA. But the (bipartisan) policy to seek entry did not change. Behind the scenes, the Prime Minister pressed on, as secretively and as exclusively as possible, preparing the ground for a third application. A White Paper on the costs of entry was published in February 1970 but not before the Prime Minister had secured the policy of unconditional commitment to Europe, marginalised opposition to it and briefed colleagues to stress the benefits of entry. All this allowed the succeeding Conservative Government to make the third application for membership just 12 days after taking office.[108]

Tactics changed, of course, after the general election defeat in June 1970. Wilson now sought to distinguish himself from Heath by attaching conditions to Britain's entry, while claiming that the Conservatives did not. This was rather obviously the best way to manage his own party, in which every conceivable opinion about the Common Market was expressed and the sensible 'middle' was defined in terms of safeguards for essential British and Commonwealth interests. Outright opponents on both left and right of the party were mollified by hearing that Labour would demand protection for the balance of payments, the cost of living, the national health and social security systems, and the preservation of independent decision-making in matters of foreign policy and economic planning.[109] Focus on the terms of entry made even more sense after the Conservative Government made rapid progress towards British accession.

Summing up the debate on the Common Market for the NEC at the 1971 annual conference, James Callaghan reflected the mood, which had grown more rather than less sceptical about the benefits of entry, in the face of what he called 'the most intensive barrage of propaganda in favour of entry that I have ever seen'.[110] A long list of objections was rehearsed ranging from the rising price of food; the constitutional and parliamentary position; the adverse impact on unemployment, regional policy, and industrial development; the greater mobility of capital (as against labour); to the absurdity of supporting inefficient French farmers with taxes on Britain. The solution proposed was to obtain the verdict of the British people in a general election, with the attendant threat that if Heath signed the Treaty of Rome in advance of such an election 'he must expect the issue to remain open'. Labour would reopen the principles and renegotiate the details when next elected to power. At no point in this process was there an honest debate about the relationship of any of these economic and social issues to European political integration.

Wilson's critics

Labour's public support for the US war in Vietnam did not falter when the bombing of the North began in February 1965 even though the Chief Whip was already complaining that it was causing him more problems than any other issue.[111] Fifty backbenchers condemned the attack. At meetings of the PLP Wilson invariably neutralised criticism by referring to his ongoing talks with the Americans and Russians.[112] Party management was probably only one of Wilson's motivations for the various 'peace initiatives' which he conducted from March 1965. While members of his own Cabinet dismissed them as 'gimmicks'[113] and the Communist states rejected them out of hand as a propaganda cover for the USA, President Johnson himself was often irritated by Wilson's presumptions. But Wilson seriously imagined himself as a mediator between the USA and the Communist world in matters of détente and was keen to stress Britain's role as a co-chair of the Geneva Conference – both as a way of resisting US pressure for direct British involvement in the war and of boosting his own mediating role. High profile peace initiatives were also useful in placating Commonwealth, as well as domestic, critics of Labour policy. This was also obviously true in Wilson's handling of the Rhodesian problem, on which he was faced from the outset by an intransigent white minority bent on independence under Ian Smith's leadership. The issue was what the Labour Government would do about it. Wilson opted for negotiations, while Smith prepared for unilateral independence on the basis of a white mandate which was renewed in an election in May 1965. In October Wilson publicly announced that there would be no recourse to armed force in preventing or responding to a white break away, even though the preferred alternative – economic sanctions – was known to be of doubtful efficacy because of Rhodesia's porous borders with South Africa and Portuguese Mozambique. Healey later described Wilson's statement ruling out force as 'a classic strategic blunder'.[114] In fact an invasion plan had been drawn up by the Conservative Government in 1961. This had served to highlight the military and political problems involved and these became the standard objections to military intervention within Whitehall, which Wilson inherited.[115] In the event Smith declared unilateral independence on 11 November and Wilson was now pressurised from most Commonwealth states and his own left-wing to use force. The General Assembly of the UN also recommended force to remove the regime, though the resolution in question was non-binding.

Wilson's failed diplomatic initiatives could not appease the critics who wondered why military intervention – so often applied by the British in colonial matters – was discounted on this occasion. Was it because the blacks did not matter so much after all, or the whites – being kith and kin – enjoyed special privileges denied to other colonial subjects? These were the suspicions and they tended to strengthen as it became apparent that sanctions were only applied half-heartedly, while Wilson himself was prepared to compromise on the principle of no independence before black majority rule. By 1968 the Government knew that British Petroleum and Shell were among the companies ignoring sanctions, but kept quiet about it.[116] Sanctions had failed to bring down the Smith regime in 'a matter of weeks' as Wilson had initially promised and now looked, at best, a long-term instrument to aid further negotiations. The Prime Minister's concessions to Smith, when they met aboard HMS *Tiger* in December 1966, to prolong white minority rule would surely have provoked further outrage from Wilson's Commonwealth and Labour critics had they been accepted. In the event their rejection led to renewed emphasis on black majority rule and a request for UN sanctions against Rhodesia. Despite this development Wilson was still prepared to guarantee that the Smith regime would remain in power during the transition – an offer that was reiterated (and again rejected) in talks with Smith on HMS *Fearless* in October 1968. As the matter dragged on in 1969 Wilson lost interest. The real significance of Rhodesia was in exposing how little had been done in the decades of rhetoric concerning native paramountcy, trusteeship, development and multiracialism. Rhodesia's unilateral declaration of independence was the logical outcome of the real history of the colony, characterised as it was by black economic, political and educational backwardness and white authoritarianism, privilege and racism.

Public opinion in Britain was not well informed about Rhodesia, and probably supported the Conservatives in opposing the use of force. But it turned against the USA in the course of 1966, especially after the bombing of Hanoi and Haiphong from which Wilson was obliged to 'dissociate' his Government. Wilson had been careful to warn Johnson in advance of his need for dissociation and won a sympathetic response from the President.[117] By this time the Government's policy on Vietnam was rejected by the party's annual conference and criticism of it was spreading, from left to right, through the PLP.[118] Sidney Silverman and other back benchers demanded dissociation from the US war without qualification but their motion was defeated at a PLP meeting 214 votes to 46.[119] Almost a third of the PLP supported U Thant's demand for an unconditional cessation of the bombing as a precondition for peace talks.[120] The Prime Minister answered the critics by denying that there was any deal with the US administration, while playing up his influence in the White House and alluding to secret talks for peace (which public denunciations of the USA would only jeopardise).[121] Michael Stewart bluntly blamed Hanoi and Peking for the failure of Britain's peace initiatives and spent much of his contribution to the annual conference debate of 1965 explaining why the UN was disqualified from playing this role.[122] His critics complained that the United States had been 'flouting the United Nations for years' by a policy of unilateral intervention in South East Asia and Latin America. They demanded an independent foreign policy 'without the strings which at present appear to be attached to it'.[123] They wanted to know how Britain could be a mediator for peace and act as an apologist for the USA at the same time. Stewart had said that he did not want to dissociate the Government from American policies; the real question was why he had made so many statements 'completely identifying the Government with American policy'.[124] Many of the critics merely demanded dissociation – not defiance, opposition or condemnation of American policy. It was rather more tepid than the criticism members of the Front Bench – including Wilson himself – had expressed during the first twenty years of the war in Vietnam, when they had recognised it as a national liberation struggle against foreign (Japanese, then French) occupation. But it was already clear that the USA was emerging in the minds of many party members – including 'unrepentant admirers' of America – as the real villain of the piece.[125]

Those who broadly approved of Wilson's Vietnam policy were also conscious of his closeness to the US administration – none more so than members of the administration itself. The US Embassy monitored Parliamentary debates, Labour Party conferences, and discussions at meetings of the PLP, sending regular reports to the Department of State which assured Dean Rusk and his colleagues of the good work being done in defence of US policy. Sometimes Rusk was moved to telegram his personal congratulations when a speech made 'a brilliant exposition of our mutual interests in Southeast Asia', as he cabled in thanks to Michael Stewart.[126] The Embassy also prepared anonymously written statements on Vietnam to support the Government which were circulated via 'selected key Labour and trade union leaders' in readiness for the annual conference.[127] On other occasions it was reported that the Prime Minister 'has accepted some of our suggestions and would use the attached text in his statement in the Commons today'.[128] A full-page advertisement published in *The Times* (25 April 1966) quoted President Johnson as 'cheered and strengthened' by Labour's re-election which he had taken as an endorsement by the electorate for Wilson's support of US policy. This interpretation was firmly repudiated by the sponsors of the advert – Labour supporters who rejected Wilson's support for the Americans. Parliamentary critics of the Government's stance complained of 'this extremely senseless and sordid war', while others pointed to 'the methods of barbarism resorted to by our American allies'.[129]

Privately, members of the Government agreed with the critics. The Foreign Office had been advising that there was no military solution in Vietnam from the moment Labour entered office.[130] Wilson himself complained of being placed in 'an intolerable position' that encouraged 'stories about satellites and the fifty-first state'.[131] He even admitted that 'the facts seem to support the jibe that HMG is the tail-end Charlie in an American bomber'.[132] This was why it was necessary, the US Ambassador explained to Washington, 'to counter the charge of being a mere puppet or satellite of the US . . . from time to time [by] assert[ing] its independence by taking exception to certain details of policies to which he [Wilson] is ready to give general support'.[133] Hence, for example, the utility of 'dissociation' from the bombing of Hanoi and Haiphong. The irascible George Brown – who in August 1965 implied criticism of Wilson by asserting that Gaitskell would already have sent troops to Vietnam – was complaining to Barbara Castle a year later that he had been 'sickened by what we have had to do to defend America – what I've had to say at the despatch box'.[134] For those members of the Government – such as Crossman – who questioned the value of the world role and the special relationship, the folly of Wilson's foreign policy was all too apparent.

Wilson's defence of US policy looked even worse in retrospect, as the conflict deteriorated up to US withdrawal in 1974, and a fuller picture emerged about American conduct of the war and the consequences for Vietnam and its neighbours such as Cambodia. In the year of Labour's centenary Wilson's support for LBJ ranked equal with MacDonald's betrayal of 1931 as the most shameful episode in the party's history, in the opinion of its MPs.[135] Wilson had once briefed Stewart to the effect that he should leave President Johnson in no doubt 'about the strength of feeling here [on Vietnam] and about the difficulties which we are facing. There is a danger of widespread anti-Americanism and of America losing her moral position.'[136] That was in 1965. When Crossman tried to raise the moral issue in Cabinet in September 1967 – arguing that most of the party saw Vietnam as an unjust war – Roy Jenkins opined that such 'crude' ideas as a 'just war' were beneath the consideration of serious politicians, and Crossman was left to reflect how rarely Cabinet even discussed great issues of principle.[137] The movement of opinion outside Government continued to change in an anti-American direction but Johnson felt able to thank Wilson, in January 1969, as he contemplated retirement, for the fact that 'one of his great comforts had been that he could always count on the UK during any crisis'.[138]

By the end of the decade anti-Americanism was embodied in theories which placed the USA at the centre of much that was wrong with the world. Vietnam contributed to the popularity on the left of 'revisionist' histories of the Cold War and accounts of US foreign policy since Pearl Harbor that emphasised American imperialism as a structured force for evil in the world. Whereas Bertrand Russell had argued in 1951 that Europe's freedom was 'only capable of being maintained by cooperation with America',[139] he now asserted that 'Whenever there is hunger, wherever there is exploitative tyranny, whenever people are tortured and the masses left to rot under the weight of disease and starvation, the forces which hold the people stem from Washington.'[140] He was not alone in this view. The United States, it was increasingly believed, 'has exercised a sustained, systematic, remorseless, and quite cynical manipulation of power worldwide, while masquerading as a force for universal good . . . [it has been] the most dangerous power the world has ever known.'[141] Others reached 'the reluctant and terrible conviction that the greatest threat to the peace of humanity is the United States. I can no longer stomach America's insidious meddling across the face of the world. Wherever I go I find myself more and more repelled by the apparently insatiable American urge to interfere in other people's business.'[142] Such conclusions were reached empirically by way of Vietnam but also theoretically, through the critique of US hegemony.

The reputation of the Labour Government for an unethical foreign policy on Rhodesia and Vietnam was reinforced by its equivocation over arms sales to South Africa and the steps that were taken to boost arms sales in general, such as the creation of the Defence Sales Organisation.[143] All these episodes stood in sharp contrast to the rhetoric of moral improvement in foreign policy which the incoming Government had made in 1964. For example, as public opinion in Britain turned against the apartheid system in South Africa, especially after the Sharpeville massacre in 1960, Labour pledged its opposition to all further arms sales to Pretoria. Meanwhile the USA committed itself at the UN to cease all shipments of weapons to South Africa by the end of 1963. Two days after Labour's victory in October 1964 Wilson instructed the Board of Trade that arms sales to South Africa should 'cease forthwith'.[144] In the event the balance of payments problem weighed heavily in the decision to honour existing contracts, as did the protection of over-flying rights and the naval base at Simonstown. Further balance of payments problems in 1967 provided the context in which it was suggested (by George Thompson and Roy Mason) that Labour should revert to the previous Conservative policy which supplied arms that supposedly could not be used to suppress internal dissent. Brown, Healey, Callaghan, Crosland, Gordon Walker, Ray Gunter and Ernie Ross supported this argument in Cabinet. It was only quashed when the PLP got wind of it and Wilson moved to reassert the old policy. By this time the public relations damage was done. Wilson rejected the idea that 'we should solve all our problems by selling arms all over the world', but had taken steps to boost British arms sales.[145] The USA and the UK had dominated this market until the USSR and France entered it in the mid-1950s. Up to this point Britain had supplied 95 per cent of all jet aircraft to the Middle East and South East Asia and additionally armed Iraq, Egypt and Kuwait with Centurion tanks. The Defence Sales Organisation was intended to restore Britain to its place as one of the two leading suppliers of arms in the world. Early evidence of its success was seen in the Biafran War (1967–9) and the military coup in Chile.[146] South Africa's nuclear capability, as Frankel notes, was virtually given to the regime by Labour's decision to allow a deal between Pretoria and Rio Tinto Zinc to mine uranium 'at the time of its most outspoken criticism of South Africa'.[147]

There was nevertheless the feeling that a turning point in British foreign policy had been reached by the end of the first two Wilson Governments. The decisions to withdraw from East of Suez and terminate sterling's role as a reserve currency had, after all, been taken – despite the fact of Wilson's pragmatic, procrastinating conduct of policy, with its emphasis on continuity and its essentially conservative character.[148] The increasingly flimsy pretence that Britain was engaged in an international division of labour with the USA in the maintenance of global order – the basis for claims of a special relationship – could no longer be maintained. Labour's illusions about the Commonwealth as a potential economic asset offering an alternative to Europe did not survive Wilson's first year in office. Since the advent first of President Nixon's administration, whose foreign policy paid little attention to European allied states; and then of

Edward Heath's Government in Britain, with its successful drive for Common Market entry, the special relationship was presumed to be dead on both sides of the Atlantic. Europe was surely Britain's future. Old convictions about its essential fragility and incapacity for real integration could no longer be sustained. Post-war assumptions about international Communism and the Soviet threat were also being questioned. Perhaps the idea of the United States as the crucial source of the West's economic and military security would fade with the fading threat of Soviet Communism. Perhaps as Britain came to terms with Europe she would give up claims of 'punching above her weight' in world politics. Such, at any rate, were some of the possibilities of the early 1970s, as they seemed to contemporaries.[149]

In fact the Labour Party was by no means committed to a European future. For most of the 1980s it was formally committed to withdrawal. One strong line of continuity among the membership was the desire for a more ethical foreign policy. Labour lost an estimated quarter of a million individual members in the years 1964–70 and one suspects that disillusionment with Labour's conduct of foreign policy – especially its public support for the USA – was a contributory factor. The defence and foreign policies of the Labour Government were defeated for the first time in the history of the party in 1966 and the experience was repeated in 1967 and 1968. The relevant issues were military expenditure (1966), Vietnam (1966 and 1967), Greece (1967), Biafra (1968) and Rhodesia (1968). Conflicts over domestic issues, however, were also important in causing the widening rift in the party. Certainly the division which opened between the Parliamentary and trade union leaderships over the future of industrial relations made a major contribution to the breakdown of authority within the organisation. After Labour's defeat in the general election of 1970 it spent 23 of the next 27 years in opposition to Conservative Governments. Unable to rely upon the votes of the affiliated trade unions the parliamentary leadership was faced throughout the 1970s, and much of the 1980s, with a rebellious annual conference leading to left-wing control of much of the party's policy-making process. On foreign policy this was reflected in resolutions carried by majorities against first use and threatened use of nuclear weapons and for the removal of all US military bases in the UK (1972, 1973) as well as the demand for new definitions of Britain's overseas interests (1973). The Labour election manifesto of February 1974 even committed the party to 'seek the removal of American Polaris bases from Great Britain'. After the formation of another Labour Government in 1974, in conditions of 'stagflation' and economic crisis, the annual conference deplored its failure to honour promises to institute cuts in defence expenditures (1975), its breaches of the arms embargo to South Africa, and its failure to prevent sanctions-busting in relation to Rhodesia (1978). Labour's Foreign Secretaries meanwhile – Callaghan, Crosland and David Owen – took up the theme of human rights. Owen even wrote a book on the subject while serving as Foreign Secretary.[150] This echoed the concerns of post-Vietnam US foreign policy and chimed in with rank and file sentiment, which was particularly outraged by human rights abuses in Chile, after the US-supported coup against Salvador Allende's socialist government on 11 September 1973. Numerous attempts were also made to commit Labour to withdrawal from NATO and the Common Market and to renounce the policy of bipartisanship in relation to Northern Ireland. All these attempts failed, as did the activists' demands for Labour to dissociate itself from the Shah of Iran's repressive regime (which it supplied with CS gas) and to oppose the American decision to deploy the neutron bomb in central Europe

But a further shift to the left, following defeat in the general election of 1979, led to the adoption of the policy of unilateral nuclear disarmament in 1981, along with the demand that all US military bases be withdrawn from Britain. In 1977 the House of Commons was told that there were 100 US military bases in Britain and another 30 sites devoted purely to accommodation of US forces.[151] The creation of a breakaway Social Democratic Party in 1981 was influenced by the perception that the left was finally and securely in control of the party's policy-making apparatus. The 'second Cold War', following the Soviet invasion of Afghanistan in 1979, ensured that the revived CND rose to new heights of public appeal and the country was divided over NATO's decision to site Cruise missiles in Britain. Though Labour's swing to the left was reversed after 1983 it was not until 1989 that nuclear disarmament was finally ditched as party policy. Throughout the 1980s the party stood for withdrawal from the European Community; it criticised US policy in Central America, demanded sanctions against South Africa and insisted that NATO adopt a 'no first use' policy on nuclear weapons. It was the experience of three consecutive general election defeats by 1987 which helped to restore the authority of the Parliamentary leadership and return foreign and defence policies to the old bipartisanship with the Conservatives, as revealed by Labour's support for the Gulf War in 1991, the decision to send troops to Bosnia in 1992 and to impose sanctions against Serbia.

Membership turnover continued at historically high levels throughout this period of turmoil, in the context of a long-term decline in the numbers of activists, which Labour shared with its domestic rivals and many of its continental counterparts. There was no evidence, however, that the party membership had been cured of its desire for an ethical foreign policy. Indeed, the idea was taken up by New Labour – which in all other respects was supposed to have broken with the party's past – and was briefly championed by a Labour Foreign Secretary (Robin Cook) in 1997. This runs somewhat counter to the argument that Labour politics evolved as 'a journey from fantasy to politics'[152] if we take 'realism' in foreign policy as the standard of commonsense in this area. Applied to Labour history the thesis of gradual political maturation begins with Labour's first taste of governmental office in the 1920s, followed by the grim reminder of the reality of power politics of the 1930s culminating in a Second World War within the space of a generation – powerful lessons which caused the leadership of the party and the trade unions to shed their pacifist illusions and embrace a realist outlook by 1940. Munich and appeasement had supplanted August 1914 as the key reference point. There is clearly some truth in this picture but as an account of the party's development it is also too simplistic. It overlooks the fact that part of the fantasy was made real in that the struggles for democracy and inter-national law, and against colonialism and dictatorship, made progress. It overlooks the fact that the Labour leadership continued to stress the role of reason, negotiation and compromise in relations between states. In this it was no doubt assisted by long spells in Opposition and popular support for these values, perhaps ultimately explained in terms of Britain's offshore status. But it would be wrong to suppose that internationalism, anti-colonialism, scepticism about the use of military force, and fear of nuclear disaster were confined to the membership of the party. It is quite clear that large sections of the parliamentary party believed that the interests of states were subject to change and not permanently in-compatible or ultimately antagonistic. In short, the party believed in the efficacy of politics in international affairs from the beginning – in the broad sense of an activity concerned with public decision-making and the resolution of conflict. Labour was also heir to a tradition which was alive to the disproportionate costs of war in an age of industrialism and technological advance, a tradition which socialist writers (like H. G. Wells and Bertrand Russell) did much to keep alive. The party's internationalism and generosity to other nations was stronger than that of any other British political party and so it continued to attract members on this basis and maintained a broadly distinctive outlook in its international policy.

This is all the more remarkable in view of the undoubted continuity of policy which marked Labour's brief periods in Government. This can also be traced back to the origins of the party in its acceptance of the need to represent the nation as a whole; to compete with a dominant Conservative Party for spells in office (which acted as a powerful incentive to adopt conventional views of the national interest); to take the Empire as a fact of life and present this enterprise as a force for good in the world; and to embrace the Westminster model of government in its entirety. Though the link between objectionable foreign policies and the secretive, highly centralised, decision-making processes at Westminster was made by Labour and Liberal critics before the First World War, the structures of power survived largely unscathed in the twentieth century. Labour Prime Ministers, like their Conservative counterparts, were inclined to by-pass their own Cabinets, let alone the Parliamentary party, in the conduct of foreign policy. They retained prerogative powers to deploy troops at home and abroad, make and ratify treaties, conduct policy, make war and negotiate for Britain within multilateral bodies ranging from the UN to NATO and the IMF. Far from being consulted, Parliament did not even have the right to know what the full extent of the prerogative powers entailed. Prime Ministers, armed with these powers, but apt to be isolated from most of their colleagues, were also caught in the webs of advice, intelligence, commitments and dependency in which they inevitably found themselves. None of this deterred Labour Party members in their expectation that a Labour Government would pursue a significantly more enlightened foreign policy than the Conservatives. But if the contradictions between expectation and performance remain, they do so in the context of Labour's diminishing significance as a social force and the fact that Britain is no longer a geostrategic player and, in the words of one US analyst, 'entertains no ambitious vision of Europe's future', unlike Germany and France:

It is America's key supporter, a very loyal ally, a vital military base, and a close partner in critically important intelligence activities. Its friendship needs to be nourished, but its policies do not call for sustained attention.[153]

Notes

1 Party and Liberal nation

1 H. Pelling, *The Origins of the Labour Party* (Oxford: Oxford University Press, second edition, 1979).

2 R. McKibbin, *The Ideologies of Class* (Oxford: Oxford University Press, 1990), p. 26.

3 Walter Bagehot remarked in *The English Constitution* (1867) on the capacity of the monarchy and state-sponsored pomp to preserve and inspire popular deference by its show of dazzle and theatre. Victoria's sulky retreat from public life after 1861 provided negative support for this hypothesis with the revival of republicanism in the early 1870s. But crown-worship was soon restored as she returned to the exercise of her duties. Many spontaneous demonstrations of its popular roots were supplied in Victoria's later years but its cultural significance continued to grow for decades after her demise.

4 See McKibbin, *Classes and Cultures* (Oxford: Oxford University Press, 1998) and his *Ideologies of Class*, pp. 259–94.

5 See T. Pakenham, *The Scramble for Africa* (London: Abacus Books, 1991).

6 The attempt has been made by J. M. McKenzie (ed.), *Imperialism and Popular Culture* (Manchester: Manchester University Press, 1986).

7 This point is made by J. Schumpeter in *Imperialism and Social Classes* (1919 and Oxford: Oxford University Press, 1951), p. 13. On the effects of Harmsworth's *Daily Mail* see R. Pound and G. Harmsworth, *Northcliffe* (London: Praeger, 1959), pp. 206–7.

8 See G. R. Searle, *The Quest for National Efficiency: A Study in British Politics and British Political Thought, 1899–1914* (Oxford: Oxford University Press, 1971), p. 96 and B. Semmel, *Imperialism and Social Reform* (London: Allen and Unwin, 1960).

9 P. Kennedy, *The Rise of the Anglo-German Naval Antagonism, 1860–1914* (London: Prometheus, 1980), p. 308.

10 Liberal Imperialists such as Lord Rosebery explicitly linked imperialism and social reform at home but unlike the Liberal Unionist followers of Joseph Chamberlain refused to countenance tariff protection. Chamberlain campaigned for an imperial customs union from 1896.

11 See his articles 'Aggression on Egypt and Freedom in the East', *Nineteenth Century*, August 1877; 'Kin Beyond Sea', *North American Review*, September 1878; and 'England's Mission', *Nineteenth Century*, September 1878.

12 See H. G. C. Matthews, *Gladstone, 1875–1898* (Oxford: Clarendon Press, 1995), pp. 56 and 123.

13 Quoted in H. Winkler, *Paths Not Taken: British Labour and International Policy in the 1920s* (London: University of North Carolina Press, 1994), p. 12.

14 A. P. Saab, *Reluctant Icon: Gladstone, Bulgaria and the Working Classes* (Cambridge, Mass.: Harvard University Press, 1991).

15 R. Shannon, *The Crisis of Imperialism 1865–1915* (London: Paladin Books, 1976), pp. 124–5.

16 See H. Cunningham, 'The Language of Patriotism', in R. Samuel (ed.), *Patriotism: The Making and Unmaking of British National Identity*, volume 1, *History and Politics* (London: Routledge, 1989), pp. 57–90.

17 Ibid., p. 77.

18 Matthews, *Gladstone*, p.135.

19 Ibid., p. 136.

20 See H. Arendt, *The Origins of Totalitarianism* (New York: Harvest, 1966 and 1994), pp. xvii–xxviii, 123–47.

21 K. Marx, *New York Daily Tribune*, 21 September 1857, quoted in L. E. Davis and R. A. Huttenback, *Mammon and the Pursuit of Empire* (Cambridge: Cambridge University Press, 1988), p. 262.

22 B. Semmel, *The Rise of Free Trade Imperialism* (Cambridge: Cambridge University Press, 1970), pp. 216–17.

23 Kennedy, *Rise of the Anglo-German Naval Antagonism*, p. 410.

24 As at Omdurman in 1898 where 48 British soldiers died as Kitchener's army slaughtered 11,000 Sudanese 'rebels' and few of a further 16,000 wounded survived. Churchill, an observer at the scene, later wrote that 'This kind of war was full of fascinating thrills. It was not like the Great War. Nobody expected to be killed.' Quoted by S. Lindqvist, *Exterminate All the Brutes* (London: Granta, 2002), pp. 53–4. Unequal force of this kind characterised most, if not all, of these colonial wars.

25 It was also given a Hegelian gloss by his British followers, such as Bernard Bosanquet, who exercised some intellectual influence within the 'progressive alliance' of the turn of the twentieth century. See D. Boucher, 'British Idealism, the State and International Relations', *Journal of the History of Ideas*, 55, 4, 1994, pp. 671–94.

26 C. Johnson, *The Sorrows of Empire* (London: Verso, 2004), p. 67.

27 See A. Hochschild, *King Leopold's Ghost* (Boston: Mariner, 1998).

28 F. Lugard, *The Dual Mandate in British Tropical West Africa* (London: 1922 and Frank Cass, 1965).

29 See B. Davidson, *The Black Man's Burden* (London: Three Rivers Press, 1992), chapter 4.

30 B. Porter, *The Lion's Share* (London: Longman, 1984), p. 289.

31 The *locus classicus* was J. A. Hobson's *Imperialism: A Study* (London: 1902 and Routledge, 1988). Even Hobson referred to 'sane' or 'legitimate' imperialism as well as 'aggressive' imperialism – the latter being the product of Great Power competition and the dominant influence of finance. Strong Cobdenite influences remained in his thinking – in the role of sinister interests, in the presumed benefits of free trade and the political interdependence it would foster. His most original argument contended that inequality of incomes and monopoly organisation of industry led to the 'underconsumption' of the masses and the need for capital export, the source of the imperialist quest for overseas markets.

32 Hobson believed that this was best done by an international body. The League of Nations carried these hopes from 1919.

33 'Lest We Forget', *The Churches and the South African War* (London: New Age, 1905), pp. 36–9.

34 For good accounts of the tradition of anti-imperialism on the British left, see S. Howe, *Anticolonialism in British Politics: The Left and the End of Empire, 1918–1964* (Oxford: Clarendon Press, 1993).

35 The articles are reprinted in R. Blatchford, *Germany and England: The War That Was Foretold* (London: Clarion pamphlet, 1914).

36 H. M. Hyndman, 'The Jews' War on the Transvaal', *Justice*, 7 October 1899.

37 B. Baker, *The Social Democratic Federation and the Boer War* (London: CPGB, 1974), p. 9.

38 George Bernard Shaw, *Fabianism and the Empire* (London: 1900).

39 J. A. Hobson, Edward Carpenter, John Burns and Michael Davitt were among those perceiving a Jewish conspiracy in the pro-war policy on South Africa in 1899–1902. See D. Lowry, '"The Boers were the beginning of the end"?: The Wider Impact of the South African War', in D. Lowry (ed.), *The South African War Reappraised* (Manchester: Manchester University Press, 2000), pp. 203–46, 205, 211.

40 J. M. Winter, 'The Webbs and the Non-White World: A Case of Socialist Racialism', *Journal of Contemporary History*, 9, 1, 1974.

41 S. Webb, 'Lord Rosebery's Escape from Houndsditch', *Nineteenth Century*, 50, 1901, pp. 375–6.

42 S. McIntyre, *Imperialism and the British Labour Movement in the 1920s* (London: CPGB, 1975).

43 Ibid., p. 12.

44 The question of the significance of racism among the imperial working class before 1914 is debated in J. Hyslop, 'The Imperial Working Class Makes Itself "White": White Labourism in Britain, Australia, and South Africa before the First World War', *Journal of Historical Sociology*, 12, 4, 1999, pp. 398–421 and N. Kirk, *Comrades and Cousins* (London: Merlin, 1994), pp. 154 and 204–5.

45 E. D. Morel (1873–1924). Campaigner against the brutal regime of Leopold II of Belgium in the Congo Free State in the first years of the twentieth century. A critic of British foreign policy under Grey and a campaigner for neutrality in 1914. Launched the UDC to oppose annexations and promote a negotiated peace. Joined the ILP in 1918 and entered Parliament in November 1922 as Labour MP for Dundee, where he defeated Winston Churchill.

46 R. C. Reinders, 'Racialism on the Left: E. D. Morel and the "Black Horrors on the Rhine"', *International Review of Social History*, 13, 1968, p. 1.

47 See C. Benn, *Keir Hardie* (London: Richard Cohen, 1997); A. Morgan, *J. Ramsay MacDonald* (Manchester: Manchester University Press, 1987); D. Marquand, *Ramsay MacDonald* (London: Cape, 1977); K. Laybourne, *Philip Snowden*; R. McKibbin, 'Arthur Henderson as Labour Leader', in *Ideologies of Class*, pp. 42–66.

48 J. Ramsay MacDonald, *Labour and the Empire* (1907), in R. E. Dowse (ed.), *From Serfdom to Socialism* (London: Harvester, 1974). See also P. Snowden, *Labour and the New World* (London: Waverley, 1921).

49 See Joll, *The Second International, 1889–1914* (London: Weidenfeld and Nicolson, 1955), pp. 126–7.

50 E. J. Hobsbawm, *Age of Empire* (London: Weidenfeld and Nicolson, 1987), p. 72.
51 Norman Angell (1872–1967). Published *Europe's Optical Illusion* (1909) to show that war, even when successfully prosecuted, was economically counterproductive because of the complex commercial, industrial and trading relationships which it inevitably dislocated. *The Great Illusion* (1910) elaborated this thesis and sold over a million copies in 25 languages. In 1914 Angell was initially isolationist but quickly came to the view that the war had to be won by Britain. Stood as a Labour parliamentary candidate in 1922 and 1923 before entering parliament for the first time in 1929.
52 N. Angell, *War and the Workers* (London: 1912), p. 60.
53 Ibid., p. 63.
54 Ibid., p. 60.
55 *An Exposure of the Armaments Ring: A Report of Snowden's Speech on the Naval Estimates* (London: Labour Party, 1914).
56 See G. H. Perris, *The War Traders: An Exposure* (London: National Peace Council, 1913), p. 31; and J. T. Walton-Newbold, *The War Trust Exposed* (London: 1913).
57 See M. Freeden, *Ideologies and Political Theory* (Oxford: Oxford University Press, 1996).
58 See K. Ingram, *Fifty Years of the National Peace Council, 1908–58* (London: 1958).
59 The term was coined in 1901 and referred to the doctrine that it is desirable and possible to settle international disputes by peaceful means.
60 N. Young, 'War Resistance and the British Peace Movement since 1914', in R. Taylor and N. Young (eds), *Campaigns for Peace: British Peace Movements in the Twentieth Century* (Manchester: Manchester University Press, 1987), p. 27.
61 H. Quelch, *Social Democracy and the Armed Nation* (London: 1900).
62 The Rainbow Circle, the Fabian Society and the South Place Ethical Society are examples of this working alliance. In different ways, so were *The Nation*, under Hugh Massingham's editorship, and C. P. Scott's *Manchester Guardian*.
63 H. Cunningham, 'The Language of Patriotism', pp. 57–89, 77.
64 B. Porter, *Critics of Empire* (London: Macmillan, 1968), pp. xi and 1.
65 J. Meerscheimer, *The Tragedy of Great Power Politics* (New York: Norton, 2001), p. 187.
66 After 1880 the Nonconformist sects became increasingly pro-empire and the Boer War revealed that, with the exception of the Quakers, none of them contained more than minorities of anti-war or 'pro-Boer' opinion. Most Nonconformists returned as Liberal MPs in the Khaki election of 1900 supported the war. See G. Cuthbertson, 'Pricking the "Nonconformist Conscience": Religion against the South African War', in D. Lowry (ed.), *The South African War Reappraised* (Manchester: Manchester University Press, 2000), pp.169–88.
67 Ibid., pp. 170–1.
68 P. Catterall, 'Morality and Politics: The Free Churches and the Labour Party between the Wars', *The Historical Journal*, 36, 3, 1993, pp. 667–85. By 1931 more Nonconformists stood as Labour candidates in the general election than as Liberals and it was here that the Nonconformist conscience resided (p. 676).

69 J. A. Hobson (1858–1940). Co-author, with A. F. Mummery, of *The Physiology of Industry* (1889). Member of the Rainbow Circle discussion group with Ramsay MacDonald, Herbert Samuel, J. M. Robertson and other liberals and socialists. Visited South Africa in 1899 as correspondent of the *Manchester Guardian* and wrote *The War in South Africa: Its Causes and Effects* (1900) which explained the conflict as the result of international financial and capitalist interests, much of it Jewish. These ideas further developed in *Imperialism* (1902) which was explained as a consequence of the maldistribution of metropolitan incomes, causing crises of under-consumption and the need for overseas markets. In 1914 Hobson was a member of the British neutrality committee, which became the Bryce group. He became a critic of the Prussian trends in British politics during the war. Thereafter he championed international cooperation, but was disappointed with the League of Nations as created in 1919. He joined the Labour Party in 1924 and worked with the ILP in preparing *The Living Wage*.

70 Norman Angell's *The Great Illusion* (1910) was the most eloquent statement of this viewpoint in English. But Rudolf Hilferding and Karl Kautsky reached similar conclusions around the same time in Germany. Hugo Haase and August Bebel also emphasised the restraints on aggression when imperialism was debated at the SPD's Chemnitz congress in 1912. Jean Jaurès expressed similar views in the French Chamber of Deputies on 20 December 1911. See G. Haupt, *Socialism and the Great War* (Oxford: Clarendon, 1972), pp. 149–51.

71 Formed in 1911 from the fusion of the Social Democratic Party and dissident factions of the ILP.

72 G. D. H. Cole, *A History of the Labour Party from 1914* (London: Routledge and Kegan Paul, 1948), p. 9.

73 The ILP claimed 672 branches but many of these were small and only 244 of them were represented at its Bradford conference of 1914.

74 J. F. Naylor, *Labour's International Policy* (London: Weidenfeld and Nicolson, 1969); before 1914 Labour was 'not greatly concerned with foreign policy', p. 2. The parliamentary party reserved the right, as formulated by Keir Hardie in 1907, to determine when (and therefore if) policies approved by annual conference would be acted upon. The 1918 constitution essentially repeated this formula, while in practice allowing the trade union leaderships to manage conference in conjunction with its parliamentary leaders. Subject to these constraints, annual conference acted as a forum for inner-party democracy to a much greater extent than its Conservative or Liberal counterparts.

2 The First World War

1 Quoted in Joll, *The Second International*, p. 109.

2 See Haupt, *Socialism and the Great War*.

3 Joll, *Second International*, p. 163.

4 *Labour Party Annual Conference Report 1916* (henceforward *LPACR*), 26 January 1916, p. 51.

5 Cole, *A History of the Labour Party*, p. 19. Among the trade union critics of the war was Robert Smillie, president of the Miners' Federation and foundation member of the ILP, who succeeded Henderson as chair of the War Emergency Workers' National Committee in May 1915. It is true that

at the end of 1918 the pro-war trade union element was prominent among the Labour MPs elected to Parliament in December 1918, and some of them had been elected on a patriotic ticket such as Arthur Hayday. But the views of many of them had altered profoundly since August 1914. John Hill, general secretary of the Boilermakers, for example, helped in guiding the TUC to accept Henderson's new foreign policy in 1917; Tom Shaw, who went on to become secretary of state for war in the second minority Labour Government, was a strong critic of the Versailles Treaty and a convinced champion of the League of Nations and the ILO; George Barnes, who resigned from the party in order to stay in the War Cabinet, could claim that he had helped to create the ILO. Men like Hayday and William Adamson, who claimed to be loyal to their class as well as their country, also provided evidence of this dual commitment by opposing MacDonald when he looked to wage and benefits cuts to solve the political and economic crisis of 1931. Class as well as party loyalties explain why these men had remained on working terms with at least some of the war's critics, thanks to the fact that men like Smillie served on the War Emergency Workers' National Committee.

6 Quoted in Joll, *Second International*, p. 181.
7 Goldsworthy Lowes Dickinson (1862–1932). Credited as the originator of the idea of a League of Nations, a term he coined within weeks of August 1914. The key member of the Bryce group and a member of the UDC. A critic of the peace settlement, joined the Labour Party's advisory committee on international questions
8 James Bryce, ennobled in January 1914 as Viscount Bryce, was ambassador to the USA 1907–13. Bryce chaired the committee which investigated German conduct in Belgium which reported in May 1915. As an establishment figure he was a useful ally for members of the UDC and other critics of the war. The Bryce memorandum submitted to the British Government on 8 August 1917 outlined a structure for the League of Nations.
9 Hardie, MacDonald, Philip Snowden, Fred Jowett and Thomas Richardson. J. R. Clynes and James Parker supported the war.
10 See J. Liddington, *The Long Road to Greenham: Feminism and Anti-Militarism in Britain since 1820* (London: Verso, 1989), p. 106.
11 'Declaration of the inter-allied conference of the socialist and labour parties', 14 February 1915, LSI 3/5/1i, Labour History Archive.
12 M. Ceadal, *Semi-Detached Idealists: The British Peace Movements and International Relations, 1854–1945* (Oxford: Oxford University Press, 2000), pp. 188–9.
13 F. L. Carsten, *War against War: British and German Radical Movements in the First World War* (London: Batsford, 1982), p. 177.
14 Ibid., p. 190.
15 Ceadal, *Semi-Detached*, p. 198.
16 C. P. Trevelyan (1870–1958). Liberal imperialist, parliamentary under-secretary at the Board of Education from October 1908, but increasingly critical of Grey's foreign policy. Resigned from the government in August 1914 and helped to establish the UDC. Joined the Labour Party in November 1918. President of the Board of Education in the 1924 Labour Government and Minister for Education in 1929.
17 Arthur Ponsonby (1871–1946). Joined diplomatic service in 1894, resigned from Foreign Office in 1902, became PPS to the Prime Minister Campbell-Bannerman. Elected Liberal MP in 1908. Specialist on foreign affairs,

advocate of parliamentary control of foreign affairs. Opposed Grey's foreign policy. Founder member of UDC. Member of the Bryce group. Advocate of League of Nations. Elected Labour MP for Sheffield Brightside in 1922. Parliamentary under-secretary at the Foreign Office in 1924. Pacifist who reorganised the peace letter campaign of 1927. Advocate of unilateral disarmament in 1928. Entered House of Lords in 1931 and became Labour leader of the House. Co-founder of the Peace Pledge Union with Dick Shephard. Resigned from Labour Party in May 1940.

18   Quoted by Ceadal, *Semi-Detached*, p. 204. Leonard Woolf (1880–1969): joined the colonial service in 1904, served for seven years in Ceylon, where he became a critic of British imperialism, and resigned from the civil service in 1912. Woolf's reports on international government written for the Fabian Society in 1916 helped to shape the League of Nations. From 1919 to 1945 he was secretary of the Labour Party's advisory committee on international and imperial questions.

19   H. N. Brailsford (1873–1958), journalist of advanced anti-imperialist views with *The Nation* (1907–22); joined ILP in 1907; opponent of the Anglo-Russian entente. Identified economic imperialism as the roots of war, notably in *The War of Steel and Gold* (1914). Favoured economic and territorial appeasement of Germany before 1914 and took the view that war guilt was shared, rather than exclusively German. Advocated a negotiated peace and generosity towards Germany. Advocated a League of Nations in 1917 in a book by that title.

20   Young, 'War Resistance', in Young and Taylor, p. 28.

21   The Open Door policy can be traced back to the end of the Spanish–American war and signified a strategy of enlarging American trade and power without the encumbrance of overseas annexations. In other words it sought to emulate the free trade imperialism practised by Britain before the era of competitive annexations began in the late nineteenth century.

22   N. Angell, *Shall This War End German Militarism?* (London: UDC, 1914), p. 1.

23   Murray was a liberal internationalist who supported the war to defend Belgium. After the war he was the leading spirit of the League of Nations Union together with Viscount Cecil.

24   Angell, *Shall This War*, p. 3.

25   By the end of 1914 France alone had suffered 900,000 casualties. In 1915 330,000 French, 170,000 German and 73,000 British soldiers were killed. The wounded were measured in millions.

26   G. Lowes Dickinson, 'The War and the Way Out', *Atlantic Monthly*, 114, December 1914, pp. 820–37.

27   L. Woolf, *International Government: Two Reports Prepared for the Fabian Research Department* (London: 1916), pp. 10–11, 90–1, 216–30. Woolf also suggested that in the British Empire 'we see the beginnings of another system of government, and one to which International Government would necessarily approximate' (p. 230).

28   H. N. Brailsford, *The Origins of the Great War* (London: UDC, 1914), pp. 3 and 18.

29   Ibid., p. 17.

30   Ibid., p. 13.

31   Ibid., p. 15.

32   A. Ponsonby, *Parliament and Foreign Policy* (London: UDC, 1914), p. 1.

33   Quoted in ibid., p. 8.
34   Ibid., p. 9.
35   J. A. Hobson, *A League of Nations* (London: 1915).
36   Ibid., pp. 6–7.
37   Ibid., p. 16.
38   *LPACR*, 1916, p. 32.
39   Karl Liebknecht was the first to break with the SPD majority by voting against a renewal of the war credits in December 1914. By March 1915 a further 31 of his colleagues were prepared to abstain. Expulsions followed in March 1916 and in April of the following year the Independent Social Democratic Party (USPD) was formed.
40   Leon Jouhaux of the CGT successfully moved a resolution insisting that the peace treaty included a raft of measures protecting European workers and trade unions. See G. D. H. Cole, *A History of Socialist Thought*, volume 4, part 1 (London: Macmillan, 1965), p. 330.
41   *LPACR*, 1916, G. J. Wardle MP, pp. 102–3.
42   J. Schneer, *George Lansbury* (Manchester: Manchester University Press, 1990).
43   *LPACR*, 23 January 1917, p. 126.
44   T. J. Knock, *To End All Wars: Woodrow Wilson and the Quest for a New World Order* (New Jersey: Princeton University Press, 1992), pp. 48–58.
45   Quoted in ibid., p. 78. See also Arno J. Mayer, *Political Origins of the New Diplomacy*; L. W. Martin, *Peace Without Victory* (New Haven, Conn.: 1958); Swartz, *The Union of Democratic Control.*
46   LPACR, 1917.
47   The full story is told in H. Meynell, 'The Stockholm Conference of 1917', *International Review of Social History*, volume 5, 1960, pp. 1–25 and 202–25. See also J. M. Winter, 'Arthur Henderson, the Russian Revolution, and the Reconstruction of the Labour Party', *Historical Journal*, 15, 4, 1972, pp. 753–73.
48   In the event a convention was held at Leeds on 3 June at which delegates called for the establishment of soviets in Britain.
49   Carsten, *War against War*, pp. 103–5.
50   The delegation was eventually issued with passports but refused permission to travel at Aberdeen by the Sailors' and Firemen's Union.
51   Ceadal, *Semi-Detached Idealists*, p. 229.
52   Press release of joint meeting of the TUC and LP on new peace offer of the Central Powers, LSI 3/4/2i
53   Henderson resigned on Saturday 11 August. It was announced in *The Times* two days later as 'the direct result of his speech in favour of the Stockholm Conference'. The cheers that greeted his resignation speech were reported as coming mainly from ' "pacifist" group' of MPs. 'Mr Henderson explains', *The Times*, 14 August 1917.
54   The argument on war aims was then taken up at an Inter-Allied Socialist Conference on 28–9 August. See 'Today's Labour Conference', *The Times*, 28 August 1917; 'Rival Socialist War Aims', *The Times*, 29 August 1917.
55   Cole, *History of Socialist Thought*, volume 4, p. 58.
56   It was redrafted by seven representatives of the TUC and seven representatives of the Labour Party of whom only Webb, Henderson and MacDonald were not serving trade union officials.
57   C. Huysmans, 'Memorandum on International Policy', LSI 3/5/1i, p. 2.

58   Ibid., p. 4.
59   Ibid., p. 4.
60   Labour Party, *Memorandum of War Aims*, 28 December 1917.
61   H. Winkler, 'British Labor and the Origins of the Idea of Colonial Trusteeship, 1914–19', *The Historian*, 13 (spring), 1951, pp. 154–72, 157. See also his *The League of Nations Movement in Great Britain, 1914–1919* (Methuen, N.J., 1952 and Scarecrow Reprint, US, 1967), especially chapter 8, pp. 199–229.
62   Ibid., p. 162.
63   *Labour and the Peace Treaty* (London: Labour Party, 1919), pp. 47–8.
64   Huysmans, 'Memorandum on International Policy', p. 6.
65   Knock, *To End All Wars*, pp. 141–3.
66   *LPACR*, 23 January 1918, p. 3.
67   See Z. Steiner, *The Lights That Failed: European International History 1919–33* (Oxford: Oxford University Press, 2005), pp. 32–3.
68   Quoted in Knock, *To End All Wars*, p. 161.
69   Ibid., p. 161.
70   *Memorandum of War Aims* as agreed at Central Hall, Westminster, 20–4 February 1918, p. 8.
71   Ibid., p. 10.
72   Quoted by Camille Huysmans, 'Memorandum on International Policy', LSI 3/5/1i, p. 2.
73   Huysmans, 'Memorandum on International Policy', pp. 9–10.
74   'Statements of national parties to the inter-allied war aims memorandum'; nd, LSI 1/21.
75   'The War Aims Memorandum of the Allied Socialists and the projected League of Nations', LSI 1/14. This document reproduces the gist of Cunow's article 'The Projected International Conference at Berne', *Die Neue Zeit*, number 10, 7 June 1918.
76   Ibid., p. xi.
77   P. J. Troelstra, 'The New Socialist Peace Conference: An Open Letter to Arthur Henderson', *Het Volk*, 3–6 July 1918, LSI 1/11.
78   M. Gilbert, *First World War* (London: Weidenfeld and Nicolson, 1994), pp. 480–1.
79   Emile Vandervelde to Arthur Henderson, 19 August 1918, LSI 2/2/2i.
80   Gilbert, *First World War*, p. 470.
81   Ibid., p. 503.
82   Henderson had called for a Wilsonian peace during the election while Lloyd George was reported to have echoed 'the immense (and very practical) interest of the public in "making Germany pay" the damages of the war', as *The Times* put it. 'Opposition Essential' and 'Making Germany Pay', *The Times*, 9 December 1918.
83   Knock, *To End All Wars*, pp. 196–7.

3   Peace in our time

1   Henderson's constitutional reforms gave increased weight to the affiliated unions on the party's executive and within its annual conference. Yet at the same time he claimed that he wanted 'to remove the idea that the party is the party of the manual wage-earners merely, and that its politics is the politics of the trade unions – a purely class-conscious demand for specific improvements in wages, hours, conditions of employment'. The aim of the

party in the revised constitution was, he said, 'to promote the political, social, and economic emancipation of the people'. A. Henderson, 'The Outlook for Labour', *Contemporary Review*, February 1918, pp. 121–30.

2   R. Blake, *The Decline of Power* (London: Grafton, 1985), p. 67.
3   *Labour and the New Social Order* (London: Labour Party, 1918), p. 3.
4   Ibid., p. 22.
5   Ibid., p. 22.
6   The Communist Party organised and led this critique. See J. Callaghan, *Rajani Palme Dutt* (London: Lawrence and Wishart, 1993).
7   *Labour and the New Social Order*, p. 22.
8   The Dominions' response to the possibility of British war with Turkey in 1922, at the time of the so-called Chanak Incident, was an early suggestion of this.
9   R. McKibbin, *The Evolution of the Labour Party* (London: Oxford University Press, 1974), p. 220.
10 An excellent account is provided by M. Macmillan, *Peacemakers: Six Months That Changed the World* (London: John Murray, 2001).
11 *LPACR*, 1918, p. 3.
12 *Labour Leader*, 20 February 1919.
13 J. A. Hobson, *The New Holy Alliance* (London: UDC, 1919).
14 *LPACR*, 1919, pp. 139–42.
15 E. D. Morel, *The Fruits of Victory* (London: UDC, 1919), p. 4.
16 'The League of Nations', resolution of the Berne conference of the Labour and Socialist International, LSI 4, Labour History Archive, Manchester. See also *Bulletin of the Second International*, English edition, May 1919, LSI 1/34.
17 Ibid., LSI 1–4.
18 Support for a Jewish state accorded with the Wilsonian idea of self-determination for ethnic groups. Lansbury, MacDonald and Brailsford were among the first socialists in Britain to give their support. From the beginning Labour showed a tendency to favour the Jewish immigrants to Palestine because of their industry and their ability to articulate their interests as trade unionists and socialists. While there was a real issue of protecting native interests which Labour recognised in the 1920s – the natives here being the Palestinians – Labour politicians were inclined to discount 'genuine patriotism' among Palestinians in the inter-war years. See, P. Keleman, 'Zionism and the British Labour Party: 1917–39', *Social History*, 21, 1, 2000, pp. 71–87.
19 J. M. Keynes, *Economic Consequences of the Peace* (1919) in *Collected Works*, volume 2 (London: Macmillan, 1971).
20 Ibid., p. 7.
21 Wilson's Fourteen Points, R. Maidment and M. Dawson (eds), *Key Documents*, second edition (London: Hodder and Stoughton, 1999), pp. 303–8.
22 C. S. Maier, *Recasting Bourgeois Europe* (Princeton, N.J.: Princeton University Press, 1975), p. 137.
23 A. Henderson, *The Peace Terms*, a manifesto of the NEC (London: Labour Party, 1919), p. 3.
24 Hobson, *The New Holy Alliance*, p. 11.
25 See *Labour and the Peace Treaty* (London: Labour Party, 1920), pp. 21–3.
26 Keynes produced a figure of £3,000 million; the Treasury finally came to the view that £2,000 million would do, the experts generally taking a more moderate stance than British and Commonwealth politicians. The Cabinet

committee on indemnity wanted £24,000 million, but it took until 1921 before
a figure of $33,000 million was arrived at by the Reparations Commission.

27 'Peace Treaty and the League of Nations', statement adopted by LSI at
Geneva, August 1920, LSI 4.

28 M. Ceadal, 'Problems of Definition', in N. Young and R. Taylor (eds),
Campaigns for Peace: British Peace Movements in the Twentieth Century
(Manchester: Manchester University Press, 1987), p. 78.

29 D. S. Birn, *The League of Nations Union 1918–45* (Oxford: Clarendon, 1981),
pp. 24–5, 55, 123.

30 A. Orde, *Great Britain and International Security, 1920–1926* (London: Royal
Historical Society, 1978), p. 209.

31 M. Cowling, *The Impact of Hitler* (London: Cambridge University Press,
1975), p. 7.

32 See *LPACR*, 1922, pp. 200–3.

33 *Unemployment: The Peace and the Indemnity* (London: Labour Party, 1921),
p. 5. This originated, under the same title, as a paper by H. N. Brailsford for
the advisory committee on international questions; see number 188, February
1921.

34 Ibid., p. 11.

35 A view expressed by N. Ferguson in *The Pity of War* (Harmondsworth:
Penguin, 2006).

36 *Unemployment*, p. 5.

37 Ibid., p. 9. Charles Roden Buxton (1875–1942). Liberal MP briefly in 1910.
Favoured a negotiated peace after 1914, founder member of UDC. Joined
the ILP in 1917. Labour MP from 1922–3 and 1929–31. Sat on the Labour
Party's advisory committee on international questions.

38 *Unemployment*, p. 9.

39 Keynes, *Economic Consequences*, p. xxv.

40 'From the Foreign Delegation of the Socialist Revolutionary Party of Russia
to the Labour Party', 16 September 1918, LSI 2/11/13–14; 'An Appeal from
the Russian Socialists to the Socialists of the whole world', published in
L'Humanité, 18 August 1918, ibid., 2/11/18i.

41 A. Henderson, 'Memo on the World Labour and Socialist Peace Conference',
11 November 1918, LSI 2/10/12i.

42 S. White, *Britain and the Bolshevik Revolution* (London: Macmillan, 1979),
p. 31.

43 *Report of the Special Conference on Labour and the Russian–Polish War*,
13 August 1920 (London: Labour Party, 1920), p. 8.

44 W. P. and Z. K. Coates, *History of Anglo-Soviet Relations* (London: Lawrence
and Wishart, 1944), p. 42.

45 See on this White, *Britain and the Bolshevik Revolution*, pp. 39–40.

46 *Report of the British Labour Delegation to Russia 1920* (London: Labour
Party, 1920), p. 8.

47 *Labour and the Peace Treaty*, p. 46.

48 The International thereafter played no role in shaping Labour policy, of course,
and functioned chiefly in various 'committees, agendas [and] reports' beyond
the experience of most party members. See C. Collette, *The International
Faith: Labour's Attitudes to European Socialism, 1918–39* (Aldershot:
Ashgate, 1998), whose exhaustive research demonstrates its irrelevance in
spite of her evident enthusiasm for the idea of internationalism.

49 Ibid., pp. 46–8.

50 Ireland was locked out of the Paris Peace Conference and denied the right of self-determination despite the fact that Sinn Fein nationalists had won most of the relevant seats in the general election of December 1918. Labour debates on Ireland deplored the violence and British military intervention which ensued while affirming the party's belief in 'a democratic self-determination, with adequate protection for minorities' – a purely theoretical formula given the circumstances. 'Labour's Irish Policy', *The Times*, 25 June 1920.

51 Egypt was not formally a part of the Empire but might be considered a semi-colony on the grounds of British control of its foreign relations and military occupation. Egypt's exclusion from the Peace Conference and the denial of its case for independence touched off the national rising of 1919. See A Hourani, *History of the Arab Peoples* (London: Faber and Faber, 1991), p. 317.

52 The third Afghan War.

53 Violent rebellions broke out in Bengal and other parts of India in 1919 in response to the Rowlatt Acts.

54 E. Kedourie, *England and the Middle East* (London: Bowes and Bowes, 1956), pp. 35–40.

55 Almost 100,000 British and Indian troops were stationed in Iraq by the end of 1919. Mustard gas bombs were nevertheless required to suppress a rebellion in 1920. See D. E. Omiss, *Air Power and Colonial Control* (Manchester: Manchester University Press, 1990).

56 D. Gilmour, *Curzon* (London: John Murray, 1994), p. 512.

57 Philip Noel-Baker (1889–1982): member of the British delegation at the Paris Peace Conference, worked with the League of Nations secretariat until 1922, secretary to the British delegation at Geneva from 1923 to 1924; responsible for League of Nations affairs in the first Labour Government; PPS to Arthur Henderson and MP for Coventry in 1929–31, then followed Henderson back to Geneva as his principal assistant at the Disarmament Conference until 1933. Member of the Labour Party's advisory committee on international questions.

58 Henry Winkler attaches more significance to the committee, claiming that Henderson, in particular, 'depended heavily' upon it. See his 'The Emergence of a Labour Foreign Policy in Great Britain, 1918–29', *Journal of Modern History*, 28, 1956, pp. 247–58.

59 'Letter to the Executive Committee', Labour Party Advisory Committee on International Questions (henceforward LPACIQ), 149a, 1920.

60 D. Marquand, *Ramsay MacDonald*, p. 285.

61 H. Arendt, *On Revolution* (1963 and Harmondsworth: Penguin, 1990), p. 13.

62 J. F. Naylor, *Labour's International Policy: The Labour Party in the 1930s* (London: Weidenfeld and Nicolson, 1969), p. 15.

63 'League of Nations', LPACIQ, 1918.

64 *LPACR*, Southport 1919, pp. 139–42.

65 *Labour and the Peace Treaty* (London: Labour Party, 1919).

66 'The International Labour and Socialist Congress, Geneva, 1920', LSI 1/38/2, p. 82.

67 See 'Labour and the League of Nations', May 1921, 207, LPACIQ where the League is simultaneously denounced for all the reasons established in 1919 – 'a paper sham', no less – but is then described as potentially 'a tremendous instrument for good'. Labour's policy is declared to be the conversion of the League into such an instrument and the test of this is to be the prevention of war by disarmament.

68 A. Henderson, *Labour and Foreign Affairs* (London: Labour Party, 1922), p. 9.
69 Winkler, *The Path Not Taken*, p. 107.
70 'Labour and the League of Nations: The Need for a League Foreign Policy', July 1923, LPACIQ, 287.
71 'Suggestions for Draft Resolutions ... by the British Section', LSI 12/4/1 and 'Resolutions of the Labour and Socialist Congress', Hamburg, 21–5 May 1923, LSI 12/1/14.
72 P. Snowden, *If Labour Rules* (London: Labour Party, 1923), p. 46.
73 Ibid., p. 46.
74 Ibid., pp. 46–7.
75 For example, McKenzie King, the Canadian Prime Minister, recorded in October 1923 that Baldwin thought 'England must get rid of some of her population'. This was also in the context of gloomy thoughts about mass unemployment. P. Williamson and E. Baldwin (eds), *Baldwin Papers* (London: Cambridge University Press, 2004), p. 112.
76 See, for example, J. R. MacDonald, *Socialism* (London: Jack, 1907); *Socialism and Government* (London: ILP, 1909); and *The Socialist Movement* (London: Williams and Norgate, 1911), by the same author.
77 See P. Williamson, *National Crisis and National Government: British Politics, the Economy and Empire, 1926–1932* (Cambridge: Cambridge University Press, 1996), pp. 34–43.
78 R. Palme Dutt, 'The General Election and British Foreign Policy', *Labour Monthly*, 6, 1, 1924, pp. 1–25.
79 Josiah Clement Wedgwood (1872–1943): Liberal joined the ILP in 1919. Championed Indian independence and the idea of the British empire as a voluntary association of free states.
80 Noel Buxton (1869–1948): Liberal MP, strong interest in Balkan (especially Bulgarian) and international affairs. Favoured a negotiated peace in 1914–18. Joined Labour Party in 1919, critic of Versailles settlement. Member Labour advisory committee on international questions. Elected Labour MP 1922; Minister of Agriculture in 1924.
81 See C. A. Cline, *Recruits to Labour: The British Labour Party 1914–31* (Syracuse: Syracuse University Press, 1963).
82 D. Howell, *MacDonald's Party: Labour Identities and Crisis 1922–31* (Oxford: Oxford University Press, 2002), pp. 60 and 65.
83 See S. Webb, 'The First Labour Government', *Political Quarterly*, 32, January–March 1961, pp. 6–44. Webb notes the 'universal approval' which greeted publication of the new Cabinet and the fact that 'no one could pretend' that it was 'likely to ruin the Empire'.
84 A. Morgan, *J. Ramsay MacDonald* (Manchester: Manchester University Press, 1987), p. 104.
85 M. Cowling, *The Impact of Labour* (Cambridge: Cambridge University Press, 1971), p. 379.
86 The Lord Chancellor, Lord Sankey, complained of Thomas: 'he would like to appear at a dinner in trousers and coat made out of a Union Jack and shout for Empire'; Ponsonby said of him: 'he has no imagination, is constitutionally orthodox and conservative, he still has the outlook of what he started as, a Liberal agent'. See Howell, *MacDonald's Party*, pp. 10–11.
87 Cowling, *Impact of Labour*, pp. 360–81.
88 Quoted by Cowling, ibid., p. 372.

89 Cline, *Recruits*, p. 66.
90 The Dawes Committee was formally put together by the Reparations Commission, weeks before the formation of the Labour Government, with the participation of US businessmen Charles Dawes and Owen Young. Montagu Norman, Governor of the Bank of England, and Hjalmar Schacht, president of the Reichsbank, were also liaising from December 1923 with a view to resolving Germany's financial problems in a way which would thwart French plans. The German foreign minister, Gustav Streseman, understood that the Dawes Plan gave Germany the chance to employ the power of Anglo-American capital against French militarism. See J. Wright, *Gustav Streseman* (Oxford: Oxford University Press, 2002), p. 284.
91 See N. Angell, 'France and Europe', *New Leader*, 25 January 1924.
92 Winkler, *Paths Not Taken*, p. 133 and Marquand, *Ramsay MacDonald*, pp. 335–6.
93 *Six Months of a Labour Government* (London: ILP, nd), p. 1.
94 Marquand, *Ramsay MacDonald*, p. 342.
95 The resolution read as follows: 'That, in the opinion of this House, no diplomatic arrangement or understanding with a Foreign State, involving, directly or indirectly, national obligations shall be concluded without the consent of Parliament, and no preparations for cooperation in war between the naval, military, or air staffs of Foreign State shall be lawful unless consequent upon such arrangement or understanding; and this resolution shall be communicated to all States with which we are in diplomatic relations and to the League of Nations', *LPACR*, 1924, p. 56.
96 Howell, *MacDonald's Party*, pp. 31–2.
97 For the advice of the party's experts see 'Draft Memorandum prepared by the special sub-committee on the Draft Treaty of Mutual Assistance', LPACIQ, March 1924, 323. The Cabinet agreed that it 'was opposed in principle' but added that the Government favoured a conference on disarmament instead. See CAB23, meeting of 30 May 1924.
98 The list of objections included the difficulty of combining the proposed regional responsibilities in Europe with Britain's existing global imperial responsibilities. See R. W. Lyman, *The First Labour Government 1924* (London: Chapman and Hall, 1924), pp. 171–2.
99 Amery spoke on 23 October 1935.
100 The Washington Naval Conference, November 1921–February 1922, established parity of capital ships between Britain and the USA, while entitling Japan to maintain a fleet three-fifths the size of Britain's.
101 G. Lansbury, 'Empire Day', *Lansbury's Labour Weekly*, 23 May 1925; Lansbury had already suggested that the empire might form the core of a future 'International Commonwealth of all Nations' in his 'A New Way of Empire', *Daily Herald*, 5 July 1924. The same idea can also be found in 'A Socialist Commentary', *Forward*, 5 September 1925 and Snowden's 'The Labour View on Emigration', *Daily News*, 18 June 1925.
102 *Labour Party Annual Conference Report* (London: Labour Party, 1926), p. 252.
103 For Bevin's ideas on this see 'Minute to Attlee from Bevin', 8 July 1947, PRO, FO 371/5666 and 'Creech Jones to Bevin', 12 August 1947 in the same file.
104 Wording of a motion put by Clynes on behalf of the NEC, *LPACR,* 1925, p. 228.

105   Ibid., contribution of Dr Haden Guest, p. 235.
106   See Steiner, *The Light That Failed*, pp. 338–40.
107   A. G. Church, 'Black and White in East Africa', *Labour Magazine*, February 1925.
108   'Popular or Parliamentary Control of Foreign Policy', A. Ponsonby, LPACIQ, 256, nd probably 1921.
109   'The Reform of Diplomacy: A Practical Programme', G. Young, May 1921, LPACIQ, 171.
110   D. Marquand, *Ramsay MacDonald*, pp. 416–18.
111   See 'The Foreign Office and Labour Governments', G. Young, January 1925, LPACIQ, 333; see also 333h, and 333h(b), March 1926, which stressed the need for parliamentary control over foreign policy.
112   'Note on the Committee of Imperial Defence', April 1925, LPACIQ, 336.
113   *Socialism in Our Time*, March 1926, co-authored by the ILP leaders and J. A. Hobson, was the product of this research, though Oswald Mosley found a Keynesian alternative.
114   Williamson, *National Crisis and National Government*, p. 45.
115   *Labour and the Nation* (London: Labour Party, 1928). See the section on the 'British Commonwealth of Nations'.
116   H. Dalton, *Towards the Peace of Nations* (London: 1928).
117   'Commentary on the British Government's Observations', 1928, Advisory Committee on International Questions.
118   Webb, 'First Labour Government', p. 20.
119   C. Barnett, *The Collapse of British Power* (Gloucester: Sutton, 1984), p. 139.
120   D. Cannadine, *Decline and Fall of the British Aristocracy* (New Haven, Conn.: Yale University Press, 1990), p. 588.
121   Ibid., pp. 264–74.
122   Ibid., pp. 280–3 and S. Bok, *Secrets: On the Ethics of Concealment and Revelation* (Oxford: Oxford University Press, 1982), chapter 12.
123   L. Woolf, 'De Profundis', *Political Quarterly*, 10, 1939, pp. 485–6.
124   T. E. Lawrence wrote to *The Times* in August 1920 complaining that British policy in Iraq had resulted in the deaths of about 10,000 Iraqis in the uprising of that summer alone. Cited in Kedourie, *England and the Middle East*, p. 193.
125   See V. G. Kiernan, *European Empires from Conquest to Collapse* (Leicester: Leicester University Press, 1982), pp. 195–200.
126   The British delegation at the Disarmament Conference successfully insisted on making an exception of the prohibition proposed for aeriel bombardment when it was used in colonies. Lloyd George observed that the British had 'insisted on the right to bomb niggers'. Quoted in Kiernan, *European Empires*, p. 200.
127   The Committee of Imperial Defence decided in June 1928 that this rule should be assumed in any given year.
128   Williamson, *National Crisis and National Government*, p. 49.
129   The Tory leaders were more obviously irritated by the USA in politics and diplomacy and more inclined to sneer at American popular culture than Labour politicians. Labour drew on a left-wing tradition of warm regard for the USA as a pioneer of democracy, populism and egalitarianism. Labour's leaders also had more positive memories of US intervention in the First World War. The Tories, with their greater fondness for the reorganisation of the

Empire as a closed trading bloc and their greater experience of actually governing Britain in the inter-war years, were more inclined to see the USA as a rival, when it was not simply unreliable. See P. Williamson, *Stanley Baldwin* (London: Cambridge University Press, 1999), p. 304; Williamson and Baldwin, *Baldwin Papers*, pp. 30–1, 199, 201, 315; R. Holland, *Pursuit of Greatness: Britain and the World Role 1900–1970* (London: Fontana, 1991), p. 109. Nevertheless Baldwin promised at the 1929 general election, just like MacDonald, to go personally to Washington to repair relations should he be re-elected.

4 Crisis of liberal internationalism

1 *Record of the Second Labour Government* (London: Labour Party, 1935), pp. 2–5.
2 *What has the Labour Government Done?* (London: Labour Party, 1930), p. 7.
3 D. Dimbleby and D. Reynolds, *An Ocean Apart* (London: Random House, 1988), pp. 98–101.
4 *Two Years of Labour Rule* (London: Labour Party, 1931), p. 43.
5 See R. G. Gregory, *Sidney Webb and East Africa: Labour's Experiment with the Idea of Native Paramountcy* (Berkeley: University of California Press, 1962). Webb placed his White Papers on Closer Union in East Africa and Memorandum on Native Policy before a Joint Committee of both Houses of Parliament which 'destroyed' his scheme 'to place the African community in a pre-eminent position'. Webb himself appears not to have noticed (p. 136).
6 See K. Robinson, *The Dilemmas of Trusteeship* (London: Oxford University Press, 1965), pp. 58–9 and J. A. Hobson, 'A Self-Contained Empire', *Labour Magazine*, 11 November 1923.
7 Compare *Labour and the Nation* (1928), *The Colonial Empire* (1933) and *The Colonies: The Labour Party's Post-war Policy for the African and Pacific Colonies* (1940).
8 M. Beloff, *Wars and Welfare: Britain 1914–45* (London, Hodder Arnold, 1984), p. 4.
9 See on this, J. M. McKenzie, *Imperialism and Popular Culture* (Manchester: Manchester University Press, 1986).
10 J. Morris, *Farewell the Trumpets* (Harmondsworth: Penguin, 1979), p. 308.
11 MacDonald's diary, entries for 9 February, 25 August, 28 September, 1 October, 13 November. Cited in Williamson, *National Crisis and National Government*, p. 81.
12 Barnett, *Collapse of British Power*, p. 203.
13 The principalities of 'independent' India numbered 563 and occupied an area of 712,000 square miles or two-fifths of the subcontinent. About one-quarter (80 million) of India's population lived in these feudatory systems which the British dispensation helped to maintain on the divide-and-rule and indirect rule principles.
14 B. Chandra, *India's Struggle for Freedom* (Harmondsworth: Viking, 1989), p. 263.
15 J. Barnes and D. Nicholson (eds), *The Empire at Bay: The Leo Amery Diaries 1929–45* (London: Hutchinson, 1988), p. 48.

16   Quoted in C. Ponting, *Churchill* (London: Sinclair Stevenson, 1994), p. 341.
17   For example by making explicit that Irwin's declaration, pointing to some distant dominion status for India, involved no change of policy. See Williamson, *National Crisis and National Government*, p. 87. Baldwin had already made clear that he would do nothing to upset the Government's delicate handling of the Indian issue. See p. 119 of Williamson.
18   Quoted in R. Palme Dutt, *India Today* (London: Gollancz, 1940), p. 439.
19   Beaverbrook began his 'Empire Crusade' in July 1929 through the medium of the *Daily Express* campaigning for a closed imperial bloc. Rothermere used the *Daily Mail* to call for the removal of Baldwin in order to fight Irwin's Declaration and halt appeasement generally of the Empire's colonial opponents.
20   A. J. P. Taylor, *English History 1914–45* (Oxford: Oxford University Press, 1965), p. 374.
21   Quoted by R. Skidelsky, *Politicians and the Slump* (London: Macmillan, 1967), p. 270.
22   Quoted in T. Cliff and D. Gluckstein, *The Labour Party: A Marxist History* (London: Bookmarks, 1988), p. 153.
23   *Report of the Proceedings*, 63rd Annual Trades Union Congress, Bristol, 7–11 September 1931, pp. 66–72.
24   *Labour Party Annual Conference Report* (London: 1931), p. 5.
25   Ibid., chairman's address, p. 156.
26   R. B. Suthers, *Socialism or Smash* (London: Labour Party, May 1932), p. 15.
27   *LPACR*, 1931, p. 5.
28   For example in W. N. Ewer and F. Williams, *The World Muddle* (London: Labour Party, 1932); and F. Williams, *Democracy and Finance* (London: Labour Party, 1932).
29   *LPACR*, 1931, p. 177. Morrison talked of the need for a 'real Socialist Left' rather than the spurious left which he now associated with doles and benefits. See also B. Donoughue and G. W. Jones, *Herbert Morrison: Portrait of a Politician* (London: Weidenfeld and Nicolson, 1973), pp. 182–3.
30   Taylor, *English History*, pp. 429–30.
31   S. H. Beer, *Modern British Politics* (London: Faber and Faber, 1965), chapter 5, pp. 126–53.
32   Taylor, *English History*, p. 430.
33   R. M. Bassett, *Nineteen Thirty-one: Political Crisis* (London: Macmillan, 1958), p. 350.
34   Ibid., pp. 217–18.
35   *LPACR*, 1931, p. 158.
36   For a sympathetic portrait see H. R. Winkler, 'Arthur Henderson', in G. A. Craig and F. Gilbert (eds), *The Diplomats, 1919–1939* (Princeton, N.J.: Princeton University Press, 1953), pp. 311–44.
37   *Daily Herald*, 2 November 1931.
38   M. Cowling, *Impact of Hitler* (London: Cambridge University Press, 1975), p. 23.
39   E. Durbin, *New Jerusalems* (London: Routledge and Kegan Paul, 1985); M. Francis, 'Old Realisms: Policy Reviews of the Past', *Labour History Review*, 56, 1, 1991, p. 14.
40   R. Dare, 'Instinct and Organisation: Intellectuals and British Labour after 1931', *Historical Journal*, 26, 3, 1983, pp. 677–97, 680.

41 R. H. Tawney, 'The Choice before the Labour Party', quoted in Dare, 'Instinct and Organisation', p. 691.
42 This does not mean that the PLP was as subservient to the unions as Henry Pelling implies in *A Short History of the Labour Party* (London: Macmillan, 1961), pp. 77–9.
43 E. J. Feuchtwanger, *From Weimar to Hitler: Germany, 1918–33* (London: Macmillan, second edition, 1995), pp. 216–17, 247.
44 A. Glyn and A. Booth, *Modern Britain: An Economic and Social History* (London: Routledge, 1996), p. 118.
45 A. Best *et al.*, *International History of the Twentieth Century* (London: Routledge, 2004), pp. 66–7.
46 *Daily Herald*, 8 August 1931.
47 D. J. K. Peukert, *The Weimar Republic* (London: Allen Lane, 1991), p. 249.
48 As reported by the *Daily Herald*, 11 September 1931.
49 Ibid.
50 Formed in 1932 by members of the ILP who refused to follow the organisation when it seceded from the Labour Party in that year to pursue a 'revolutionary' path. The Socialist League acted as a socialist ginger group within the Labour Party until its dissolution in 1939.
51 F. Wise, 'The Control of Finance and the Financiers', in C. Addison *et al.* (eds), *Politics of a Socialist Government* (London: Gollancz, 1933), pp. 83–4.
52 S. Cripps, 'Can Socialism Come by Constitutional Methods?', in ibid., p. 38.
53 Taylor, *English History*, p. 431.
54 Quoted in A. Bullock, *The Life and Times of Ernest Bevin: Trade Union Leader* (London: Heinemann, 1960), p. 508.
55 'Report of the NEC, 1934–5', *LPACR* (London: Labour Party, 1935), pp. 7–8.
56 G. D. H. Cole, *Economic Tracts for the Times* (London: Macmillan, 1932).
57 B. Pimlott, *Hugh Dalton* (London: Cape, 1985), p. 213.
58 D. Blaazer, *The Popular Front and the Progressive Tradition: Socialists, Liberals and the Quest for Unity, 1884–1939* (London: Cambridge University Press, 1992), p. 18.
59 Ibid., p. 145.
60 P. M. Williams, *Hugh Gaitskell* (Oxford: Oxford University Press, 1982), p. 47.
61 Taylor, *English History*, p. 433.
62 G. Orwell, review of Harold Laski's *Faith, Hope and Civilization*, in P. Davison (ed.), *The Complete Works of George Orwell*, volume 16 (London: Secker and Warburg, 1998), pp. 122–3.
63 See J. Callaghan, 'The Left and the "Unfinished Revolution": Bevanites and Soviet Russia in the 1950s', *Contemporary British History*, 15, 3, 2001, pp. 63–83.
64 See M. Newman, *Harold Laski: A Political Biography* (London: Macmillan, 1993).
65 H. J. Laski, *A Grammar of Politics*, preface to the third edition (London: Allen and Unwin, 1934).
66 H. J. Laski, *Democracy in Crisis* (London: Allen and Unwin, 1933), p. 233.
67 H. J. Laski, 'Communism as a World Force', *International Affairs*, January 1931, p. 25.
68 Philip Noel-Baker to Leonard Woolf, 8 March 1934, quoted in Newman, *Harold Laski*, p. 163.

69 Ibid., p. 163.
70 M. Adams (ed.), *The Modern State* (London: Allen and Unwin, 1933), p. 18.
71 L. Woolf, *Barbarians at the Gate* (London: Gollancz, 1939), p. 13.
72 Woolf, *Barbarians*, pp. 156–7.
73 Ibid., pp. 172–3.
74 Ibid., pp. 191–3.
75 Ibid., pp. 208–9.
76 Nye Bevan was an eloquent spokesman for both views within the Labour Party in the 1950s.
77 Williams, *Hugh Gaitskell*, p. 65.
78 Vansittart was appointed head of the American Section of the Foreign Office in February 1924, in which capacity he had dealings with MacDonald, who took a keen interest in Anglo-American relations. When MacDonald returned to power in 1929 he found Vansittart installed in the Prime Minister's private office where he had worked with Baldwin. MacDonald then appointed Vansittart Permanent Under Secretary in December 1929, privately telling him, in reference to the Labour Party, that 'the amateurs must be controlled'. See B. J. C. McKercher, 'The Foreign Office, 1930–39: Strategy, Permanent Interests and National Security', *Contemporary British History*, 18, 3, 2004, pp. 87–109, 89. See also I. Tombs, 'The Victory of Socialist "Vansittartism": Labour and the German Question, 1941–5', *Twentieth Century British History*, 7, 3, 1996, pp. 287–309.
79 E. Durbin, *The Politics of Democratic Socialism* (London: Routledge, 1940), pp. 240–4.
80 See P. Williamson and E. Baldwin (eds), *Baldwin Papers: A Conservative Statesman, 1908–1947* (London: Cambridge University Press, 2004). Baldwin's strategy was to assist MacDonald in defeating the Labour left and marginalising the Liberal Party (pp. 159, 445, 482–3).
81 Durbin, *Democratic Socialism*, pp. 288–9.
82 *For Socialism and Peace: The Labour Party's Programme of Action* (London: Labour Party, 1934).
83 'Report of the National Executive Committee, 1934–5', p. 8.
84 The normally safe Conservative seat was lost amid allegations that Labour had played the peace card and raised doubts in the voters' minds about the Conservatives' commitment to peace and disarmament. The Labour victor, John Wilmot, told the House that Government rearmament policy was as aggressive as the one advocated by the *Daily Mail*.
85 Ten days after Hitler came to power, on 9 February 1933, the Oxford Union Society voted 275 to 153 in favour of the motion 'That this House will in no circumstances fight for its King and Country'.
86 Birn, *The League of Nations Union*, pp. 142–3.
87 Ibid., p. 150.
88 M. Ceadal, *Pacifism in Britain 1914–45: The Defining of a Faith* (Oxford: Clarendon, 1980), pp. 124 and 134.
89 See L. Woolf, 'Labour's Foreign Policy', *Political Quarterly*, 4, 1933, pp. 504–24 and his 'The Labour Party's Policy with Regard to Sanctions', LPACIQ, March 1933, document 431a.
90 Even in 1945 Labour took the view that Conservative policy in the 1930s 'was to let Fascist aggressors get away with their crimes because they wanted to keep Fascism and its oriental ally Japanese militarism strong enough to hold down the working class in Europe and to bolster up Imperialism in Asia

and Africa', *Labour Party Speaker's Handbook* (London: Labour Party, 1945), p. 179.

91 Lansbury published a letter calling for the appeasement of Italy in *The Times*, 19 August 1935, which suggested that a fairer distribution of the world's resources would prevent the threatened aggression against Abyssinia.

92 *House of Commons Debates*, volume 304, 1 August 1935, column 2894.

93 *TUC Report: Weymouth 1934*, p. 320.

94 *TUC Report: Margate 1935*, p. 345.

95 'Report of the National Executive Committee, 1934–5', *LPACR*, 1935, pp. 3–4.

96 Bevin famously accused Lansbury of carting 'his conscience round from conference to conference asking to be told what to do with it'. After the debate, in reply to someone who said he'd been rough on the 'old boy' he replied that 'Lansbury has been going about dressed up in saint's clothes for years waiting for martyrdom. I set fire to the faggots.'

97 'Report of the National Executive Committee, 1934–5', p. 8.

98 T. Buchanan, *The Spanish Civil War and the British Labour Movement* (Cambridge: Cambridge University Press, 1991), p. 5.

99 Dalton took the same view and added, in response to criticism, that British rearmament against fascist aggression should be the priority. The public, in any case, would not stand for a real intervention in Spain by British forces. See D. Carlton, 'Eden, Blum, and the Origins of Non-Intervention', *Journal of Contemporary History*, volume 6, 1971, fn 27, p. 54.

100 Ibid., pp. 41, 42, 58–9.

101 Meeting of NCL, IFTU and LSI, Paris, 26 October 1936, NEC Minutes, 24 June 1936–23 June 1937, Box 15, LPA.

102 H. Graham, *The Spanish Republic at War 1936–39* (Cambridge: Cambridge University Press, 2002), p. 125.

103 The Leninist view was now championed by ILP-ers such as George Orwell who argued that a war between Britain and Germany would be a war between rival imperialisms. See his 'Not Counting Niggers', in S. Orwell (ed.), *Collected Essays, Journalism and Letters of George Orwell*, volume 1 (Harmondsworth: Penguin, 1970), pp. 434–8.

104 M. Foot, *Aneurin Bevan, 1897–1945* (London: Paladin, 1975), p. 220.

105 NCL, March 1936, 'Points of Policy', by C. R. A[ttlee], Box Foreign/Defence Policy 1936–44.

106 NCL, *Labour and the Defence of Peace* (London: Labour Party, May 1936), p. 5.

107 'Memorandum on the attitude which the Party should adopt to proposed reforms of the League', Advisory Committee on International Questions, July 1936, Box Foreign/Defence Policy 1936–44.

108 Ibid., p. 5.

109 Ibid., p. 6.

110 Attlee, *The Labour Party in Perspective*, p. 220.

111 Ibid., pp. 270–1.

112 'The Labour Party's International Policy', March 1939, NEC Minutes, 27 July 1938–30 May 1939, Box 17.

113 National Council of Labour, 'Labour and the Defence of Peace', 21 April 1936, 28 April 1936 and 5 May 1936.

114 Joint meeting of NEC, General Council and PLP Executive, 4 September 1936. 'Memorandum on the Attitudes which the Party should Adopt to

Propose Reforms of the League', LPACIQ 468A, July 1936, Box Foreign/
Defence Policy, 1936–44.

115 It is not true that Labour recognised abolition of national airforces and
internationalisation of civil aviation were unfeasible by 1936 as is said in
J. H. Brookshire, '"Speak for England", Act for England: Labour's
Leadership and British National Security under the Threat of War in the
Late 1930s', *European History Quarterly*, 29, 2, 1999, p. 263. Attlee, who
was after all the leader of the party, was still arguing for these measures in
1937. See his *Labour Party in Perspective*, p. 269, where he says 'I do not
believe that the scheme of an international air force is chimerical. I think
that it is supremely practical ... With it necessarily goes the
internationalisation of civil aviation.'

116 R. A. C. Parker, 'British Rearmament 1936–9: Treasury, Trade Unions and
Skilled Labour', *English Historical Review*, 96, 1981, pp. 306–43.

117 See B. Donoughue and G. W. Jones, *Herbert Morrison: Portrait of a
Politician* (London: Weidenfeld and Nicolson, 1973), pp. 264–5.

118 Ibid., p. 334.

119 Morrison reminded the Government that the Opposition had 'often' accused
the Government of having a pro-Fascist bias in their foreign policy'.
'Imperialist Agreement: The Labour Amendment', *The Times*, 3 May 1938.

120 'Proposals for Economic Action against Japan', 7 January 1938, NEC
Minutes 28 July 1937–22 June 1938, Box 16.

121 'Labour and the International Situation', leaflet, September 1938, NEC
Minutes 27 July 1938–30 May 1939, Box 17.

122 NEC minutes, 28–9 September 1938, ibid.

123 Joint meeting of General Council, NEC and PLP executive, 21 September
1938, NEC minutes, ibid.

124 'Labour's Claim to Power', leaflet, NEC Minutes, October 1938, ibid.

125 Vansittart recorded this thought in his diary on 7 December. Quoted in Finkel
and Leibovitz, *Chamberlain–Hitler Collusion*, p. 190.

126 'The Labour Party's International Policy', March 1939, NEC Minutes, 27
July–30 May 1939, Box 17.

127 *LPACR*, 1939, p. 243.

128 Ibid., p. 250.

129 See Bullock, *Ernest Bevin: Trade Union Leader*, pp. 622–34.

130 Dalton expressed the same idea in 'The Dominions and Foreign Policy',
Political Quarterly, 9, 1938, in which he observed that the Dominions had
strongly supported Labour's efforts to improve Anglo-American relations
in 1929–31. The influence of the Dominions, he continued, 'urges us away
from Europe . . . it urges us towards the United States'. Britain was the only
country in the world which could unlock the 'store of moral force' in that
country.

131 Bevin put the same point to an audience at Chatham House on 22 November
1938. See E. Bevin, 'Impressions of the British Commonwealth Relations
Conference, 1938', *International Affairs*, 18, 1938, pp. 63–6.

132 Ibid., pp. 243–5.

5   The Second World War

1 Mass Observation reported in November 1940 that 'it has been hard to find,
even among women, many who do not unconsciously regard this war as in

some way revolutionary, or radical'. Quoted in A. Calder, *The People's War* (London: Cape, 1969), p. 139. See also H. Arendt, *On Revolution*, p. 17.

2 R. H. S. Crossman, 'Labour and Compulsory Military Service', *Political Quarterly*, 10, 1939, pp. 319–20.

3 L. Woolf, 'De Profundis', *Political Quarterly*, volume 10, 1939, p. 485.

4 Cato, *Guilty Men* (London: Gollancz, 1940). It sold a quarter of a million copies.

5 See A. Finkel and C. Leibovitz, *The Chamberlain–Hitler Collusion* (London: Merlin, 1997). The authors amass enough circumstantial evidence to keep the alleged collusion at least an open question.

6 R. H. S. Crossman, 'Labour and Compulsory Military Service', *Political Quarterly*, 10, 1939, p. 311.

7 Dalton records that the agreement on the government of post-fascist Italy was 'evidence that the Russians are now most anxious to get down to detail with us on all points'. B. Pimlott (ed.), *The Second World War Diary of Hugh Dalton, 1940–45* (London: Cape, 1986), p. 649. Around the same time, when his thoughts had turned to the question of the 'international post-war settlement in the summer of 1943 Dalton also records the misgivings of those such as Douglas Jay and Gladwyn Jebb about future American policy, with Jay and others worried about US economic imperialism and Jebb giving vent to fears of the "tidal waves of sentiment, prejudice and hysteria" to which American foreign policy was allegedly subject'. See pp. 612, 621, 649. Eden and Halifax also expressed doubts about the 'confusion of woolliness' of US foreign policy in 1943. See Kimball, *The Juggler: Franklin Roosevelt as Wartime Statesman* (Princeton, N.J.: Princeton University Press, 1991), p. 14.

8 J. Campbell, *Nye Bevan: And the Mirage of British Socialism* (London: Weidenfeld and Nicolson, 1987), p. 121.

9 *Tribune*, 7 April 1944.

10 P. Clarke, *The Cripps Version: The Life of Sir Stafford Cripps 1889–1952* (Harmondsworth: Penguin, 2003), p. 292.

11 W. F. Kimball, *The Juggler*, p. 127.

12 Ibid., p. 144.

13 Wm. Roger Louis and Ronald Robinson, 'The United States and the Liquidation of the British Empire in Tropical Africa, 1941–51', in P. Gifford and W. R. Louis (eds), *The Transfer of Power in Africa: Decolonization 1940–1960* (New Haven, Conn.: Yale University Press, 1982), p. 36.

14 P. J. N. B (Noel-Baker), 'Memorandum on the Principle of Colonial Trusteeship', nd (1945), NECISC. Noel-Baker believed that the old Mandates scheme had supported 'native interests' by making the imperial Power conscious of the consequences of bad publicity if it fell short on this matter. But he also thought the opportunity to extend the principle should be taken. The governments of New Zealand and Australia supported the idea of international supervision in October 1944, as Noel-Baker pointed out, as well as the regional commissions proposed by the Colonial Office.

15 J. G. Darwin, *Britain and Decolonisation* (London: Macmillan, 1988), p. 48.

16 M. Crowder, 'The Second World War', in M. Crowder (ed.), *The Cambridge History of Africa*, volume 8, 1940–75 (Cambridge: Cambridge University Press, 1984), p. 33.

17 Ibid., pp. 34–5.

18   See P. Wilson, *The International Theory of Leonard Woolf* (London: Palgrave, 2003), p. 102.
19   Ibid., p. 109.
20   B. Davidson, *Africa in Modern History* (Harmondsworth: Penguin, 1978), p. 118.
21   H. S. Wilson, *African Decolonisation* (London: Oxford University Press, 1994), p. 35; P. Fryer, *Black People in the British Empire* (London: Pluto, 1988), p. 35.
22   See P. J. Cain and A. G. Hopkins, *British Imperialism: Crisis and Deconstruction, 1914–1990* (London: Longman, 1993), pp. 224–5; D. Berman, *Control and Crisis in Colonial Kenya* (London: James Currey, 1990), p. 193, note 109.
23   B. Porter, *The Lion's Share: A Short History of British Imperialism* (London: Longman, 1984), p. 281; see also I. M. Drummond (ed.), *British Economic Policy and the Empire 1919–39* (London: Allen and Unwin, 1972), pp. 47–8.
24   'Jamaica Agitation', *The Times*, 6 May 1938; Sir Leonard Lyle (of Tate and Lyle) predictably attributed the disturbances to Communists and was rebuked by Lord Olivier for asserting that the West Indian labourer did not remotely resemble his British counterpart either in mentality or his mode of life. *The Times*, letters to the editor, 9 and 10 May 1938.
25   Fryer, *Black People in the British Empire*, pp. 102–6 and 30–2.
26   'The position in the West Indies', Advisory Committee on Imperial Questions, 247a, November 1942. This paper advocated schemes of swamp reclamation to create jobs and greater rice production in the Caribbean but after an intervention by Sir Frank Stockdale (member of the Anglo-American Caribbean Commission set up in March 1942) the NEC agreed that no further action should be taken, ISCNEC minutes 26 January 1943.
27   Quoted in Buchanan, *The Spanish Civil War and the British Labour Movement*, pp. 40–1.
28   *TUC Report: Blackpool 1938*, 5–9 September 1938, pp. 201–6.
29   P. Weiler, *British Labour and the Cold War* (Stanford: Stanford University Press, 1988), pp. 38–9. In 1943 Citrine offered the TUC's services to the Foreign Office to do the same in Italy. See Weiler, *British Labour and the Cold War*, p. 62.
30   Ibid., p. 52.
31   Thus its lack of interest in the British campaign to publicise the Meerut Conspiracy trial of 1929 and the subsequent punitive sentences handed out to the accused.
32   This is dealt with in detail in P. Weiler, *British Labour and the Cold War* (Stanford: Stanford University Press, 1988), pp. 36–52.
33   W. R. Louis, *Imperialism at Bay, 1941–45* (Oxford: Oxford University Press, 1977), pp. 33 and 192–3.
34   Quoted in C. Thorne, *Allies of a Kind* (London: Hamish Hamilton, 1978), p. 61.
35   Louis, *Imperialism at Bay*, pp. 212, 15–17, 464; Thorne, *Allies of a Kind*, p. 209; J. P. D. Dunbabin, *The Post-Imperial Age: The Great Powers and the Wider World* (London: Longman, 1994), p. 26.
36   See Lord Hailey, *Native Administration and Political Development in Tropical Africa* (London: 1942).
37   Louis, *Imperialism at Bay*, p. 51; see also C. Pratt, 'Colonial Governments and the Transfer of Power in East Africa', in P. Gifford and W. M. Louis

(eds), *The Transfer of Power in Africa: Decolonization, 1940–1960* (London: Yale University Press, 1982), pp. 250–4.

38 J. D. Hargreaves, 'Towards the Transfer of Power in British West Africa', in Gifford and Louis, *Transfer of Power*, p. 133.

39 See on this F. Furedi, *Colonial Wars and the Politics of Third World Nationalism* (London: I. B. Tauris, 1994), pp. 72–3.

40 D. Silverfarb, *The Twilight of British Ascendancy in the Middle East* (New York: St Martin's Press, 1994), p. 19.

41 B. R. Tomlinson, *The Political Economy of the Raj* (London: Macmillan, 1979), p. 94; J. Barnes and D. Nicholson (eds), *The Empire at Bay*, pp. 910–12.

42 See J. Saville, *The Politics of Continuity: British Foreign Policy and the Labour Government 1945–6* (London: Verso, 1993), pp. 176–204.

43 G. Kolko, *The Politics of War: The World and United States Foreign Policy, 1943–1945* (New York: Pantheon, 1970), p. 291.

44 See R. Skidelsky, *John Maynard Keynes: Fighting for Britain, 1937–1946* (London: Macmillan, 2000), pp. 326–7.

45 Dalton, *Second World War Diary*, July 1943 – by which time the debt stood at over £800 million and was growing at the rate of £250 million per year, p. 622.

46 Arthur Lewis, Professor of Political Economy at Manchester University, complained of this colonial exploitation in a letter to the *Financial Times* in January 1952. Cited in Saville, *Politics of Continuity*, p. 159.

47 Skidelsky, *Keynes: Fighting for Britain*, p. 313.

48 For Roosevelt's attitude see Kimball, *The Juggler*, p. 164.

49 A month after the Yalta Conference of February 1945 Churchill was petitioning Roosevelt to stand up to Stalin over Poland, claiming that they had been deceived.

50 See Saville, *The Politics of Continuity*, pp. 183, 186, 200.

51 PRO, FO 371/50912, 'Stocktaking after VE Day', memorandum by Orme Sargent, 11 July 1945.

52 See J. Callaghan, *Socialism in Britain* (Oxford: Blackwell, 1990), pp. 120–50.

53 P. M. H. Bell, *John Bull and the Bear: British Public Opinion, Foreign Policy and the Soviet Union, 1941–45* (London: Edward Arnold, 1990), p. 103.

54 J. Schneer, *Labour's Conscience* (London: Unwin Hyman, 1988), p. 44.

55 G. D. H. Cole, *Europe, Russia, and the Future* (London: Gollancz, 1941), pp. 31–2.

56 H. Laski, *Faith, Reason and Civilization* (London: Gollancz, 1944), p. 62.

57 'Are We Bolshevising Europe?', *New Statesman and Nation*, 8 January 1944; see *Tribune*, 7 April 1944 for Bevan's argument.

58 The NEC received appeals from the General Federation of Jewish Labour in Palestine demanding active intervention 'for rescue action', including reports of Bund leaders executed by the Russians. NECISC meeting 26 January 1943, paper by S. Zygielbojm, 1 March 1943, NECISC minutes and documents 1942–9.

59 H. Laski, 'Comments on Mr Gillies' Draft Circular', 22 August 1943; W. Gillies, 'Notes in Reply to Harold J. Laski', nd, NECISC minutes and documents 1942–9.

60 Dalton, *Second World War Diary*, April 1944, p. 673.

61 'Post-war settlement', NECISC, nd, minutes and documents 1942–9. In October 1944 the advisory committee on imperial questions observed that the Arabs insisted that Britain should adhere to the White Paper of 1939

which envisaged a single Palestinian state for Arabs and Jews. Since there was little hope of a compromise, it was suggested that the UN would have to arbitrate a solution. See 'Economic Approach to the Palestine Problem', October 1944, Advisory Committee on Imperial Questions. The rest of this paper is concerned with Jewish economic achievements and prospects.
62 P. Keleman, 'Zionism and the British Labour Party: 1917–39', *Social History*, 21, 1, p. 77. Keleman points to Poale Zion and the lack of an Arab equivalent to help explain the success of this doctrine.
63 See Saville, *Continuity of Policy*, pp. 120–4.
64 See J. Charmley, *Churchill's Grand Alliance: The Anglo-American Special Relationship 1940–57* (London: Hodder and Stoughton, 1995), p. 89.
65 D. Mayers, 'Soviet War Aims and the Grand Alliance: George Kennan's Views 1944–46', *Journal of Contemporary History*, 21, 1, January 1986, p. 57; for American figures see S. Ambrose, *Rise to Globalism: American Foreign Policy since 1938* (Harmondsworth: Penguin, 1985), p. 30.
66 Schneer, *Labour's Conscience*, p. 44.

6   Great Power strategies

1   See Chiefs of Staff report 'British Strategic Interests in the Far East', 1 November 1945, FO 371/46415/F9628.
2   Quoted by Saville, *Continuity of Policy*, p. 4.
3   Skidelsky, *Keynes: Fighting for Britain*, p. 307.
4   Ibid., p. 406.
5   Skidelsky, *Keynes: Fighting for Britain*, p. 452.
6   By 1949 the Labour Government was calling upon the USA to intervene in South East Asia with economic and military assistance to prevent the spread of Communism. See A. J. Rotter, 'The Triangular Route to Vietnam: The United States, Great Britain, and Southeast Asia, 1945–50', *International History Review*, 6, 3, 1984, pp. 333–506.
7   D. K. Fieldhouse, 'The Labour Governments and the Empire Commonwealth', in R. Ovendale (ed.), *The Foreign Policy of the British Labour Governments, 1945–51* (Leicester: Leicester University Press, 1984), p. 95.
8   Labour wanted a stable democracy in Greece but the exclusion of the Communists took precedence even if that meant working with Greek reactionaries in both the unions and the state. See T. D. Sfikas, *The British Labour Government and the Greek Civil War: The Imperialism of Non-intervention* (Keele: Keele University Press, 1994); H. Richter, *British Intervention in Greece: From Varkiza to Civil War* (London: Merlin, 1985); J. Iatrides (ed.), *Greece in the 1940s* (1981); E. O'Ballance, *The Greek Civil War, 1944–49* (New York: Faber and Faber, 1966).
9   Sir Orme Sargent, 'Stocktaking after VE Day', Public Record Office (PRO), FO371/50912.
10 Dalton was constantly pressing for cuts in military expenditure in 1946 and 1947. See B. Pimlott (ed.), *The Political Diary of Hugh Dalton, 1918–40, 1945–60* (London: Cape, 1986), pp. 368–9, 389, 405, 406, 413, 421.
11 Quoted in J. Kent, 'The British Empire and the Origins of the Cold War', in A. Deighton (ed.), *Britain and the First Cold War* (London: Macmillan, 1990), p. 171.
12 Dalton observed in February 1946 that Cadogan and Sargent had feared for their jobs shortly before Bevin took office but says that they need not have

worried given the latter's ignorance of the alternatives on offer in the Foreign Office, *Political Diary Hugh Dalton*, p. 367.

13 PRO, FO371/50920: Memorandum from Secretary of State for Foreign Affairs (Ernest Bevin), 4 October 1945.

14 PRO, FO371/57170: Italian Colonies and UNO Collective Trusteeship, January 1946; memorandum from J. G. Ward, 6 February 1946.

15 FO371/49069: Letter from South African High Commissioner, 26 January 1946; Bevin to Attlee, 9 February 1946.

16 Quoted in Saville, *Continuity of Policy*, p. 136.

17 FO371/57171: Telegram from General Paget, 8 February 1946.

18 FO371/57278: Proceedings of the Second Plenary Conference of the Council of Ministers, Paris, 25 April–16 May 1946, p. 103; CAB 128, volume 12, 5 February 1948.

19 G. Balfour-Paul, *The End of Empire in the Middle East* (Cambridge: Cambridge University Press, 1991), pp. 9 and 14.

20 FO 800/476, memorandum from Attlee to Bevin, 5 January 1947.

21 G. Kolko and J. Kolko, *The Limits of Power* (New York: Harper and Row, 1972), p. 312.

22 Quoted in W. I. Hitchcock, *The Struggle for Europe* (London: Profile, 2003), p. 59.

23 Quoted in M. Walker, *The Cold War* (London: Fourth Estate, 1993), p. 42.

24 H. Dalton, *Diary*, end of November 1946.

25 Yet the TUC was already alarmed that the WFTU was a Soviet front. The evidence included demands for Franco's international isolation and criticisms of British imperialism from delegates to the WFTU conference. Extrication from the WFTU was achieved in 1948. A rival International Confederation of Free Trade Unions (ICFTU) was established in 1949 and with government aid it assisted global anti-Communism.

26 Pimlott (ed.), *Political Diary Hugh Dalton*, pp. 368–9.

27 Ibid.

28 The story of Attlee's resistance is told by R. Smith and J. Zametica, 'The Cold Warrior: Clement Attlee Reconsidered, 1945–7', *International Affairs*, 61, 2, 1985, pp. 237–52.

29 R. H. S. Crossman *et al.*, *Keep Left* (London: New Statesman pamphlet, May 1947).

30 An amendment and an Early Day Motion supporting this idea were put before the House in 1946 and 1947 respectively, gaining the support of 72 MPs. Another Early Day Motion in favour of European political integration was supported by 100 MPs in March 1948 and the party's annual congress adopted a federalist resolution in the same year.

31 FO371/67673: Record of Conversation between the Secretary of State and M. Renadier, 22 September 1947.

32 Weiler, *British Labour and the Cold War*, pp. 195–6.

33 Ibid., p. 208.

34 FO371/67673, record of Foreign Office meeting, 8 October 1947.

35 Ibid., Anglo-French co-operation: meeting of Bevin, Oliver Harvey, Edmund Hall-Patch, and Esler Dening, 26 September 1947.

36 FO371/168: Memorandum on European Recovery Programme, prepared for the Cabinet Economic Policy Committee, 23 December 1947.

37 Quoted in M. J. Hogan, *The Marshall Plan: America, Britain and the Reconstruction of Western Europe, 1947–52* (Cambridge: Cambridge University Press, 1987), pp. 46–9.

38 Pimlott (ed.), *Political Diary Hugh Dalton*, p. 443.
39 Quoted in B. Pimlott, *Hugh. Dalton* (London: Cape, 1985), p. 577.
40 FO371/62740: Cabinet Economic Policy Committee, 7 November 1947.
41 Some historians persist in the error of depicting Labour as 'ragged-trousered philanthropists' in colonial matters, focusing on the comic wrong-headedness of the groundnuts scheme and the apparent generosity of the Colonial Development and Welfare Act as amended in 1945, to the exclusion of the main business. For these typical errors see K. O. Morgan, *Labour in Power, 1945–51* (Oxford: Oxford University Press, 1984), pp. 201, 230 and F. S. Northedge, *Descent From Power: British Foreign Policy, 1945–73* (London: Allen and Unwin, 1974), p. 221. For the main business see Fieldhouse, above, and D. A. Low and A. Smith (eds), *Oxford History of East Africa*, volume 3 (Oxford: Oxford University Press, 1976).
42 J. Tomlinson, 'The Attlee Governments and the Balance of Payments', *Twentieth Century British History*, 2, 1, 1991, pp. 61–3.
43 FO371/5666: Minute to Attlee from Bevin, 8 July 1947 and Creech Jones to Bevin, 12 August 1947.
44 CO 847/25/7, 'Factors affecting native administration policy', January 1946, in R. Hyam (ed.), *The Labour Government and the End of Empire: Part 1, High Policy and Administration* (London: HMSO, 1992), p. 98.
45 CO 847/35/6, 'Minute', 1 November 1946, ibid., pp. 117–18.
46 CO 847/35/6, nos 15–24, 'Circular despatch from Mr. Creech Jones to the African governors', 25 February 1947, ibid., pp. 119–29.
47 CO 847/35/6, no 88, 'Despatch from Sir P. Mitchell', 30 May 1947, ibid., pp. 129–41.
48 CO 847/36/1, no 9, 'Report of the [CO Agenda] Committee on the conference of African Governors', 22 May 1947, ibid., pp. 203–4.
49 CO 852/1053/1, no 18, 'Opening address to summer conference', 19 August 1948, ibid., pp.162–72, 166, 168.
50 CAB 124/1007, no 62, 'Projection of Britain overseas', as revised by Herbert Morrison, 17 August 1946, ibid., p. 309.
51 CO 847/36/4, no 24, 'Economic development in Africa', Sir Stafford Cripps, 12 November 1947, ibid., p. 299.
52 CO 847/36/4, no 18, 'The colonies and international organisations', November 1947, ibid., pp. 283–4.
53 CO 847/36/1, no 9, 'Report of the [CO Agenda] Committee on the Conference of African Governors', 22 May 1947, ibid., p. 199.
54 CAB 128/1, CM 38 (45) 6, 'Middle East: future policy', 4 October 1945, in R. Hyam (ed.), *The Labour Government and the End of Empire, 1945–51*, Part 1, 'High Policy and Administration', British Documents on the End of Empire, Series A, volume 2 (London: HMSO, 1992), p. 2.
55 CAB 128/5, CM 57 (46) 1, 'Anglo-Egyptian negotiations', 6 June 1946, in Hyam, *Labour Government and the End of Empire*, p. 12.
56 CAB 128/19, CM24(51)3, 'Egypt: Anglo-Egyptian Treaty', 5 April 1951, in Hyam (ed.), *Labour Government and the End of Empire*, p. 84.
57 CAB 128/20, CM 60 (51)6, 'Persia: Cabinet conclusions on decision not to use force at Abadan and to refer the dispute to the UN', 27 September 1951.
58 W. Laqueur, *A History of Zionism* (New York: Schocken Books, 2003), p. 564.
59 W. R. Louis, *The British Empire in the Middle East* (Oxford: Oxford University Press, 1984), p. 44.

60 Ibid., pp. 214–15, 307, 632, 640.
61 See A. Howard, *Richard Crossman: The Pursuit of Power* (London: Pimlico, 1990), pp. 108–26 and R. Crossman, *Palestine Mission* (London: Hamish Hamilton, 1947).
62 CAB 129/11, CP (46) 267, 'Palestine: Anglo-US report – military implications', in Hyam, *Labour Government and the End of Empire*, p. 21.
63 Ibid., p. 21.
64 CAB 128/11, CM 6 (47) 3 and 4, 15 January 1947, in Hyam (ed.), *Labour Government and the End of Empire*, pp. 44–51.
65 Laqueur, *History of Zionism*, p. 574.
66 FO371/5132, documents UE 11531 and UE 12502.
67 CAB 128, volume 12, 8 January 1948.
68 CAB 129/37, CP(49)208, 'European Policy', memo from Bevin, 18 October 1949.
69 Ibid.
70 CAB 128/19, CP(49)208, 'Brief for the UK Delegation: A Third World Power or Western Consolidation', 19 April 1950.
71 Ibid.
72 Sir Otto Franks telegram to Foreign Office, 30 March 1950, in R. Bullen and M. E. Pelly (eds), *Documents on British Policy Overseas: Series 2, Volume 2: The London Conferences, January–June 1950* (London: HMSO, 1987), pp. 33–4.
73 'Brief for the UK Delegation', 21 April 1950, in ibid., p.70.
74 'Record of Third Bipartite meeting', 25 April 1950, ibid., p. 124.
75 'Anglo-American Relations: Present and Future', memorandum for the Permanent Under-Secretaries Committee, 22 April 1950, ibid., p. 84.
76 'Brief for the UK Delegation', 24 April 1950, ibid., p. 97.
77 'Brief by Sir E. Plowden for Sir S. Cripps', 25 April 1950, ibid., pp. 131–2.
78 'Note of informal meeting of Ministers', 4 May 1950, ibid., pp. 210–15. Cripps came back to this issue the next day, arguing that the language used in the briefing paper implied that these 'Deputies' to NATO would have the power to override ministers. See pp. 231–2, ibid.
79 'Memorandum from Sir N. Brook to Attlee', 5 May 1950, ibid., pp. 227–8.
80 F. Hutchins, 'India Leaves Britain, in T. Smith (ed.), *The End of European Empire: Decolonisation after World War Two* (London: D. C. Heath, 1975), p. 35.
81 Quoted in B. R. Tomlinson, *The Political Economy of the Raj*, p. 142.
82 A. Bullock, *Ernest Bevin: Foreign Secretary* (London: Heinemann, 1983), pp. 359–61.
83 Darwin, *Britain and Decolonisation*, p. 89.
84 PRO, CAB 128/8, CM 108(46), 'India: constitutional position', 31 December 1946.
85 CAB 129/19, CP(47) 158, 22 May 1947.
86 W. R. Louis, *The British Empire in the Middle East* (Oxford: Oxford University Press, 1984), p. viii.
87 Ibid., pp. 32–3.
88 F. Stonor Saunders, *Who Paid the Piper? The CIA and the Cultural Cold War* (London: Granta, 1999), pp. 58–9.
89 NEC, International Sub-Committee Minutes and Documents (henceforward NECISC), 1950–2.
90 'The International Situation', Sam Watson and Morgan Phillips, 2 October 1950, NECISC. The 'Horsham Resolution', distributed to all constituency

parties in December 1950 by party activists, meanwhile questioned the conduct of the Korean War and the nature of the Anglo-American relationship.

91 C 5845/27/18, Sir Gladwyn Jebb to Mr. Younger, 13 September 1950, in R. Bullen and M. E. Pelly (eds), *Documents on British Policy Overseas, Series 2, Volume 3, German Rearmament, September–December 1950* (London: HMSO, 1989), p. 43.

92 Younger to Jebb, 14 September 1950, ibid., p. 44 and Rickett to Attlee, 14 September 1950, p. 52. On German attitudes, see Kirkpatrick to Bevin, 11 November 1950, ibid., p. 261.

93 Jebb to Attlee, 23 September 1950, ibid., p. 92.

94 Memorandum by Sir Otto Franks, 27 September 1950, ibid., p. 111.

95 Ibid., p.113.

96 As reported in Franks to Bevin, 7 December 1950, ibid., p. 350.

97 CAB 128/18 CM(50) 87th Conclusions, 18 December 1950, ibid., pp. 382–3.

98 See Harvey to Bevin, 14 October 1950, ibid., p. 206; Bevin to Franks, 28 October 1950, ibid., p. 230.

99 See J. Callaghan, *Socialism in Britain* (Oxford: Blackwell, 1990), pp. 147–61.

7   A party divided

1 The administration fabricated evidence of unprovoked attacks against US shipping – the so-called Gulf of Tonkin incident – to justify American bombing of North Vietnam.

2 Gaitskell is cited in L. Black, ' "The Bitterest Enemies of Communism": Labour Revisionists, Atlanticism and the Cold War', *Contemporary British History*, 15, 3, 2001, p. 27.

3 As in the pamphlet *One Way Only* (London: Tribune, 1952).

4 Denis Healey, quoted in debate, *LPACR*, 1951, p. 131. The conference began two weeks before Labour lost the general election. Healey repeated this point in 1952, adding that the US alliance was essential for keeping the Commonwealth together and for solving Britain's and the world's economic problems. See *LPACR,* 1952, p. 123.

5 James Callaghan, ibid., p. 132.

6 *LPACR*, 1944, NEC statement, *The International Post-War Settlement*, p. 5.

7 'A Statement by the National Executive Committee of the Labour Party', 1 October 1950, NECISC Minutes and Documents.

8 'European Unity and the Council of Europe', NEC statement, nd, National Executive Committee, International Sub-Committee (henceforward NECISC), p. 7.

9 *LPACR*, 1952, p. 126.

10 As in 'Foreign Policy', revised draft, NECISC, nd (probably 1952).

11 *LPACR*, 1958, p. 223.

12 R. H. S. Crossman, M. Foot, I. Mikardo *et al.*, *Keep Left* (London: New Statesman, May 1947).

13 J. Schneer, *Labour's Conscience: The Labour Left 1945–51* (London: Allen and Unwin, 1988), p. 45.

14 *Tribune*, 5 March 1948, p. 8.

15 *Tribune*, 23 April 1948, editorial.

16 See the preface to D. Healey, *Cards on the Table* (London: Labour Party, 1947).

17 *Tribune*, 7 July 1950, editorial and p. 4.
18 Quoted in M. Foot, *Aneurin Bevan, 1945–60* (London: Paladin, 1975), p. 322.
19 Constituency activist J. Fagan, *LPACR*, 1953, p. 90.
20 As above, D. Finch, p. 92.
21 'Overseas Military Commitments', NECISC, 1952.
22 'Britain's Overseas Obligations', CAB 129 series, C(52)202, document reproduced in S. Lucas (ed.), *Britain and Suez* (Manchester: Manchester University Press, 1996), p. 116.
23 Harold Wilson, *LPACR*, 1952, p. 147.
24 Ibid., p. 144.
25 For example, Christopher Mayhew MP speaking at the 1952 annual conference. See *LPACR*, 1952, p. 122.
26 See J. Callaghan, 'The Left and the "Unfinished Revolution": Bevanites and Soviet Russia in the 1950s', *Contemporary British History*, 15, 3, 2001, pp. 63–83.
27 Bevan wrote the preface to Denis Healey's account of the Communist repression in Eastern Europe in *The Curtain Falls: The Story of the Socialists in Eastern Europe* (London: Lincolns–Praeger, 1951).
28 A. Bevan, *In Place of Fear* (London: Quartet, 1978, and 1952), p. 23.
29 See on this P. Krugman, 'The Myth of Asia's Miracle', *Foreign Affairs*, November–December 1994, pp. 62–3 and fn. p. 65.
30 *Tribune*, 6 July 1956 and 26 October 1956.
31 Quoted by Zilliacus, *LPACR*, 1956, p. 136.
32 See the issues of 10 May 1957, p. 6; 12 July 1957, p. 5; 6 September 1957, p. 7; 11 October 1957, p. 5; and 18 October 1957, p. 6.
33 See K. M. Jensen (ed.), *Origins of the Cold War: The Novikov, Kennan and Roberts 'Long Telegrams' of 1946* (Washington, D.C.: United States Institute of Peace, 1991), p. 56; D. Healey, *The Time of My Life* (Harmondsworth: Penguin, 1990), p. 101.
34 Quoted by M. Foot, *Aneurin Bevan, 1945–60*, pp. 646–7.
35 Cited in Black, '"The Bitterest Enemies of Communism"', p. 30.
36 Quoted in Pells, *Not Like Us*, p. 87.
37 R. H. S. Crossman, *Planning for Freedom* (London: Hamish Hamilton, 1965); see also his 'The Spectre of Revisionism: A Reply to Crosland', *Encounter*, March 1960, pp. 24–8; on Wilson see B. Pimlott, *Harold Wilson* (London: HarperCollins, 1993), pp. 236–7.
38 See R. Pells, *Not Like Us: How Europeans Have Loved, Hated and Transformed American Culture Since World War Two* (New York: Basic Books, 1997), p. 156 and F. Stonor Saunders, *Who Paid the Piper?: The CIA and the Cultural Cold War* (London: Granta, 1999), pp. 165–89.
39 See J. Callaghan, *Cold War, Crisis and Conflict: The History of the CPGB 1951–68* (London: Lawrence and Wishart, 2003).
40 See Black, "The Bitterest Enemies of Communism", pp. 53–4.
41 J. Callaghan, *Time and Chance* (London: Collins, 1987), pp. 89–90.
42 R. Pells, *Not Like Us*, pp. 50–4.
43 C. A. R. Crosland, 'About Equality II: Is Equal Opportunity Enough?', *Encounter*, August 1956, pp. 39, 43–4; see also the first part of this analysis in the July 1956 issue, p. 9.
44 The Fulbright programme 'was entangled from the beginning in the tentacles of the State Department' according to Pells, p. 60; the Smith–Mundt Act of

January 1948 involved the US state directly in the cultural war with the Soviet Union. Both schemes were targeted at 'potential opinion moulders and policymakers overseas', Pells, *Not Like Us*, p. 63.

45   Quoted in L. Black, '"The Bitterest Enemies of Communism": Labour Revisionists, Atlanticism and the Cold War', *Contemporary British History*, 15, 3, 2001, pp. 26–62, 39–40.

46   Ibid., p. 40.

47   Cited in Stonor Saunders, pp. 134–5. The Ford Foundation had itself donated $7 million to the Congress for Cultural Freedom by the early 1960s (p. 142).

48   Quoted in S. Fielding, '"But westward, look, the land is bright": Labour's Revisionists and the Imagining of America, c. 1945–64', in J. Hollowell, *Twentieth-century Anglo-American Relations* (London: Palgrave, 2001), pp. 87–103, 87.

49   Stonor Saunders, *Who Paid the Piper?*, pp. 330–1.

50   P. Williams (ed.), *Diary of Hugh Gaitskell, 1945–56* (London: Cape, 1983), pp. 316–18.

51   Healey, *Time of My Life*, pp. 196, 238–9.

52   See Williams, *The Diary of Hugh Gaitskell*, pp. 42, 159.

53   See editorial, *Socialist Commentary*, June 1960, pp. 2–3; D. Marquand, 'The Shape of the West', *Socialist Commentary*, October 1962, pp. 18–20; and F. Pickstock, 'The Sickness of American Society', *Socialist Commentary*, April 1964, pp. 15–17. Cited in Fielding, "But westward look", p. 103.

54   See P. Foot, *The Politics of Harold Wilson* (Harmondsworth: Penguin, 1968), pp. 207–10.

55   D. Goldsworthy, 'Britain and the International Critics of British Colonialism, 1951–6', *Journal of Commonwealth and Comparative History*, 29, 1, 1991, pp. 1–24.

56   As in Hugh Dalton's contribution to the debate on 'Labour's Foreign Policy' and 'Towards World Plenty' at the 1952 annual conference. See *LPACR*, 1952, p. 113.

57   The expression was used at the Bandung Conference in 1955. It was coined by Alfred Sauvy in 1952 to suggest an analogy with the Third Estate prior to the French Revolution of 1789.

58   *LPACR,* 1952, 'Challenge to Britain', p. 63.

59   CAWU resolution, 1953 conference. Left critics depicted the TUC as engaged in prolonging British colonialism. See J. Woddis, *The Mask Is Off: An Examination of the Activities of Trade Union Advisers in the British Colonies* (London: Thames Publications, 1954).

60   'The Constitutional Advances in the Colonies, 1945–54', 15 February 1955', MSS 292/930/2 file 3. TUC archive Modern Records Centre, Warwick University. See also TUC Colonial Advisory Committee, 13 March 1950, in which a variety of colonies were represented by trade union activists describing the problems they were confronted with.

61   'TUC: Re-assessment of Situation in British Africa', Victory Tewson, Colonial Advisory Committee, 4 February 1959, MSS 292/932.9/4.

62   TUC Colonial Advisory Committee, meetings of 15 July 1954 and 4 May 1955, MSS 292/932.9/1, where Operation Anvil in Kenya and the West Indies are discussed respectively.

63   Resolutions of this sort can be found in MSS 292/930/2 file 1, forwarded by Arthur Horner, Frank Haxell, Alan Birch and others.

64   *Daily Telegraph,* 5 December 1956.

65 'TUC: Reassessment of the situation in Africa'.
66 'TUC: Informal Meetings with OEF and Colonial Office, suggested reappraisal', 6 January 1960, MSS 292/930/2 file 2, ibid.
67 TUC, Colonial Advisory Committee, 29 October 1953, MSS 292/932.9/1.
68 'Colonial Office Labour Notes', March 1956, MSS 292/930/2 file m2.
69 'TUC: Informal Meetings with the OEF'.
70 *LPACR*, 1953, p. 64.
71 Taken from 'The Colonial Employer, 1947–8', report presented to Parliament by the Secretary of State for the Colonies, restated by Oliver Lyttelton, and repeated by Labour's NEC in 'Statement of Policy on Colonial Affairs', presented to the Labour conference of 1854.
72 *LPACR*, 1952, p. 119. One supposes that such criticisms would have carried added force if more members of the Labour Party had known about these repressive policies and others that were taking place around the same time in Kenya, British Guiana, and Iran. For example, the US-sponsored coup which deposed the Iranian nationalist prime minister, Mohammed Mossadeq, in 1953 – another event justified in terms of a spurious Communist threat – was first contemplated by the Labour Foreign Secretary Herbert Morrison in the summer of 1951 at a time when the USA was opposed to military action.
73 'Russia, China, Japan, Malaya, Burma: Labour Party delegation report number three', 26 January 1955, NECISC.
74 The Socialist International was also 'in imminent danger', according to Morgan Phillips, of becoming a merely Western or 'white' International and needed to pay urgent attention to the danger of a separate Asian Socialist International (SI) being formed from the Congress of Asian Socialist Parties scheduled for November 1952. Phillips acknowledged that the Socialist International was associated with colonialism and alignment with the USA, while the Asian socialists stood for neutralism and anti-colonialism. Nevertheless, the SI had to expand its membership and seek to assist in the emergence of appropriate socialist parties where they did not exist. 'The Socialist International', M. Phillips, nd (1952), NECISC.
75 D. McKnight, 'Western Intelligence and SEATO's War on Subversion, 1956–63', *Intelligence and National Security*, 20, 2, 2005, pp. 288–303, 289.
76 See R. J. McMahon, 'Eisenhower and Third World Nationalism: A Critique of the Revisionists', *Political Science Quarterly*, 101, 3, 1986, pp. 453–73, for a review of the literature.
77 A. Hourani, *A History of the Arab Peoples* (London: Faber and Faber, 1991), p. 360.
78 'Problems of Foreign Policy', NECISC, nd (1952), pp. 12–13. The rest of the paragraph is drawn from this document.
79 Hourani, *History of the Arab Peoples*, pp. 397–8.
80 Charmley, *Churchill's Grand Alliance,* pp. 254–5.
81 S. Lucas, *Divided We Stand: Britain, the US and the Suez Crisis* (1991), pp. 14–17.
82 S. Lucas and A. Morey, 'The Hidden "Alliance": The CIA and MI6 before and after Suez', *Intelligence and National Security*, 15, 2, 2000, p. 98.
83 Quoted in Charmley, *Churchill's Grand Alliance*, pp. 282–3.
84 D. Little, 'Mission Impossible: The CIA and the Cult of Covert Action in the Middle East', *Diplomatic History*, 28, 5, 2004, pp. 663–700.
85 Healey, *Cards on the Table*, p. 4.

86　'European Unity and the Council of Europe: A Statement by the National Executive Committee', nd (probably 1952), NECISC.

87　D. Healey, 'Britain and Europe', *Socialist Commentary*, May 1951, p. 111.

88　'Questions of International Policy', Morgan Phillips, nd (probably 1952), NECISC. Phillips casually acknowledged in this document (p. 4) that the USA 'is already engaged in subversive activities in Eastern Europe' while Britain's activities were restricted to intelligence gathering.

89　'Problems of Foreign Policy: A Discussion Pamphlet' (1952), NECISC.

90　Ibid., p. 6.

91　'Development of Labour Party Policy towards Western Europe, 1945–1953', nd (1953), NECISC.

92　'Britain and Europe: A Draft Report', March 1961, NECISC.

93　'A Note: Britain's Relationship to the Common Market', T. Balogh, May 1961, NECISC.

94　'Note from Nicholas Kaldor', June 1961, NECISC.

95　D. Healey, 'The Crisis in Europe', *International Affairs*, 38, 2, 1962, p. 145.

96　State Department papers, record group 59, 1964–66, Politics and Defence, box 1692, memorandum of conversation, 22 March 1964.

97　'Problems of Foreign Policy', p. 10.

98　See R. G. Hughes, '"We are not seeking strength for its own sake": The British Labour Party, West Germany and the Cold War, 1951–64', *Cold War History*, 3, 1, 2002, pp. 67–94.

99　See 'Report on the SPD Conference, Hamburg, 20–26 May 1950', NECISC, in which 'Dr. Schumacher was quite definite in his contention that the British Labour Government had deserved criticism for not supporting the SPD in developing the Social Ownership of the industries of the Ruhr and Saar. He was very bitter about this.'

100　Report on SPD Congress, Dortmund, 24–8 September 1952, by Saul Rose, NECISC.

101　'Conference of British, French and German Socialists at Bonn, 27 April 1952', report by Hugh Dalton, NECISC, 30 April 1952. See also 'Summary of the SPD Action Programme adopted at Dortmund, September 1952', NECISC, September 1952.

102　Complaints about the number of ex-Nazis involved in running the Bonn administration would continue into the 1960s.

103　The Brussels Treaty had been 'the sprat to catch the mackerel' of NATO, according to Bevin. Quoted in P. Jones, *America and the British Labour Party: The Special Relationship at Work* (London: I. B. Tauris, 1997), p. 62.

104　D. Healey, *A Neutral Belt in Europe* (London: Labour Party, 1957). See also 'Draft Pamphlet on Labour's Foreign Policy', 1958, p. 7, NECISC.

105　E. L. Woodward, *Some Political Consequences of the Atomic Bomb* (Oxford: Oxford University Press, November 1945). Woodward held the Montague Burton chair in International Relations at Oxford University.

106　D. Healey, 'The Cominform and World Communism', *International Affairs*, 24, 1948, p. 341; D. Healey, 'When Shrimps Learn to Whistle: Thoughts after Geneva', *International Affairs*, 32, 1, 1956, p. 6.

107　Healey, 'When Shrimps Learn to Whistle', p. 6.

108　D. Healey, 'Prometheus Bound: A Review of Henry Kissinger's *Nuclear Weapons and Policy*', *Encounter*, 9 December 1957, p. 75.

109　D. Healey, 'The Sputnik and Western Defence', *International Affairs*, 34, 2, 1958, pp. 147–8.

110 H. Kissinger, *The White House Years* (London: Weidenfeld and Nicolson, 1979), p. 219. Kissinger had given up limited nuclear war turning to limited conventional war in the early 1960s. With Nixon, however, he seems to have believed that the USA could win the war in Vietnam if they could persuade the Communists that they would stop at nothing. For this 'Madman Theory' see the Pullitzer prize-winning investigation by W. Shawcross, *Sideshow: Kissinger, Nixon and the Destruction of Cambodia* (New York: Simon and Schuster, 1979). For Mountbatten's views see P. Lashmar, 'Healey Plan was "Terrifying", Said Royal', *Independent*, 1 January 2000, p. 17.

111 *Defence Outline of a Future Policy* (London: HMSO, April 1957), in R. Ovendale (ed.), *British Defence Policy Since 1945* (Manchester: Manchester University Press, 1994), p. 115.

112 See Black, ' "The Bitterest Enemies of Communism" ', p. 52.

113 J. B. Priestley, 'Russia, the Atom, and the West', *New Statesman*, 2 November 1957.

114 On 26 March 1956 Russell had written to the *Manchester Guardian* expressing this opinion and denouncing the 'atrocities committed by the FBI' during the Rosenberg trial. Cited in Stonor Saunders, *Who Paid the Piper?*, p. 231.

115 'Draft Declaration for Consideration by Labour Party and TUC', nd (1959), NECISC.

116 'Defence and Disarmament: Some Points for Consideration', May 1960, NECISC.

117 *LPACR*, 1960, p. 173.

118 Ibid., p. 186, contribution of Harold Davies MP.

119 The case for positive neutralism was put in 1960 by Peter Worsley in 'Imperial Retreat', in E. P. Thompson (ed.), *Out of Apathy* (London: Steven and Sons, 1960).

120 L. Freedman, *The Evolution of Nuclear Strategy* (London: Macmillan, second edition, 1989), pp. 320–4.

121 *Let's Go with Labour for the New Britain* (London: Labour Party, 1964), p. 23.

122 P. Keleman, 'Looking the Other Way: The British Labour Party, Zionism, and the Palestinians', in C. Collette and S. Bird (eds), *Jews, Labour and the Left, 1918–48* (London: Ashgate, 2000), pp. 141–57, 142.

123 C. Cohen of Poale Zion, *LPACR*, 1955, p. 178.

124 Herbert Morrison, House of Commons, 4 April 1955; cited in 'Israel–Arab Relations', NECISC, September 1955.

125 Sam Watson, *LPACR*, 1955, p. 184.

126 There was an Arab Socialist Movement and on 15 February 1955 Clovis Maksoud – later a distinguished UN representative of the League of Arab states – tried to put its case to the NEC, stressing Israel as a blockage on the evolution of a progressive Middle East. Memorandum, nd (1955), NECISC.

127 The NEC noted this in March 1955. See 'The Israel–Arab Problem', March 1955, NECISC, where Nasser is quoted to the effect that Israel 'must disappear'.

128 *Hansard*, 2 August 1956, volume 557, column 1613.

129 Cited in J. Campbell, *Nye Bevan: And the Mirage of British Socialism* (London: Weidenfeld and Nicolson, 1987), p. 319.

130 *LPACR*, 1956, p. 70.

131 Ibid., p. 71.
132 See S. Lucas (ed.), *Britain and Suez* (Manchester: Manchester University Press, 1996), p. 38.
133 'Analysis of resolutions on Foreign Policy received for September Sub-Committee', NECISC, 1958.
134 Blackwell, 'Pursuing Nasser', pp. 86–7; Mountbatten, First Sea Lord, advised against continuation of the old policy. See p. 92.
135 'Draft Pamphlet on Labour's Foreign Policy', November 1958, NECISC.
136 Ibid., p. 10.
137 Quoted in Blackwell, 'Pursuing Nasser', p. 98.
138 Tom Driberg MP introduced this policy to the 1956 annual conference. See *LPACR*, 1956, pp. 155–6.
139 'Statement of Policy on Colonial Affairs: from colonies to Commonwealth', presented to annual conference 1954, NECISC.
140 'Lasting friendship between Britain and the peoples of Africa depends on treating the interests of the native majority as paramount', 'Foreign Policy', revised draft, nd (1952), NECISC, p. 5.
141 See *Tribune*, 5 December 1952 and 27 March 1953.
142 The TUC's Colonial Advisory Committee objected to the MCF's 'interference in the trade union field', at home and abroad; its propaganda claiming that the colonies denied free trade unionism and that Britain was engaged in repression in Malaya and British Guiana; and the fact that 'undesirables' were associated with it. Meeting of 6 February 1957, MSS 292/932.9/1, TUC archive.
143 CO 822/437, untitled document of 10 September 1952.
144 Ibid., correspondence of 19 September 1952.
145 CO 822/444, Baring to Lyttelton, 9 October 1952.
146 CO 822/471, telegram from Deputy Governor to Secretary of State, 15 December 1953.
147 CO 822/471, see the evidence from Canon Bewes; CO 822/499, see the case of Brian Hayward convicted of violence against 20 prisoners.
148 C. Elkins, *Britain's Gulag: The Brutal End of Empire in Kenya* (London: Cape, 2005), pp. 99–100.
149 Ibid., p. 117.
150 B. Castle, *Fighting All the Way* (London: Macmillan, 1993), p. 264.
151 Elkins, *Britain's Gulag*, pp. 287–8.
152 Documents relating to this *coup* can be found at http://www.guyana.org/govt/declassified_british_documents_1953.html; Labour's and the TUC's role is discussed in http://www.guyana.org/features/guyanastory/chapter134.html.
153 Britain suspended the Guianan constitution until 1957. Jagan was re-elected in 1961 and independence was expected two years later. US opposition to independence led Harold Macmillan to remark on the 'pure Machiavellism' of the 'anti-colonial' zealots of the Kennedy administration who made clear that independence under Jagan must not be allowed to happen. See J. Tratt, 'Harold Macmillan and the "Golden Days" of Anglo-American Relations Revisited, 1957–63', *Diplomatic History*, 29, 4, 2005, pp. 691–711.
154 *LPACR*, 1956, p. 166.
155 CO 822/1237, see documents of 9 January 1957 and 4 February 1959.
156 CO 822/1787, 'Kenya News', press office handout, number 789.
157 Elkins, *Britain's Gulag*, p. 309.

158 See FO 371/1990. Ministers were advised to stress the 'precision' of air strikes involving the use of fragmentation bombs.
159 See F. Halliday, *Arabia Without Sultans* (Harmondsworth: Penguin, 1974), pp. 274–6.
160 *This Week*, volume 5, supplement 2, 4 April 1963, NECISC minutes and documents.
161 Tredgold was Chief Justice of the Federation of Nyasaland and Rhodesia.

8   The last pretence

1 CAB 129/100, Defence White Paper, 8 February 1960.
2 CAB 128/35, part 1, discussion of 17 January 1961.
3 CAB 129/100, 'Sovereign Base Areas in Cyprus', 7 March 1960.
4 See B. O'Malley and I. Craig, *The Cyprus Conspiracy: America, Espionage and the Turkish Invasion* (London: I. B. Tauris, 2004).
5 See PREM 11/3737.
6 PREM 11/3737, see the correspondence between Harold Macmillan and Lord Selkirk of 14 August, 12 September, and 14 October 1961. The Indonesian problem was perceived this way until Sukarno was overthrown in 1965. See CAB 128/38, part 2, meeting of 23 January 1964.
7 CAB 128/41, part 1. By the end of 1964 Britain had around 54,000 military personnel in Malaysia. See D. Easter, *Britain and the Confrontation with Indonesia, 1960–66* (London: I. B. Tauris, 2004), p. 1.
8 'The Middle East', 17 April 1963, NECISC.
9 Ibid., p. 2.
10 Ibid., p. 11.
11 DO/193/52, 'Prime Minister's Minute of 30 July', 16 September 1963; 'Commonwealth Links', 6 September 1963.
12 CAB 128/38, part 2, meeting of 9 April 1964.
13 G. Cunningham, 'Southern Rhodesia', 10 June 1963, NECISC minutes and documents.
14 J. Tomlinson, *The Labour Governments, 1964–70: Economic Policy* (Manchester: Manchester University Press, 2004), pp. 22–4.
15 Quoted in Pimlott, *Harold Wilson*, p. 247.
16 B. Castle and T. Driberg, report on the fifth congress of the socialist parties of the member countries, Paris, 5–6 November 1962, NECISC minutes and documents.
17 'Message from the fifth congress', November 1962, ibid.
18 FO 371/177812. These thoughts were provoked by the suggestion that a new statement of foreign policy was required to emulate and supplant the Crowe memorandum of 1907.
19 PREM 11/3737, Lord Selkirk to Macmillan, 14 August 1961.
20 Ibid.
21 A. Varsori, 'Britain and US Involvement in the Vietnam War during the Kennedy Administration, 1961–63', *Cold War History*, 3, 2, 2003, pp. 83–112.
22 See R. Steininger, '"The Americans Are in a Hopeless Position": Great Britain and the War in Vietnam, 1964–65', *Diplomacy and Statecraft*, 8, 3, 1997, pp. 237–85.
23 See for example CAB 134/1932 for discussions on the need for defence economies of £200 million in 1961.

24   FO 371/177830, 'Anglo-American Special Relationship', 10 July 1964.
25   E. J. W. Barnes, Head of the Western and Coordinating Department, expressed such doubts in June 1964 but they were removed from the last draft of the relevant paper. See FO 371/177812, minute of 10 June 1964 and CAB 128/118 part 2, CP(64)164, 2 September 1964.
26   PREM 11/41888, see correspondence of Harold Macmillan and Lord Selkirk of 24 June 1962 and 12 March 1962.
27   CAB 129/118, part 2, CP(64)143, 'Prospects for Expenditure', 15 July 1964.
28   Ibid.
29   CAB 129/105, 'Economic Situation', memorandum from the Chancellor of the Exchequer, 29 June 1961.
30   *Let's Go With Labour For the New Britain* (London: Labour Party, 1964), p. 23. See also Healey, *Time of My Life*, p. 245.
31   Chapman Pincher in the *Daily Express*, 5 June 1964. Privately Home admitted that once Wilson was apprised of the 'facts' he would not scrap Polaris because he was 'reliable in terms of the national interest'. Quoted in P. Hennessy, *Muddling Through* (London: Gollancz, 1998), p. 114.
32   See R. Pearce (ed.), *Patrick Gordon Walker: Political Diaries* (London: Historical Press, 1991), p. 299.
33   PREM 11/4332, 'Confidential Note for Record', 24 November 1963.
34   Full convertibility of sterling had been restored in 1958.
35   S. Dockrill, 'Forging the Anglo-American Global Defence Partnership: Harold Wilson, Lyndon Johnson and the Washington Summit, 1964', *Journal of Strategic Studies*, 23, 4, 2000, p. 111.
36   P. Ziegler, *Wilson: The Authorized Life of Lord Wilson of Rievaulx* (London: Weidenfeld and Nicolson, 1993), pp. 218–19.
37   Crossman reflected on Wilson's 'predominant' interest in foreign and defence issues as early as November 1964, later complaining that Gordon Walker was 'hopeless' and Healey in the hands of his officials and chiefs of staff. Not only had the Cabinet become part of the 'dignified' element in the constitution, as he had always supposed, but even its sub-committees were 'completely paralleled at the official level' and apt to be by-passed by bilateral deals struck between the PM and the relevant Ministers. R. H. S. Crossman, *Diaries of a Cabinet Minister: Volume One, Minister of Housing, 1964–66* (London: 1975 and Baylis Trinity Press,1977), pp. 68, 203, 382, 189, 198, 201. While Michael Stewart was Foreign Secretary, according to Crosland, the Foreign Office didn't matter much 'because the PM maintained his control'. *Diaries of a Cabinet Minister: Volume 2, Lord President of the Council, 1966–68* (London: Cape, 1976), p. 295. Callaghan informed the US Embassy that Stewart was 'a little on the pedestrian side' (US National Archive, Maryland, Box 2780, file POL 15–1, telegram Embassy to Department of State, 22 January 1965).
38   See Anthony Eden's observations of June 1952, 'Britain's Overseas Obligations', CAB 129, C(52)202, reproduced in S. Lucas (ed.), *Britain and Suez* (Manchester: Manchester University Press, 1996), p. 116; for the Communist analysis see R. P. Dutt, *The Crisis of Britain and the British Empire* (London: Lawrence and Wishart, 1953), pp. 303–4. The most influential case was put by A. Shonfield, *British Economic Policy since the War* (London: Penguin, 1958).
39   For a recent Conservative statement of this argument see J. Charmley, *Churchill's Grand Alliance: The Anglo-American Special Relationship, 1945–57* (London: Hodder and Stoughton, 1996).

40 See R. Pryke, *Though Cowards Flinch: An Alternative Economic Policy* (London: McGibbon and Kee, 1967).

41 See C. Ponting, *Breach of Promise: Labour in Power, 1964–70* (London: Hamish Hamilton, 1989), especially chapter 3.

42 Ibid., p. 44.

43 Quoted in Ponting, *Breach of Promise*, p. 44.

44 See M. Jones, 'A decision delayed: Britain's withdrawal from Southeast Asia reconsidered, 1961–8', *English Historical Review*, 67, 472, 2002, pp. 569–95.

45 PREM 13/18, 'Defence Policy – Chequers Discussions', 19 November 1964.

46 Britain had more troops deployed in the Far East and Middle East than Europe when Labour came to power. The eventual decision to focus on Europe had nothing to do with any perceived threat from that quarter, as these early discussions show. See G. Wyn Rees, 'British Strategic Thinking and Europe, 1964–1970', *Journal of European Integration,* 5, 1, pp. 57–71. For a review of the explanations for Britain's withdrawal from East of Suez, see T. T. Petersen, 'Crossing the Rubicon? Britain's Withdrawal from the Middle East, 1964–1968: A Bibliographical Review', *International History Review*, 35, 4, 2000, pp. 619–39.

47 PREM 13/18, 'Defence Policy – Chequers Discussions', 19 November 1964, p. 3.

48 FO 371/177824, 'British Policy towards South East Asia', December 1964.

49 CAB 130/213, Cabinet meeting, 21 November 1964.

50 B. Reed and G. Williams, *Denis Healey and the Policies of Power* (London: Sidgwick and Jackson, 1971), p. 169.

51 Crossman, *Diaries*, volume 1, p. 105. Crossman himself recognised that the ANF scheme functioned as a dodge to retain nuclear weapons, p. 73.

52 See L. Freedman, *Britain and Nuclear Weapons* (London: Macmillan, 1980), pp. 31–2, where it is pointed out that Polaris could have been cheaply scrapped. Wilson repeated his deception in *The Labour Governments 1964–70* (London: Hamish Hamilton, 1989), p. 40.

53 Ibid., 22 November 1964.

54 *Hansard*, 23 November 2964, column 1028.

55 PREM 13/18, 'Defence Policy', 25 November 1964.

56 PREM 13/2450, 'Record of a Conversation' between Wilson and George Ball, 30 November 1964.

57 PREM 13/103, 'Strategy for Washington', 2 December 1964.

58 PREM 13/104, 'Record of a Meeting . . .', Washington, DC, 7 December 1964.

59 In January 1964 British military intervention in Kenya and Tanzania quashed rebellions in the local armed forces.

60 PREM13/104, 'Record of a Meeting', Washington, DC, 7 December 1964.

61 Rusk had already congratulated the British earlier that day for making allowances on behalf of the USA in their guidance of British Guiana. Gordon Walker assured him that there could be no question of independence yet. PREM 13/104, 'Record of a Meeting . . .' at the White House, 7 December 1964.

62 R. G. K. Thompson was the architect of the British strategy in Malaysia and acted as consultant to the US involvement in Vietnam. In 1961 he recommended the 'strategic hamlet programme' which the British had employed in Malaysia for use in the Mekong Delta.

63 The US Embassy was alarmed when the *Sunday Telegraph* referred to these arrangements for fear that 'it stimulates Parliamentary interest in the British

Indian Ocean Territory' (Telegram to Department of State, 4 December 1966, Box 1693).

64   Crossman, *Diaries*, vol 1, p. 94.
65   PREM 13/252, 'Record of US–UK meeting', 7 December 1964.
66   See for example Ponting, *Breach of Promise*; J. Dumbrell, *A Special Relationship* (London: Macmillan, 2001); Pimlott, *Harold Wilson*; and C. Wrigley, 'Now You See It, Now You Don't: Harold Wilson and Labour's Foreign Policy', in R. Coopey, S. Fielding and N. Tiratsoo (eds), *The Wilson Governments, 1964–70* (London: Pinter, 1993). Crossman records Cabinet discussions alluding to understandings with the USA linking financial assistance to Britain with deflationary policies at home and support for the USA in Vietnam and maintenance of the East of Suez role. *Diaries*, volume 1, pp. 321, 456 and volume 2, p. 156.
67   PREM 13/431, 'Singapore', P. Rogers, 27 August 1965.
68   J. Young, *The Labour Governments, 1964–70* (Manchester: Manchester University Press, 2003), p. 67.
69   PREM13/431, 'Record of a Conversation . . . ', 8 September 1965.
70   PREM 13/2450, 'Meeting of Wilson, Callaghan and Ball', 9 September 1965.
71   PREM 13/431, 'Singapore: Quadripartite Talks'.
72   CAB 190/239; see the reports of 13 August and 26 August 1965.
73   PREM 13/431, 'Foreign Office telegram No 6981 to Washington', 9 September 1965.
74   Ibid., 'Repercussions on British Policy in South East Asia . . . ', OPD(65)131.
75   FO 371/190785, record of meeting of Denis Healey, Michael Stewart, Dean Rusk, George Ball and Robert McNamara, 27 January 1966.
76   See P. Scott, 'The United States and the Overthrow of Sukarno, 1965–67', *Pacific Affairs*, 58, 2, 1985, pp. 239–64; P. Lashmar and O. James, *Britain's Secret Propaganda War* (Stroud: Sutton Publishing, 1998).
77   See the survey of evidence in D. Easter, ' "Keep the Indonesian Pot Boiling": Western Covert Intervention in Indonesia, October 1965–March 1966', *Cold War History*, 5, 1, 2005, pp. 55–73.
78   PREM 13/799, 'Meeting at the White House', 16 December 1965.
79   PREM 13/216, meeting of 30 June 1965.
80   CAB 129/124, Part Two, C(66)33, 'Defence Review', 11 February 1966.
81   FO 371/190785, record of a meeting, 27 January 1966. The implication was that Pakistan was only interested in its own security vis-à-vis India.
82   Crossman, *Diaries*, volume 2, pp. 215–16.
83   B. Castle, *The Castle Diaries 1964–70* (London: Weidenfeld and Nicolson, 1984), p. 147.
84   Powell advocated withdrawal from East of Suez at the Tory conference of October 1965. Gladwyn is cited in Young, *The Labour Governments*, p. 46.
85   PLP Minutes 15 June 1966.
86   Ibid., p. 9.
87   Castle, *Diaries 1964–70*, pp. 273–4 and Crossman, *Diaries*, volume 2, pp. 403 and 411–12.
88   CAB 130/213, 18 November 1964.
89   H. Parr and M. Pine, 'Policy towards the European Economic Community', in P. Dorey (ed.), *The Labour Governments 1964–1970* (London: Routledge, 2006), p. 109.
90   Crossman records Stewart telling Wilson to apply for entry in early December 1965. Wilson himself was worried that Britain could not remain an

'independent power' outside the Common Market. Crossman, *Diaries*, volume 1, pp. 443 and 461.

91 PREM 13/1617, 'British Policy towards the Arab/Israel Dispute', 29 March 1966.
92 Hourani, *History of the Arab Peoples*, p. 407.
93 PREM 13/1617, telegram 22 May 1967.
94 PREM 13/1618, 'Middle East Crisis: Some Basic Considerations', 26 May 1967.
95 PREM 13/1617, note of meeting of Harold Wilson and George Thompson (Minister for Foreign Affairs), 23 May 1967.
96 PREM 13/1618, telegram Kuwait to Foreign Office, 27 May 1967.
97 PREM 128/42, Part Two, memorandum from the Foreign Secretary on 'Arab Attitudes and British Economic Interests in the Middle East', 11 July 1967.
98 R. Roy, 'The Battle for Bretton Woods: America, Britain and the International Financial Crisis of October 1967–March 1968', *Cold War History*, 2, 2, 2002, pp. 38–9.
99 PREM 13/1447, Wilson to Callaghan, 6 November 1967; Wilson to Crossman, 13 November 1967.
100 PREM 13/1447, Brown to Wilson, 15 November 1967.
101 B. Castle, *The Castle Diaries, 1964–70* (London: Weidenfeld and Nicolson, 1980), p. 325.
102 PREM 13/1854, telegram from Wilson to Johnson, 17 November 1967.
103 PREM 13/1854, telegram from Sir P. Dean, Washington to Foreign Office, 8 November 1967.
104 See PREM 13/1856 for reaction to devaluation.
105 Roy, 'The Battle for Bretton Woods', p. 46.
106 CAB 128/43/CC6(68).
107 PREM 13/1999, telegram from Johnson to Wilson, 15 January 1968.
108 Parr and Pain, 'Policy Towards the European Economic Community', pp. 126–9.
109 As enumerated by Jack Jones, *LPACR*, 1969, p. 309.
110 *LPACR*, 1971, p. 138.
111 E. Short, *Whip to Wilson* (London: MacDonald, 1989), p. 160.
112 See examples in the PLP Minutes for 17 December 1964, 8 December 1965, 15 June 1966 and 3 April 1968.
113 Crossman, *Diaries*, volume 1, p. 253.
114 Healey, *Time of My Life*, p. 332.
115 It has recently been argued that the objections were exaggerated. See C. Watts, 'Killing Kith and Kin: The Viability of British Military Intervention in Rhodesia, 1964–5', *Twentieth Century British History*, 16, 2005, pp. 382–415 and J. R. T. Wood, *So Far and No Further! Rhodesia's Bid for Independence during the Retreat from Empire, 1959–1965* (Victoria, B.C.: Trafford Publishing, 2005). For operation KINGFISHER see P. Murphy, '"An intricate and distasteful subject": British Planning for the Use of Force against the European Settlers of Central Africa, 1952–65', *English Historical Review*, 121, 492, 2006, pp. 746–77.
116 Pimlott, *Wilson*, pp. 455–7; Young, *The Labour Governments*, p. 181; Ziegler, *Harold Wilson*, p. 319.
117 S. Ellis, *Britain, America, and the Vietnam War* (London: Praeger, 2004), pp. 160–79.
118 Crossman, *Diaries*, volume 2, p. 498 (September 1967).

119 PLP Minutes, 6 July 1966.
120 Ibid., 2 February 1967.
121 Ibid., 15 June 1966. The same formula was used on 14 February 1967 when the bombing was resumed after a short-lived cessation.
122 *LPACR*, 1965, p. 177.
123 Ibid., contributions from Alex Kitson and R. Wadsworth, pp. 182–3.
124 Ibid., contribution of J. J. Mendelson, pp. 184–5.
125 *LPACR*, 1967, pp. 223–5.
126 Telegram from Rusk to Stewart, 17 June 1965, US National Archive, Record Group 59, Box 1696; on other occasions he left it to the discretion of the Embassy as to whether his 'personal compliments and appreciation' should be conveyed, for example telegram, Rusk to Embassy, 19 December 1966, Box 2783, File POL 15.
127 Embassy to Department of State, 27 September, 1965, Box 2780, file POL 12, signed by James R. Cheek, second secretary.
128 Box 2782, POL 15–1, 3 September 1965, message from Leonard Unger, Deputy Assistant Secretary for Far Eastern Affairs, to George Ball. On 9 March 1965 a telegram from the Embassy to the Department of State reported that 'Wilson's statement on South Viet Nam in Commons this afternoon conformed closely to text agreed with Washington'. Box 2782, POL 15–1. Rusk exchanged telegrams to spell out the important distinctions Wilson should make in the House. See PREM13/693, telegram FO to Washington and Washington to FO, 9 March 1965.
129 Jeremy Thorpe and Michael Foot respectively during Prime Minister's Question Time, 21 June 1966.
130 PREM 13/692, FO Memorandum, 'Visit to Washington by Prime Minister and Foreign Secretary: Viet Nam', 3 December 1964. See also FO371/180580, 'Seeking a Solution in Viet-Nam', memorandum 15 February, 1965; and PREM13/693, minute on 'Vietnam', 1 March 1965.
131 PREM 13/693, 'Record of a conversation between Wilson and David Bruce', 12 March 1965.
132 PREM 13/693, draft telegram to the Foreign Secretary, nd.
133 US Embassy to Department of State, telegram 11 July 1966, Box 2782, POL 15–1, US National Archives.
134 Memo from Richard Neustadt to McGeorge Bundy, 'Round-up on Trip to England', 9 August 1965, NSF Name File, Box 7, LBJ Library. Castle, *The Castle Diaries 1964–70*, p. 148.
135 C. Wheeler, 'Half the Way with LBJ', *New Statesman*, 10 April 2000, p. 33.
136 Quoted in J. Colman, *A Special Relationship? Harold Wilson, Lyndon B. Johnson and Anglo-American Relations 'At the Summit'* (Manchester: Manchester University Press, 2004), p. 67.
137 Crossman, *Diaries*, volume 2, p. 499.
138 Quoted in Colman, *A Special Relationship?*, p. 163.
139 Quoted in Pells, *Not Like Us*, p. 61.
140 Quoted in B. Rubin and J. C. Rubin, *Hating America: A History* (Oxford: Oxford University Press, 2004), p. 153.
141 Harold Pinter, quoted in ibid., p. 128.
142 Jan Morris, quoted in ibid., p. 153.
143 M. Phythian, *The Politics of British Arms Sales* (Manchester: Manchester University Press, 2000), pp. 691–711.

144 Ibid., p. 8.
145 T. Bale, 'A Deplorable Episode? South African Arms and the Statecraft of British Social Democracy', *Labour History Review*, 62, 1, 1997. Wilson is quoted on p. 32.
146 Phythian, *Politics of British Arms Sales*, pp. 105–13.
147 J. Frankel, *British Foreign Policy, 1945–73* (London: Oxford University Press, 1975), p. 141.
148 These are characteristic of the style of British foreign policy as a whole according to M. Waltz, *Foreign Policy and Democratic Politics: The American and British Experiences* (London: Longmans, 1967), p. 157.
149 Frankel, *British Foreign Policy*, p. 92.
150 See D. Owen, *Human Rights* (London: Cape, 1978); but also Callaghan, *Time and Chance*, p. 296; K. Jeffreys, *Anthony Crosland: A New Biography* (London: Politico's, 2000), p. 201.
151 D. Campbell, *The Unsinkable Aircraft Carrier*, p. 15.
152 S. Pierson, *British Socialists: The Journey from Fantasy to Politics* (London: Harvard University Press, 1979).
153 Z. Brzezinski, *The Grand Chessboard* (New York: Basic Books, 1997), p. 43. Brzezinski was National Security Advisor to President Carter, 1977–81, and currently a professor of American foreign policy.

Selected bibliography

Place of publication is London unless otherwise stated.

Documents

Labour Party (Labour History Archive and Study Centre, Manchester)

Annual Conference Reports
Labour and Socialist International (LSI), documents from 1914 to 1925
LPACIQ, memoranda and minutes of the advisory committee on international questions
NEC Minutes
NEC International Sub-Committee Minutes and Documents
National Council of Labour minutes and memoranda
Minutes of the Parliamentary Labour Party

Trades Union Congress (Modern Records Centre, University of Warwick)

Colonial Questions 1928–60, 62: MSS 292/930/1 – 932.91/4
TUC Annual Report

UK National Archive (Kew)

CAB 23: War Cabinet and Cabinet: Minutes, 1916–1939
CAB 128: Cabinet: Minutes (CM and CC series), 1945–1975
CAB 129: Cabinet: Memoranda (CP and C series), 1945–1975
CAB 130: Miscellaneous Committees: Minutes and Papers (GEN, MISC and REF Series), 1945–1976
CAB 134: Cabinet: Miscellaneous Committees: Minutes and Papers (General Series), 1945–1978
CAB 190: Cabinet Office: Central Intelligence Machinery: Joint Intelligence Committee: Working Groups and Working Parties Minutes and Reports (INT Series), 1970–1975
DO 193: Commonwealth Relations Office: Planning and Research Unit: Registered Files (PLA Series), 1957–1966

FO 371: Foreign Office: Political Departments: General Correspondence, 1906–1966
CO822: Colonial Office: East Africa: Original Correspondence, 1927–1964
CO847: Colonial Office: Africa: Original Correspondence, 1932–1965
CO852: Colonial Office: Economic General Department and predecessors: Registered Files, 1935–1966
PREM 11: Prime Minister's Office: Correspondence and Papers, 1944–1964
PREM 13: Prime Minister's Office: Correspondence and Papers, 1964–1970

US archives

Department of State papers, National Archive, College Park, Maryland
Lyndon Baines Johnson Library and Museum, Austin, Texas

Collections of documents

Baylis, J. (ed.), *Anglo-American Relations since 1939: The Enduring Alliance* (Manchester: 1997)
Bullen, R. and Pelly, M. E. (eds), *Documents on British Policy Overseas: Series 2, Volume 2: The London Conferences, January–June 1950* (1987)
—— *Series 2, Volume 3: German Rearmament* (1989)
Greenwood, S. (ed.), *Britain and European Integration since the Second World War* (Manchester: 1996)
Hyam, R. (ed.), *The Labour Government and the End of Empire: Part 1: High Policy and Administration* (1992)
Lucas, S. (ed.), *Britain and Suez* (Manchester: 1996)
Ovendale, R. (ed.), *Defence Policy since 1945* (Manchester: 1994)

Pamphlets

Angell, N., *War and the Workers* (1912)
—— *Shall This War End German Militarism?* (1914)
Baker, B., *The Social Democratic Federation and the Boer War* (1974)
Blatchford, R., *Germany and England: The War That Was Foretold* (1914)
Brailsford, H. N., *The Origins of the Great War* (1914)
Crossman, R. *et al., Keep Left* (1947)
Ewer, W. N. and Williams, F., *The World Muddle* (1932)
Healey D., *Cards on the Table: An Interpretation of Labour's Foreign Policy* (1947)
—— *The Curtain Falls: The Story of the Socialists in Eastern Europe* (1951)
—— *A Neutral Belt in Europe* (1957)
Henderson, A., *The Peace Terms* (1919)
—— *Labour and Foreign Affairs* (1922)
Hobson, J. A., *A League of Nations* (1915)
—— *The New Holy Alliance* (1919)
Independent Labour Party, *Six Months of a Labour Government* (1924)
—— *Socialism in Our Time* (March 1926)

Ingram, K., *Fifty Years of the National Peace Council, 1908–58* (1958)
Labour Party, *An Exposure of the Armaments Ring: A Report of Snowden's Speech on the Naval Estimates* (1914)
—— *Labour and the New Social Order* (1918)
—— *Labour and the Peace Treaty* (1919)
—— *Unemployment: The Peace and the Indemnity* (1921)
—— *Report of the Special Conference on Labour and the Russian–Polish War* (1920)
—— *Report of the British Labour Party Delegation to Russia 1920* (1920)
—— *Labour and the Nation* (1928)
—— *What Has the Labour Government Done?* (1930)
—— *Two Years of Labour Rule* (1931)
—— *The Colonial Empire* (1933)
—— *For Socialism and Peace: The Labour Party's Programme of Action* (1934)
—— *Record of the Second Labour Government* (1935)
—— *The Colonies* (1940)
'Lest We Forget', *The Churches and the South African War* (1905)
McIntyre, S., *Imperialism and the British Labour Movement in the 1920s* (1975)
Morel, E. D., *The Fruits of Victory* (1919)
National Council of Labour, *Labour and the Defence of Peace* (1936)
Perris, G. H., *The War Traders: An Exposure* (1913)
Ponsonby, A., *Parliament and Foreign Policy* (1914)
Quelch, H., *Social Democracy and the Armed Nation* (1900)
Snowden, P., *If Labour Rules* (1923)
Socialist Union, *Socialism and Foreign Policy* (1953)
Suthers, R. B., *Socialism or Smash* (1932)
Tribune, *One Way Only* (1952)
Walton-Newbold, J. T., *The War Trust Exposed* (1913)
Williams, F., *Democracy and Finance* (1932)
Woddis, J., *The Mask Is Off: An Examination of the Activities of Trade Union Advisers in the British Colonies* (1954)
Woodward, E. L., *Some Political Consequences of the Atomic Bomb* (Oxford: November 1945)

Books

Adams, M. (ed.), *The Modern State* (1933)
Addison, C. (ed.), *Politics of a Socialist Government* (1933)
Ambrose, S., *Rise to Globalism: American Foreign Policy since 1938* (1985)
Angell, N., *The Great Illusion* (1910)
Arendt, H., *On Revolution* (1963)
—— *The Origins of Totalitarianism* (New York: 1966 and 1994)
Attlee, C. R., *The Labour Party in Perspective* (1937)
Balfour-Paul, G., *The End of the Empire in the Middle East* (Cambridge: 1991)
Barnes, J. and Nicholson, D. (eds), *The Empire at Bay: The Leo Amery Diaries, 1929–45* (1988)
Barnett, C., *The Collapse of British Power* (Gloucester: 1984)
—— *The Audit of War* (1986)

Bassett, R. M., *Nineteen Thirty-One: Political Crisis* (1958)
Beer, S., *Modern British Politics* (1965)
Bell, P. M. S., *John Bull and the Bear: Public Opinion, Foreign Policy and the Soviet Union* (1990)
Beloff, M., *Wars and Welfare: Britain 1914–45* (1984)
Benn, C., *Keir Hardie* (1997)
Benn, T., *Out of the Wilderness: Diaries 1963–67* (1987)
Berman, D., *Control and Crisis in Colonial Kenya* (1990)
Best, A., Henhimaki, J. M., Miolo, J. A. and Schulze, K. E., *International History of the Twentieth Century* (2004)
Bevan, A., *In Place of Fear* (1952 and 1978)
Birn, D. S., *The League of Nations Union 1918–45* (Oxford: 1981)
Blaazer, D., *The Popular Front and the Progressive Tradition: Socialists, Liberals and the Quest for Unity, 1884–1939* (Cambridge: 1992)
Blake, R., *The Decline of Power* (1985)
Bok, S., *Secrets: On the Ethics of Concealment and Revelation* (Oxford: 1982)
Brailsford, H. N., *The War of Steel and Gold* (1914)
Brzezinski, Z., *The Grand Chessboard* (New York: 1997)
Buchanan, T., *The Spanish Civil War and the British Labour Movement* (Cambridge: 1991)
Bullock, A., *Life and Times of Ernest Bevin: Trade Union Leader* (1960)
—— *Ernest Bevin: Foreign Secretary* (1983)
Cain, P. J. and Hopkins, A. G., *British Imperialism: Crisis and Deconstruction 1914–1990* (1993)
Calder, A., *The People's War* (1969)
Callaghan, J., *Time and Chance* (1987)
—— *Socialism in Britain* (1990)
—— *Rajani Palme Dutt* (1993)
—— *Cold War, Crisis and Conflict: The History of the CPGB 1951–68* (2003)
Campbell, D., *The Unsinkable Aircraft Carrier: American Military Power in Britain* (1986)
Campbell, J., *Nye Bevan and the Mirage of British Socialism* (1987)
Cannadine, D., *Decline and Fall of the British Aristocracy* (Yale: 1990)
Carlton, D., *Anthony Eden* (1981)
Castle, B., *The Castle Diaries 1964–70* (1984)
—— *Fighting all the Way* (1993)
Cato, *Guilty Men* (1940)
Ceadal, M., *Pacifism in Britain 1914–45: The Defining of a Faith* (Oxford: 1980)
—— *Semi-Detached Idealists: The British Peace Movements and International Relations* (Oxford: 2000)
Chandra, B., *India's Struggle for Freedom* (1989)
Charmley, J., *Churchill's Grand Alliance: The Anglo-American Special Relationship 1940–57* (1995)
Clarke, P., *The Cripps Version: The Life of Sir Stafford Cripps 1889–1952* (2003)
Cliff, T. and Gluckstein, D., *The Labour Party: A Marxist History* (1988)
Cline, C. A., *Recruits to Labour* (Syracuse: 1963)
Coates, W. P. and Z. K., *History of Anglo-Soviet Relations* (1944)

Cole, G. D. H., *Economic Tracts for the Times* (1932)
—— *Europe, Russia and the Future* (1941)
—— *A History of the Labour Party from 1914* (1948)
—— *A History of Socialist Thought*, volume 4, part 1 (1965)
Collette, C., *The International Faith: Labour's Attitude to European Socialism, 1918–39* (1998)
Collette, C. and Bird, S. (eds), *Jews, Labour and the Left, 1918–48* (2000)
Colman, J., *A Special Relationship? Harold Wilson, Lyndon B. Johnson and Anglo-American Relations 'At the Summit'* (Manchester: 2004)
Coopey, R., Fielding, S. and Tiratsoo, T. (eds), *The Wilson Governments 1964–70* (1993)
Cowling, M., *The Impact of Hitler* (1975)
Crossman, R. H. S., *Palestine Mission* (1947)
—— *Planning for Freedom* (1965)
—— *Diaries of a Cabinet Minister: Volume 1, Minister of Housing, 1964–66* (1975)
—— *Diaries of a Cabinet Minister: Volume 2, Lord President of the Council* (1976)
—— *Diaries of a Cabinet Minister: Volume 3, Secretary of State for Social Services, 1968–70* (1977)
Crossman, R. H. S. (ed.), *New Fabian Essays* (1952)
Crowder, M. (ed.), *The Cambridge History of Africa: Volume 8, 1940–75* (Cambridge: 1984)
Dalton, H., *Towards the Peace of Nations* (1928)
Darwin, J. G., *Britain and Decolonisation* (1988)
Davidson, B., *Africa in Modern History* (1978)
—— *The Black Man's Burden* (1992)
Davis, L. E. and Huttenback, R. A., *Mammon and the Pursuit of Empire* (Cambridge: 1988)
Deighton, A. (ed.), *Britain and the First Cold War* (1990)
Dimbleby, D. and Reynolds, R., *An Ocean Apart* (1988)
Donoughue, B. and Jones, G. W., *Herbert Morrison: Portrait of a Politician* (1973)
Dorey, P. (ed.), *The Labour Governments 1964–70* (2006)
Dowse, R. E. (ed.), *From Serfdom to Socialism* (1974)
Drummond, I. M. (ed.), *British Economic Policy and the Empire 1919–39* (1972)
Dumbrell, J., *A Special Relationship* (2001)
Dunbabin, J. P. D., *The Post-Imperial Age: The Great Powers and the Wider World* (1994)
Durbin, E., *New Jerusalems* (1985)
Durbin, E. F., *The Politics of Democratic Socialism* (1940)
Dutt, R. Palme, *India To-Day* (1940)
Dutton, D., *Anthony Eden* (1997)
Easter, D., *Britain and Confrontation with Indonesia, 1960–66* (2000)
Elkins, C., *Britain's Gulag: The Brutal End of Empire in Kenya* (2005)
Ellis, S., *Britain, America and the Vietnam War* (2004)
Feuchtwanger, E. J., *From Weimar to Hitler: Germany 1918–33* (1995)
Finkel, A. and Leibovitz, C., *The Chamberlain–Hitler Collusion* (1997)

Foot, M., *Aneurin Bevan 1897–1945* (1975)
—— *Aneurin Bevan 1945–60* (1975)
Foot, P., *The Politics of Harold Wilson* (1968)
Frankel, J., *British Foreign Policy 1945–73* (1975)
Freeden, M., *Ideologies and Political Theory* (Oxford: 1996)
Freedman, L., *Britain and Nuclear Weapons* (1980)
—— *The Evolution of Nuclear Strategy* (1981)
Fryer, P., *Black People and the British Empire* (1989)
Furedi, F., *Colonial Wars and the Politics of Third World Nationalism* (1994)
Gifford, P. and Louis, W. R. (eds), *The Transfer of Power in Africa: Decolonization 1940–60* (1982)
Gilbert, M., *First World War* (1994)
Gilmour, D., *Curzon* (1994)
Glyn, A. and Booth, A., *Modern Britain: An Economic and Social History* (1996)
Graham, H., *The Spanish Republic at War 1936–39* (Cambridge: 2002)
Gregory, R. G., *Sidney Webb and East Africa* (Berkeley: 1962)
Gupta, P. S., *Imperialism and the British Labour Movement* (1975)
Hailey, Lord, *Native Administration and Political Development in Tropical Africa* (1942)
Halliday, F., *Arabia without Sultans* (1974)
Harris, K., *Attlee* (1982)
Hathaway, R. M., *Ambiguous Partnership: Britain and America 1944–47* (Columbia: 1981)
Haupt, G., *Socialism and the Great War: The Collapse of the Second International* (Oxford: 1972)
Healey, D., *The Time of My Life* (1990)
Hennessy, P., *Muddling Through* (1998)
Hitchcock, W. I., *The Struggle for Europe* (2003)
Hobsbawm, E. J., *Age of Empire* (1987)
Hobson, J. A., *Imperialism: A Study* (1902 and 1988)
Hogan, M. J., *The Marshall Plan: America, Britain and the Reconstruction of Western Europe 1947–52* (Cambridge: 1987)
Holland, R., *Pursuit of Greatness: Britain and the World Role 1900–1970* (1991)
Hollowell, J. (ed.), *Twentieth-Century Anglo-American Relations* (2001)
Hourani, A., *A History of the Arab Peoples* (1991)
Howard, A., *Richard Crossman: The Pursuit of Power* (1990)
Howe, S., *Anticolonialism in British Politics: The Left and the End of Empire, 1918–64* (1993)
Howell, D., *MacDonald's Party: Labour Identities and Crisis 1922–31* (Oxford: 2002)
Iatrides, J. (ed.), *Greece in the 1940s* (1981)
James, L., *Imperial Rearguard: Wars of Empire 1919–1985* (1988)
Jeffreys, K., *Anthony Crosland: A New Biography* (2001)
Jensen, K. M. (ed.), *Origins of the Cold War: The Novikov, Kennan, and Roberts 'Long Telegrams' of 1946* (Washington, D.C.: 1991)
Johnson, C., *The Sorrows of Empire* (2004)

Joll, J., *The Second International, 1889–1914* (1955)

Jones, P., *America and the British Labour Party: The Special Relationship at Work* (1997)

Kedourie, E., *England and the Middle East* (1956)

Kennedy, P., *The Rise of the Anglo-German Naval Antagonism, 1860–1914* (1980)

Keynes, J. M., *The Economic Consequences of the Peace* (1919)

Kiernan, V., *European Empires from Conquest to Collapse* (Leicester: 1982)

Kirk, N., *Comrades and Cousins* (1994)

Kissinger, H., *The White House Years* (1979)

Knock, T. J., *To End All Wars: Woodrow Wilson and the Quest for a New World Order* (New Jersey: 1992)

Kolko, G., *The Politics of War: The World and United States Foreign Policy 1943–45* (New York: 1970)

Kolko, G. and Kolko, J., *The Limits of Power: The World and United States Foreign Policy* (New York: 1972)

Laquer, W., *A History of Zionism* (New York: 2003)

Lashmar, P. and James, O., *Britain's Secret Propaganda War* (Stroud: 1998)

Laski, H., *Democracy in Crisis* (1933)

—— *A Grammar of Politics* (third edition, 1934)

—— *Faith, Reason and Civilization* (1944)

Laybourne, K. and James, D., *Philip Snowden* (Bradford: 1987)

Liddington, J., *The Long Road to Greenham: Feminism and Anti-Militarism in Britain since 1820* (1989)

Lindqvist, S., *Exterminate All the Brutes* (2002)

Louis, W. R., *Imperialism at Bay, 1914–45* (Oxford: 1977)

—— *The British Empire in the Middle East* (Oxford: 1984)

Low, D. A. and Smith, A. (eds), *Oxford History of East Africa*, Volume 3 (Oxford: 1976)

Lowry, D. (ed.), *The South African War Reappraised* (Manchester: 2000)

Lugard, F., *The Dual Mandate in British Tropical West Africa* (1922)

Lyman, R. W., *The First Labour Government 1924* (1924)

MacDonald, J. Ramsay, *Labour and the Empire* (1907)

—— *Socialism* (1907)

—— *Socialism and Government* (1909)

—— *The Socialist Movement* (1911)

McKenzie, J. M., *Imperialism and Popular Culture* (Manchester: 1986)

McKibbin, R., *The Ideologies of Class* (Oxford: 1990)

—— *Classes and Cultures* (Oxford: 1998)

Macmillan, M., *Peacemakers: Six Months That Changed the World* (2001)

Maier, C. S., *Recasting Bourgeois Europe* (New Jersey: 1975)

Marquand, D., *Ramsay MacDonald* (1977)

Martin, L. W., *Peace Without Victory* (New Haven: 1958)

Matthews, H. G. C., *Gladstone, 1875–1898* (Oxford: 1995)

Mayer, A. J., *Political Origins of the New Diplomacy* (1959)

Meerscheimer, J.,*The Tragedy of Great Power Politics* (New York: 2001)

Morgan, A., *J. Ramsay MacDonald* (1977)

Morgan, K. O., *Labour in Power, 1945–51* (Oxford: 1984)

Morris, J., *Farewell the Trumpets* (1979)

Naylor, J. F., *Labour's International Policy* (1969)

Newman, M., *Harold Laski: A Political Biography* (1993)

Northedge, F. S., *Descent from Power: British Foreign Policy 1945–73* (1974)

O'Ballance, E., *The Greek Civil War 1944–49* (New York: 1966)

O'Malley, B. and Craig, C., *The Cyprus Conspiracy: America, Espionage and the Turkish Invasion* (1999)

Omiss, D. E., *Air Power and Colonial Control* (Manchester: 1990)

Orde, A., *Great Britain and International Security 1920–26* (1978)

Orwell, S. (ed.), *Collected Essays, Journalism and Letters of George Orwell* (1970)

Ovendale, R. (ed.), *The Foreign Policy of the British Labour Governments 1945–51* (Leicester: 1984)

Owen, D., *Human Rights* (1978)

Oxford University Socialist Discussion Group (ed.), *Out of Apathy: Voices of the New Left 30 Years On* (1989)

Pakenham, T., *The Scramble for Africa* (1991)

Pearce, E., *The Lost Leaders* (1997)

—— *Denis Healey: A Life in Our Times* (2002)

Pearce, R. (ed.), *Patrick Gordon Walker: Political Diaries, 1932–71* (1991)

Pelling, H., *A Short History of the Labour Party* (1961)

—— *The Origins of the Labour Party* (Oxford: second edition, 1979)

—— *The Labour Governments 1945–51* (1984)

Pells, R., *Not Like Us: How Europeans Have Loved, Hated and Transformed American Culture since World War 2* (New York: 1997)

Peukert, D. J., *The Weimar Republic* (1991)

Pimlott, B., *Hugh Dalton* (1985)

—— *The Second World War Diary of Hugh Dalton, 1940–45* (1986)

—— *Harold Wilson* (1993)

Pimlott, B. (ed.), *The Political Diary of Hugh Dalton 1918–40, 1945–60* (1986)

Ponting, C., *Breach of Promise* (1989)

—— *Churchill* (1994)

Porter, B., *Critics of Empire* (1968)

—— *The Lion's Share: A Short History of British Imperialism* (1984)

Pound, R. and Harmsworth, G., *Northcliffe* (1959)

Preston, P., *Franco* (1993)

Pryke, R., *Though Cowards Flinch: An Alternative Economic Policy* (1967)

Reed, B. and Williams, G., *Denis Healey and the Policies of Power* (1971)

Richter, H., *British Intervention in Greece* (1986)

Robinson, K., *The Dilemmas of Trusteeship* (1965)

Rubin, B. and Rubin, J. C., *Hating America: A History* (Oxford: 2004)

Saab, A. P., *Reluctant Icon: Gladstone, Bulgaria and the Working Classes* (Cambridge, Mass.: 1991)

Saville, J., *The Politics of Continuity* (1993)

Schneer, J., *Labour's Conscience* (1988)

—— *George Lansbury* (Manchester: 1990)

Searle, G. R., *The Quest for National Efficiency: A Study in British Politics and British Political Thought, 1889–1914* (Oxford: 1971)

Semmel, B., *Imperialism and Social Reform* (1960)
Sfikas, T. D., *The British Labour Government and the Greek Civil War* (Keele: 1994)
Shannon, R., *The Crisis of Imperialism 1865–1915* (1976)
Shaw, G. B., *Fabianism and the Empire* (1900)
Shonfield, A., *British Economic Policy since the War* (Harmondsworth: 1958)
Short, E., *Whip to Wilson* (1989)
Silverfarb, D., *The Twilight of the British Ascendancy in the Middle East* (New York: 1994)
Skidelsky, R., *Politicians and the Slump* (1967)
—— *John Maynard Keynes: Fighting for Britain 1937–46* (2001)
Smith, T. (ed.), *The End of European Empire: Decolonisation after World War Two* (1975)
Snowden, P., *Labour and the New World* (1921)
Stonor Saunders, F., *Who Paid the Piper? The CIA and the Cultural Cold* War (1999)
Swartz, M., *The Union of Democratic Control in British Politics during the First World War* (Oxford: 1971)
Taylor, A. J. P., *English History 1914–45* (Oxford: 1965)
Taylor, R. and Young, N. (eds), *Campaigns for Peace* (Manchester: 1987)
Thompson, E. P. (ed.), *Out of Apathy* (1960)
Thorne, C., *Allies of a Kind* (1978)
Tomlinson, B. R., *The Political Economy of the Raj* (1979)
Tomlinson, J., *The Labour Governments, 1964–70: Economic Policy* (Manchester: 2004)
Walker, M., *The Cold War* (1993)
Waltz, K. N., *Foreign Policy and Democratic Politics: The American and British Experience* (1968)
Weiler, P., *British Labour and the Cold War* (Stanford: 1988)
White, S., *Britain and the Bolshevik Revolution* (1979)
Williams, P. M., *Hugh Gaitskell* (Oxford: 1982)
—— (ed.), *The Diary of Hugh Gaitskell, 1945–56* (1983)
Williamson, P., *National Crisis and National Government: British Politics, the Economy and the Empire, 1926–1932* (1996)
—— *Stanley Baldwin* (1999)
—— *Baldwin Papers* (2004)
Wilson, H., *The Labour Governments 1964–70: A Personal Memoir* (1989)
Wilson, H. S., *African Decolonisation* (1984)
Wilson, P., *The International Theory of Leonard Woolf* (2003)
Winkler, H., *The League of Nations Movement in Great Britain, 1914–1919* (New Jersey: 1952)
—— *Paths Not Taken: British Labour and International Policy in the 1920s* (1994)
Wood, J. R. T., *So Far and No Further! Rhodesia's Bid for Independence during the Retreat from Empire 1959–1965* (Victoria, British Columbia: 2005)
Woolf, L., *International Government: Two Reports Prepared for the Fabian Research Department* (1916)
—— *Barbarians at the Gate* (1939)

Wright, J., *Gustav Streseman* (Oxford: 2002)
Yapp, M. E., *The Near East Since the First World War* (second edition, 1996)
Young, J., *The Labour Governments 1964–70: International Policy* (Manchester: 2003)
Young, M. B., *The Vietnam Wars 1945–90* (New York: 1991)
Ziegler, P., *Wilson: The Authorized Life of Lord Wilson of Rievaulx* (1993)

Articles

Angell, N., 'France and Europe', *New Leader*, 25 January 1924
Bale, T., 'A Deplorable Episoide? South African Arms and the Statecraft of the British Social Democracy', *Labour History Review*, 62, 1, 1997
Black, L., '"The Bitterest Enemies of Communism": Labour Revisionists, Atlanticism and the Cold War', *Contemporary British History*, 15, 3, 2001
Blackwell, S., 'Pursuing Nasser: The Macmillan Government and the Management of British Policy towards the Middle East Cold War, 1957–63', *Cold War History*, 4, 3, 2004
Boucher, D., 'British Idealism, the State and International Relations', *Journal of the History of Ideas*, 55, 4, 1994
Brookshire, J. H., '"Speak for England", Act for England: Labour's Leadership and British National Security Under Threat of War in the Late 1930s', *European History Quarterly*, 29, 2, 1999
Callaghan, J., 'The Left and the "Unfinished Revolution": Bevanites and Soviet Russia in the 1950s', *Contemporary British History*, 15, 3, 2001
Catterall, P., 'Morality and Politics: The Free Churches and the Labour Party between the Wars', *Historical Journal*, 36, 3, 1993
Crosland, A., 'About Equality II: Is Equal Opportunity Enough?', *Encounter*, August 1956
Crossman, R. H. S., 'Labour and Compulsory Military Service', *Political Quarterly*, 10, 1939
—— 'The Spectre of Revisionism: A Reply to Crosland', *Encounter*, March 1960
Cunningham, H., 'The Language of Patriotism', in R. Samuel (ed.), *Patriotism: The Making and Unmaking of British National Identity* (1989)
Cuthbertson, G., 'Pricking the Non-Conformist Conscience: Religion against the South African War', in D. Lowry (ed.), *The South African War Reappraised* (Manchester: 2000)
Dare, R., 'Instinct and Organisation: Intellectuals and British Labour after 1931', *Historical Journal*, 26, 3, 1983
Dockrill, S., 'Forging the Anglo-American Global Defence Partnership: Harold Wilson, Lyndon Johnson and the Washington Summit, December 1964', *Journal of Strategic Studies*, 23, 4, 2000
Dutt, R. Palme, 'The General Election and British Foreign Policy', *Labour Monthly*, 6, 1, 1924
Easter, D., '"Keep the Indonesian Pot Boiling": Western Covert Intervention in Indonesia, October 1965–March 1966', *Cold War History*, 5, 1, 2005
Fielding, S., '"But westward, look, the land is bright": Labour's Revisionists and the Imagining of America, c. 1945–64', in J. Hollowell (ed.), *Twentieth Century Anglo-American Relations* (2001)

Foster, A., 'The Politicians, Public Opinion and the Press: The Storm over British Military Intervention in Greece in December 1944', *Journal of Contemporary History*, 19, 3, 1983

Francis, M., 'Old Realisms: Policy Reviews of the Past', *Labour History Review*, 56, 1, 1991

Gladstone, W. E., 'Aggression on Egypt and Freedom in the East', *Nineteenth Century*, August 1877

—— 'Kin Beyond the Sea', *North American Review*, September 1878

—— 'England's Mission', *Nineteenth Century*, September 1878

Goldsworthy, D., 'Britain and the International Critics of British Colonialism, 1951–56', *Journal of Commonwealth and Comparative History*, 29, 1, 1991

Healey, D., 'The Cominform and World Communism', *International Affairs*, 24, 1948

—— 'Britain and Europe', *Socialist Commentary*, May 1951

—— 'The Defence of Western Europe', *Socialist Commentary*, October 1951

—— 'The Bomb That Didn't Go Off', *Encounter*, July 1955

—— 'When Shrimps Learn to Whistle', *International Affairs*, 32, 1, 1956

—— 'Prometheus Bound', *Encounter*, 1957

—— 'The Sputnik and Western Defence', *International Affairs*, 34, 2, 1958

—— 'The Crisis in Europe', *International Affairs*, 38, 2, 1962

Henderson, A., 'The Outlook for Labour', *Contemporary Review*, 1918

Hughes, R. G., ' "We are not seeking strength for its own sake": The British Labour Party, West Germany and the Cold War, 1951–64', *Cold War History*, 3, 1, 2002

Hyndman, H. M., 'The Jews' War on the Transvaal', *Justice*, 7 October 1899

Hyslop, J., 'The Imperial Working Class Makes Itself "White"', *Journal of Historical Sociology*, 12, 4, 1999

Jones, M., 'A Decision Delayed: Britain's Withdrawal from South East Asia reconsidered, 1961–8', *English Historical Review*, 67, 472, 2002

Keleman, P., 'Zionism and the British Labour Party: 1917–39', *Social History*, 21, 1, 1996

—— 'Looking the Other Way: The British Labour Party, Zionism, and the Palestinians', in C. Collette and S. Bird (eds), *Jews, Labour and the Left, 1918–48* (2000)

Krugman, P., 'The Myth of Asia's Miracle', *Foreign Affairs*, November–December 1994

Lansbury, G., 'Empire Day', *Lansbury's Labour Weekly*, 23 May 1925

Laski, H., 'Communism as a World Force', *International Affairs*, January 1931

Little, D., 'Mission Impossible: The CIA and the Cult of Covert Action in the Middle East', *Diplomatic History*, 28, 5, 2004

Lowes Dickinson, G., 'The War and the Way Out', *Atlantic Monthly*, 114, December 1914

Lowry, D., ' "The Boers were the beginning of the end": The Wider Impact of the South African War', in D. Lowry (ed.), *The South African War Reappraised* (Manchester: 2000)

McKercher, B. J. C., 'The Foreign Office, 1930–39: Strategy, Permanent Interests and National Security', *Contemporary British History*, 18, 3, 2004

McKnight, D., 'Western Intelligence and SEATO's War on Subversion 1956–63', *Intelligence and National Security*, 20, 2, 2005

McMahon, R. J., 'Eisenhower and Third World Nationalism: A Critique of the Revisionists', *Political Science Quarterly*, 101, 3, 1986

Meynell, H., 'The Stockhom Conference of 1917', *International Review of Social History*, volume 5, 1960

Murphy, P., '"An intricate and distasteful subject": British Planning for the Use of Force against the European Settlers of Central Africa, 1952–65', *English Historical Review*, 121, 492, pp. 746–77

Myers, D., 'Soviet War Aims and the Grand Alliance: George Kennan's Views 1944–46', *Journal of Contemporary History*, 21, 1, 1986

Parker, R. A. C., 'British Rearmament 1936–9: Treasury, Trade Unions and Skilled Labour', *English Historical Review*, 96, 1981

Petersen, T. T., 'Crossing the Rubicon? Britain's Withdrawal from the Middle East, 1964–1968: A Bibliographical Review', *International History Review*, 22, 2, 2000

Reinders, R. C., 'Racialism on the Left: E. D. Morel and the "Black Horrors on the Rhine"', *International Review of Social History*, 13, 1968

Rotter, A. J., 'The Triangular Route to Vietnam: The United States, Great Britain and Southeast Asia, 1945–50', *International History Review*, 6, 3, 1984

Roy, R., 'The Battle for Bretton Woods: America, Britain and the International Financial Crisis of October 1967–March 1968', *Cold War History*, 2, 2, 2002

Scott, P., 'The United States and the Overthrow of Sukarno, 1965–67', *Pacific Affairs*, 58, 2, 1985

Smith, R. and Zametica, J., 'The Cold Warrior: Clement Attlee Reconsidered, 1945–7', *International Affairs*, 61, 2, 1985

Steininger, R., '"The Americans are in a hopeless position": Great Britain and the War in Vietnam, 1964–65', *Diplomacy and Statecraft*, 8, 3, 1997

Tombs, I., 'The Victory of Socialist "Vansittartism": Labour and the German Question, 1941–5', *Twentieth Century British History*, 7, 3, 1996

Tomlinson, J., 'The Attlee Governments and the Balance of Payments 1945–50', *Twentieth Century British History*, 2, 1, 1991

Tratt, J., 'Harold Macmillan and the "Golden Days" of Anglo-American Relations Revisited, 1957–63', *Diplomatic History*, 29, 4, 2005

Varsori, A., 'Britain and US Involvement in the Vietnam War during the Kennedy Administration, 1961–63', *Cold War History*, 3, 2, 2003

Watts, C., 'Killing Kith and Kin: The Viability of British Military Intervention in Rhodesia, 1964–5', *Twentieth Century British History*, 16, 2005, pp. 382–415

Webb, S., 'Lord Rosebery's Escape from Houndsditch', *Nineteenth Century*, 50, 1901

Webb, S., 'The First Labour Government', *Political Quarterly*, 32, January–March 1961

Winkler, H., 'British Labour and the Origins of the Idea of Colonial Trusteeship, 1914–19', *The Historian*, 13, spring, 1951

—— 'Arthur Henderson', in G. A. Craig and F. Gilbert (eds), *The Diplomats, 1919–1939* (New Jersey: 1953)

Winter, J. M., 'The Webbs and the Non-White World: A Case of Socialist Racialism', *Journal of Contemporary History*, 9, 1, 1974

Woolf, L., 'Labour's Foreign Policy', *Political Quarterly*, 4, 1933

—— 'De Profundis', *Political Quarterly*, 10, 1939

Worsley, P., 'Imperial Retreat', in E. P. Thompson (ed.), *Out of Apathy* (1960)

Wyn Rees, G., 'British Strategic Thinking and Europe, 1964–70', *Journal of European Integration*, 5, 1, 1999

Young, N., 'War Resistance and the British Peace Movement since 1914', in R. Taylor and N. Young (eds), *Campaigns for Peace: British Peace Movements in the Twentieth Century* (Manchester: 1987)

Index